SECRET WILL

*How People, Events and a Dancing
Horse Inspired Shakespeare*

Paul Chapman

Little Donkey Publishing

ISBN-9798723258969
ISBN-10: 1477123456

Cover design by: Paul Chapman
Library of Congress Control Number: 2018675309
Printed in the United States of America

He was not of an age, but for all time

BEN JONSON

CONTENTS

FOREWORD

Throughout this book I have used the standard protocol for identifying passages from Shakespeare's plays: i.e. numeral – full point – numeral. For example, *Richard III*, Act 1 Scene 1 is represented as *Richard III*, 1.1. Dating many of the plays is problematical and the subject of much debate. I have therefore sought to follow the broadest consensus of scholarly opinion when doing so.

My grateful thanks are due to my wife Liz for keeping the ideas, encouragement and cups of coffee flowing, in addition to her tireless proofreading. Thanks also to Sue Gibson for diligently checking the manuscript and making many helpful observations, and to Lati Moodie who provided both inspiration and invaluable assistance. Finally, I acknowledge my good friends at the U3A Tauranga Shakespeare Group, in whose company I have spent many happy hours. All that said, any errors in the text are entirely down to me.

This book is dedicated to Liz.
We are such stuff as dreams are made on.

Email: littledonkeypublishing@gmail.com
www.secretwill.net

PROLOGUE: ROAR OF THE CROWD

ON A summer's day in 1587, a glove-maker's son from War-wickshire did something unbelievably exciting. He ran away to the playhouse. Call it good luck, for him and us, but the most famous troupe of actors in the land had just arrived in William Shakespeare's home town with a big problem. The Queen's Men were on tour from their base in London, staging comedies, histories and tragedies in town halls and inn yards, wherever they could draw a crowd. After a performance in the market town of Thame, two of the players had fallen into a quarrel. The dispute quickly escalated into a swordfight. By the time the company reached Stratford-upon-Avon, one actor was dead and the other was facing arrest for murder.

William Knell, the young man who died of stab wounds, was noted for his performance as the dashing Prince Hal in *The Famous Victories of Henry V*. The play called for thirty-eight characters and, while actors regularly doubled and tripled up on roles, there were only a dozen of them even when the company had been at full muster. Now they needed to find someone who could act, in however basic a way, and quickly. Essential qualifications: male (by law females were not allowed on the stage), young (but mature), energetic (it was a demanding business), intelligent with a prodigious memory (for lines and cues), able to start at once a considerable advantage. And keen. Definitely keen.

Something about the theatre fired the imagination of the twenty-three year old Will (only his mother ever called him William). It had done so for a long time. He remembered being captivated when, as an eleven year old boy sitting on the grass beside his father at Kenilworth Castle, he watched the spectacular outdoor performances put on by actors entertaining Elizabeth I. He had been entranced every time companies of players came to Stratford, as they donned their gaudy costumes and assumed the identities of anguished kings, strutting tyrants and weeping maidens.

As high bailiff, or mayor, his father had been in charge of granting permits to touring theatrical groups and paying them from the civic treasury. Now the Queen's Men, the very performers who entertained Her Majesty in her gorgeous palaces, were in town. Among their number was the incomparable Richard Tarlton. People came from miles around to see him. Celebrated as 'the wonder of his time', Tarlton was the consummate funnyman, described as having a 'wondrous plentiful, pleasant extemporal wit'. Even the simple act of poking his head out from behind a curtain and screwing up his face was enough to set a crowd roaring with laughter. Elizabeth loved him. So did everybody else.

Theatrical life was a world away from all Shakespeare knew. After a hurried wedding to Anne Hathaway when, at the age of eighteen he was shocked to discover she was pregnant, he was now the father of Susanna, aged four, and the two-year-old twins Hamnet and Judith. Anne was eight years older than he was, and they all lived together in his parents' crowded home in Henley Street. As the eldest son it was assumed he would follow his father into the family glove-making business, one day taking over the house and shop. Yet he found the siren call of the playhouse somehow irresistible. The idea of making audiences weep or laugh with the power of words thrilled him and made his heart beat faster. Joining the Queen's Men would also give him the opportunity to travel – he had never been further afield than neighbouring Gloucestershire – and get to know people outside the confines of the dull market town where he had grown up. Even better, somewhere over the horizon the great city of London beckoned, with all its promise and excitement.

Before he realised quite what he was doing, he had volunteered his services to the company of actors, begging them to take a chance on him. Whenever he could get away, he promised Anne, he would bring the money he had earned back home to support her and the children. His pledge did nothing to mitigate her horror. Actors had long been regarded as little better than vagabonds, with no secure employment. The theatres in London were notorious dens of thievery, prostitution and disease, and those Protestant zealots the Puritans wanted them closed down altogether. It was only because the Queen so enjoyed seeing plays at court that the kill-joys had not yet got their way. The powerful preacher John Stockwood had railed against the theatres in an address he gave at Paul's Cross, an open-air pulpit in the grounds of London's great cathedral, lamenting:

Will not a filthy play, with the blast of a trumpet, sooner call thither a thousand, than an hour's tolling of a bell bring to sermon a hundred?

Stockwood went on to condemn the Theatre itself, built by the enterprising James Burbage in 1576 to be the first permanent theatrical structure in London, saying it was constructed ...

Even after the manner of the old heathenish theatre at Rome, a show-place of all beastly and filthy matters, to the which it cannot be chosen that men should resort without learning thence much corruption.

In 1583, the staunchly Christian pamphleteer Philip Stubbes had delivered an even more blistering barrage against the playhouses and everyone involved with them:

Do they not maintain bawdry, insinuate foolery, and renew the remembrance of heathen idolatory? Do they not induce whoredom and uncleanness? Nay, are they not rather plain devourers of maidenly virginity and chastity?

Ouch. Shakespeare would argue that times were a-changing, that players were gaining a new-found respectability, especially a company as prestigious as the Queen's Men. As the historian John Stow would put it:

> Comedians and stage-players of former times were very
> poor and ignorant ... but being now grown very skillful
> and exquisite actors for all matters, they were entertained
> into the service of diverse great lords: out of which there
> were twelve of the best chosen, and ... [they] were sworn the
> Queen's servants and were allowed wages and liveries as
> Grooms of the Chamber.

The Queen's Men, for their part, would soon have cause to congratulate themselves on the wisdom of their choice. They would realise that the new fellow's talent for writing plays, and improving on old ones, surpassed even his skills as an actor. Today, in a way neither he nor they could have foreseen, Shakespeare's name is celebrated around the world.

At least, that is how it all may have happened.

✽ ✽ ✽

The Elizabethans present us with what appears an irreconcilable paradox. How could an age that cheerfully employed sadistic tortures in order to extract confessions, and silenced political and religious dissent through public disembowelling or burning at the stake, have left us some of the most sublime poetry written anytime, anywhere and in any language? How did an era whose citizens whooped with delight at seeing blinded bears mercilessly whipped, and horses carrying terrified, shrieking apes on their backs while being chased by packs of slavering dogs, come to bequeath us some of the finest – arguably *the* finest – accomplishments in the history of world theatre? The first Elizabethan era was in many respects – like the second, through which we have lived – the worst of times and the best of times, so that we might say, with Hamlet: 'This was sometime a paradox, but now the time gives it proof.'

The answer, of course, is that the age of Elizabeth I, like that of James I which followed, was not an isolated snapshot in time, as history lessons and biographers might beguile us into thinking. It was, rather, a point along the continuum of cultural development, with Europe emerging from the bleakness of the Middle Ages into the light of the Renaissance. It was also a time of great turbulence. England was being wrested apart by the opposing forces of Protestantism and Catholicism, the young Elizabeth's reign having begun only twenty-four years after her father Henry VIII upended everyone's settled world by declaring that he, not the Pope, was head of the Church within his realm. In the meantime, her half-sister 'bloody' Mary had turned the clock fully back to Catholicism during a murderous five-year reign, before Elizabeth herself succeeded to the throne.

In 1588, the Spanish king, Philip II, seeing himself as the Pope's champion, launched his massive Armada towards England's coasts in an attack designed to depose Elizabeth and drag her subjects back to the old faith. In that ambition he had many covert English supporters. James I would, in his turn, be fortunate to survive the most audacious attempted regicide in British history – what in modern times has been called the country's 9/11 – a desperate conspiracy by diehard Catholics to restore the old order. It is known to us as the Gunpowder Plot and even Shakespeare became caught up on its periphery.

Nor was that all. Other certainties that had anchored past generations were under siege. In astronomy, the divinely ordained universe with an immovable earth at the centre of everything, originally laid down by Claudius Ptolemy fifteen hundred years earlier, was being challenged by the radical notions of Copernicus. He insisted, if you please, that the earth itself was travelling through space around the sun. The vast potential of chemistry was emerging from the shadow of its vacuous parent alchemy, whose quest for the elixir of life and the philosopher's stone that would turn base metals into gold had proved futile. Medicine was evolving from the second-century precepts of Galen into a discipline that would one day stand more chance of making sick people well than causing them harm.

In exploration, after Ferdinand Magellan's expedition had circumnavigated the globe early in the sixteenth century, an unquenchable thirst for knowledge of unknown peoples and lands – and the fame and wealth it brought – drove Sir Francis Drake to follow in his wake around the world. Raleigh, Frobisher, Barents and others probed waters closer to home and continued to push back the frontiers of *terra incognita*, giving map makers ever more coastal outlines to add to their charts. The spice trade with the East Indies boomed, as did the shipping of cotton from India and sugar from the West Indies, and the grim business of transporting slaves in their thousands from Africa to work the burgeoning plantations of the New World. There were rich pickings to be had when Spanish or Portuguese galleons, groaning with gold and treasures purloined from South America, were forcibly boarded and relieved of their valuable loot. England, becoming increasingly aware of her place in the world, began to foster fledgling colonies such as Virginia with an eye to profit.

An emphasis on education, at least for the sons of the wealthy and the emerging middle classes of merchants and tradesmen, meant more people could read and write than ever before. Within a century of Gutenberg's death, the printing presses in London were working overtime to cope with demand from a public that was increasingly literate and insatiable. Copies, authorised or otherwise, of popular poems and plays, journals telling of implausible adventures and discoveries, new translations into English of Greek and Roman classical tales, pamphlets on the latest controversies (government censors permitting), and broadside ballads that salivated over the most salacious gossip were all snapped up.

It was an exciting – albeit dangerous – time to be alive.

* * *

Into this world was born William Shakespeare, destined to play a unique and revolutionary role of his own. When he arrived on or about 23 April 1564, the theatre that would become his lifeblood had at last shaken off the straitjacketed format of the Medieval Mystery Plays, with their rigid moralising directed at keeping a God-fearing population in line. It had discovered its own identity, providing secular entertainment for the masses, and the masses responded by queuing up to part with their hard-earned cash.

By the time Shakespeare turned twenty-five, he would be leading the art form on to unprecedented heights of accomplishment. Where the feted Christopher Marlowe had laid the foundations of modern drama, the man from Stratford constructed an edifice that would become the theatre as we know it. He encountered many trials along the way, suffered unbearable grief in the death of his young son Hamnet, faced the loss of his beloved Globe to the flames, and acquired enemies, famously coming under attack from the playwright Robert Greene as 'an upstart crow'. He also cultivated enduring friendships, and carved an unassailable place for himself in the history of literature and the dramatic arts.

In many ways we are lucky to have Shakespeare and his works at all. Child mortality was already shockingly high but, in the year he was born, the plague – dreaded curse of so many ages – swept through Stratford and wiped out around a fifth of the town's population. The plague would visit London many times in the twenty-five years or so he lived in the city, often closing the theatres that were his livelihood and scattering the actors on yet more tours of the countryside until each outbreak subsided.

There were other dangers too. Several of his contemporary writers fell foul of the authorities. Ben Jonson was thrown into Marshalsea Prison for 'leude and mutynous behaviour' over a satirical play titled *The Isle of Dogs.* Jonson's co-writer Thomas Nashe escaped incarceration only by fleeing to Great Yarmouth. Thomas Kyd died at the age of thirty-five, never having recovered from the brutal torture he endured after being accused of possessing blasphemous papers. Even the great Kit Marlowe, Kyd's former room-mate in shared lodgings, was murdered by government secret agents in the most murky of circumstances. Shakespeare himself, raised in an unrelentingly Catholic family, must have felt trepidation on more than one occasion because of his own association with dangerous traitors involved in conspiracies against the Crown.

Indeed, we might not even have many of his plays were it not for the unstinting efforts of two of his dearest friends and fellow actors. For some years after Shakespeare's death in 1616, John Heminges and Henry Condell took upon themselves the herculean task of gathering his scripts together, finally publishing them in 1623 as the *First Folio.* Eighteen of the plays had appeared previously as quarto editions (the term refers to the size of the paper they were printed on, a quarto being a sheet folded twice to produce four leaves, or eight printed sides, each page having about the same dimensions as a modern paperback book). But many of these quartos were 'pirated,' published by greedy printers cashing in on a play's popularity, and were riddled with inaccuracies. Copyright as we know it did not exist. The *First Folio*, in contrast, was what we might now term a 'coffee table' book. It contains an introduction in which Heminges and Condell give us a hint of the trouble to which they went in order to ensure the plays as printed were faithful to the scripts Shakespeare had written:

Where before you were abus'd with diverse stolne and sur-

reptitious copies, maimed and deformed by the frauds and stealthes of iniurious imposters that expos'd [published] them: even those [plays] are now offer'd to your view cur'd and perfect of their limbes; and all the rest, absolute in their numbers, as he conceived them.

'All the rest' were a further eighteen plays – among them such perennial favourites as *Twelfth Night, As You Like It, The Taming of the Shrew, Macbeth, Julius Caesar, Antony and Cleopatra, The Tempest* and *The Winter's Tale* – which might never have survived were it not for their inclusion. Of around seven hundred and fifty copies of the *First Folio* that were printed, some two hundred and thirty-five are known to survive today, with previously unknown copies coming to light from time to time. Eighty-two copies, by far the biggest single collection, are in the Folger Shakespeare Library in Washington, DC. Posterity owes Heminges and Condell an immeasurable debt of gratitude.

In a touching preface that allows us an insight into the character of the playwright, the pair say they have undertaken their task solely 'to keep the memory of so worthy a friend and fellow alive as was our Shakespeare'. The *First Folio* also gives us one of the few reliable portraits we have of Shakespeare (*pictured*), an engraving by Martin Droeshout, an English artist of Flemish descent, which appears on the book's title page, and a generous tribute from Ben Jonson, who so memorably summed up the man from Stratford in the line: 'He was not of an age, but for all time.'

Today, Shakespeare is many different things to many different people. To those who pick up on an easy familiarity with legal terms and phrases glimpsed in several of the plays, he surely underwent training as a legal clerk. They note, for instance, Hamlet's graveyard ruminations over a skull he supposes to be that of a lawyer, in which he speaks of legal 'quiddities', 'quillities', 'tenures', 'statutes', 'recognizances', 'convey-

ances' and an 'action of bat-
tery'.

Then there is the grave-
digger's explanation in *Hamlet*
of an arcane Elizabethan court
ruling on suicide. Tense trial
scenes in several plays, notably
The Merchant of Venice and *The
Winter's Tale*, show us Shakespeare was well aware of their
potential for drama. (There is

even a mock trial in *King Lear*.) The theory that Shakespeare
had a background in the legal profession was first advanced in
1788 by the scholar Edmund Malone, although it is difficult to
conclude whether his argument is supported or contradicted
by the rebellious Dick the Butcher's lusty cry in *Henry VI, Part
2*: 'The first thing we do, let's kill all the lawyers.'

Shakespeare mentions ships and the sea often in his
writing, which to some suggests he had experience of seafar-
ing. Shipwrecks are pivotal to the plots of *The Comedy of
Errors*, *Twelfth Night*, *The Tempest*, *Pericles* and, indirectly, *The
Merchant of Venice*, where Antonio's fortunes are undone by
the loss in a storm of an 'argosy', or merchant vessel. In the
dramatic opening scene of *The Tempest,* Shakespeare appears
to reveal a detailed knowledge of the actions mariners must
take in the face of a ferocious storm, and the correct sequence
in which they should be performed. Sixteen years after *The
Tempest* appeared, the shouted commands of the Boatswain in
the play would be echoed among the rules of good practice
prescribed in a definitive manual of seamanship titled *A Sea
Grammar*. That book was written by no less a mariner than
John Smith, Admiral of New England and Governor of Virginia.

Shakespeare also alludes in *The Tempest* to the detach-
able topmast, a spar which was hoisted to provide extra speed
in good weather and stowed away when heavy seas struck.

It was the relatively recent innovation of Admiral Sir John Hawkins, Treasurer of the Navy until 1595. A line in the comedy *As You Like It* could reflect seagoing experience on an altogether more personal level, when Jacques describes the jester Touchstone's wit as being 'as dry as the remainder biscuit after a voyage'. Shakespeare's interest in the sea seems all the more remarkable, coming as it does from a native of Warwickshire, among the most distant of English counties from the coast. Did he glean what he knew from questioning the seamen who drank in London's taverns?

Those with medical knowledge may express surprise that the Ghost in *Hamlet*, when speaking of the poison coursing through his body, appears to know about the circulation of the blood almost three decades before it was described by the physician William Harvey. Or that Shakespeare mentions the *pia mater*, the delicate inner membrane covering the brain and spinal cord, in no fewer than three plays (*Love's Labour's Lost*, *Twelfth Night* and *Troilus and Cressida*).

In a letter published in *Clinical Infectious Diseases* on 15 January 2006, three clinicians at the Walter Reed Army Medical Center in Washington, DC suggested Shakespeare may have made the earliest known reference to variant Creutzfeldt-Jakob Disease (vCJD). To support their case they appended an exhaustive table of lines spoken by Macbeth, tracing his decline into delusions, hallucinations and paranoia, together with the associated clinical diagnoses. In an allusion to the putative link between vCJD and bovine spongiform encephalopathy ('mad cow disease,' as it became known to Britain's headline writers in the early 1990s), the writers also pointed to Sir Andrew Aguecheek's line in *Twelfth Night*: 'I am a great eater of beef and I believe that does harm to my wit.' Their conclusion: 'Shakespeare showed an uncannily prescient understanding of prion disease transmission via exposure to neural tissues.'

Other commentators point to Shakespeare's impressive knowledge of how to construct a building, or of the sport of falconry, not to mention the fineries of the glove-making industry of his father. Freemasons have long claimed him as one of their own, based on his use of words and phrases in which they detect masonic symbolism. Students of religion can find in the Shakespearean canon at least a thousand biblical allusions, far more than in any other playwright of his time (and probably ever). Indeed, familiarity with the scriptures is so much a part of who Shakespeare was that the late Jesuit priest and scholar Father Peter Milward was moved to say his plays, despite their secular appearance, 'conceal an undercurrent of religious meaning which belongs to their deepest essence'.

Certainly Shakespeare's bucolic upbringing never left him. There are colourful allusions everywhere in his works to birds, plants, wildlife and rustic traditions. His evocation of the natural world – from the bank where wild thyme blows of *A Midsummer Night's Dream* to that other tranquil bank where moonlight sweetly sleeps in *The Merchant of Venice* – yields some of his most ravishing poetry. Yet not only does he wax lyrical about how nature looks, with the keen eye and intimate knowledge of a countryman he tells us how she behaves. In *The Winter's Tale*, for instance, Perdita describes how a favourite garden flower closes its petals at sunset but opens them again when the dew settles at dawn: 'The marigold, that goes to bed wi' the sun and with him rises weeping.' The same play contains an animated discussion on the merits of grafting plants in order to improve their stock.

Richard II features a scene in which a gardener gives horticultural instructions to his assistant. We hear in *The Merchant of Venice* how the martlet, or house martin, builds its nest 'in the weather on the outward wall, even in the force and road of casualty'. In *As You Like It*, set in the idyllic Forest of Arden, a lord describes how he watched the melancholy Jacques grieve over a weeping stag which had been mortally wounded by a hunter's arrow, as 'the wretched animal heav'd forth such groans that their discharge did stretch his leathern coat almost to bursting'. Shakespeare may have spent most of his adult life in London, but his heart never strayed far from the Warwickshire countryside he loved.

As for the concepts he espouses, there is no shortage of interpretations. Some see Hamlet (who attended university at Wittenberg, spiritual home of Martin Luther), as personifying Renaissance man, a deeply thoughtful Protestant hero raging against a world of Catholic symbolism (the Ghost's Purgatory, Ophelia's funeral rites and an oblique reference to the Diet of Worms). Others claim to have discovered within *Hamlet* a series of coded messages championing Copernican 'heresies' as being more convincing than the orthodox Ptolemaic universe.

One academic paper posted online contends that, both in *Hamlet* and his love poem *Venus and Adonis*, Shakespeare covertly argues England should resist the new fashion of burning coal instead of timber for heating because of the intolerable pollution it caused. 'As an artist,' the author writes, 'he realised that if he wished to support the dying (but always latent) sun economy (what we call renewable energy today), he would need to disguise his message and hope that future generations would appreciate it more.' I am not making this up.

There are those who argue that, because no fewer than thirteen plays are set in Italy, either in whole or in part, Shakespeare must have lived, or at least spent time, in that lovely country. It has even been suggested he *was* Italian. All of which overlooks the fact that several of his references contain notable geographical inaccuracies. In *The Taming of the Shrew*, for instance, Lucentio proudly announces: 'I am arriv'd for [in] fruitful Lombardy, the pleasant garden of great Italy,' while at the same time telling us he has come 'to see fair Padua, nursery of arts'. Padua, while it was a noted centre of learning, is not in Lombardy. However, all is explained when we know that a map of Europe in what is considered to be the first modern atlas, published by the cartographer Abraham Ortelius in 1570, had the name 'Lombardy' inscribed right across northern Italy.

In truth, wherever and whenever any of Shakespeare's plays are notionally set, the action is always really taking place in the Elizabethan or Jacobean England with which his audiences were familiar. The oxlips and nodding violets of the enchanted Athenian wood in *A Midsummer Night's Dream* are as English as a May morning. Mistress Overdone's brothel in *Measure for Measure* is never in the Vienna it purports to be, but rather in the seamier suburbs of London.

Many people with an interest in Shakespeare have engaging cases to make, whether you agree with them or not. Many, that is, except those misguided cynics who sniffily insist that a grammar school boy from Stratford could not possibly write in the way Shakespeare does, and who then waste countless hours seeking to prove their facile arguments that he was some kind of impostor. Ben Jonson started his working life as a bricklayer's apprentice and, like Shakespeare, missed out on a university education, but no one to my knowledge has yet argued he was a pretender. It is a mark of Shakespeare's incomparable greatness that he attracts such scepticism. The fact is, of course, genius knows no boundaries.

❊ ❊ ❊

Precious few anecdotes about Shakespeare which date from his own lifetime have come down to us. One that has survived is an entry in the diary of a London law student named John Manningham for 13 March 1601. Manningham tells how the celebrated actor Richard Burbage was propositioned by a woman in the audience when she became enamoured after seeing his performance in Shakespeare's *Richard III*. Manningham writes:

Upon a time when Burbage played Richard the Third, there was a citizen grew so far in liking with him that before she went from the play she appointed him to come that night unto her by the name of Richard the Third. Shakespeare, overhearing their conclusion, went before, was entertained and at his game ere Burbage came. Then message being brought that Richard the Third was at the door, Shakespeare caused return to be made that William the Conqueror was before Richard the Third.

Manningham adds helpfully: 'Shakespeare's name was William.'

It would be impossible to count the attempts at defining Shakespeare, from the legion of excellent biographies to the plethora of scholarly essays. Yet somehow the man himself always avoids being pinned down. Just when you think you are catching up with him, you find he is already one step ahead. A N Wilson may have put it best when he wrote: 'Shakespeare has that Macavity knack of eluding historians. He remains alive in the plays, but as a man we can sense him as someone who has just left the room.' We might, however, reasonably conclude that every writer incorporates something of what he or she knows in their work. Shakespeare was shaped by, as well as being a shaper of, the world in which he lived. This simple fact should give us a clue to getting closer to him.

Consider for a moment two of his characters. Bardolph, noted for his drunkard's red nose, is a lackey of that wastrel Sir John Falstaff and appears in no fewer than four plays, the two parts of *Henry IV* as well as *Henry V* and *The Merry Wives of Windsor*. Fluellen is a soldier, fiercely proud of his Welshness (Fluellen being a crudely anglicised version of the Celtic name Llewellyn), who plays a key role in *Henry V*. They are not historical characters and Shakespeare could have given them any names he chose. As it happens, during Will's boyhood two Stratford-upon-Avon men named George Bardolph and William Fluellen show up in a list of recusants – Catholics who committed an offence by refusing to regularly attend Protestant church services – along with his father John Shakespeare.

Ponder also how in *Henry IV, Part 2* we learn that a certain 'William Visor of Woncote' is bringing a court case against one 'Clement Perkes o' th' hill'. Sure enough, generations of a family named Visor or Vizard had lived in the Gloucestershire village of Woodmancote (pronounced Woncot) for hundreds of years, while a man named Perkes or Perchas owned a house on nearby Stinchcombe Hill, which was known to locals simply as 'the hill'. William Visor and Clement Perkes may even have been wool dealers who had a business association with Shakespeare's father over in the next county.

Shakespeare's genius for getting inside his characters' heads and articulating their conflicting points of view with an eloquence beyond anything they themselves could have commanded in life, his matchless ability to mould the English language and turn mere words into exquisite symphonies of sound and meaning, and his profound understanding of the human condition, defy any attempt at explanation on my part. He undoubtedly had what has been described as a 'magpie' mind, picking up shiny trinkets of knowledge here, sparkling nuggets of information there, and storing them away to put to good use at a later time. He was, without peer, a snapper up of unconsidered trifles.

More than four centuries have passed since Shakespeare's plays were written, and it is little wonder that the true meaning of many references in them escapes modern audiences. That's a shame because they are packed with allusions to the fascinating people, dramatic events, juicy morsels of gossip, lurid scandals, gripping court battles, treacherous conspiracies and outrageous acts of insolence he encountered during his lifetime. To know these background stories is to understand and enjoy his plays so much more. In this book we shall peel back the curtain to reveal the secret Shakespeare who lies hidden behind those quill-scratched pages. 'All the world's a stage,' he wrote. We will uncover the astonishing story of how he really did put his world on the stage. Our technique will be to examine key passages from the plays and then ask searching questions about how they relate to the tempestuous times in which he lived.

For instance, did that childhood visit to the Earl of Leicester's extravaganza at Kenilworth produce some of the most exquisitely beautiful verses as well as the funniest scene in *A Midsummer Night's Dream*? Did one of the most violent earthquakes ever to shake the British Isles, which rocked Stratford-upon-Avon when Will Shakespeare was sixteen years old, inspire the way the Nurse in *Romeo and Juliet* calculates Juliet's age in years 'since the earthquake' and speaks of running in terror from beneath a shaking dovecote? Has Shakespeare immortalised as Ophelia a young woman named Katherine Hamlett, who drowned in the River Avon? How is a speech in *Hamlet* connected to the brazen daylight abduction of an Elizabethan schoolboy in a London street? Does the playwright pour out the raw grief he feels over the death of his son in a handful of heartbreaking lines in *King John*, the historical drama he is thought to have been writing at the time the boy died?

Should Shakespeare's most famous stage direction – 'Exit, pursued by a bear' – actually read 'Exit, pursued by a *polar* bear'? Is he teasing us with a cryptic clue to the identity of the mysterious 'Dark Lady' of his desires in *Twelfth Night*? What do his plays expose of London's sleazy sex industry, with its legions of prostitutes known as Winchester Geese? Why did his famous Globe theatre become entangled in a courtroom drama alleging it was built using timbers stolen during an armed midnight raid? How did the shipwrecking of settlers on their way to Virginia shape *The Tempest*? Did a rancorous legal battle between three feuding sisters over their senile father's estate inspire *King Lear*? What frenzy of communal madness lay behind the appearance of the witches in *Macbeth*? And what in the world was the dancing horse?

Our quest will lead us on a captivating trail. While all the historical events described actually happened, their connection with the playwright must often be speculative. After all these centuries, how could it be otherwise? Having notched up fifty years in a career as a journalist, and been a devotee of Shakespeare for forty of them, I reserve the right to indulge in a little speculation – with a suitable degree of caution, of course. I have pursued the leads I follow in this book, often treading appreciatively in the footsteps of generations of doughty researchers, by employing the same investigative techniques I used throughout my journalistic career: with one eye on a good story and the other on integrity.

I trust fellow Shakespeare lovers will find my efforts enhance their enjoyment next time they watch a play by our favourite writer. More than that, I hope those readers who are only vaguely familiar with the man from Stratford when they pick up this book will be inspired to explore the overflowing cornucopia of his works, which is waiting to delight them too. Now, welcome to the wonderful world of Will Shakespeare.

Dancing horse and all.

1. THE MERMAID AND THE DOLPHIN

A popular comedy hints at the illicit love affair between Elizabeth I and Robert Dudley

My gentle Puck, come hither. Thou rememberest since once I sat upon a promontory and heard a mermaid on a dolphin's back, uttering such dulcet and harmonious breath that the rude sea grew civil at her song and certain stars shot madly from their spheres, to hear the sea-maid's music.

(A Midsummer Night's Dream, 2.1, 1595-6)

OBERON, King of the Fairies, a figure who swings between vengeful tyrant and adoring lover to his wife Titania, is in reflective mood in the enchanted forest outside Athens. The tempestuous nature of the couple's relationship is not unlike that which flourished between Elizabeth I and Robert Dudley, Earl of Leicester, although the Queen and Dudley were never to marry despite his best efforts.

Whether Elizabeth's claim to be the 'Virgin Queen' meant she had never been intimate with a man is an open question. If she had been, Robert Dudley must be the number one suspect. The two had been friends since their childhood – when Elizabeth was eight years old she is said to have confided to Dudley 'I will never marry' – and they shared the same tutor. Their bond grew even closer when they were imprisoned together in the Tower of London during the reign of Elizabeth's half-sister Mary.

When Elizabeth became Queen in 1558 at the age of twenty-five, one of her first acts was to appoint Dudley (*pictured*) as her Master of the Horse, a prestigious position which involved regular attendance upon her. Within a year, she had

a bedchamber organised for him next to her private rooms and it was well known that they enjoyed frequent clandestine meetings together. Tongues started wagging – the handsome, six-foot (1.82m) tall Dudley had no shortage of envious enemies – not least because he was by then a married man. Rumours ran wild and a woman known as Old Mother Dowe of Brentwood was even jailed for spreading gossip that 'My Lord Robert hath given Her Majesty a red petticoat' – in other words, had taken her virginity.

After his wife died in 1560, Dudley launched an unrelenting campaign to win the Queen's hand. The prospect of Her Majesty agreeing to marry him filled Dudley's enemies with horror. They were well aware that, if he succeeded, the presumptuous courtier would consider himself 'king' by any other name. After all, they noted, when the Queen fell ill with smallpox in 1562 she instructed the Privy Council to appoint him Lord Protector of the Realm, along with an eye-watering salary of twenty thousand pounds a year (equivalent to more than six million pounds today), in the event of her death. There was much relief among courtiers that she survived, if only to see Dudley's ambitions thwarted.

In 1564, the year of Will Shakespeare's birth, the Queen created Dudley Earl of Leicester, his seat being the splendid Kenilworth Castle in Warwickshire, and as a Privy Councillor he became one of the most powerful – and unpopular – statesmen in the land. Throughout her reign, the spinster Elizabeth (*pictured*) would be besieged by a line of noble suitors, all of whom would be turned away. Dudley believed his big chance of finally melting Elizabeth's resolve had arrived in July 1575. The Queen was to embark on a summer 'progress,' one of the tours of her realm that she undertook from time to time, sojourning at the palaces of various noblemen and putting them to the enormous cost of entertaining the royal presence along with her considerable retinue. When she informed Dudley that she would be staying with him at  Kenilworth, he resolved to pull out all the stops in order to win her heart.

The trouble and expense to which he went are truly astonishing. Elizabeth was to stay for nineteen days and Dudley set about devising a lavish programme of entertainment to keep her entertained and amused on every one of them. The cost was estimated at a thousand pounds a day (the equivalent of three hundred thousand pounds today), and that was after he had already forked out the staggering sum of sixty thousand pounds (eighteen million pounds today) on improvements to the castle to ensure the Queen's absolute comfort. By comparison, a farmhand at that time would earn no more than a few pounds a year.

From the moment Elizabeth arrived on 9 July she was assailed with grandiloquent speeches, some in Latin, by welcoming parties of actors dressed as heroic figures such as Hercules. Trumpeters sounded a royal salute and a fusillade of cannon fire rang out, which was so loud it could be heard twenty miles (32km) away. She was assured that 'the Lake, the Lodge and the Lord' were at her disposal at all times. As the Queen entered the grounds she was approached by 'the Lady of the Lake', attended by two silk-clad nymphs, who told her that she had presided over the castle lake since King Arthur's day and was now pleased to offer it to Her Majesty. Elizabeth, who had gifted Kenilworth to Dudley in the first place, thanked her then added with dry humour: 'We had thought indeed the lake had been ours, and do you call it yours now? Well, we will herein commune more with you hereafter.'

During her stay, Elizabeth was treated to elaborate displays of colourful and highly inventive fireworks, a performance by an acrobat lured from Italy specifically for the occasion, musicians playing their instruments, finely costumed figures dancing and singing in pageant-like masques, deer hunting, and her favourite 'sport' of bear baiting, the unfortunate bears having been especially brought into the castle. There were sumptuous feasts, for which provision of corn, meat, fish and other victuals had been ordered in from the countryside for many miles around. Large quantities of wine and beer flowed freely. Dudley also proudly unveiled two sets of portraits he had commissioned from respected artists, depicting the Queen and himself (separately).

Among the other attractions, a group of artisan tradesmen from Coventry asked to be allowed to perform their city's traditional 'Hocktide' play. The drama had been presented on the second Tuesday after Easter since ancient times but performances were forbidden during the reign of Henry VIII and remained so. The official reason for the ban was the public disorder that came to be associated with Hocktide festivities, although at the time England's newly installed Protestant authorities were enthusiastically abolishing many long-standing Catholic holidays, the number of which they considered excessive. The Coventry men were delighted to be granted permission and Elizabeth's assent marked nothing less than the play's first revival in a generation. Their presentation apparently celebrated the massacre of the Danes by Ethelred the Unready in the year 1002, and consisted largely of a mock battle in which men dressed as English and Danish knights knocked the living daylights out of each other.

On 18 July, the 'princely pleasures' of Kenilworth reached their climax. As part of the preparations, Dudley had arranged for an area of low-lying land beside the castle to be flooded. It was to be the stage for the biggest extravaganza of the whole stay. That evening rounded off a hot Monday and, after the Queen returned from hunting, she found herself greeted by a spectacular water pageant. The newly created lake had become an enchanted seascape and, as Elizabeth watched, a mermaid with a tail fully 18ft (5.5m) long appeared, blowing on a trumpet fashioned into the shape of a large whelk. The figure was followed by a 24ft-long mechanical dolphin, in reality a specially constructed boat from the sides of which oars protruded. Riding on the dolphin was an amateur actor named Harry Goldingham dressed as Arion, a figure known to students of the classics as an ancient Greek singer and lyre player of legendary skill. Hidden from sight within the vessel was a small orchestra and, as they struck up a tune, Arion began to sing. We owe valuable knowledge of what happened next to an officer of the royal court named Robert Langham (or Laneham), who set down the events in a letter to a friend.

Langham says Arion sang 'a delectable ditty of a song, well adapted to melodious noise, compounded of six several instruments all covert, sounding from the dolphin's belly within'. Although the assembled crowd seemed happy enough with his performance, Goldingham's confidence wavered and he considered his voice had sounded unduly harsh. No doubt to the horror of Dudley looking on, the singer tore off his elaborate disguise and directly addressed the Queen, announcing in reassuring tones that he was 'none of Arion, not he, but eene [only] honest Harry Goldingham'. Dudley need not have worried. Elizabeth roared with laughter and was later to confess she considered that moment to have been the highlight of her entire stay at Kenilworth. After further events on the lake, the evening ended with an impressive display of fireworks.

The public had been invited to gather in the grounds to watch the pageant, for Dudley could not resist showing off his wealth and influence. In addition to the performance, the invitation would give them the opportunity to gain a coveted glimpse of their Queen, Gloriana herself. We can reasonably surmise that among the thousands present was John Shakespeare, mayor of Stratford-upon-Avon, a town just fourteen miles (23km) from Kenilworth, accompanied by his eleven-year-old son Will. So was Shakespeare casting his mind back to that warm July evening when he came to write those lines of Oberon's about 'a mermaid on a dolphin's back' in *A Midsummer Night's Dream* twenty years later? Where else might he have seen such a sight, and heard 'the sea-maid's music'? The certain stars that 'shone madly from their spheres' were the fireworks that closed the show to delighted gasps from the crowd.

Now consider this exchange from *A Midsummer Night's Dream*, which takes place when the 'rude mechanicals' (as the workmen are called) agonise, during rehearsals for the play they hope to present before Duke Theseus and his wedding party, over whether to bring Snug the joiner on stage disguised as a lion:

> *Bottom:* **Masters, you ought to consider with yourselves: to bring in – God shield us! – a lion among ladies, is a most dreadful thing; for there is not a more fearful wildfowl than your lion living; and we ought to look to 't.**

> *Snout:* **Therefore another prologue must tell he is not a lion.**

> *Bottom:* **Nay, you must name his name, and half his face must be seen through the lion's neck: and he himself must speak through, saying thus, or to the same defect**

[effect]: **'Ladies,' or 'Fair-ladies – I would wish you' – or 'I would request you' – or 'I would entreat you – not to fear, not to tremble: my life for yours.** If you think I come hither as a lion, it were pity of my life [it would be dangerous for me]: **no I am no such thing; I am a man as other men are';** and there indeed let him name his name, and tell **them plainly he is Snug the joiner.** (3.2)

When the nervous Snug finally makes his appearance in the play, dressed in the lion costume, he duly pauses to bare his head and give the audience this assurance:

You, ladies, you, whose gentle hearts do fear the smallest monstrous mouse that creeps on floor, may now perchance both quake and tremble here, when lion rough in wildest rage doth roar. Then know that I, one Snug the joiner, am a lion-fell [wearing a lion skin], **nor else no lion's dam; for, if I should as lion come in strife into this place, 'twere pity on my life.** (5.1)

Is this not Harry Goldingham speaking as he tore off his disguise as Arion? Snug's audience are highly amused by this impromptu disclaimer, just as the Queen had been by Goldingham at Kenilworth. Perhaps the whole idea of the rude mechanicals' play, which causes so much hilarity in *A Midsummer Night's Dream*, had itself been inspired by those bumbling amateur Hocktide Play artisans from Coventry.

In an interesting historical footnote, at a feast in Stirling Castle on 30 August 1594 to celebrate the baptism of Prince Henry, eldest son of King James VI of Scotland (later James I of England), there had been a plan to include a decidedly risky spectacle as part of a tableau. According to an account of events that night, *A True Reportarie of the Baptisme of the Prince of Scotland*, a chariot carrying six women adorned as goddesses 'should have been drawn by a Lyon'. But 'because his presence might have brought some feare to the nearest, or that the sight of the lights and torches might have commoved his tameness,' it was decided a Moorish warrior should take the animal's place. The organisers had clearly concluded, to quote Bottom, that 'a lion among ladies' would indeed have been 'a most dreadful thing'. Shakespeare began writing *A Midsummer Night's Dream* in 1595, the year after those royal baptism celebrations took place and the *True Reportarie* was published in Edinburgh and London.

As for the story of Arion, that is told by the Greek historian Herodotus. He recounts that the god Apollo sent a pod of dolphins to rescue Arion after he was kidnapped by pirates. Arion threw himself into the sea and one of the animals obligingly carried him to safety on its back. Shakespeare mentions the legend again in *Twelfth Night*, when a captain reassures the shipwrecked Viola that he had caught sight of her brother fighting for life in the raging seas, just before they themselves were cast ashore on the coast of Illyria. He tells Viola:

Like Arion on the dolphin's back, I saw him hold acquaintance with the waves, so long as I could see. (1.2)

As it turned out, Dudley's extravagance did him no good. On Wednesday, 20 July, the twelfth day of the visit, something went badly wrong. The Queen was meant to have gone to nearby Wedgnock Park to see yet another spectacle he had laid on, featuring 'goddesses and nymphs'. She declined to go and, although her decision was blamed on the weather being 'not so clearly disposed', Langham reveals there was much talk of Elizabeth departing from Kenilworth there and then. George Gascoigne, a courtier taking part in the tour, made his own record of events that day, writing:

There was nothing but weeping and wailing, crying and howling, dole and desperation, mourning and moan.

Gascoigne too formed the impression that Her Majesty intended to leave the castle without delay. What can have happened?

* * *

Despite the arrogant Dudley's best efforts to woo the Queen, a skeleton in his cupboard had already made such a match out of the question. On 8 September 1560 his first wife, Amy Robsart, who had been alone at Cumnor Place, near Oxford, was found dead under mysterious circumstances. Her body was discovered at the foot of a small flight of stairs with her neck broken and wounds to her head. She was twenty-eight years old.

Although a coroner's jury returned a verdict of death by 'misfortune', in other words accidental, the finger of suspicion was soon pointed at Dudley. He had arranged for Amy's murder, so the scuttlebutt ran, in order to be free to marry Elizabeth. Whether there was any foundation to the rumours or not, they meant that all his future efforts to win the Queen's hand would be futile. If she had accepted Dudley's proposal, Elizabeth's enemies would go so far as to suggest that she had been complicit in Amy's death, and such a scandal could have cost her the throne.

While professing his undying love for Elizabeth, Dudley was covertly bedding Lettice Knollys, one of the Queen's ladies-in-waiting. A great-niece of Elizabeth's mother, Anne Boleyn, Lettice was described by all who saw her as stunningly attractive. She was a member of the royal party staying at Kenilworth that July, and it helped that her husband, Walter Devereux, first Earl of Essex, was away fighting in Ireland on the Queen's behalf. In fact, Dudley and Lettice were consummating an acquaintance first forged ten years earlier. On that occasion the Queen had flown into a jealous rage upon learning he had been seen flirting with Lettice. What some historians believe happened on the twelfth day of the visit to Kenilworth in 1575 was that Elizabeth got wind of Dudley's renewed dallying with her lady-in-waiting and reacted with furious indignation.

Despite the latest set-back, Elizabeth decided to remain at the castle for the rest of her scheduled stay. A detailed itinerary had long been organised to accommodate her elsewhere at the appointed dates on her 'progress,' and it would prove difficult to change. In a bitter irony, the next stop was due to be Chartley in Staffordshire, home of Lettice (*pictured*) in her cap-

acity as Countess of Essex. The atmosphere when the Queen did arrive must have been decidedly awkward.

In the meantime, a gloomy mood appears to have descended at Kenilworth. The festivities largely fizzled out until the farewell ceremony that had been arranged for Elizabeth's send-off. When, three years later, Dudley secretly married Lettice after she became pregnant with his child and her husband had died of dysentery – Dudley was inevitably rumoured to have poisoned him – the Queen was incandescent with rage. She reportedly boxed Lettice's ears and banished the 'flouting wench' from her sight forever.

Look what Oberon goes on to tell Puck shortly after those lines about the mermaid on the dolphin's back:

> **That very time I saw, but thou couldst not, flying between the cold moon and the earth, Cupid all arm'd. A certain aim he took at a fair vestal throned by the west, and loosed his love-shaft smartly from his bow, as it should pierce a hundred thousand hearts. But I might see young Cupid's fiery shaft quench'd in the chaste beams**

of the watery moon, and the imperial votaress passed on, in maiden meditation, fancy-free. Yet mark'd I where the bolt of Cupid fell. It fell upon a little western flower, before milk-white, now purple with love's wound, and maidens call it love-in-idleness. (2.1)

Cupid aimed his arrow at 'a fair vestal' (one who has vowed virginity like the Vestal Virgins of ancient Rome) who was 'throned by the west' (this is none other than Elizabeth herself). It missed, and 'the imperial votaress' (the royal vow-taker pledged to chastity) passed on 'in maiden meditation, fancy-free' (free from the power of love). The arrow did, however, fall upon 'a little western flower'. While Shakespeare has in mind for dramatic purposes the *viola tricolor* or pansy, then also known as love-in-idleness, the flower is here also a metaphor for Lettice Knollys. (Lettice was portrayed as a character named Floscula – which means 'little flower' — in a play titled *Endymion* written by John Lyly around 1588.) Cupid's arrow may have missed the Queen, at whom it was aimed on Dudley's behalf, but it hit Lettice instead.

Before her affair with Dudley, Lettice had indeed maintained a spotless 'milk white' reputation for fidelity to her husband. Oberon boasts that he knew what was going on behind closed doors between Lettice and Dudley – 'that very time I saw, but thou couldst not' – even though Puck, like so many others, remained in ignorance.

The pansy itself, a name derived from the French *pensée* for 'thought', was additionally known as 'hearts-ease' (meaning 'peace of mind') and 'call-me-to-you' by the Elizabethans. Because it represented love, Oberon sends Puck on an errand to fetch the little flower so that he can smear its juice on the sleeping eyelids of Titania, in order to make her fall in love with the first thing she sees upon waking (which turns out to be Bottom wearing an ass's head). Legend held that the pansy, which proliferated in wild meadows, had once been 'milk white' but obtained its dash of colour after becoming stained with the blood of a lover's heart pierced by Cupid's arrow. The flower was a known favourite of Elizabeth.

Despite all the turmoil, the Queen still felt deeply for Dudley, the only true love she had ever known, and her attitude towards him eventually softened. In 1586, Sir Walter Raleigh wrote to Dudley: 'The Queen is on very good terms with you ... and you are again her sweet Robin.' The pair grew closer once more, and he was given the honour of walking beside her horse as she rode into Tilbury, at the mouth of the Thames, on 8 August 1588 to address the troops standing ready to defend London against the expected arrival of invading soldiers from the Spanish Armada. Within a month of that speech, however, Dudley was taken ill and, when he died on 4 September at the age of fifty-five, Elizabeth was inconsolable. She barricaded herself in her chambers for days on end, kept his letters to her in a locked casket for the rest of her life, and it was said that her eyes filled with tears at the very mention of his name.

Shakespeare may have been making passing references to Dudley when Ophelia in her madness sings a snatch of 'For bonny sweet Robin is all my joy' in *Hamlet*, and the jester Feste trills 'Hey, Robin, jolly Robin, tell me how thy lady does' in *Twelfth Night*. Robert Dudley's love affair with Elizabeth was the sensation of the age. Shakespeare was hardly likely to miss a chance of alluding to it, and his audiences, from the penny groundlings to the great and good sitting high in the theatre galleries, knew exactly who he was talking about.

2. THE DAY THE EARTH MOVED

The young Will is shaken by two of the most violent earthquakes in Britain's history

Diseased nature oftentimes breaks forth in strange eruptions. Oft the teeming earth is with a kind of colic pinch'd and vex'd by the imprisoning of unruly wind within her womb; which, for enlargement striving, shakes the old beldam [old lady] **earth, and topples down steeples and moss-grown towers. At your birth our grandma earth, having this distemperature** [disorder], **in passion shook.** (*Henry IV, Part 1*, 3.1, 1596-7)

CYNICAL Harry Hotspur scoffs at the grandiose claims of the Welsh wizard Owen Glendower that the earth itself trembled in fear at the moment of his birth. Hotspur counters that the shaking would have taken place anyway. He goes on to espouse his own theory about what causes earthquakes. It may amuse us today that seismic upheavals might be blamed on flatulence, comparing the planet to an incontinent elderly grandmother but, long before shifting tectonic plates were conceived of, that is probably as close to a scientific explanation as anyone was going to get. At least it has more going for it than the fiery Welsh chieftain's alternative. Glendower's trumpeting in the same scene that :

> **At my nativity the front of heaven was full of fiery shapes, of burning cressets** [flaming torches, here meaning meteors]; **and at my birth the frame and huge foundation of the earth shaked like a coward**

gets a further knockback with Hotspur's dismissive:

Why, so it would have done at the same season, if your mother's cat had but kittened, though yourself had never been born.

The British Isles are not noted for large earthquakes but two of the most violent in the history of northwest Europe struck when Shakespeare was young. The first, with a magnitude of 5.0 on the Richter Scale, hit directly beneath the West Midlands, not far from his Warwickshire home, in 1575 when he was ten years old. Stratford-upon-Avon would have been among the towns and villages to experience strong shaking. The contemporary historian John Stow tells how widespread the effects were felt:

On xxvj [26] February, betweene foure and sixe of the clocke in the afternoone, great Earthquakes happened in the Cities of Yorke, Woorcester, Glocester, Bristow, Hereford and in the Countreys about, which caused the people to runne out of their houses, for feare they [the buildings] should have fallen on their heads.

Part of a castle fell down, chimneys tumbled, dishes flew off shelves, while church bells rang out of their own accord as the ground swayed beneath them. In a place Stow calls Norton Chappell:

The people beeing on their knees at evening prayer, the ground mooving, caused them to runne away, in great feare that the dead bodyes woulde have risen, or the Chappell to have fallen.

Just five years later an even bigger earthquake struck. It appears to have been the largest to rock Britain throughout the entire second millennium AD. At around 6pm on the evening of 6 April 1580 – which was the Wednesday of Holy Week, the week before Easter – the Dover Straits Earthquake notched up a bone-shaking magnitude of 5.9 on the Richter scale. It had a shallow focal depth of about twelve miles (20km). Will Shakespeare was now almost sixteen years old and still living in Stratford. The earthquake severely rattled towns and villages across southern and central England, as well as northern France and the Low Countries. The epicentre was a point on the seabed between Dover and Calais, with shaking felt as far north as York and possibly even Edinburgh, and as far west as Bristol, leading to extensive panic and an outburst of fervent prayers.

Terrified people demanded all the news they could get about the earthquake, and over the next few days and weeks a large number of pamphlets full of lurid accounts were rushed into print for sale to eager customers. The writer Thomas Churchyard, who was in London when the quake struck, wrote that the effects could be felt all across the capital and its suburbs. He reported 'a wonderful motion and trembling of the earth,' then added:

Churches, Pallaces, houses and other buildings did so quiver and shake that such as were then present in the same were tossed too and fro as they stoode, and others, as they sate on seates, driven off their places.

Widespread damage to buildings occurred, particularly in Kent. The tower of the Church of St Peter's, Broadstairs, cracked from top to bottom, and a section of the famous chalk cliffs collapsed near Dover, taking with it a chunk of the walls of the eleventh-century Dover Castle. Near Hythe, Saltwood Castle, notorious as the place where the murder of Thomas Becket had been plotted in 1170, was so badly damaged as to render it uninhabitable. It remained so for three hundred years until restoration began in the 1880s. Chimney stacks were sent tumbling and masonry toppled from buildings, especially church steeples. The extent of damage to the hovels of the poor was not thought worth recording, not because there was none but simply because their inhabitants' wretched social status did not merit it.

In London, John Stow tells us that while a sermon was being delivered at Christ's Church, Newgate, the capital's largest place of worship after St Paul's Cathedral:

A stone fell from the toppe of the Church whiche killed out of hand one Thomas Grey an apprentice, & another stone also brused his felowe servaunte named Mabel Everet, so that she lived but foure dayes after; diverse other were sore hurt with running out of the Church.

Masonry crashed down from St Paul's Cathedral itself, a pinnacle fell off Westminster Abbey and, in Cambridgeshire, stonework plummeted from Ely Cathedral. Many people around the country were injured and it is impossible to know how many more, if any, died other than the unfortunate youngsters Thomas Grey and Mabel Everet. Remarkably, accounts suggest that in some places the ground continued shaking for between seven and eight minutes, with three or four ground waves seen rippling across the landscape like waves in water.

Thomas Churchyard describes the chaotic scenes at the crowded Theatre and its nearby rival the Curtain (the Globe was not yet conceived of). Telling how the audiences watching plays at the time 'a fearful frightening goett', he says:

A number being at the Theatre and the Curtain at Hollywell [Holywell Street in Shoreditch], beholding the plays, were so shaken, especially those that stood in the highest rooms and standings [upper and lower galleries], that they were not a little dismayed, considering that they could no way shift for themselves, unless they would, by leaping, hazard their lives or limbs, as some did indeed, leaping from the lowest standings.

The fact that the earthquake hit during Easter week was

taken as an ill omen and there were widespread calls for repentance. Unlike Hotspur's 'flatulence' explanation, to many people the trembler was nothing less than the wrathful act of an angry God. A special prayer book was urgently issued to be used in all churches, aimed at calming worried parishioners. It rejoiced under the snappy title of *The order of prayer, and other exercises, upon Wednesdays and Frydayes, to avert and turne God's wrath from us, threatned by the late terrible earthquake: to be used in all parish churches and housholdes throughout the realme, by order given from the Queenes Maiesties most honourable Privie Counsel.*

The Puritans, for their part, had no hesitation in triumphantly attributing the disastrous events to divine anger over the ungodly goings-on in London's theatres. In his *The Anatomie of Abuses*, the religious pamphleteer Philip Stubbes indulges in more than a hint of *schadenfreude* as he puts his own slant on Churchyard's account:

> *The like judgement (almost) did the Lord shew unto them a little befor, being assembled at the Theaters, to see their bawdie enterluds and other trumperies practised. For he caused the earth mightily to shake and quaver, as though all the world would have fallen down, whereat the People stood sore amazed. Some leapt down from the top of turrets, pinnacles, and towers wher they stood to the ground, whereof some had their legs broke, some their arms, some their backs, some hurt one where, some another, & many sore crusht and brusd: but not any, but they went away sore afraid & wounded in conscience.*

For good measure, Stubbes adds this earnest plea:

> *The Lord of his mercie, open the eyes of the maiestrats [magistrates] to pluck down these places of abuse, that God may be honoured, and their consciences disburthened.*

The clergyman Abraham Fleming weighed into the debate with his treatise, *A Bright Burning Beacon, forewarning all wise Virgins to trim their lampes against the coming of the Bridegroome*, declaring:

> As much is God glorified in the pulling downe of polluted
> places, as in the building up of holie temples.

By 'polluted places' he meant, of course, the theatres. Shakespeare and his fellow thespians would be forced to do battle against such prejudice all through their working lives. Only the writer Gabriel Harvey, in a letter to his friend Edmund Spenser, sounded a note of light relief. Recounting how he was playing cards with two 'gentlewomen' at the time the quake struck, he says his female companions had been quarrelling so vehemently that he quipped:

> Good Lord, is it not wonderful strange that the delicate
> voices of two so proper fine Gentlewomen should make such
> a sudden terrible Earthquake?

As 'the Earth under us quaked, and the house shaked above,' Harvey continued, one of the women declared: 'I beseech you heartily, let us leave off playing and fall a-praying.'

The earthquake caused further deaths, injuries and serious damage in France and Belgium, and seismic effects were observed on the waters of the English Channel. Stow says the sea 'foamed' at Sandwich and 'shippes tottered' both there and in the port of Dover. It is unclear whether a tsunami actually struck the English coast but records show a destructive inundation in France, which cost hundreds of lives. A contemporary French account reports:

> In the city of Calais such a horrible and terrible earthquake
> did come to pass that a great part of the houses fell, and even
> the sea overflowed into the city and did ruin and drown a
> great number of houses, and numerous persons perished,
> and a great multitude of beasts lost which were at pasture
> outside this city.

Adding strength to the suggestion of a tsunami, the account goes on to say that up to thirty ships, English, French and Flemish, 'perished by the great and awful tempestuousness of the sea'. It adds:

> One passenger that came from Dover to Calais relates that his ship did touch the bottom of the sea five times, and the waves mounting higher than six heights of a spear above his ship, but God preserved him.

Two aftershocks struck later the same day as the main quake, and two more early the following morning, causing further damage. The largest aftershock came almost a month later on 1 May 1580, with a magnitude of around 4.4. Earthquakes were clearly on Shakespeare's mind when he came to write *Romeo and Juliet*. Asked about Juliet's age, the down-to-earth nurse says:

> **On Lammas-eve at night shall she be fourteen; that shall she, marry** [by the Virgin Mary, a common oath]; **I remember it well. 'Tis since the earthquake now eleven years; and she was wean'd – I never shall forget it – of all the days of the year, upon that day.** (1.3)

The nurse is verifying the age of Juliet by recalling the very day she ceased to breast-feed the babe as a wet nurse, her own infant daughter having died. She remembers it well, not only – as she goes on to tell us – because she had smeared the bitter herb wormwood on her nipples in order to discourage the child from taking her milk any longer (an Elizabethan practice), but because 'the earthquake' struck on that day. Shakespeare would have known that Italy was subject to earthquakes and the reference adds a degree of realism to his setting of Verona. He also clearly recalled from his own experience how country folk would speak of past events based on how many years 'since the earthquake' they had occurred. It was a method of calculating the passing years to which the groundlings in his audience would probably have related.

That reference to 'eleven years' since the earthquake has puzzled scholars, leading some to question whether Shakespeare wrote *Romeo and Juliet* in 1591, which was eleven years after the 1580 shake felt in England. No evidence exists that the play was performed before 1595, however, and for a variety of reasons that year seems the likeliest in which it was written.

But there is another possible explanation. In March 1584, an earthquake with a magnitude of 5.9 rocked Switzerland and northern Italy, its effects severe enough to be reported in Britain. At the epicentre was the small town of Aigle, near Geneva. In addition to the injuries and damage caused by the initial quake, an aftershock created a massive landslide of rocks and mud which, according to *The History of the City and State of Geneva* (published in 1647 from older manuscripts) 'poured down like a shower of rain and overwhelmed in an instant the valleys and neighbouring plains'.

The landslide destroyed several villages, killing more than three hundred inhabitants, and at even its shallowest point the wall of moving earth measured 10ft (3m) deep. According to the *History*:

All the ground which it covered was made so smooth that a man would have thought it to have been run over by a rolling stone, there being not the least appearance of any houses.

The quake also caused a tsunami on nearby Lake Geneva, which swamped settlements along the shoreline and led to further deaths. The Aigle earthquake is mentioned by the English clergyman William Covell in his 1595 polemical treatise, *Polimanteia.* It is likely Shakespeare was familiar with Covell's book, not least because it contains a reference to his recently published poems *Venus and Adonis* and *The Rape of Lucrece.* So if the nurse has the 1584 Swiss-Italian earthquake in mind, her reckoning of Juliet's age eleven years later would fit exactly with 1595 as the year *Romeo and Juliet* was written and first performed.

In her description of the earthquake, Juliet's nurse adds an interesting footnote when she says:

> **Shake quoth the dove-house: 'twas no need, I trow** [declare], **to bid me trudge** [be on my way].

The terrified woman had witnessed a dovecote shaking so severely in the earthquake that, she tells us, she needed no instructing to run for her life in case it collapsed on her. Dovecotes had been a feature of the English countryside for centuries, the birds being bred as a source of fresh meat in winter (in *The Merchant of Venice*, Bassanio is offered 'a dish of doves'), their eggs, and their droppings for fertiliser. Pigeons, closely related to doves in the family *Columbidae*, were also used in medicine. *The English Huswife*, a book of cookery and cures written by Gervase Markham in 1615, advises victims of the plague to apply to their feet a pigeon 'cut in two parts' (gruesomely known as 'pigeon slippers'). *The London Pharmacopoeia*, published by the College of Physicians in 1618, recommends pulling the feathers off a live pigeon and applying the bald patch on the bird's body to the sores of sufferers in the hope of remedy.

Stratford-upon-Avon boasts a dovecote, which is today preserved as a heritage building. The free-standing brick structure in Grove Road dates from the seventeenth century, at which time there were an estimated twenty-six thousand dovecotes in England. Did it, perhaps, replace an earlier timber-built dovecote on the same site, little more than five minutes' walk from the Shakespeare family home in Henley Street? Shakespeare mentions earthquakes in several other plays – *All's Well That Ends Well*, *As You Like It*, *Henry V*, *King John*, *Much Ado About Nothing*, *The Tempest*, *Pericles*, and in his poem *Venus and Adonis* – but something about the nurse's remark intrigues me. It is such a fine point of detail. Did the youthful Will just happen to be loitering beside a dovecote when the massive Dover Straits Earthquake jolted his home town on that April evening in 1580?   And did that graphic image of the ground shaking, the structure rocking, and the panicked birds flying off in all directions stay with him, to be put to good use when he came to write *Romeo and Juliet*?

3. THE GIRL WHO WAS OPHELIA

The death of Hamlet's lover echoes the tragic drowning of a young woman in the River Avon

There is a willow grows aslant the brook, that shows [reflects] **his hoary** [silver-grey] **leaves in the glassy stream. There with fantastic** [intricately fashioned] **garlands did she come, of crowflowers, nettles, daisies, and long purples, that liberal shepherds give a grosser name, but our cold** [chaste] **maids do dead men's fingers call them. There on the pendant** [overhanging] **boughs her coronet weeds clamb'ring to hang, an envious sliver broke, when down her weedy trophies and herself fell in the weeping brook. Her clothes spread wide and, mermaid-like, awhile they bore her up; which time she chanted snatches of old tunes, as one incapable** [insensible] **of her own distress, or like a creature native and indued** [accustomed] **unto that element. But long it could not be till that her garments, heavy with their drink, pull'd the poor wretch from her melodious lay** [song] **to muddy death.**

(Hamlet, 4.7, 1601-2)

WITH these exquisite lines, some of the most heart-rending Shakespeare would write, Hamlet's mother Gertrude reports the shocking death of the young Ophelia. They depict a scene so poignant that it has inspired paintings by numerous artists down the years. The girl who loved the Prince of Denmark has met her untimely end by drowning. Curiously, her death appears to bear uncanny similarities to an incident that became the talk of Stratford-upon-Avon when Will was just fifteen years old. Perhaps, as he was writing his great tragedy, his mind turned back to that dark day.

On 17 December 1579, a young woman tragically died when she fell into the River Avon at Tiddington, then a mile or so upriver from Stratford itself, but long since absorbed within the urban boundary. The river at that point was noted for its overhanging willow trees. The drowned girl's parents insisted that she had simply lost her footing while attempting to fill a bucket with water. She was duly given a proper Christian burial in the churchyard at nearby Alveston. But as the weeks went by, ugly rumours started to fly. People began questioning if her death was accidental after all, and asking whether she had instead taken her own life. The name of the unfortunate young woman was, somewhat remarkably, Katherine (or Kate) Hamlett.

The gossip around town became so persistent that Henry Rogers, Stratford's coroner, took it upon himself to empanel a jury of 'three gentlemen' from Alveston and ten other parishioners to investigate the case and thereby put an end to the speculation one way or another. The inquest opened on 11 February 1580. After seven weeks in the earth, poor Katherine's body was hauled out of its resting place and minutely examined in a search for clues that might suggest she had died a violent death. We do not know now what events in her brief lifetime had led to such unhappy speculation, but we can imagine the horror her grieving family must have been going through as her corpse was exhumed to be pored over.

The Elizabethans considered suicide both a mortal sin and a crime as serious as murder. Indeed, in law it *was* murder – of oneself. If the jurors should find that Katherine had died at her own hands, her body would not be allowed to return to her grave in the hallowed ground of the churchyard. She would instead have been cast naked and without any further religious ceremony into a hole dug in the ground beside a crossroads, broken pottery and stones being thrown into the poor girl's grave with her. Having committed the legal offence of *felo de se* (the Latin phrase means 'felon of oneself'), her death would bring everlasting shame to her family, who would then be required to forfeit their possessions to the Crown. What was more, Katherine's soul – so it was claimed – would be denied a place in heaven by the Almighty. Ironically, anyone surviving a suicide attempt could expect to be put to death as punishment.

Much to the relief of Katherine's family, coroner Rogers at length declared in his findings:

> *The deceased was going with a milk pail to draw water at the River Avon and was standing on the bank when she slipped and fell in, and was drowned, meeting her death in no other wise or fashion.*

He recorded a verdict that Katherine had died '*per infortunium*' – by accident. There was much relief in Tiddington and Alveston that no scandal would besmirch their villages' good names. Her body could at last be re-interred in the sanctified ground from which it had been so rudely ripped.

The description of Katherine Hamlett's death and its aftermath offers striking parallels to those of Ophelia in Shakespeare's play. While Gertrude gives no indication that Ophelia's demise was anything other than an unhappy accident, the two gravediggers who open Act Five of *Hamlet* have clearly heard something to the contrary, as their conversation reveals:

> *First Gravedigger:* **Is she to be buried in Christian burial when she wilfully seeks her own salvation** [has killed herself]?
>
> *Second Gravedigger:* **I tell thee she is. Therefore make her grave straight** [facing East-West in the Christian tradition]. **The crowner** [coroner] **hath sate on her and finds it Christian burial.** (5.1)

The gravediggers' discussion on the subject of suicide continues. Later in the same scene, Ophelia's distressed brother Laertes protests at her graveside that the burial service has been too cursory. 'What ceremony else?' he demands. And again: 'What ceremony else?' The officiating priest gives him short shrift, replying:

> **Her obsequies** [funeral rites] **have been as far enlarg'd as we have warranty** [as permitted by Church liturgy]. **Her death was doubtful; and, but that great command o'ersways the order** [prescribed practice], **she should in ground unsanctified have lodg'd till the last trumpet. For** [instead of] **charitable prayers, shards, flints, and pebbles should be thrown on her. Yet here she is allow'd her virgin crants** [a garland worn as a sign of maidenhood], **her maiden strewments** [flowers strewn on the grave, often a sign of chastity], **and the bringing home** [to her last resting place] **of bell and burial** [the tolling of the church bell and formal solemnities]. (5.1)

In other words, Ophelia's death was considered to be suicide and only the direct command of the King and Queen, Claudius and Gertrude, had overruled Church custom and allowed her even those burial rites she has received. The fact that Ophelia may have drowned herself while the balance of her mind was disturbed was unlikely to be considered an excuse in Elizabethan England. Even though we have seen earlier in the play that she had been driven to madness by the murder of her father Polonius, and Hamlet's rejection of her as a lover, the law was largely intolerant of pleas of mitigation in such cases. Two researchers, Michael MacDonald and Terence Murphy, have established that out of eight hundred and three suicide verdicts delivered to the King's Bench between 1590 and 1599, the decade before *Hamlet* was written, in only five cases was a mitigating plea of '*non compos mentis*' allowed. They go on to say that this tiny proportion is consistent with all verdicts returned between 1500 and 1650.

Relating the horror of Ophelia's death, Gertrude first

pauses to give an account of the willow tree with its pendant branches hanging out above a stream and the wild flowers the girl was collecting. It is an odd interruption to her narrative, considering the gravity of the news she is about to relate, but that image too is pure rural Warwickshire. Gertrude names crow-flowers (thought to mean either the marsh marigold or a wetland bloom known as ragged robin), nettles, daisies and long purples (some botanists suggest this means the early-purple orchid or *orchis mascula*, though another view prefers the cuckoo-pint or wild arum, also known as lords-and-ladies). Shakespeare's term 'dead men's fingers' would have been familiar in and around his native county although, as Gertrude says, there were also 'grosser names' for plants whose appearance struck 'liberal [free with their language] shepherds' by their similarity to a distinctive part of the male anatomy.

There is symbolism in the tree from which Ophelia fell being a willow, which in Shakespeare's time would be the common 'white' willow (*Salix alba*), the weeping willow not having been introduced into England until early in the eighteenth century. (Despite that, the weeping willow appears in several popular artistic portrayals of her death.) The willow had been associated with mourning since Biblical times, where Psalm 137 tells of the captive Israelites weeping for their lost lands as they lay beneath willows alongside the rivers of Babylon. The phrase 'to wear the willow' denoted someone experiencing great sadness. By Elizabethan times, the tree had also become symbolic of jilted lovers mourning their lost loves. The seventeenth-century clergyman Thomas Fuller tells in his *History of the Worthies of England* how the willow 'is a sad tree, whereof such who have lost their love make their mourning garlands'. Shakespeare refers to the tree in several of his plays, most memorably when the broken-hearted Desdemona sings the 'willow, willow, willow' song on the night her husband Othello goes on to murder her in a fit of jealous rage.

Ophelia's own spirit had been crushed. As tragic a figure as she is, she was at least fortunate not to have been treated as harshly in death as she was in life. Like poor Katherine Hamlett, she was finally allowed to rest in peace.

* * *

Not only does Shakespeare appear to have been casting his memory back to his boyhood in recalling the tragedy of Katherine when he portrayed Ophelia's death and burial, he almost certainly had in mind a celebrated court case. 'Hales versus Petit' gripped the nation's attention when it was heard in court in 1560. The thrust of the arcane argument that had taxed some of the finest legal brains in England is articulated in *Hamlet* by the worker who digs Ophelia's grave, as he and his companion discuss whether she was guilty of her own death:

> *First Gravedigger:* **It must be se offendendo** [felo de se], **it cannot be else. For here lies the point: if I drown myself wittingly, it argues an act; and an act hath three branches – it is to act, to do, and to perform; argal** [ergo or therefore], **she drown'd herself wittingly.** (5.1)

Their discussion continues:

> *First Gravedigger:* **Give me leave. Here lies the water – good. Here stands the man – good. If the man go to this water and drown himself, it is, will he nill he, he goes, mark you that. But if the water come to him and drown him, he drowns not himself. Argal** [ergo], **he that is not guilty of his own death shortens not his own life.**
>
> *Second Gravedigger:* **But is this law?**
>
> *First Gravedigger:* **Ay, marry is't, crowner's quest** [coroner's inquest] **law.**

In 1554, a judge named Sir James Hales had drowned himself in the river at Canterbury. The coroner conducting an inquest into his death returned a verdict of *felo de se*. As a suicide, his estate was automatically forfeit to the Crown, which in turn intended to bestow part of it upon one Cyriac Petit of Kent, about whom little else is known. Four years after Sir James' death, his widow Margaret instigated legal proceedings against Petit for the recovery of a lease on land at Graveney, near Faversham, which she had held jointly with her husband before his death.

The case revolved around the abstruse point of whether the offence of committing suicide had actually occurred during Sir James' lifetime or after his death. Lady Hales' counsel argued that Sir James 'cannot be *felo de se* till the death is fully consummate, and the death precedes the felony and the forfeiture'. In other words, because a felony could only be committed by a person who was alive, and one would have to be dead before self-murder could be attributed, no felony had been committed at the instant Sir James' interest in the lease had passed to his widow as the surviving partner.

Like the gravedigger, counsel for Petit countered that the act of committing suicide consisted of three parts:

> *The first is the imagination, which is a reflection or meditation of the mind, whether or not it is convenient for him to destroy himself, and what way it can be done; the second is the resolution, which is a determination of the mind to destroy himself; the third is the perfection, which is the execution of what the mind had resolved to do. And of all the parts, the doing of the act is the greatest in the judgment of our law, and it is in effect the whole.*

The case attracted considerable attention because of the fine legal nuance it presented. Lord Browne, one of the presiding justices, summed up the dilemma magnificently:

Sir James Hales was dead, and how came he to his death? It may be answered by drowning – and who drowned him? Sir James Hales – and when did he drown him? In his lifetime. So that Sir James Hales being alive caused Sir James Hales to die, and the act of the living man was the death of the dead man. And then for this offence it is reasonable to punish the living man who committed the offence, and not the dead man. But how can he be said to be punished alive when the punishment comes after his death?

For his part, Lord Chief Justice Dyer concluded with:

Wherefore all the Justices agreed that the forfeiture of the goods and chattels, real and personal, of Sir James Hales shall have relation to the act done in his lifetime, which was the cause of his death, viz: the throwing himself into the water ... He therefore committed felony in his lifetime, although there was no possibility of the forfeiture being found in his lifetime, for until his death there was no cause of forfeiture.

Confused? Petit won, and the case was significant enough for the distinguished lawyer Sir Edmund Plowden to include a full report of it in his authoritative collection of legal papers titled *Commentaries*, published in 1571. Plowden's book appeared again after his death in an abridged edition that was circulated in 1597, just a few years before Shakespeare wrote *Hamlet*. The revived case would undoubtedly have been the subject of much discussion in London's Inns of Court and Inns of Chancery, the law schools and offices where all lawyers received their training.

Shakespeare himself was familiar with the Inns, gala performances of several of his plays having been staged in their halls. He set one act of the history play *Henry VI, Part 1* in their gardens. The habitués of Clement's Inn, in particular, acquired notoriety as a wild lot, given to partying and causing 'the honest burghers of Westminster much concern'. Shakespeare knew of its reputation, which is why in *Henry IV, Part 2* he has the old fool Justice Shallow boast while reminiscing:

I must, then, to the Inns o' Court shortly. I was [at] Clement's Inn, where I think they will talk of mad Shallow yet. (3.2)

In the nineteenth century, the tale of Ophelia almost claimed an unlikely victim in the shape of Elizabeth ('Lizzie') Siddall. She was the model hired to pose as Shakespeare's tragic heroine by the Pre-Raphaelite artist John Everett Millais. His portrayal (*pictured*) has become the most celebrated depiction of Ophelia's drowning – and it very nearly cost poor Lizzie her life. In the course of modelling for his painting, she was required to lie for hours on end in a bath. Oil lamps were placed beneath the bath to keep the water warm, but on one occasion the lamps went out and Millais had become so engrossed in his work that he did not notice. Lizzie ended up lying in a tub of cold water, as a result of which she contracted pneumonia.

Her furious father engaged a doctor to treat her and sent Millais the bill, threatening legal action if it was not paid. Lizzie went on to marry the poet Dante Gabriel Rossetti and refused to work for Millais ever again. After losing her first child in a stillbirth, she fell into a deep depression. On 11 February 1862, she committed suicide by taking an overdose of the opiate laudanum. She was just thirty-two years old. A distraught Rossetti is said to have burned the suicide note she left him in order to prevent Lizzie, like Katherine Hamlett and Ophelia before her, facing the grim prospect of being refused a Christian burial.

4. UNDERNEATH THE ARCHES

Lines in one of Will's poems appear to recall a curious sight he witnessed in Stratford

As through an arch the violent roaring tide / Outruns the eye that doth behold his haste, / Yet in the eddy boundeth in his pride / Back to the strait that forc'd him on so fast, / In rage sent out, recall'd in rage, being past. / Even so his sighs, his sorrows, make a saw / To push grief on and back the same grief draw.

(*The Rape of Lucrece,* 1594)

WILL Shakespeare's fledgling career as an actor and writer almost came to a juddering halt in the summer of 1592, only a few years after he had left Stratford-upon-Avon for London, so full of hope. A severe outbreak of bubonic plague gripped the capital in the spring of that year, and in June the desperate authorities ordered all theatres to close in an attempt to slow the spread of the disease. Indeed, according to Puritan preachers the fact that theatres were such god-forsaken dens of iniquity was the very reason God was smiting the populace with such gruelling punishment.

Suddenly the theatre companies faced catastrophe. Not only were the actors at risk from the infection like everyone else, but the closures threatened financial ruin. The one option left was to haul their baskets of props and lavish costumes on to horse-drawn carts, grab their scripts and take to the road, touring provincial towns and cities to present their plays far away from the disease-ravaged metropolis. The players tentatively returned that autumn, when the outbreak looked as if it was easing with the chillier weather, but the respite was short. On 2 February 1593, the theatres were closed again as the infection returned with a vengeance. They remained shut through most of that year while plague carried away up to a thousand victims a week in London.

Shakespeare had another string to his bow. He picked up his quill and began to write poetry, hoping to please Henry Wriothesley (pronounced Rizely), third Earl of Southampton, a wealthy sponsor of the arts. Southampton may even have allowed him to take refuge from the plague on his country estate at Titchfield, in Hampshire. In 1593, Shakespeare's narrative poem *Venus and Adonis* appeared in print, prefaced by a gushing dedication to the generous and clearly somewhat vain young earl. Rich in erotic imagery, the book proved an instant success. Its appeal was so enduring that it would be reprinted eight times during the author's lifetime. The following year, Shakespeare, then aged thirty, struck again with a classical narrative titled *The Rape of Lucrece*, once more dedicated to Southampton.

The new poem told a far more tragic and moralistic tale than had *Venus and Adonis*, drawing on Ovid and Livy, about how the beautiful Lucretia – her name anglicised to Lucrece – was cruelly raped by Sextus Tarquinius, the king of Rome's son, circa 509 BC. The crime had a shattering effect on ancient Rome, at least according to legend. Lucrece committed suicide out of shame but revulsion over the outrage led to a bloody uprising, banishment of the royal family and the founding of the Roman republic. We know the story fascinated Shakespeare because he alludes to it in no fewer than five of his plays, *Cymbeline, Titus Andronicus, Macbeth, The Taming of the Shrew* and *Twelfth Night*.

Of the poem's 1,855 lines, one verse in particular is of interest to us here. The stanza expresses the agonising of Lucrece's husband Collatine, after she urgently summons him home to reveal that his one-time friend Tarquin has violated her. Tarquin is long gone and, as Collatine listens to his wife's heart-rending tale, his anger rushes forth 'as through an arch the violent roaring tide outruns the eye that doth behold his haste' – only to rebound as impotent rage and grief, like an eddy returning 'back to the strait that forced him on so fast, in rage sent out, recall'd in rage, being past.' There is further symbolism in the lines: 'Even so his sighs, his sorrows, make a saw to push grief on, and back the same grief draw.' The allusion is to a carpenter's saw, which to the poet, while pushing grief away, just as promptly draws it back again by the return stroke.

All of which brings us to Clopton Bridge. Sir Hugh Clopton, who died in 1496, was Stratford's worthiest son until Shakespeare came along. A merchant and self-made man, who had himself gone off to seek his fortune in the capital and even became its Lord Mayor, Sir Hugh succeeded in accumulating great wealth. He used some of it to purchase land in and around his home town, and in about 1483 built one of the largest houses in Stratford. The splendid mansion boasted five handsome gables, ten fireplaces, gardens, barns and an orchard. A little over a century later Shakespeare, by then a successful playwright, would buy that same house and turn it into the family home called New Place.

Chief among Sir Hugh's benevolences to the town of his birth was the splendid masonry bridge that still bears his name as it carries the thundering traffic of the A3400. It was desperately needed. Stratford had been a busy market town since Anglo-Saxon times but by the fifteenth century its fortunes were beginning to decline. Until Sir Hugh came along, the problem was that the Avon, running through the town's heart, could be crossed only by an ancient rickety wooden bridge, which became impassable whenever the river was particularly high.

After visiting the town in 1530, the antiquarian John Leland wrote:

*Afore the time of Hugh Clopton there was but a poor bridge
of timber and no causey [causeway] to it, whereby many
poor folks and other refused to come to Stratford when Avon
was up, or coming thither stood in jeopardy of life.*

In contrast, Leland tells us Clopton's structure was

*A great and sumptuous bridge upon Avon at the east ende
of the towne, which hath 14 great arches of stone and long
causey made of stone, low walled on each side.*

Growing up beside the Avon must have left a deep impression on Shakespeare, never more so than in the very wet summer of 1588 – the year a ferocious storm wrecked the Spanish Armada – when the river rose higher than had ever been known before, swamping homes, mills and hay barns at Warwick. The flooding in Stratford was so severe that both ends of even Sir Hugh's staunch bridge were swept away, and three men trying to cross it at the time found themselves stranded. According to one account:

*When they cam to the midle of the Bridge they could not goe
forwardes and then returned presently but they could not go
backe for the watter was soe risen.*

Shakespeare uses dozens of river images as similes in his works, and floods in particular seem to captivate him. Perhaps the memory of those shocked men huddling on Clopton Bridge, with rising waters swirling around them on either side, came into his mind years later when he wrote Macbeth's lament:

**I am in blood stepp'd in so far that, should I wade no
more, returning were as tedious** [difficult] **as go o'er.** (*Macbeth*, 3.4)

In her book *Shakespeare's Imagery*, published in 1935, Caroline Spurgeon suggests it was the young Will's experience gazing over the walls of Clopton Bridge that inspired the so-called 'back eddy' verse in *The Rape of Lucrece.* Spurgeon tells how, during a visit to Stratford while compiling her research, she wandered into the bookshop in Sheep Street belonging to Captain William Jaggard, a descendant of the William Jaggard who had been one of the foremost printers in London at the dawn of the seventeenth century. The original Jaggard's printing works were chosen by Shakespeare's old friends John Heminges and Henry Condell to produce the *First Folio* of his collected plays in 1623.

Captain Jaggard reacted with excitement when Spurgeon said she was anxious to stand on Clopton Bridge and watch the movement of the current. He told her to be sure to stand above a particular arch at the southern end of the bridge and look down, explaining:

> *I have often stood there and watched the current being forced back beneath the narrow Tudor arch, on to the right bank at an angle which produces a swirling eddy, so that the water is then forced back through the arch equally swiftly and in an exactly contrary direction to that in which it has just come. I have sometimes hardly been able to believe my eyes when I have seen sticks or straws, which I have just noticed swirled on the flood downward through the arch, being brought back again just as swiftly in the opposite direction and against the flood weight.*

There, says Spurgeon, was a 'present-day Stratfordian' describing in minute detail exactly what the Stratford man Shakespeare had set down in that verse in *The Rape of Lucrece* three hundred and fifty years earlier. She later sat on the bank and drew a sketch showing the eddy, which she included as a frontispiece to her book (*pictured*). Her account offers us a touching image of how a detail that might otherwise have gone unnoticed could have impressed the finely tuned sensibilities of Shakespeare. We can perhaps picture him as a boy dropping sticks into the water over one side of the bridge and running to the other side to watch what became of them.

Clopton Bridge – the only place to cross the Avon as it carried the road that took travellers south to Banbury and thence London – was, after all, only a short walk from his childhood home in Henley Street. It was a bridge he was destined to use many times more during the years he would travel on horseback between the Stratford that was home to his family and the capital city that was home to the theatres, and memories of the Avon were something he would never forget.

July, 1930./

The 18th arch
Old Clopton Bridge
Stratford-on-Avon
The black line shows approximately the
movement of the current, with the eddy in front.

5. THREE-AND-TWENTY

Does Will secretly celebrate the age at which his life took a crucial turn?

I would [wish] there were no age between sixteen and three-and-twenty, or that youth would sleep out the rest. For there is nothing in the between but getting wenches with child, wronging the ancientry, stealing, fighting. (*The Winter's Tale*, 3.3, 1610-11)

AN OLD shepherd bemoans the fecklessness of youth in a voice that sounds almost like Shakespeare speaking about his own life. 'Getting wenches with child' would certainly apply to him, if we consider how he was apparently strong-armed into a hastily arranged wedding at the age of eighteen. Anne Hathaway was eight years his senior and old enough to be considered 'on the shelf' in an era when life expectancy was much lower than today. It was an odd arrangement, as men usually married women younger than themselves. But Anne was pregnant with his child, and young Will was expected to do the right thing. The product of their passion was a daughter named Susanna, who was baptised in Holy Trinity Church, Stratford-upon-Avon on Sunday, 26 May 1583.

Baptism usually took place within a few days of birth, which suggests Susanna was conceived the previous August or September, possibly during a romp the lovers enjoyed in the late summer meadows surrounding the Hathaway farmhouse in Shottery, a mile (1.6km) or so to the west of Shakespeare's home in Stratford ('It was a lover and his lass, with a hey, and a ho, and a hey nonino,' in the words of the song in *As You Like It*). Or perhaps even among the corn fields ('Between the acres of the rye, with a hey, and a ho, and a hey nonino, these pretty country folks would lie,' the same song continues) that clothed the low hills towards Temple Grafton, five miles (8km) from town, where Anne was living with relatives at the time.

The discovery of an entry in the episcopal register showing that a certain William Shakespeare was granted a licence to marry one Anne Whateley in Temple Grafton parish church late in November 1582 has led to excited speculation over the years that he had intended to marry another Anne altogether, but their marriage was thwarted at the last minute because of Anne Hathaway's condition. The less glamorous truth appears to be that 'Whateley' was simply a misspelling of 'Hathaway' by a careless or tired clerk in an age when the spelling of names (and much else besides) was notoriously imprecise.

Almost two years after Susanna was born, the twins Hamnet and Judith followed, and were baptised on 2 February 1585. Susanna's was an unusual name, deriving from the story of 'Susanna and the Elders', now included in the *Apocrypha* but in Shakespeare's day within the Old Testament. Since the name implied purity and innocence, the biographer Peter Ackroyd muses that 'it may have been an assertion of virtue after a birth perilously close to the wrong side of marriage'. The choice of Hamnet and Judith for the twins was, however, much more mundane. They were named in honour of two neighbours and close friends of the Shakespeare family in Henley Street, the baker Hamnet Sadler and his wife.

As for 'wronging the ancientry, stealing, fighting,' if we can believe notes left by the seventeenth-century churchman Richard Davies, who lived in the Cotswold village of Sapperton, the young Will Shakespeare did his share of that too. According to Davies, Shakespeare

Was much given to all unluckiness in stealing venison and rabbits, particularly from Sir Thomas Lucy, who oft had

him whipped and sometimes imprisoned, and at last made him fly his native county to his great advantage.

Lucy was the local Member of Parliament and a generally unpopular local bigwig. The writer Nicholas Rowe takes up the story about Shakespeare poaching deer from Lucy's lavish Charlecote estate in biographical notes he included in an edition of the plays published in 1709. Rowe writes of Shakespeare:

He had, by a misfortune common enough to young fellows, fallen into ill company; and amongst them, some that made a frequent practice of deer-stealing, engag'd him with them more than once in robbing a park that belong'd to Sir Thomas Lucy of Cherlecot, near Stratford. For this he was prosecuted by that gentleman, as he thought somewhat too severely; and in order to revenge that ill usage, he made a ballad upon him. And tho' this, probably the first essay of his poetry, be lost, yet it is said to have been so very bitter that it redoubled the prosecution against him to that degree that he was oblig'd to leave his business and family in Warwickshire for some time, and shelter himself in London.

Whatever the truth of the poaching legend, Shakespeare had reason enough to resent his alleged persecutor. The zealous Lucy, a Justice of the Peace and staunch Protestant, relished the task of rounding up suspected Catholic conspirators living in his patch. In 1583 his dragnet hauled in several members of the Arden family, who were relatives of Will's mother Mary (her maiden name being Arden). Trouble started after a young man named John Somerville, who was married to an Arden girl, was arrested after declaring in a wayside inn at Aynho, near Oxford, that he was on his way to London to assassinate the Queen. Under interrogation by the authorities, Somerville implicated his father-in-law Edward Arden, patriarch of the prominent Warwickshire family, along with several other close relatives.

Lucy's home at Charlecote became the base from which government agents were despatched to arrest the suspects. Edward Arden was found guilty of treason and publicly hanged, drawn and quartered. Somerville either hanged himself or was strangled by jailers in his cell at the Tower of London before sentence could be carried out. Both men were later decapitated, with their heads being displayed on poles above the gateway at the southern end of London Bridge as a chilling example to other 'traitors'. In future years Will would have to pass under his relatives' heads every time he crossed the only bridge over the Thames.

Perhaps it was in John Somerville's memory that Shakespeare would give the name Sir John Somerville to a 'gentleman' from Warwickshire in one of his earliest plays, *Henry VI, Part 3*. As for Sir Thomas Lucy, the playwright almost certainly took his revenge by lampooning him in the shape of the boasting dotard Justice Shallow. Apart from a bit of comic wordplay on the name Lucy in *The Merry Wives of Windsor*, when Shallow's coat of arms is described as bearing 'a dozen white luces' ('luce' being another word for the fish we call a pike), Sir John Falstaff makes a particularly interesting comment in *Henry IV, Part 2*. Amid a barrage of scathing comments about Shallow, Falstaff complains that the old fool

> **Talks as familiarly of John a** [of] **Gaunt as if he had been sworn brother** [companion in arms] **to him; and I'll be sworn 'a** [he] **ne'er saw him but once in the Tiltyard** [a place in Westminster where tournaments and jousts took place]**; and then he** [John of Gaunt] **burst his head** [cut Shallow's head with his sword] **for crowding among the marshal's men.** (3.2)

It can surely be no coincidence that in real life two of Sir Thomas Lucy's forebears, Sir William Lucy and his son and successor, another Sir Thomas Lucy (the latter died in 1415), were indeed among the retinue of John of Gaunt, father of

Henry IV. Shakespeare delighted in making such cryptic connections.

What then are we to make of the significance the old shepherd in *The Winter's Tale* attaches to the age of twenty-three or, as it was often expressed in Shakespeare's day, 'three-and-twenty'? While Davies and Rowe surmised that Lucy's tyrannical aggression drove young William out of town, an interesting turn of events offers a more tempting explanation as to why he left for London and the theatre. In 1587, no fewer than five touring companies of actors visited Stratford. Foremost among them were the Queen's Men, the troupe founded four years earlier at the express command of Elizabeth I.

The company's appearance in Shakespeare's home town came as part of a tour, pressing inn yards and town halls into service as theatres for performances of the most popular plays of the day, which included *The Famous Victories of Henry V*, *King Leir*, *The Troublesome Reign of King John*, and *The True Tragedy of Richard III*, all by now unknown authors (Shakespeare would later rewrite all four plays and turn them into the classics we know today), as well as Robert Greene's *Friar Bacon and Friar Bungay*.

Before travelling to Stratford the Queen's Men appeared in Abingdon, where a minor riot took place as eager townsfolk scrambled to see them perform, and then moved on to Thame, thirteen miles (21km) from Oxford. In that market town an ugly event occurred that was at first sight a major setback for the players, but which may instead have marked a turning point in both their fortunes and Shakespeare's. Between nine and ten o'clock on the evening of 13 June a quarrel broke out between William Knell and John Towne, two of the actors. Perhaps they had been drinking too freely after the show on that long summer evening because Knell, a fiery young man who played juvenile leads such as Prince Hal, drew his sword and chased Towne into a close behind an inn. An account of what happened next survives in the words of the Thame coroner:

> *John Towne late of Shoreditch, yeoman, was in a close called White Hound in Thame when William Knell came and had in his right hand a sword, and jumped upon John Towne intending to kill him. Towne in fear and despairing of his life and of the mutilation of his limbs by the aforesaid Knell, drew back to a certain mound of earth, which he could neither cross nor ascend without peril of his life. William Knell continuing his attack as before, so maliciously and furiously, and Towne on the hillock, to save his life drew his sword of iron (price five shillings), and held it in his right hand and thrust it into the neck of William Knell and made a mortal wound three inches deep and one inch wide.*

Towne, it would turn out, was cleared of murdering Knell with his five-shilling sword because he was found to have acted in self-defence. The immediate aftermath for the Queen's Men meant they arrived at Stratford, their next stop, at least one and possibly two actors short. Biographers have speculated that Shakespeare, with little prospect of advancement in his home town and oppressed by the overbearing Sir Thomas Lucy, volunteered his services as an actor.

Within eight months of William Knell's death his widow Rebecca, then still aged just sixteen, married another member of the Queen's Men, the actor John Heminges. Shakespeare and Heminges would go on to become close friends. They are known to have acted together often, including in Ben Jonson's plays *Sejanus* and *Every Man in His Humour*.

Shakespeare would remember Heminges in his will, and it was Heminges and his fellow actor Henry Condell who would collect and publish the playwright's manuscripts in the *First Folio*.

Shakespeare's age in that fateful year of 1587? Twenty-three.

He may have left us another clue by recalling his first nervous public appearance after the Queen's Men had agreed to give him a trial. One of his sonnets begins:

As an unperfect actor on the stage / Who with his fear is put besides his part [forgets his lines] ...

The number of that sonnet? Twenty-three.

See also: 14. He Was But One Hour Mine
27. The Geese and the Golden Eggs
45. Alas, Poor Tarlton

6. THERE STANDS THE CASTLE

Curious details reveal an intimate knowledge of a historic corner of England

Duncan: **This castle hath a pleasant seat; the air nimbly and sweetly recommends itself unto our gentle senses.**

Banquo: **This guest of summer** [summer bird], **the temple-haunting martlet** [house martin], **does approve by his loved mansionry** [building his nests] **that the heaven's breath** [the breeze] **smells wooingly here** [is sweetly scented]: **no jutty, frieze, buttress, nor coign** [corner] **of vantage but this bird hath made his pendent bed and procreant cradle** [hanging nests in which to breed]. **Where they most breed and haunt, I have observed, the air is delicate.** (*Macbeth*, 1.6, 1606)

DUNCAN, King of Scotland, is approaching Macbeth's castle with his trusty lieutenant Banquo. They pause to admire the edifice, their resting place for the night, its appearance made the more wholesome by the house martins nesting along the outside of its sturdy walls. Little does either of them know of the bloody events that are but a few hours away, with the malevolent Macbeths having regicide in mind. The presence of the little migratory birds bodes well, Banquo suggests, since they often build their nests around monasteries and churches ('temple-haunting'). In fact, the 'martlets' like the castle walls so much they have colonised every available corner of the masonry.

It is a touching image of tranquillity but perhaps Duncan and Banquo would have been better advised to keep in mind Shakespeare's only other mention of the 'martlet'. The allusion comes in *The Merchant of Venice* when the swaggering

Prince of Arragon, a suitor to the fair lady Portia, speaks scornfully of the bird's lack of good sense because it …

Builds in the weather on the outward wall, even in the force and road of casualty. (2.9)

During her studies in the 1930s, the scholar Caroline Spurgeon became convinced Shakespeare's description of the masses of house martins' nests on the castle walls in *Macbeth* could not simply have come from his imagination, but that he must have seen such a sight for himself. But where? She set about investigating Warwickshire castles – Kenilworth and Warwick were the obvious suspects – without success. At Berkeley Castle in neighbouring Gloucestershire she also drew a blank. No one could recall house martins ever having nested on the walls of any of them. Then something rather interesting happened.

Spurgeon says that a few weeks after making her inquiries she was contacted by a Mr O'Flynn, private secretary to the eighth Earl of Berkeley. O'Flynn told her that he had recently come across a reference to the *Note Books* of Edward Jenner while reading a biography of that eminent scientist. Jenner, a Fellow of the Royal Society, is known as the 'father of immunology' because of the pioneering work he did in developing the world's first vaccine (against smallpox) in 1796. The advances he made possible in medicine arguably have saved more lives than those of anyone else in history. Jenner was also an eminent ornithologist. It was through his patient observations that the newly hatched cuckoo's murderous activities in pushing a host's own eggs and fledgling chicks out of a colonised nest were documented, in a paper published by the Royal Society in 1788. Previously it had been thought only the adult cuckoo was responsible for the savagery. Jenner's observations of bird life were to be taken seriously.

As it happened, Jenner was born in the village of Berkeley, his father having been the local vicar. O'Flynn pointed out that in his *Note Books* Jenner records making a visit back to Berkeley on 9 June 1787, during which he examined house martins' nests on the castle walls, noting that they 'exhibit every variety with regard to the forwardness of the eggs'. If house martins had been reliably reported at the castle as late as 1787, it supports Spurgeon's theory that Berkeley was the very place Shakespeare could have seen them.

The link with Berkeley strengthens when we consider lines from *Richard II*, as Henry Percy, Earl of Northumberland, and his son Harry Hotspur appear in a scene set amid 'Wilds in Gloucestershire':

> *Northumberland:* **How far is it to Berkeley and what stir keeps good old York there with his men of war?**
>
> *Hotspur:* **There stands the castle, by yon tuft of trees.**
> (2.3)

Harry Hotspur's words perfectly describe the view of Berkeley Castle, nestling amid its 'tuft of trees,' from the top of Stinchcombe Hill, less than five miles (8km) away. The hill towers to 719ft (219m) on the scarp of the Cotswolds, overlooking the coastal plain beyond. Stinchcombe lies on the route the Earl of Northumberland and Hotspur would have taken on their journey from Ravenspurgh in Yorkshire to Berkeley. The earl has already complained about their uncomfortable ride along 'high wild hills and rough uneven ways' to get there.

The view Shakespeare conjures remains pretty much unchanged today, and it is tempting to think he may have stood on Stinchcombe Hill himself, gazing across at the castle with the River Severn as a backdrop. There are several other intriguing strands of evidence that suggest he had an intimate knowledge of Stinchcombe and the neighbouring villages of Dursley and Woodmancote, an area about sixty miles (97km) from his home in Stratford-upon-Avon.

A scene set at the Gloucestershire home of Justice Shallow in *Henry IV, Part 2* features this exchange:

> *Davy:* **I beseech you, sir, to countenance** [favour] **William Visor of Woncot against Clement Perkes o' th' hill.**
>
> *Shallow:* **There is many complaints, Davy, against that Visor. Visor is an arrant knave, on my knowledge.** (5.1)

The servant Davy is asking Justice Shallow to favour 'William Visor of Woncot' when judging a legal case against 'Clement Perkes o' th' hill'. Shallow, on the other hand, makes it clear that he holds a low opinion of the said Visor. There are records of a family named Visor or Vizard dating back more than four hundred years in Woodmancote (locally pronounced Woncot), which adjoins Dursley.

During Shakespeare's lifetime the Vizards had made their fortune as dealers in wool, which was the boom commodity of the sixteenth and seventeenth centuries in the way oil was of the twentieth. Today local gravestones and memorial plaques bear witness to generations of Vizards having lived in the area. A Vizard is recorded as bailiff (mayor) of Dursley in 1612. A short street that runs beside the ancient parish church of St Mark in Woodmancote is called Vizard Close. Along the street is a row of almshouses built by the Vizard family in the Victorian era.

We cannot say what led Justice Shallow to call William Visor 'an arrant knave' – arrant meaning absolute or downright – but perhaps Shakespeare had his reasons. The playwright's father John is known to have dabbled illegally in the strictly controlled wool trade and could have had his own fractious dealings with a William Visor or Vizard of 'Woncot'. There was also a Shakespeare family living in the area at the time – a James Shakespeare was buried fourteen miles (23km) away in Bisley in 1570, and a Thomas Shakespeare married one Joan Turner in Dursley in 1578 – although whether they had any connection with the playwright, or ever clashed with any of the Vizards, it is impossible to tell.

As for 'Clement Perkes o' th' hill', Stinchcombe Hill is known by local people simply as 'the hill' and a family named Perkes or Perchas owned a house there in Shakespeare's time. A Clement Perkes is recorded as having been born in the village of Fladbury, in neighbouring Worcestershire, in 1568, though we have no way of knowing whether he ended up at Stinchcombe. Family links with the area did endure, however, with an obituary appearing in the *Gentleman's Magazine* as late as 1812 which recorded the death 'At Margate, in his seventy-fifth year, J Purchas, Esq, of Stinchcombe Hill, near Dursley, Gloucestershire.'

Shakespeare reveals yet more detailed knowledge of Gloucestershire in *Henry IV, Part 2*, when Justice Shallow instructs Davy to sow his land with 'red wheat'. This reddish variety of the grain, also known locally as 'red lammas' since it was sown around 1 August or Lammas Day, was particularly popular in the county. What's more, Berkeley itself stands only a few miles from the River Severn and, according to the biographer D H Madden, writing in 1907: 'When Shakespeare writes of Severn, he affords local knowledge absent from references to Thames or Wye.' In support of his argument, Madden quotes references in *Henry VI, Part 1* to 'gentle Severn's sedgy bank', 'swift Severn's flood' and the 'sandy bottomed Severn'.

Shakespeare's links with this delightful part of England may not end there either. For much of his acting and writing career he worked with Richard Burbage and the Lord Chamberlain's Men, who became known as the King's Men on the accession of James I. The company had been founded in 1594 under the patronage of Henry Carey, the first Baron Hunsdon, a cousin of Elizabeth I. When Henry Carey died in July 1596, his son and heir George took over the patronage. On 19 February 1596, George Carey's daughter Elizabeth was married. Her new husband was none other than Sir Thomas Berkeley of Berkeley Castle, and according to one account Shakespeare wrote his joyous comedy *A Midsummer Night's Dream* as entertainment for their nuptial celebrations.

Generations of biographers have struggled to fill in the blanks in our knowledge of where Shakespeare spent the so-called 'lost years' before he turns up in London's theatre world. The seventeenth-century antiquarian John Aubrey claimed in his *Brief Lives* to have been told that Shakespeare 'had been in his younger years a schoolmaster in the country'. The suggestion that he could have spent at least some of those 'lost years' in the Berkeley area of Gloucestershire has a seductive appeal.

7. GREENE WITH ENVY

Has Will taken subtle revenge on the playwright who scorned him as an 'upstart crow'?

I have a daughter – have while she is mine – who in her duty and obedience, mark, hath given me this. Now gather and surmise. [Reads] 'To the celestial, and my soul's idol, the most beautified Ophelia' – That's an ill phrase, a vile phrase, 'beautified' is a vile phrase.

(Hamlet, 2.2, 1599-1601)

THE tiresome meddler Polonius is reading a love-letter written to his daughter Ophelia by Hamlet. It is this love, he insists, that is the cause of Hamlet's apparent madness. Claudius, the usurping king, and Gertrude, Hamlet's mother, remain unconvinced. Polonius is a pedant but it may seem curious to us that he should break off from his discourse to fume about Hamlet's use of 'beautified' in a letter. The word sounds innocuous enough. So why might Polonius – and perhaps Shakespeare himself – have found it offensive? For a possible explanation, let us turn the clock back ten years or so, from the time Shakespeare was writing *Hamlet* to shortly after he had arrived as a newcomer on the London theatre scene.

The country boy from Warwickshire found himself suddenly pitched into a world of intense rivalry, jealousy and intellectual snobbery. The plays that pulled punters into the theatres, and the poetry written in hope of appealing to wealthy aristocratic sponsors, came almost entirely from a coterie of highly educated men whom historians have labelled 'the university wits'. Chief among them were Christopher Marlowe, Robert Greene and Thomas Nashe, all Cambridge men, as well as John Lyly, Thomas Lodge and George Peele from Oxford. Greene and Nashe, who were close friends, appear to have taken particular exception to the rising fortunes of Shakespeare, regarding him as a precocious actor turned playwright wannabe from the provinces with little education to speak of and ideas well above his station.

Shakespeare may have been making his mark as early as 1589. His first stab at writing a romantic comedy – *The Two Gentlemen of Verona*, in which a servant named Launce delivers moving monologues to his oblivious pet dog Crab – was a hit with the penny-paying groundlings. *The Taming of the Shrew*, which Shakespeare appears to have rewritten from an older play and vastly improved in the process, and his gory *Titus Andronicus* proved even bigger successes. By 1591 he was working on the first of his English history dramas, the massive Henry VI trilogy, possibly in collaboration with Christopher Marlowe. But then Will really showed off his true talent with the tale of a hunchbacked tyrant who slashes his way to the throne through a sea of blood. *Richard III* was greeted with thunderous applause and established beyond all doubt that the man from Stratford was a writer of exceptional ability.

It all proved too much for Robert Greene, author of the comedy *Friar Bacon and Friar Bungay*. In 1592, sickening and close to death although still in his early thirties, he summoned up the energy to vent his bitterness in a jealous tirade. The first targets of his wrath were actors in general, the 'showbiz' celebrities of the day who, in Greene's view, stole for themselves the plaudits that were due to the writers of the lines they spoke. Launching his withering attack, Greene warns fellow university-educated playwrights:

> O that I might intreat your rare wits to be employed in more
> profitable courses: and let those Apes [actors] imitate your
> past excellence, and never more acquaint them with your
> admired invention [writing]. Seek you better, Masters: for it
> is pity men of such rare wits [playwrights] should be subject

to the pleasures of such rude grooms [actors].

If there was one thing worse in Greene's eyes than preening actors, it was actors who thought they could write. He had one johnny-come-lately in particular in mind.

Yes, trust them not, for there is an upstart Crow, beautified with our feathers, that, with his Tyger's heart wrapt in a Player's hide, supposes he is as well able to bombast out a blanke verse as the best of you; and being an absolute Johannes Factotum [jack of all trades], is in his owne conceit the onely Shake-scene in a countrie.

If 'Shake-scene' were not clue enough, Greene's phrase 'Tyger's heart wrapt in a Player's hide' leaves no doubt who he is talking about. It is a sneering parody of a line in Shakespeare's own *Henry VI, Part 3*:

O tyger's heart wrapt in a woman's hide! (1.4)

In the history play, the captive Richard, Duke of York – father of the future Richard III – screams the line in rebuke to the merciless Margaret of Anjou as she torments him. 'Upstart crow' is an allusion to one of Aesop's fables, in which the crow dresses up in the stolen brighter plumage of more glamorous birds. In that sentence of Greene's we also see the word 'beautified'. Words were constantly being added to the English language as it evolved at the hands of writers, but the use of 'beautified' was still something of a rarity.

Dr Samuel Johnson, himself a notable scholar of Shakespeare's works, had trouble with that line when studying *Hamlet*, and suggested Polonius's objection to the 'vile phrase' was due to its ambiguity of meaning. The insulting implication of the word is that Ophelia's beauty was not natural but merely the result of applying make-up. ('God hath given you one face, and you make yourselves another,' Hamlet tells her in 3.1). Yet we have to ask: When Shakespeare came to write

Hamlet, did he introduce Polonius's revulsion at the word 'beautified' in a mischievous note of payback for Greene's merciless polemic directed at the new boy in town all those years earlier? Somewhere deep in Will's psyche, did Greene's attack still rankle? Was his revenge a dish served cold at the pinnacle of his career as a writer?

As it turned out, Greene unwittingly did an immense favour to later generations of biographers by including those references to a 'tyger's heart' and 'Shake-scene'. His is the earliest known written reference we have to Shakespeare as a playwright. Greene's bilious rant means we can say with some certainty where Shakespeare was and when, and the impact he was having on those around him.

The diatribe appeared in a pamphlet titled *Greene's Groats-worth of Witte, Bought with a Million of Repentance.* It was published shortly after Greene *(grimly pictured wearing his death shroud as he wrote)* died in poverty on 3 September 1592, from a surfeit 'of Rhenish [Rhineland white] wine and pickled herring'. Greene's demise in itself may have prompted a later allusion by Shakespeare in *Twelfth Night*, when a drunken Sir Toby Belch lives up to his name and emits a show-stopping belch, thumps his chest with his fist, and declares:

A plague o' [on] **these pickle herring!** (1.5)

Shakespeare had already made powerful friends by the time *Greene's Groats-worth of Witte* appeared in print. Henry Wriothesley, Earl of Southampton, who had been impressed enough with Will's early poetry to become his patron, took offence. The celebrated Christopher Marlowe, still the most eminent tragedian of the day, even as rumours about his atheism and homosexuality were raising eyebrows, also appears to have taken exception. With Greene freshly in his grave, some cynics suggested the attack might have actually been written by his good friend Thomas Nashe, using the dead man's name as a cover. A clearly rattled Nashe rushed out a denial, declaring:

> A scald, trivial, lying pamphlet called Greene's Groats-worth of Witte is given out to be of my doing. God never have care of my soul, but utterly renounce me, if the least word or syllable in it proceeded from my pen or if I were any way privy to the writing or printing of it.

The printer of the pamphlet, Henry Chettle, was accused by others of being the real author. He too vigorously denied the claims of authorship and, probably in response to Southampton's protests, issued a grovelling apology for his part in the controversy:

> With neither of them that take offence [Marlowe and Shakespeare] was I acquainted, and with one of them [Marlowe] I care not if I ever be. The other [Shakespeare] whom at that time I did not so much spare as since I wish I had, for that I have moderated the heat of living writers and might have used my own discretion (especially in such a case, the Author being dead), that I did not, I am as sorry as if the original fault had been my own fault, because myself have seen his [Shakespeare's] demeanour no less civil than he excellent in the qualities he professes.

Just in case there was any doubt that Shakespeare had the support of people of influence, Chettle adds:

> Besides, divers of worship have reported his uprightness of dealing which argues his honesty, and his facetious [easy] grace in writing, which approves his art.

Robert Greene's star had risen through the 1580s as he scratched out plays and popular novels. He had also made a reputation as a writer of graphic pamphlets detailing the world of the coney-catchers. 'Coneys' was the name country folk gave to rabbits but in London 'coney-catchers' was a slang term for the thieves, pickpockets and cutpurses who preyed on their victims in the capital's public places. Shakespeare would in time plunder Greene's pamphlets to add colour to the character of the thieving pedlar Autolycus in *The Winter's Tale* (he also borrowed the basic plot of the play itself from a novel by Greene).

The disreputable life Greene led unquestionably allowed him a first-hand acquaintance with the world of crime. He was said to have married a 'gentleman's daughter' whom he called 'Doll,' before abandoning her after she had a child by him and he had spent his way through her bridal dowry. According to the contemporary writer Gabriel Harvey, who viewed his lifestyle with deep distaste, Greene took up with a mistress named Emma, the sister of a notorious cut-throat known as 'Cutting' Ball. Harvey describes her as 'a sorry ragged quean [prostitute] of whom he [Greene] had his base [bastard] son, Infortunatus Greene'. The aptly named Infortunatus died in infancy. At one time Greene appears to have found it necessary to hire Ball as a personal bodyguard. Ball ended his days on the gallows at Tyburn when the authorities finally caught up with him.

Harvey launched his own attack on Greene in a 1592 publication titled *Four Letters*, writing:

> I was altogether unacquainted with the man, and never once saluted him by name, but who in London hath not heard of his dissolute and licentious living?

In a long list of Greene's alleged faults, including consorting with dubious companions, vainglorious bragging, cheating and thieving, swearing, profaning sacred texts, blasphemy and 'outrageous surfeiting', Harvey goes on to condemn 'his beggarly departing in every hostess's [inn-keeper's] debt, his infamous resorting to Bankside, Shoreditch, Southwark [all notorious for their brothels] and other filthy haunts' and 'his obscure lurking in the basest corners' among other faults. An incensed Nashe later hit back on behalf of his late friend, claiming Greene had 'inherited more virtues than vices' and was 'a good fellow', and branding Harvey a liar.

The scholar Stephen Greenblatt has suggested Greene's dissolute lifestyle may have been Shakespeare's inspiration for Falstaff, the obese glutton and incorrigible reprobate who frequents the seediest haunts in London. While Falstaff is a figure filled with good-humoured *bon homie*, in contrast to Greene's evident moroseness, there are interesting parallels. Falstaff does indeed swindle the good-hearted hostess Mistress Quickly, not only out of what he owes her for rent, food and drink, but out of money from her own purse. He consorts at the Boar's Head tavern in Eastcheap with a prostitute, with whom he professes to be in love, known as 'Doll'. If Professor Greenblatt is right, then Greene not only left us a vital clue to sketch on to the sparsely inked canvas that is Shakespeare's life, he was the catalyst for the most colourful scoundrel ever created in the history of theatre.

8. PESTILENCE HANGS IN THE AIR

Plague was a constant threat in Will's lifetime. So why does no one die from it in his plays?

Friar John: **Going to find a barefoot brother** [a fellow priest] **out, one of our order** [Franciscans], **to associate** [accompany] **me, here in this city** [Verona] **visiting the sick, and finding him, the searchers of the town** [health officers who enforced quarantine], **suspecting that we were both in a house where the infectious pestilence** [plague] **did reign, seal'd up the doors and would not let us forth; so that my speed** [journey] **to Mantua there was stay'd** [halted].

Friar Laurence: **Who bare** [carried] **my letter, then, to Romeo?**

Friar John: **I could not send it – here it is again – nor get a messenger to bring it to thee, so fearful were they of infection.** (*Romeo and Juliet*, 5.2, 1595)

THIS brief exchange between two friars can pass almost unnoticed by audiences engrossed in the unfolding drama that is *Romeo and Juliet*. Yet it is the crucial pivot around which the entire plot of Shakespeare's most frequently performed tragedy hinges. Friar Laurence is the lovers' confidante and this is the chilling moment we learn that his artfully contrived plan has unravelled and the star-crossed lovers are doomed. The reason? Bubonic plague, the deadly curse that held Europe in its grip throughout Will's lifetime and beyond. Not because either of the young heroes has caught the pestilence, but as a consequence of a terrified society's reaction to the outbreak.

It is a situation all too easy for us to understand in light of the lockdowns with which authorities have responded to the Covid-19 pandemic in our own troubled times. We too have become familiar with the unwelcome concept of quarantine. In Shakespeare's day quarantine meant anyone suspected of being infected with the plague could find themselves sealed up without notice inside their homes, together with any visitors who happened to be present at the time.

Doors were nailed firmly shut and daubed with a large red Christian cross as a warning to the healthy to keep away. Windows were boarded over to prevent anyone escaping. A watchman might even be set to guard the house. Food and drink could be passed through a gap between the boards by friends or relatives on the outside. Whole families would remain incarcerated, either until a suitable length of time was deemed to have passed or everyone inside had died. It really was as stark as that.

Juliet's domineering family have been led to believe that she is dead but we, the audience, know better. In Verona, Friar Laurence had written a letter to Romeo, then living in exile in Mantua, explaining the plan: she has drunk a soporific potion which merely simulates the appearance of death. Juliet will in fact be lying in the burial crypt, expecting Romeo to greet her with a loving kiss when she awakes from her drug-induced stupor and all will end happily. But Friar Laurence is mortified to be handed his crucial letter back unopened. He learns that it did not even leave Verona, let alone reach Mantua.

Friar John, to whom delivery was entrusted, reports that he had sought out a companion to join him on the journey to Mantua (the term 'a barefoot brother' tells us they were members of the Franciscan order, who travelled shoeless and always in pairs). He located his friend visiting the home of someone who was sick.

The alarmed men then suddenly found themselves being boarded up, along with the occupants, inside the house. Their protests were in vain. No exemption was allowed for the pair to leave. Friar John could not even pass the letter out of the house so it could be returned to Friar Laurence, and thereby warn him of the problem. No one would take it from his hands for fear of the infection. It is sobering to reflect that without the short 'plague scene' *Romeo and Juliet* would be a triumphant love story rather than a tragedy.

Shakespeare perhaps gives us a hint of the plot device that is coming when, earlier in the play, the dying Mercutio calls down a curse upon the feuding families of the Montagues and the Capulets. Three times within less than two minutes he cries:

A plague on both your houses! (3.1)

Bubonic plague was a truly horrifying affliction. In *King Lear*, the enraged monarch heaps a terrible insult on his daughter Goneril when he scolds her:

Thou art a boil, a plague-sore, an embossed carbuncle in my corrupted blood. (2.4)

Plague sores, or buboes, were among the many distressing symptoms of the highly contagious infection, caused by the bacterium *Yersinia pestis*. It has long been believed that the bacteria entered their human victims through the bites of fleas spread by rats, although more recent research suggests body lice lurking in clothes and bedding may also have been culprits. Buboes were extremely painful swellings which resulted when the infection reached the sufferer's lymph nodes.

They could become as big as chicken's eggs, and usually appeared around the groin and under the armpits. Other symptoms included a raging fever, chills, racing heart, diarrhoea, vomiting, and bleeding from the mouth, nose or rectum. Death in the most excruciating agony was usually inevitable, and often came as a welcome relief. No one, of course, had any idea how the disease originated. It would not be until 1894 that the French bacteriologist Alexandre Yersin discovered rodents were the mode of infection.

A few weeks after Shakespeare was born in April 1564, the church in which he was christened, Holy Trinity, recorded the death of one Oliver Gunne, a weaver's apprentice. In the margin next to the entry are inscribed the ominous Latin words '*Hic incipit pestis*' ('Here begins the plague'). Before that year's outbreak had passed it would claim more than two hundred of Stratford's citizens. Will's parents John and Mary Shakespeare had already mourned the loss of two daughters in infancy, the elder sisters he would never know. There can be no doubt the couple did everything they could to shield their newborn son from becoming yet another casualty. Danger passed close by their door. A neighbour in Henley Street named Roger Green lost four of his children to the pestilence that year.

Plague continued to cast a long shadow over Shakespeare's life. After he moved to London, it would ravage the city again and again. In 1592, even as he was beginning to make his mark as a playwright, a particularly severe outbreak struck. The authorities ordered all theatres to close in an effort to curb the spread of infection. There was a flurry of activity that autumn when the pestilence appeared to ebb and the theatres reopened. They were closed again the following February and would remain shut for most of 1593. The disease carried away more than ten thousand souls in London alone that year.

The threat from plague was ever present and the closures were a headache Shakespeare and his fellows were forced to live with throughout their theatrical careers. Further particularly severe outbreaks occurred in 1603-4 – when almost one-fifth of London's population died – in 1606, and again in 1608-9. One scholar has calculated that in the four years between 1606 and 1610 the theatres were open for only nine months in total. If the outbreaks had any upside at all, they allowed Shakespeare time to create some of his greatest masterpieces. The author James Shapiro has pointed out that the epics *King Lear*, *Macbeth* and *Antony and Cleopatra* were all written in the years 1605-6.

Despite all the imaginative fates Shakespeare devises for his characters (stabbed, strangled, hanged, beheaded, poisoned, drowned, torn apart by a mob, jumping off a castle wall, bitten by a snake and eaten by a bear among them), it is perhaps remarkable that no one dies of the plague. Not one. Indeed, *Romeo and Juliet* is the only work in which the pestilence plays a decisive role.

Although the word 'plague' or 'plagues' occurs more than a hundred times in the plays and poems, in almost every instance it is used as a curse or invocation. As a writer, Will was shrewd enough to understand that the theatre represented an escape from people's everyday cares and worries. The spectre of a disease that could strike anyone down at any moment was something his audiences needed no grim reminder of. Indeed, the presence of the plague had become such an accepted fact of daily life that on occasions the ever versatile Shakespeare succeeds in turning it to comic effect. In *Much Ado About Nothing*, Beatrice sounds a mocking caveat over the danger Claudio faces if he is befriended by Benedick, the man she loves to hate:

> **Oh Lord! He will hang upon him like a disease. He is sooner caught than the pestilence, and the taker runs presently mad ... If he have caught the Benedick it will cost him a thousand pound ere a' [he] be cured.** (1.1)

While in that other delightful comedy *Twelfth Night*, the lady Olivia marvels at how suddenly she has fallen in love, declaring:

> **How now? Even so quickly may one catch the plague!** (1.5)

9. A GREAT RECKONING

Will pays his own tribute to the great Kit Marlowe, murdered by government secret agents

When a man's verses cannot be understood, nor a man's good wit seconded with the forward child understanding, it strikes a man more dead than a great reckoning in a little room. Truly, I would the gods had made thee poetical. (*As You Like It*, 3.3, 1599)

THE eloquent but haughty jester Touchstone, having fled the royal court and ended up amid the rustic surroundings of the Forest of Arden, has professed a desire to marry Audrey, a simple country girl. He does, however, rue the fact that his intended appears singularly unable to appreciate his sharp-witted musings. But what does he mean when he complains that her unreceptive ear strikes him 'more dead than a great reckoning in a little room'? To understand Touchstone's remark we must look back six years before the delightful comedy *As You Like It* was written – to one of the most seismic events in the history of English literature.

On the evening of 30 May 1593, the man widely regarded as the greatest writer of plays and poetry in the land – not William Shakespeare but Christopher Marlowe – died instantly after being stabbed just above the right eye. He was just twenty-nine years old. The story quickly spread that he had been killed during a drunken tavern brawl over the bill, or the 'reckoning' as the Elizabethans called it. The shocking news that the life of such a towering figure had been squandered over so trivial a matter shook London's theatre world to its core. But all was not as it seemed. Marlowe's untimely demise was the result of no alcohol fuelled dust-up in a seedy inn. Rather, it was connected with his entanglement in the underworld of government spies and double agents. Most people settled for the account of his death as reported. It paid not to ask too many questions.

Christopher (or 'Kit') Marlowe (*pictured*) had been born in February 1564, just a couple of months before Shakespeare. Although the two playwrights' paths were destined to cross in London, their lives were very different. Unlike Shakespeare, Marlowe was a high-flying university graduate. Born in Canterbury, he graduated at Corpus Christi College, Cambridge, where he gained a Master of Arts degree. He was also an early recruit into what became something of a Cambridge tradition that has lasted well into modern times – espionage. As a writer, Marlowe dominated the stage, producing epic tragedies such as *Tamburlaine the Great*, *The Jew of Malta*, and *Doctor Faustus* that unfailingly pulled in the crowds. As a secret agent for Sir Francis Walsingham, powerful 'spymaster' to Elizabeth I, he was immersed in murky secret missions to entrap seditious Catholics plotting to overthrow the Queen and thereby return Protestant England to the hegemony of Rome.

On that fateful Wednesday in May, Marlowe had spent the day not in a tavern but at the house of a respectable widow named Dame Eleanor Bull, on the Strand in Deptford, a busy area of docklands southeast of London. The area seethed with sailors and travellers of all nationalities coming and going. He was in the company of three other men, Ingram Frizer, Nicholas Skeres and Robert Poley.

Dame Eleanor, who had connections at Elizabeth's court, ran some sort of private victualling establishment – it may even have been a 'safe house' for government agents – and had provided meals and drink for Marlowe and his companions. The men spent some of their eight or so hours in her 'little room' playing at 'tables' (as backgammon was known). Sometime after they had eaten supper, a struggle appears to have broken out between Frizer and Marlowe, which resulted in the playwright's death.

On Friday, 1 June, only two days later, an inquest into the affair was hastily convened by William Danby, Coroner to the Royal Household. That fact in itself is curious. Danby's role was to conduct inquests when a death took place 'within the verge', which meant within twelve miles (19km) of the royal presence. If Elizabeth had been three miles away at Greenwich Palace, the inquest would indeed have fallen within his remit. But at the time the Queen was at Nonsuch Palace, near Cheam in Surrey, fifteen miles away, so Marlowe's death should rightly have been the responsibility of a coroner for the county of Kent. Danby may have held such a position in addition to his royal duties. If he did, it is unfortunate he does not mention the fact in his report of the inquest. It would have put the legitimacy of his jurisdiction in the matter beyond argument among subsequent generations of scholars, not to mention those conspiracy theorists who insist Marlowe's death was faked and that he carried on living in hiding to write the plays credited to Shakespeare.

The three witnesses were called to give evidence. They related what sounded like a well-rehearsed story of how they had been seated together along one side of a table. Frizer was in the middle and they had their backs to Marlowe, who was lounging on a couch. The men said an argument broke out about the bill and 'divers malicious words' were exchanged. According to their testimony, Marlowe leapt up from the couch, seized Frizer's dagger from its sheath and wounded him on the head. Frizer was seated 'in such a manner' as he 'in no wise could take flight' but he succeeded in grappling with

Marlowe and, in the struggle that ensued, stabbed the playwright just above the right eye. The outcome was a wound two inches (5cm) deep and one inch wide, which killed Marlowe instantly.

Few other details were supplied and the inquest raised more questions than it answered. Why were the three men sitting together along one side of the table, and how could they have had their backs to Marlowe when Frizer was supposedly arguing with him? Why, indeed, had they met with Marlowe and what had they been talking about all day? The inquest cleared Frizer of murder on the grounds of self-defence and he was granted a full pardon by the Queen within the astonishingly short time of a month. Marlowe was buried in an unmarked grave in the churchyard of St Nicholas, Deptford, with little ceremony, immediately after the inquest ended.

Each of the witnesses was glibly described as a 'gentleman' in the official report of the inquest. The truth was they were three very nasty pieces of work. What they had in common with Marlowe was that they were government agents. They had all, in one way or another, worked for either Sir Francis Walsingham or his young relative Thomas Walsingham.

Ingram Frizer was a wealthy but unquestionably crooked businessman with a track record of shady dealings. He bought and sold property. Described as 'a fixer for gentlemen of good worship' he was also an accomplished confidence trickster who had gulled many trusting victims out of their money. Records show he was born at Kingsclere in Hampshire, where he was christened on 26 September 1561.

Robert Poley was an accomplished liar who had once been heard bragging 'I will swear and forswear [perjure] myself, rather than I will accuse myself to do me any harm.' Immersing himself into a group of Catholic conspirators by purporting to be an avid supporter, he had been instrumental in exposing the Babington Plot of 1586, which aimed to assassinate Elizabeth I and replace her on the English throne with her cousin Mary, Queen of Scots. Discovery of the plot led directly to Elizabeth ordering Mary's execution after nineteen years of imprisonment. In 1597, Poley would be planted by the government in London's Marshalsea Prison to spy on Ben Jonson, who was jailed for his allegedly seditious writing in the play *The Isle of Dogs*.

Nicholas Skeres was unashamedly a conman and trickster who had a history of operating swindles in partnership with Frizer. He appears to have been a law student before becoming an agent for usurious loan sharks, luring in hapless borrowers on commission. Like Poley, Skeres had been infiltrated as a government agent among the Babington conspirators.

Not one of them, in other words, was remotely trustworthy as a witness to what had actually happened in Eleanor Bull's house. Who might have wanted Marlowe dead? One thing is for sure: Marlowe was a self-professed atheist and homosexual who had been heard on more than one occasion making scurrilous remarks about the teachings of Christianity. Blasphemy – and atheism was the greatest of those because it effectively undermined the inherent authority of the 'divinely ordained' monarch – had been declared by Parliament to be tantamount to treason. Blasphemous papers, said to be Marlowe's, had been discovered only days earlier, and a warrant for his arrest was issued on 18 May on accusations that he was a treasonous and irreligious reprobate.

Had he not died when he did, he was due to appear before the Privy Council to answer the charges against him. Despite several perilous scrapes with the law in the past, Marlowe had always been protected by his powerful connections. Now he had become an embarrassment to his handlers and his luck was running out. That luck ended altogether on 30 May. Did he know too much? Was someone in authority afraid of what Marlowe might reveal if his case went to trial?

For his part, Ingram Frizer had a good friend in the influential wife of his employer, Sir Thomas Walsingham. (One theory has it that she commissioned Marlowe's murder because she was jealous of the close relationship the playwright had developed with her husband.) For whatever reason, Lady Audrey Walsingham, who served as Lady of the Bedchamber to Elizabeth I, would subsequently ensure Frizer's personal advancement under James I shortly after the new king succeeded Elizabeth in 1603. It may simply be coincidence, but Touchstone addresses his line about 'a great reckoning in a little room' to a character named Audrey. There is even a touch of Marlowe about the phrase itself: it echoes a line from *The Jew of Malta* in which the Jewish merchant Barabas describes the jewels over which he is gloating as 'infinite riches in a little room'.

Touchstone is not the only character to allude to Marlowe in *As You Like It*. A little later in the play a country lass named Phoebe falls in love with Rosalind, the play's heroine who is disguised as a youth named Ganymede. Gazing on Rosalind, Phoebe sighs:

Dead shepherd, now I find thy saw of might: 'Who ever lov'd that lov'd not at first sight?' (3.5)

A 'saw' was a wise saying, the 'dead shepherd' is Marlowe (remember the Forest of Arden is an idyllic rustic world), and the quote is taken from Marlowe's classic poem *Hero and Leander*.

Marlowe gets another nod from Shakespeare, this time in *The Merry Wives of Windsor*. The Welsh parson Sir Hugh Evans bursts into song, slightly misquoting a verse from Marlowe's popular poem *The Passionate Shepherd to His Love*. Evans warbles:

To shallow rivers, to whose falls / Melodious birds sing madrigals; / There will we make our peds [beds] **of roses, / And a thousand fragrant posies.** (3.1)

The loss of Marlowe at such a young age proved an incalculable blow to English literature, and we are left wondering what other great works he might have bequeathed us had he lived longer. Shakespeare began his theatrical career under Marlowe's shadow and recent analysis suggests the two may even have collaborated on the Henry VI trilogy. Clearly Shakespeare, the writer who was to succeed to Marlowe's undisputed crown – and go on to surpass him – never quite forgot his debt to the flawed man of genius.

See also: 48. The Stranger's Case

10. SUMMERS ARE NO SUMMERS

Atrocious weather and disastrous harvests are blamed on trouble in fairyland

Therefore the winds, piping to us in vain, as in revenge, have suck'd up from the sea
contagious fogs; which falling in the land have every pelting [paltry] **river made so proud**
that they have overborne their continents [burst their banks].
The ox hath therefore stretch'd his yoke in vain, the plough-man lost [wasted] **his sweat** [labour], **and the green corn hath rotted ere his youth** [before he] **attain'd a beard. The fold** [pen for cattle or sheep] **stands empty in the drowned field, and crows are fatted with** [feeding on] **the murrion flock** [diseased animals].

(*A Midsummer Night's Dream*, 2.1, 1595)

THESE disturbingly beautiful lines are spoken by Titania, the fairy queen. The climate has turned topsy-turvy. Despite the time of year nominally being summer, people have become so confused by the turbulent weather that they no longer know which season they are in. 'Hoary-headed frosts' now fall into 'the fresh lap of the crimson rose'. Winter's 'icy crown' is set as a garland on 'sweet summer buds' as if in cruel mockery. Incessant rain has led to cattle and sheep dying of the infectious disease known as murrain, while humans are plagued by rheumatic illnesses. Harvests are ruined. 'Nine men's morris', a traditional game played by country folk on a grid of squares cut into the village green, 'is fill'd up with mud'. The 'human mortals' are enduring untimely winter-like conditions when they should be enjoying their summertime, without even the cheer that the Christmas season would bring to lift the darkness. Titania is in no doubt about the cause: it is the bitter dispute that has riven the fairy kingdom she shares with her husband Oberon. Hammering home the point, she says:

The spring, the summer, the childing [prolific] **autumn, angry winter, change their wonted liveries** [accustomed appearance], **and the mazed** [bewildered] **world, by their increase, now knows not which is which.** (2.1)

All in all, it is a calamitous state of affairs. And so indeed it was. The weather in the British Isles during the last two decades of the sixteenth century saw some remarkable extremes – for which, in the summer of 1588 at least, the inhabitants had reason to be grateful when a ferocious storm scattered the Spanish Armada and crushed Phillip II's attempt to invade Elizabeth's kingdom. On 18 July that year, just one day before the Spanish fleet appeared off The Lizard in Cornwall, the rainfall was so heavy and sustained that severe floods swept across southern and central England.

In Shakespeare's home town of Stratford-upon-Avon, the river rose at the rate of a yard (0.9m) every hour for at least eight hours, a contemporary writer tells us, reaching 'higher than ever yt was knowne, by a yeard and a halfe and something more'. That was the year both ends of the stone bridge built by Sir Hugh Clopton were submerged, trapping three men who were crossing it at the time. The flooding left a trail of devastation all along the Avon valley.

The weather extremes continued through the following years, ranging from a parching drought in the summer of 1592, so great that horsemen could ride across the bed of the Thames near London Bridge and cattle died for want of water, to a winter of continual snowfall and frosts that only ended when a rapid thaw set in on 8 April 1593, leading to yet more flooding. The terrible summers that immediately preceded Shakespeare writing *A Midsummer Night's Dream* brought a succession of disastrous harvests due to the continual heavy downpours, and it is to these Titania is referring. A contemporary account from 1594 records:

May, June and July very wet and cold. Many great floods this summer.

Dr John King, the Chaplain to Elizabeth I who was to become Bishop of London in 1611, lamented the country's plight under the yoke of foul weather, famine due to spoiled harvests, and outbreaks of plague. He also pointedly mentions a comet ('a blazing star') that was seen over Britain in July and August of 1593, with all the air of foreboding such a visitation entailed. He writes:

The months of the year [1593 and 1594] have not yet gone about, wherein the Lord hath bowed the heavens, and come down about us with more tokens and earnests of his wrath intended, than the agedest man of our land is able to recount of so small a time. For say, if ever the winds, since they blew one against the other, have been more common and more tempestuous; as if the four ends of heaven had conspired to turn the province of the earth upside down. Thunders and lightnings, neither seasonable for the time, and withal most terrible with such effects brought forth, that the child unborn shall speak of it.

The anger of the clouds hath been poured down upon our heads, both with abundance, and ... with incredible violence. The air threatened our miseries with a blazing star. The pillars of the earth tottered in many whole countries and tracts of our land. For the arrows of the woful pestilence have been cast abroad at large in all the quarters of our realm, even to the emptying and dispeopling of some parts thereof.

Dr King goes on to bemoan:

Our July hath been like to a February; our June even as an April: so that the air must needs be corrupted. God amend

*it in his mercy, and stay this plague of waters. But yet the
pestilence [bubonic plague] is not ceased.*

He then describes the starvation that has followed the
disastrous harvests:

*Behold! What a famine God hath brought upon our land;
and making it to persevere yet hitherto, doth increase it.
One year there hath been hunger: the second there was a
dearth: and a third there was great cleanness of teeth [noth-
ing to be eaten]. And see, whether the Lord doth not threaten
us much more, by sending such unseasonable weather
and storms of rain among us. Which if we will observe,
and compare it with that which is put, we may say, that
the course of nature is very much inverted. Our years are
turned upside down. Our summers are no summers: our
harvests are no harvests: our seeds-times [sowing times] are
no seeds-times. For a great space of time, scant any day hath
seen that it hath not rained upon us. And the nights are like
the days.*

Yet more trouble was in store for the summer of 1596.
The historian John Stow tells us:

*In this moneth of May (as afore) fell continuall raines every
day or night, wherethrough the waters, growne deep, brake
over the highways ... so that market people riding towards
London hardly escaped, but some were drowned. Also towards Lambeth, in the highway, people not on horsebacke
were borne on men's backs or rowed in wherries [rowing
boats] ... This moneth of June and also the moneth of July,
was every day raine (as afore) more or less to the end ...
This yeare, like as in the moneth of August, so in September,
October and November fell great raines, where upon high
waters followed.*

Parish registers across England record a marked increase
in the number of burials after the ruinous harvests of 1593,

1596 and 1597. Titania's speech would have struck a painful chord with the Globe's weather-beaten audiences. Shakespeare gives voice to the sense of exasperation felt by everyone – the downpours must have significantly reduced the number of the groundlings who turned up to see plays during what should have been the theatres' busiest season – in the refrain from the song Feste the jester sings at the close of *Twelfth Night*:

For the rain it raineth every day ... (5.1)

And listen to the resigned sigh in another of the lines:

With hey, ho, the wind and the rain ...

A jarring snatch of the same song is discordantly echoed by the Fool in the midst of the raging storm in *King Lear* (3.2).

✳ ✳ ✳

As if crop failures and pestilence were not bad enough, a third factor combined to create a perfect storm of calamities for common folk. Throughout the sixteenth century, the ancient freedoms of villagers and townsfolk to graze their animals and grow food crops on open countryside were imperilled by the growing imposition of 'enclosures'. Wealthy businessmen were forcing subsistence farmers off the land by buying up large areas and enclosing them with fences and hedgerows in order to keep sheep.

There were huge profits to be made from the sale of wool, but the effect was a drastic reduction in the amount of land available for everyone else. Families were forced out of their homes by starvation and loss of work, with many deciding to make for London in the hope of eking out a living in the city. To make matters worse, rich landowners were accused of hoarding grain and storing it in their barns until it could be sold at extortionate prices as the scarcity of food increased.

Starvation and rising unemployment tightened their grip. Tempers boiled over in June 1595 when a thousand angry apprentice boys rioted on Tower Hill, the soaring cost of food being chief among their grievances. The riot, the biggest uprising seen in the City of London within living memory, took on a personal element when the demonstrators accused the mayor and other leading citizens of deliberately creating the situation through their greed. The response of the authorities was sharp. Five of the protest leaders were arrested for treason and met the grim fate of being hanged, drawn and quartered as an example to others.

Discontent still grew and in September 1596 Edward Hext, a justice of the peace in Somerset, wrote in panicked tones to Lord Burghley, the Lord High Treasurer, expressing his fears that social order was in imminent danger of collapsing altogether. 'Rapynes [pillage] and thefts ... multiplye daily,' Hext complained, and he estimated there were three hundred to four hundred 'wandering souldiers and other stout roages [rogues]' running rampage in every county. Giving an example of the breakdown in law and order in his own rural district – and at the same time unwittingly demonstrating just how dire things had become for the poor – he gripes:

> And this year there assembled eighty rogues in a company
> and took a whole [wagon] load of cheese from one driving
> it to a fair, and dispersed it amongst them, for which some
> have endured long imprisonment and fine.

Hext goes on to say that idle, wandering people and robbers complain 'that the rich men have gotten it all in their hands and will starve the poor' then he adds bitterly:

> And when these lewd people are committed to the jail, the
> poor country that is robbed by them are enforced there to
> feed them, which they grieve at.

By 1597 there were at least ten thousand 'vagabonds' in London and two thousand in Norwich, the second biggest city. That year William Cecil, Lord Burghley, introduced the controversial Vagabonds Act, intended to control their numbers, which for the first time prescribed penal transportation of offenders to England's fledgling colonies in North America. In his address to Parliament, Burghley spoke of 'the lamentable cry of the poor who are like to perish' and included measures intended to prevent the hoarding of grain, although the practice continued.

The enclosure of land sparked an even more worrying uprising in May 1607, when 'a great number of common persons' began tearing up the fences and hedges newly installed by landowners. What is now known as the Midland Revolt started in Northamptonshire, then spread like wildfire across the neighbouring counties of Leicestershire and Shakespeare's own Warwickshire. The protesters were widely known as 'Diggers', although the name they gave themselves was the 'Levellers'. According to the chronicler Edmund Howes:

> They violently cut and brake downe hedges, filled up ditches, and laid open all such enclosures of Commons, and other grounds as they found enclosed, which of ancient time hadde bin open and imploied to tillage.

James I promptly issued orders for the revolt to be put down, and on 8 June around fifty people were killed in a pitched battle with the military at the village of Newton, near Kettering. The uprising so close to his home town of Stratford appears to have shaken Shakespeare, who clearly had it in mind when he came to write *Coriolanus* the following year. While that tragedy, taken from a story of Plutarch's, is set in ancient Rome, the parallels with the Midland Revolt in the opening scene are striking. A mob of plebeians confront Rome's patricians, the ruling class, whose powers extend to controlling the supply of grain. A citizen ringleader complains to the rest of the crowd that the wealthy prefer to keep the poor starving because their wretchedness allows them to gloat over how well off they themselves are. He declares:

> **We are accounted poor citizens, the patricians good.**
> **What authority** [the ruling class] **surfeits on would**
> **relieve us: if they would yield us but the superfluity,**
> **while it were wholesome** [fit to eat], **we might guess**
> **they relieved us humanely. But they think we are too**
> **dear** [valuable as we are]: **the leanness that afflicts us, the**
> **object** [spectacle] **of our misery, is as an inventory to par-**
> **ticularise** [compare with] **their abundance. Our suffer-**
> **ance** [distress] **is a gain to them. Let us revenge this with**
> **our pikes ere** [before] **we become rakes** [as lean as rakes].
> **For the gods know I speak this in hunger for bread, not in**
> **thirst for revenge.** (1.1)

An elderly aristocrat named Menenius Agrippa attempts to calm the crowd, seeking to convince them that their rulers really do care for them and blaming the elements. He says:

> **For the dearth** [of food], **the gods, not the patricians,**
> **make it.**

But the mob are not persuaded, as the citizen hurls back an accusation of hoarding:

> **They** [the rich] **ne'er cared for us yet – suffer us to famish,**
> **and their store-houses crammed with grain.**

When the arrogant general Coriolanus himself appears, he displays the same contempt for the masses that England's rulers had shown the Levellers, opening with a calculated insult:

> **What's the matter, you dissentious rogues, that rubbing**
> **the poor itch of your opinion, make yourselves scabs?**

In 1614, the continuing confrontation came to affect Will personally. Having retired to Stratford-upon-Avon, he learned that two local landowners named William Combe and Arthur Mainwaring proposed to enclose open fields, in which he had a financial interest, in the villages of Welcombe and Old Stratford. The Combe family had long-established links with the Shakespeares and, when protesters started ripping up the enclosures with the support of Stratford town council, the playwright found himself in the middle of a dispute between friends on either side. His answer was to remain studiously neutral. The case went to Warwick Assizes and eventually the Chief Justice of the King's Bench put a stop to the plan to enclose the fields in question.

Between 1586 and 1631, England saw no fewer than forty food riots resulting from widespread starvation caused by the combination of bad weather, grain hoarding and the creeping enclosures.

See also: 4. Underneath the Arches
26. Tom o' Bedlam

11. FIRE ON THE ICE

Europe's 'Little Ice Age' produces winters so cold the River Thames freezes over

When icicles hang by the wall / And Dick the shepherd blows his nail / And Tom bears logs into the hall / And milk comes frozen home in pail, / When blood is nipp'd and ways be foul, / Then nightly sings the staring owl. Tu-whit; / Tu-who, a merry note, /   While greasy Joan doth keel [stir] the pot.

When all aloud the wind doth blow / And coughing drowns the parson's saw [homily] / And birds sit brooding in the snow / And Marian's nose looks red and raw, / When roasted crabs [crab-apples] hiss in the bowl, / Then nightly sings the staring owl. Tu-whit; / Tu-who, a merry note, / While greasy Joan doth keel the pot.

(Love's Labour's Lost, 5.2, 1594-5)

SHAKESPEARE often rejoices over the joys of spring and summer but in these verses he captures a frosty winter's scene in charming detail. How readily we can picture Dick the shepherd blowing warm breath on to his frozen fingers, and the milk that has turned to ice in the bucket only a matter of minutes after being squeezed from the cow. We can almost hear the chorus of incessant coughing in the draughty medieval church that renders the parson's carefully worded homilies inaudible, the hissing of freshly roasted crab-apples in a kitchen bowl, while Joan the cook keeps stirring the big pot of thick stew that is bubbling over a fire.

Crab-apples, which grew as wildings, were traditionally roasted then mashed and added with nutmeg to ale to make a favourite hot wassailing drink known as 'lambs-wool'. And what could be more redolent of a snow-blanketed winter's night than the hoot of the owl? At least the owl in *Love's Labour's Lost* strikes 'a merry note,' unlike the haunting one heard in *Macbeth* just after the murder of King Duncan, which causes Lady Macbeth to declare:

It was the owl that shriek'd, the fatal bellman [night-watchman] **which gives the stern'st good night.** (2.2)

The shiver-inducing fact is that many Elizabethan and Jacobean winters were very cold indeed. The era fell smack into what is now termed the 'Little Ice Age', when average temperatures are estimated to have been as much as two degrees Celsius lower than those experienced in the twentieth century. The winter of 1564, the year in which Shakespeare was born, was the coldest of the sixteenth century and, indeed, one of the coldest of the entire millennium. A harsh frost set in on 7 December and clung on relentlessly until early the following January.

In London, for weeks the river was 'frozen over as hard as dry land' with ice as thick as a foot (0.3m), a phenomenon created by the combination of sub-zero temperatures and the twenty stone piers that supported London Bridge. The narrow archways between the bridge's piers had a tendency to become blocked by large pieces of ice, which then acted as a dam to restrict the river's tidal ebb and flow, leading even more ice to form upstream. At the end of December 1564, Raphael Holinshed tells us in his *Chronicle*, London's river – normally a busy highway for the passenger-carrying boatmen with their cries of 'Westward ho!' and Eastward ho!' – became a pedestrian thoroughfare:

People went over and alongst the Thames on the ise, from London Bridge to Westminster. Some plaied at the football as boldlie there as if it had been on the drie land. Divers of the court being then at Westminster, shot dailie at prickes

*[markers] set upon the Thames; and the people, both men
and women, went on the Thames in greater numbers than
in anie street of the Citie of London.*

In the west of England, the rivers Severn and Wye froze
so hard that people could walk across the ice from bank to
bank where water usually separated England and Wales. Just
as suddenly, the frost relented. Holinshed writes:

*On the third daie of January, at night, it began to thaw, and
on the fifth there was no ise to be seene betweene London
Bridge and Lambeth, which sudden thaw caused great
floods, and high waters, that bare downe bridges and houses,
and drowned manie people in England, especiallie in Yorkshire. Owes [Ouse] Bridge [in York] was borne awaie, with
others.*

Whenever ice covered the Thames during those bitter
winters, Londoners found a way of making the best of a bad
situation. They began a tradition of festive events, which
from 1607 became known as Frost Fairs. Amid several days, or
even weeks, of festivities, stalls and tents were set up on the
frozen river selling food and all manner of goods, including
souvenir certificates specially printed to mark the occasion.

Makeshift taverns on the ice served eager drinkers.
There were puppet shows, games of bowling and displays of
dancing. People skated, youngsters played football, and even
popular attractions such as bull-baiting were staged for spectators – all the fun of the fair, in fact. The ice was so thick that
coal fires were even daringly lit in pans resting on its surface.
Shakespeare uses the perils implicit in such a foolhardy venture as a metaphor for unreliability in *Coriolanus*, when the
Roman warrior scathingly addresses a mob of unruly citizens:

**He that trusts to you, where he should find you lions,
finds you hares; where foxes, geese. You are no surer, no,
than is the coal of fire upon the ice, or hailstone in the**

sun. (1.1)

On 21 December 1564, the Queen herself turned up at a Thames fair and walked on the ice. Among the delights she indulged in on that occasion was 'shooting at marks' or archery practice. The glittering royal presence, along with her large retinue of courtiers, caused much excitement among her subjects. In the years between the old London Bridge being completed in 1209, and demolished in 1831, there were at least twenty-four winters in which the Thames is recorded as having frozen over, most of them in the sixteenth and seventeenth centuries. The first event to actually be called a 'frost fair' took place in 1608 and it features on the cover of a commemorative pamphlet printed at the time (*pictured*).

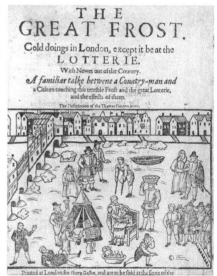

The rest of northwest Europe was also badly affected, and the heavy frosts of the 'Little Ice Age' are credited with inspiring those familiar snow-filled Flemish winter scenes painted by the Breughels. Sadly, where nature threw up challenges, the temptation to blame witchcraft could never be far away. In Brittany in 1586, the Archbishop of Treves had no fewer than one hundred and eighteen women and two men burned to death after they were found guilty of chanting incantations intended to prolong a harsh winter.

There were plenty more such winters to come. In that of 1592-3, at the time Shakespeare was creating Richard III for Richard Burbage to play, continual snowfall between 23 December and 31 March produced snowdrifts so deep they threatened 'to bury the city' of Oxford. In 1594, areas of sea froze as far south as Marseilles and Venice, and the so-called 'Great Winter' of 1607 saw the sea freeze for several miles out from the English coast. Commerce with the mainland of Europe ground to a halt as icebound ships became stranded in the English Channel and the North Sea. Inland, countless trees died.

The answer for irrepressible revellers in London was again to celebrate with a Frost Fair. In York, a horse race was run along the frozen River Ouse. The winter of 1608 brought more severe frosts, starting on 8 December and continuing, albeit broken by several brief thaws, until the following February. In London, it also heralded another Frost Fair at which, the historian Edmund Howes tells us:

People were many that set up boothes and standings upon the ice as fruit-sellers, victuallers, that sold beere and wine, shoemakers, and a barber's tent, etc.

Frosts began as early as October in the winter of 1609. In 1614, snow began falling on 16 January, 'at which time [in York] was such a heavy snow upon the earth as was not remembered by any man then living,' according to *Eboracum* by the writer Francis Drake (not to be confused with the famous explorer). In 1615, 'great snow' lay across Britain for seven weeks until 7 March and there was widespread loss of livestock.

While the owl evokes the melancholy of winter, Shakespeare reminds us in the first part of the same song from *Love's Labour's Lost* that spring could bring perils of a quite different sort. In an age now noted for its remarkably relaxed approach to sexual mores, he reminds us that many a husband lived in fear of being made a 'cuckold' by his errant wife.

The cuckoo then, on every tree, / Mocks married men, for thus sings he, / Cuckoo; / Cuckoo, cuckoo: O word of

fear, / Unpleasing to a married ear! (5.2)

Simply put, the call of the cuckoo could strike more terror into a man's heart than even the screech of the owl.

12. THE DANCING HORSE

A sensational four-footed attraction lures astonished crowds away from the theatre

Now here is three studied, ere ye'll thrice wink. And how easy it is to put 'years' to the word 'three,' and study three years in two words, the dancing horse will tell you. (*Love's Labour's Lost*, 1.2, 1594-5)

A SERVANT named Moth is teasing his dull-witted master Don Adriano de Armado, a 'fantastical Spaniard,' with word-play in which he refers to 'the dancing horse'. Everyone in the audience would have known exactly which animal Moth was talking about. For at the time Shakespeare was writing *Love's Labour's Lost*, his courtly comedy of unrequited love, just down the road an unlikely four-footed entertainer was drawing excited crowds. Marocco's act was unlike anything that had gone before, and Will was no doubt as impressed and amused as everybody else.

Astonished spectators gasped to see the horse, named after the Morocco leather from which saddles were often made, beating out with stomps of his hooves the number of coins a man had taken from his purse, or how many dots were showing on a large pair of dice. They would applaud wildly as the bay-coloured nag launched into his celebrated speciality of dancing the Canary – a lively Spanish jig popular all over Europe – then walked around the arena on his hind legs as an encore. On the command of William Banks, his owner, Marocco would collapse on to the ground and play dead, remaining there completely motionless. His performance was so convincing that many in the crowd believed the horse had actually died, until the moment came for Banks to invite them all to beg him to get up again. Then Marocco would suddenly come back to life and spring on to his hooves, to be rewarded with more delighted applause and an apple.

The horse would obey instructions from Banks to pull out of the audience with his teeth anyone who had spectacles or was wearing clothing of a certain colour. The coarsest laughter came at the expense of women watching the show, when the horse was told first to pick out the 'maids' or chaste virgins in the crowd, and then find the 'maulkins' or harlots. During their routine, Banks would address the horse as 'Señor'. Upon being ordered to bow to the name of the Queen, Marocco would oblige, dutifully scraping his hoof as he did so. But when Philip II, hated king of the Spanish, was mentioned, the horse would neigh, bare his teeth, whinny, and angrily chase his trainer right out of the staging ring.

Marocco was unfailingly earning fame and fortune for the canny Staffordshire man William Banks (also spelt Bankes). Banks had been an employee of Robert Devereux, the Earl of Essex, probably working in his lordship's stables, until he met Marocco. Realising he had a particularly intelligent animal on his hands, he purchased the horse for himself and began training him. According to one story, he saved up enough money to have Marocco shod with silver horseshoes. The pair were going places. They had apparently achieved a degree of celebrity even before the much-loved comic Richard Tarlton died in September 1588, if we are to believe an account in a popular book called *Tarlton's Jests* (first published around 1592 and later reprinted). It relates how:

There was one Banks, in the time of Tarlton, who served the Erle of Essex, and had a horse of strange qualities, and being at the Crosse-keyes [inn] in Gracious [Gracechurch] streete, getting mony [earning money] with him, as he was mightily resorted to [popular with the crowds]. Tarlton then, with

his fellowes, playing at the Bel [the Bell Inn, licensed for
dramatic performances] by [nearby], came into the Cross-
keyes, amongst many people, to see fashions, which Banks
perceiving, to make the people laugh, saies: 'Seignior,' to his
horse, 'go fetch me the veriest [biggest] foole in the company.'
The jade comes immediately, and with his mouth drawes
Tarlton forth. Tarlton with merry words, said nothing but,
'God a [have] mercy, horse.' In the end Tarlton, seeing the
people laugh so, was angry inwardly, and said: 'Sir, had I
power of your horse as you have, I would doe more than
that.' 'What ere it be,' said Banks, to please him, 'I will charge
him to do it.' 'Then,' said Tarlton, 'charge him bring me the
veriest whore-master in the company.' The horse leades his
master [Banks] to him. Then 'God a mercy, horse, indeed,'
saies Tarlton. The people had much ado to keep peace; but
Banks and Tarlton had like to have squar'd, [were ready to
fight] and the horse by to give aime. But ever after it was a by
word [catch-cry] thorow [throughout] London, 'God a mercy,
horse!' and is so to this day.

For all Tarlton's reputation as a funny man, he was known to be somewhat irascible and Banks may well have seen commercial value in baiting him in public. On the other hand, although the two men gave the impression of squaring up to each other, the whole thing could have been an elaborate publicity stunt cooked up between them beforehand. Banks knew Tarlton would draw a crowd wherever he went and vice versa. By the mid-1590s, Banks and his horse were among London's biggest attractions in their own right. As the money rolled in, Banks moved into the Belle Sauvage, an upmarket coaching inn on what is now Ludgate Hill. He housed Marocco in the inn's stables and at length became wealthy enough to build his own arena nearby, engaging a full-time musician both as a warm-up man and to accompany the horse during his dance routine.

Rumour had it that in private Banks and his horse talked

to each other, and in 1595 a satirical pamphlet appeared, titled *Maroccos Exstaticus, or Bankes Bay Horse in a Traunce; a Discourse set down in a Merry Dialogue between Bankes and his Beast.* It contained a woodcut print showing the performing animal with his owner. The print still exists. A ballad about them was also published in the same year, apparently to be sold at the shows, although unfortunately no copy of that is known to have survived. (*Banks and Marocco are pictured, as depicted in Maroccos Exstaticus.*)

Banks became a victim of his own success when others began copying what he had done with Marocco and, as the seventeenth century dawned, the novelty of their act was fading. Competition had emerged from, among others, the owners of a performing monkey, a trained elephant, a camel, a donkey and a bear. In a desperate attempt to assert the pre-eminence of his act, Banks resolved to stage a feat even more sensational than anything he had accomplished so far. In February 1601, he led Marocco up the thousand steps of the spiral staircase to the top of the tower of St Paul's Cathedral, which before it was destroyed in the Great Fire of London in 1666 had a flat roof. Emerging on to the rooftop before a crowd of excited spectators on the ground below, anxious clergymen included, Marocco performed his famous dance. Even more amazing, to anyone who has ever tried to lead a horse down steps, the pair then calmly descended the spiral staircase and emerged out of the cathedral door to be greeted with cheers.

The following month, Banks took Marocco to Paris, moving into the Lion d'Argent inn on the Rue Saint-Jacques. Renaming the animal 'Monsieur Moraco', the pair became a huge success in a city that had seen nothing like them before. For one magistrate, however, it was all too much of a novelty. Convinced some sort of witchcraft was involved, he arrested Banks on a charge of sorcery. Banks managed to argue his way out of the accusation by convincing the city authorities that his success with Marocco was all the result of training the animal. From Paris, the double act went on a tour of other French cities.

All went well until they reached Orléans. When a group of priests and monks from local monasteries saw the show they were outraged, and became convinced that Banks was a sorcerer and Marocco a demon in the form of a horse. Banks was again arrested and this time both he and Marocco were threatened with burning at the stake. He asked permission to prove their innocence with one more performance, during which he ordered Marocco to bow down before a crucifix. The horse did as he was told and Banks' accusers immediately relented, satisfied that the devil could never abide the sign of the cross. The pair were finally allowed to leave the city, with a gift of 'money and great commendations'.

Banks and his horse continued to criss-cross the Continent with their routine, attracting eager audiences wherever they went. Marocco appears to have died around 1606, after which Banks finally revealed his secrets to the English writer Gervase Markham, who published them the following year in *Cavelarice*, a study of 'all the Arte of Horsemanship'. While Marocco's training was achieved with rewards of hunks of bread and slices of apple, Banks taught the horse to look for signals as subtle as a flick of the wrist, an expression on his face, and even the movement of his eyes.

In 1608, Banks was hired to work in the royal stables of James I, and is later heard of in London's Cheapside as an innkeeper who had a lively wit. Never again would he encounter an animal capable of taking Marocco's place. He did, however, establish a precedent for a whole genre of circus acts in the centuries that followed. Banks might also be considered a forerunner of Sir William Cavendish (1593-1676), first Duke of Newcastle, who is credited with introducing the art of dressage to England.

See also: 45. Alas, Poor Tarlton

13. THE MAN WHO WAS SHYLOCK

The trial and execution of Elizabeth I's personal physician revives a tide of anti-Semitism

He hath disgraced [insulted] **me, and hindered** [cost] **me half a million** [ducats]; **laughed at my losses, mocked at my gains, scorned my nation, thwarted my bargains** [deals], **cooled my friends, heated mine enemies; and what's his reason? I am a Jew. Hath not a Jew eyes? Hath not a Jew hands, organs, dimensions, senses, affections, passions? Fed with the same food, hurt with the same weapons, subject to the same diseases, healed by the same means, warmed and cooled by the same winter and summer, as a Christian is? If you prick us, do we not bleed? If you tickle us, do we not laugh? If you poison us, do we not die? And if you wrong us, shall we not revenge?**

(*The Merchant of Venice*, 3.1, 1596-7)

SHAKESPEARE lived in an anti-Semitic world. All Jews living in England – numbering about three thousand – had been expelled by Edward I under the Edict of Expulsion in 1290. Although the ban was still on the statute books, by Elizabethan times London had again become home to a handful of Jewish residents. Jews were grudgingly tolerated on condition they publicly professed conversion to Christianity, while it was assumed with a nudge and a wink that they would follow their own faith in private. Shylock, the vengeful money-lender of *The Merchant of Venice* who seeks a pound of the merchant Antonio's flesh – and therefore his death – as the penalty for defaulting on a debt, fits the harsh image Elizabethans held of the Jewish race.

It was a stereotype that had been enthusiastically stoked six years before *The Merchant* by Christopher Marlowe in *The Jew of Malta* with its villainous anti-hero, the Machiavellian figure Barabas. Marlowe's play was so popular that it was guaranteed to pull in full houses at any theatre where it played, and it was therefore frequently revived. Yet where Barabas is a character with no redeeming qualities, Shylock, for all his faults, evokes at least some empathy from all but the most stony-hearted in the audience. 'We Jews are human too,' Shylock is saying, 'would you not expect us to treat you as you treat us?' When Shakespeare gave such voice to Shylock, a token victim of the anti-Semitic discrimination prevalent in Elizabethan society, he was breaking daring new ground where Marlowe had never gone.

There was good reason for Shakespeare to be affected by the plight of one Jew in particular. Dr Roderigo Lopez, despite being of Jewish descent and raised as a Catholic in his native Portugal, had risen from his post as physician at St Bartholomew's Hospital in London to become the Queen's personal physician-in-chief. Elizabeth I thought so highly of him that she granted him a retainer of fifty pounds a year, a lucrative monopoly in the importing of aniseed and other herbs essential to apothecaries, as well as land in Worcestershire. Lopez was fluent in five languages, treated some of the most powerful and best connected people in London, and lived in a comfortable house he owned in Holborn. The scholar Gabriel Harvey writes of him in somewhat barbed tones:

> *Doctor Lopus, the Queenes physitian, is descended of Jewes: but himselfe A Christian, & Portugall. He none of the learnedest, or expertest physitians in ye Court: but one that maketh as great account of himself as the best: & by a kind of Jewish practis, hath growen to much wealth & sum reputation: as well with ye Queen herselfe as with sum of ye greatest Lordes & Ladyes.*

As an important member of a circle of Portuguese exiles in London, Lopez also dabbled in diplomatic intrigue. Unfortunately for him, he got on the wrong side of the petulant Robert Devereux, Earl of Essex, whose animosity had increased in direct proportion to the talented Jewish doctor's influence at court. Things came to a head when Essex suspected Lopez was spreading tittle-tattle that he had been treated for sexually transmitted disease.

Perhaps inspired by an anonymous vitriolic pamphlet which had appeared in 1584, claiming 'Lopez the Jewe' was an agent of Robert Dudley, Earl of Leicester, and was notorious 'for poysoning & for the arte of destroying children in women's bellies,' Essex began digging for dirt on the good doctor. He set about constructing a case that Lopez was plotting to murder Elizabeth I as part of a conspiracy. Unknown to Essex, however, Lopez was secretly working for William Cecil, Lord Burghley, the Lord High Treasurer and Elizabeth's closest advisor, as a double agent, charged with keeping tabs on any cunning plots the perfidious Spanish might be cooking up. Concerned about having one of his key sources compromised, Cecil hurried to assure the Queen there was nothing in the allegations. Her Majesty accordingly delivered a sharp rap over the knuckles to the interfering Essex.

According to the *Memoirs of the Reign of Queen Elizabeth* by the Reverend Thomas Birch, published in 1754, she told the twenty-eight year old Essex he was a

Rash and temerarious youth to enter into a matter against the poor man which he could not prove, and whose innocence she knew well enough; but malice against him, and no other, hatch'd all this matter, which displeased her much, and the more, for that, she said, her honor was interested herein.

With that royal rebuke still ringing in his ears, the furious earl rushed to Essex House, his London home. There, says

Birch, he locked himself in his bedchamber and did not come out for two whole days. The outcome of Essex's sulking was a resolution to redouble his efforts to undo Lopez. Late in 1593 he had his 'gotcha' moment, delightedly discovering a cache of secret correspondence from which he concluded that Lopez had been promised fifty thousand crowns by Philip II of Spain to murder Elizabeth. Essex promptly arranged for a messenger named Manuel Luis Tinoco to be interrogated under torture. Gomez d'Avila, a courier for Lopez, was also hauled in, and both men implicated Lopez. Estevão Ferreira da Gama, the Portuguese man who had been involved in the correspondence in question – with officials in the Spanish Netherlands – was also arrested and threatened with torture unless he confessed his part in a secret plot involving Lopez. When asked if Lopez might have been willing to poison the Queen, Ferreira da Gama agreed that he would. On 21 January 1594, a shocked Lopez was arrested by Essex on a charge of high treason. On 28 January, Essex proudly declared in a letter to his friend Anthony Bacon, elder brother of Sir Francis:

> *I have discovered a most dangerous and desperate treason. The point of conspiracy was Her Majesty's death. The executioner should have been Dr Lopez. The manner by poison. This I have so followed that I will make it as clear as the noon day.*

Shakespeare even cheekily alludes in *The Merchant of Venice* to the rack – that notorious instrument of state torture in the Tower – and accusations of treason. It comes in a light-hearted exchange when Bassanio rejects Portia's plea for him to delay opening one of three caskets in his quest to win her love. She is worried he may choose wrongly.

Bassanio: Let me choose, for as I am I live upon the rack.

Portia: Upon the rack, Bassanio? Then confess what treason there is mingled with your love.

Bassanio: **None but that ugly treason of mistrust which makes me fear th'enjoying of my love. There may as well be amity and life 'tween snow and fire, as treason and my love.**

Portia: **Ay, but I fear you speak upon the rack, where men enforcèd do speak anything.** (3.2)

How telling, in the circumstances, is that line 'where men enforcèd do speak anything'? This time the evidence appeared damning. Lopez, Tinoco and Ferreira da Gama went on trial at the Guildhall in London on 28 February. Nothing more is heard of d'Avila, who was probably breathing a heavy sigh of relief at being left out of the case. The tone was set when Sir Edward Coke, the prosecutor, thundered that Lopez was 'a perjured, murdering villain, and a Jewish doctor, worse than Judas himself' (there goes the anti-Semitism again) who was involved in 'a plot more wicked, dangerous and detestable' than any that had gone before. Coke went on for good measure:

He was Her Majesty's sworn servant, graced and advanced with many princely favours ... permitted often access to her person, so not suspected, especially by her, who never fears her enemies nor suspects her servants.

Despite their protests of innocence, all three were found guilty and sentenced to be hanged, drawn and quartered. The Queen harboured doubts and held off signing their death warrants for three whole months. The court case had caused a sensation and the delay was described as stirring 'the general discontent of the people, who expected this execution'.

An illustration (*pictured*) by the German engraver Esaias van Hulsen purports to show Lopez receiving his instructions from a Spanish agent. A quote bubble emerging from the mouth of Lopez reads in Latin '*Quid dabitis*' or 'What will you give?', a reference to the doctor's alleged reward for turning traitor. At right, the gallows and the word '*Proditorum*' or 'traitors' alludes to the fate that awaits such treachery.

Finally, on 7 June 1594, the three men were lined up on the gallows at Tyburn for the ghastly sentence to be carried out in front of a baying crowd that roared its approval. According to the historian William Camden, on the scaffold Lopez declared in his final words that 'he loved the Queen as well as he loved Jesus Christ,' which – Camden adds wrily – 'coming from a man of the Jewish profession moved no small laughter in the standers-by'. Contrary to custom, Elizabeth allowed Lopez's widow to keep his estate, which should rightfully have been forfeit to the Crown, except for a valuable ring that had been given to his daughter by Spanish officials. The Queen had clearly taken a fancy to the sparkler.

The Lopez case led to yet another revival of *The Jew of Malta* (although Marlowe had died the previous year) and inspired Shakespeare to write *The Merchant of Venice*, which culminates in a tortuous trial scene and Shylock's humiliation, if not his death. In case we miss the connection, the playwright cannot resist inserting one of those tongue-in-cheek hints of which he was so fond. In the tense trial scene, Antonio's friend Gratiano rounds on Shylock, declaring:

Thy currish spirit govern'd a Wolf who, hang'd for human slaughter, even from the gallows did his fell soul fleet and, whilst thou lay'st in thy unhallow'd dam, infused itself in thee. (4.1)

To paraphrase: 'Your currish soul once belonged to a Wolf that was killed for slaughtering humans. When he died, his cruel soul passed out of his body and, while you were lying in your unholy mother's womb, entered yours.' The Latin for wolf is *lupus*, here a play on the name Lopez, which the English often spelled and pronounced Lopus. Significantly, the word 'Wolf' took an initial capital, as in the proper name, when the play was first published in a quarto edition in 1600. Because it includes stage directions with several seemingly superfluous remarks, the quarto is thought to have been printed directly from Shakespeare's own rough manuscript.

The Merchant of Venice includes another speech which, like Shylock's, remains one of the most quoted among Shakespeare's plays. It is delivered by Portia, in the role of a lawyer – 'a Daniel come to judgement' as Shylock describes her – when she appeals to the Jew to show mercy and spare Antonio.

The quality of mercy is not strain'd [constrained], **it droppeth as the gentle rain from heaven upon the place beneath. It is twice blest; it blesseth him that gives and him that takes.** (2.5)

Shakespeare found his source for Portia's words in a holy

book called *The Wisdom of Sirach*, otherwise known as *Ecclesiasticus* (not to be confused with *Ecclesiastes*), which was at the time included in the *Holy Bible* but is today considered apocryphal. The verse in question reads:

> *O how fair a thing is mercy in the time of anguish and trouble! It is like a cloud of rain that comes in time of drought.*

Was Lopez actually guilty of planning to poison Elizabeth? A decade after the trial, a Spanish diplomat named Count Gondomar confirmed in a letter to King Phillip III, who had succeeded his father Philip II on the throne of Spain in 1598, that there never had been any plot involving Lopez. Gondomar wrote:

> *The King our master [Philip II] had never conceived nor approved such measures. It is understood that Dr Lopez never passed through his thoughts, because he was a friend of the Queen.*

Roderigo Lopez retains the dubious distinction of being the only royal physician ever executed by an English monarch. He was also almost certainly immortalised by Shakespeare as Shylock.

14. HE WAS BUT ONE HOUR MINE

The death of Will's young son rocks his world. How is that grief reflected in his writing?

Grief fills the room up of my absent child, lies in his bed, walks up and down with me, puts on his pretty looks, repeats his words, remembers me of all his   gracious parts, stuffs out his vacant garments with his form; then, have I reason to be fond of grief?

(King John, 3.4, 1596)

CONSTANCE, Duchess of Brittany, believes her young son Arthur has been cruelly murdered while held captive by King John. To be sure, John had good reason for wanting Arthur out of the way, since the boy arguably had a greater right to the throne he had seized for himself. John had issued orders for Arthur's death but they were secretly defied by the merciful jailer Hubert. (Ironically, Arthur would die by leaping from a castle wall while attempting to escape captivity.)

For her part, Constance is convinced John has killed her son, and her heart-rending words inject a moment of high passion into what is otherwise Shakespeare's least performed history play. It is difficult to date *King John* with certainty, partly because the first printed version does not appear until the *First Folio* of 1623. The script was influenced by a revised edition of *Holinshed's Chronicles* published in 1587 and, since the play is mentioned in a list of Shakespeare's works compiled by Francis Meres in 1598, we know it must have been written between those years. Act 3 Scene 4, however, suggests he may have been writing it at the time the most painful event of his life occurred.

On a summer's day in 1596, unspeakable tragedy struck the family and led to Shakespeare immediately riding home to Stratford-upon-Avon. Hamnet, only son of Will and Anne, died at the age of eleven. The boy's loss had a devastating effect on his parents and sisters, Susanna and Judith. Hamnet was buried on 11 August in the graveyard of the town's Holy Trinity church, where the matter-of-fact note a clerk made in the parish register can still be read: '*Hamnet filius William Shakspere*.' His father may have been unable to arrive in time to see him buried, since news of Hamnet's death had first to reach him and the journey by horseback from London took three days.

Along with the agony of the family's loss, Shakespeare's hopes of a male heir were crushed. His son's death came while the now successful playwright was in the process of applying to the College of Heralds for a coat of arms for his own father John, which Will would in turn hand on to Hamnet. When the coat of arms was finally granted, it would die with Will himself, his daughters not being permitted to retain it under the laws of heraldry. Anne, now forty years old, was unlikely to bear more children.

The poignancy of the scene in *King John* goes even deeper than Constance's haunting words about grief. Moments earlier, the callous papal legate Cardinal Pandulph has rebuked her, snarling:

You hold too heinous a respect of grief. (3.4)

To which she snaps back:

He talks to me that never had a son.

Constance then corners the pompous churchman:

Father cardinal, I have heard you say that we shall see and know our friends in heaven. If that be true, I shall see my boy again. For since the birth of Cain, the first male child,

to him that did but yesterday suspire [breathe], **there was not such a gracious creature born.**

Later she gives voice to a cry that comes from her very soul:

O Lord! My boy, my Arthur, my fair son! My life, my joy, my food, my all the world!

Substitute the name Hamnet for Arthur and these all sound very much like words penned by a freshly grief-stricken father. We do not know what caused Hamnet's death because unfortunately the Holy Trinity parish register does not include such details. Some biographers have suggested it may have been the plague, which was a constant threat in sixteenth-century England. But the fact that the parish register records only five deaths in the month of August 1596, which is no more than an average number, must cast doubt on that theory. Many more people would be expected to have died in the town if the plague were responsible.

Life was, of course, a decidedly uncertain prospect in that age before modern medicine, when one in three children died before the age of ten. In *KingJohn*, Constance goes so far as to wish that she was mad, so she would be unaware of her unbearable loss. Her distress grows and her words become more harrowing as she laments:

But now will canker-sorrow [grief that gnaws like a worm] **eat my bud** [my son] **and chase the native beauty from his cheek; and he will look as hollow as a ghost, as dim and meagre as an ague's fit, and so he'll die; and, rising so again, when I shall meet him in the court of heaven I shall not know him. Therefore never, never must I behold my pretty Arthur more.**

Ague (pronounced ā-gyu) was the name Elizabethans gave to malaria and an 'ague's fit' was the fearsome, uncontrollable fever that came with it. It was an all-too-common infection in England, acquired particularly around low-lying wetlands and marshes. Before science was to identify the carrier as mosquitoes, the disease was thought to be caused by breathing in 'bad air,' hence it acquired the name 'malaria' from the Latin words meaning exactly that. The River Avon runs through Stratford, of course, but whether Shakespeare's use of the word 'ague' here is any sort of clue to the cause of his own son's death is unknown.

There is a particularly heart-rending moment in *The Winter's Tale* when the king Leontes is reminded of his own dead son Mamillius. He lets out an anguished cry that will be at once understood by anyone who has experienced the painful loss of a loved one:

Prithee, no more! Cease! Thou know'st he dies to me again when talk'd of. (5.1)

Scholars believe they have detected the influence of Hamnet's death in other works, citing everything from Shakespeare's story of twins who become agonisingly separated in *Twelfth Night* – Hamnet and Judith had been twins – to the love between a father and his daughter in *King Lear* (Cordelia), *Pericles* (Marina), *Cymbeline* (Imogen), *The Winter's Tale* (Perdita), and *The Tempest* (Miranda). Both of Shakespeare's surviving children were daughters. Perhaps the raw grief of Hamnet's death returned most tellingly to him nine years later as he was writing *King Lear*, when the despairing Lear howls over the body of his beloved Cordelia:

No, no, no life! Why should a dog, a horse, a rat, have life, and thou no breath at all? Thou'lt come no more, never, never, never, never, never! (5.3)

Others have sought a connection in the celebrated father-son relationship that is central to *Hamlet*, written in 1599-1601. The names Hamnet and Hamlet were interchangeable in an Elizabethan world where there was little consistency in spelling, proper names included. Both would have been pronounced something like 'Hamblet' in the Warwickshire dialect. The twins Hamnet and Judith had been named after the family's Stratford friends and neighbours, Hamnet and Judith Sadler. (The Sadlers returned the compliment when they christened their own son William.) Hamnet Sadler's name has also been found spelt 'Hamlet' and 'Hamlette' in surviving documents. *Hamlet*, however, is likely to have been named after Amleth, of which it is an anagram, the hero of the ninth-century Nordic saga on which the tragedy is loosely based.

Finally, the historian and broadcaster Michael Wood has posited a theory about a less obvious declaration of the pain Shakespeare felt over Hamnet's death, his *Sonnet 33*. Noting the poet's love of punning on the words 'sun' and 'son,' Wood cites as evidence these touching lines:

Even so my sun one early morn did shine / With all-triumphant splendour on my brow; / But, out, alack! He was but one hour mine, / The region cloud hath mask'd him from me now.

15. FULL OF EASTERN PROMISE

The exotic travels of a colourful English adventurer capture the public's imagination

Why, man, he's a very devil; I have not seen such a firago [virago, the term was applied to a ferocious warrior]. **I had a pass** [bout of fencing] **with him, rapier, scabbard and all, and he gives me the stuck in** [winning thrust] **with such a mortal motion** [deadly movement] **that it is inevitable; and on the answer** [when you return his thrust], **he pays you as surely as your feet hit the ground they step on. They say he has been fencer to the Sophy.** (*Twelfth Night*, 3.4, 1601)

WITH these chilling words the old rogue Sir Toby Belch torments his foppish victim Sir Andrew Aguecheek. Sir Toby has gulled Aguecheek into believing there is no escaping a duel to the death with Viola, who is disguised as a man named Cesario. Worse still, Sir Toby warns, this Cesario is a superb swordsman. The truth is both Aguecheek and Viola/Cesario are trembling with fear at the prospect of fighting each other. What follows is the most comical swordfight in any of Shakespeare's plays, with the two reluctant combatants spending the entire time assiduously trying to avoid each other's blades. But who was the Sophy to whom Sir Toby so ominously refers and why would the groundlings at the Globe have heard of him?

In the late spring of 1598, a swashbuckling braggart of an English aristocrat by the name of Sir Anthony Shirley (*pictured*), also spelt Sherley, set off by sea on a half-baked adventure through the Mediterranean. He subsequently struck out overland to Aleppo in Syria, and thence to the Persian capital Isfahan, hoping to befriend the Shah, Abbas 'the Great,'

ANTONIVS SCHERLEYNS ANGLVS, E-
ques aurat Magni Sophi Perfarum ad Cæfarem &
Chriſtianos Principes cæteros, Legatus.

Antoni Orator Perſæ, Angliæ, regit, ad ſtud
Excelſo munus ſerianis ingenis.

the man known to Elizabethans as the Sophy. Sir Anthony's brothers, Sir Robert and Sir Thomas, joined him on the journey. Officially, their aim, on the government's behalf, was to promote trade between England and Persia and stir up the Sophy against a common enemy, the reviled infidel Turks. Unofficially, it was to cover themselves in glory and riches.

Abbas was a ruthless autocrat who had seized absolute power. He was notoriously happy to carry out executions and castrations personally, and did so with abandon. He was also fabulously wealthy. When they reached Isfahan, Sir Anthony made the most of his tenuous relationship to Robert Devereux, Earl of Essex (his wife was Essex's cousin), in order to impress the Sophy with his supposed influence at Elizabeth's court. The Sophy greeted his unlikely visitors regally, going so far as to install the delighted Sir Anthony as a *mirza*, or prince, and grant him certain exclusive trading rights.

Between December 1599 and May 1600, Sir Anthony and Sir Robert reportedly trained the Persian army, with its five thousand horses, in the methods of the English military. Sir Anthony later returned to Europe to visit several capitals as the Sophy's ambassador, seeking to forge a wider anti-Ottoman alliance. Unfortunately, an allegation that he had stolen gifts the Sophy intended for European leaders cast a shadow over this sojourn. It was during a stay in Rome that he is said to have encountered Will Kempe, who had stormed out of Shakespeare's theatre company, the Lord Chamberlain's Men, after a serious disagreement.

The brothers' colourfully embellished reports of their adventures caused a sensation when they were recounted in a pamphlet titled *The True Report of Sir Anthony Shirley's Journey*. It was published anonymously in 1600 by two members of the expedition who had returned to London just before Shakespeare wrote *Twelfth Night*. The first pamphlet proved so popular that it was followed in 1601 by another, titled *A New and Large Discourse of the Travels of Sir Anthony Shirley*. Shakespeare almost certainly read one or both.

The pamphlets claimed that Sir Anthony's brother Sir Robert had been appointed the Sophy's personal fencing master, hence Sir Toby Belch's comment: 'They say he has been fencer to the Sophy.' Sir Toby's telltale use of the word 'surely' in his warning to Aguecheek is a play on the name 'Shirley', in the sort of punning we have come to expect from Shakespeare. The Sophy was also said to have granted Sir Anthony the generous sum of thirty thousand crowns a year to train his army, and that too gets a mention in *Twelfth Night* when the servant Fabian, chuckling with fellow conspirators at the success of a plot to trick the preening Malvolio, says:

I will not give my part of this sport for a pension of thousands to be paid from the Sophy. (2.5)

Public fascination with the Shirleys continued and in 1607 they were rewarded with a play about their legendary adventures, titled *The Travailes of the Three English Brothers*, which was performed at the Curtain theatre. Sir Anthony wrote his own account in *Sir Anthony Sherley: His Relation of His Travels into Persia*, published in 1613, the original manuscript of which survives in Oxford's Bodleian Library.

He experienced many other remarkable rises and falls in his fortunes, including a spell languishing in prison in Venice in 1603, being refused permission by James I to return to England, and facing allegations of defrauding several noblemen of funds to help pay for his journeys. He was appointed by the Holy Roman Emperor Rudolph II to head a mission to Morocco, and subsequently installed as an admiral of the Spanish fleet to serve in the Levant. Sir Anthony died a lonely pauper's death in Spain sometime around 1635.

As a testimony to the pitiful downfall that marked the final years of an extraordinary life, Francis Cottington, the English ambassador in Madrid, said of him:

> *The poor man comes sometimes to my house and is as full of vanity as he ever was, making himself believe that he shall one day be a great prince, when for the present he wants [needs] shoes to wear.*

* * *

Five years before Shakespeare wrote *Twelfth Night* he had already given the Sophy a mention in order to evoke a touch of Oriental exoticism in *The Merchant of Venice*, when the Prince of Morocco, an unsuccessful suitor to the desirable Portia, brags:

> **By this scimitar that slew the Sophy and a Persian prince that won three fields of Sultan Solyman, I would outstare the sternest eyes that look, outbrave the heart most daring on the earth, pluck the young sucking cubs from the she-bear, yea, mock the lion when he roars for prey, to win thee, lady.** (2.1)

The Prince of Morocco's braggadocio was an outrageous fantasy, and audiences would have recognised it as such. No one had ever succeeded in slaying a Shah of Persia, let alone defeating Suleyman the Magnificent, Sultan of the Ottoman Turks. Shakespeare's inspiration for the boastful prince in *The Merchant of Venice* appears to have been the real-life Sultan Ahmad al-Mansur, a powerful ruler of northern Africa, who spent the last two decades of the sixteenth century badgering Elizabeth I to agree an alliance between Morocco and England against their common enemy Spain.

Al-Mansur's efforts cul-
minated in a six-month mission to Elizabeth's court in
1600 led by his ambassador,
the splendidly named Abd al-
Wahid bin Messaoud bin Mohammed al-Annuri, desper-
ately seeking the support of
the English fleet for an invasion of Spain. While in London, al-Annuri arranged to
have his portrait painted in oil
on an oak panel (*pictured*). It is
now in the collection of Birmingham University. The

flamboyant al-Annuri's presence at Elizabeth's court was widely talked about, although he was eventually turned away disappointed. His visit may, however, have provided the inspiration for Shakespeare to later write his tragedy *Othello, The Moor of Venice* (1603-4).

16. ALLIGATORS AND APOTHECARIES

Romeo's strange account of the forerunner of today's pharmacies is grippingly accurate

I do remember an apothecary – and hereabouts he dwells – which late I noted in tatter'd weeds [dressed in ragged clothes], **with overwhelming brows** [bushy eyebrows], **culling of simples** [gathering medicinal herbs]; **meagre were his looks, sharp misery** [acute poverty] **had worn him to the bones: and in his needy** [shabby] **shop a tortoise hung, an alligator stuff'd, and other skins of ill-shaped** [grotesque] **fishes; and about his shelves a beggarly account** [thin scattering] **of empty boxes, green earthen pots, bladders** [leather bottles] **and musty seeds, remnants of packthread** [lengths of string] **and old cakes of roses** [rose-scented blocks], **were thinly scatter'd** [spread around] **to make up a show.** (*Romeo and Juliet*, 5.1, 1595)

ROMEO resolves to seek a potent poison with which to kill himself, wrongly believing that Juliet is already dead, in Shakespeare's tragic tale of 'star cross'd lovers'. What better place than the shop of an apothecary who has fallen on such hard times that he is likely to risk the death penalty by agreeing to sell such a lethal concoction? In his description Romeo tells us that the man had bushy eyebrows (perhaps Shakespeare was thinking of someone he knew) and that his shop boasted a tortoise shell, a stuffed alligator, and a variety of fish skins.

It sounds a bizarre collection of artefacts but surviving drawings do indeed confirm Romeo's description of such premises. Having an exotic stuffed alligator or crocodile hanging from the ceiling, usually upside down with its glassy eyes staring down at the customer, was almost *de rigueur* for any self-respecting apothecary. If you couldn't get either of those, a stuffed lizard would have to do, the bigger the better. Incidentally, Shakespeare's use of 'alligator' here is the first time the word appears in its modern form (it is actually spelled 'allegator' in the *First Folio* of 1623). The *Oxford English Dictionary* cites the earliest recorded use as 'lagarto' in 1568, and 'aligarto' in 1591. The word occurs nowhere else in any of Shakespeare's works. It derives from the Spanish '*el legarto*' (meaning 'lizard') and was coined by the explorers who first encountered the creatures while navigating the coasts of Central America.

Alligators and crocodiles – although belonging to quite different biological families – were relatively easy to preserve as stuffed specimens because of their hard carapaces, and were considered to have mystical associations with the knowledge to treat diseases. The oldest known example in a collection is a 13 ft (4m) long Nile crocodile that dates back to 1623, in the Natural History Museum in St Gallen, Switzerland. In medieval Italy, stuffed crocodiles were suspended from the vaults of some churches in an attempt to ward off demons.

An illustration (*pictured*) in the book *Historia Naturale di Ferrante Imperato*, published in Venice in 1672, shows an alligator's carapace affixed, together with a galaxy of sea creatures, to the ceiling of a so-called 'cabinet' of natural history curiosities in Naples. The collection was amassed by the Italian apothecary Ferrante Imperato (died c.1615).

Perhaps the most direct connection between the creatures and apothecaries was established by the English cleric Edward Topsell in his *The History of Four-footed Beasts*, published in 1607. The book was an early attempt to categorise the animal kingdom in a scientific way, and Topsell claimed that the crocodile was a source of many efficacious medicines. Anointing a person's eyes with crocodile's blood, he says:

> *Cureth both the dregs or spots of bloud in them, and also restoreth soundness and clearness to the sight, taking away all dulnesse or deadnesse from the eyes.*

The apothecaries were on to something. In our own

time, scientists are studying the medicinal potential alligators and crocodiles may hold for the human race. The animals live in highly unsanitary environments, such as swamps that are teeming with bacteria, they scavenge germ-infested food sources like rotten meat and, despite at times sustaining serious wounds in fights with one another, rarely suffer infections. They also appear to be immune to cancers of all sorts, despite individuals having a lifespan of up to a hundred years. Having survived as species for at least thirty-seven million years (lizards have been around even longer at more than two hundred million years) the creatures have clearly developed immensely powerful immune systems.

In 2008, researchers in Louisiana reported they had discovered that alligator blood contains a compound capable of destroying twenty-three strains of bacteria, including some that are resistant to antibiotics. Similarly, lizard saliva has been found to contain a hormone that stimulates insulin and may also be useful in the fight against superbugs. A letter from three specialists published in the Canadian medical journal *Current Oncology* in 2018 postulated that alligators and crocodiles had developed mechanisms to defend themselves against developing cancer. The writers noted that gut bacteria from the animals produce anti-tumour molecules that can thwart various cancers.

In 2019, other researchers announced they had shown that white blood cells from crocodiles can reduce the growth of cancer cells in humans, pointing the way to develop a whole new generation of anti-cancer drugs. Work is also going on to explore how proteins extracted from crocodiles could be used to combat flesh-eating bacteria, ironic as that may seem in a notorious predator. Meanwhile, academics at a Thai university claim an extract from crocodile blood could be used to repair damaged skin as well as in the cosmetic anti-ageing industry. That's just for starters. It seems the ancients may have known rather more about these remarkable creatures' medicinal value than we had suspected.

＊ ＊ ＊

The expression to shed 'crocodile tears' means to falsely weep for someone's fate while secretly enjoying it. Several of Shakespeare's plays mention what was a very old myth even in his day: that the crocodile weeps for its prey while cheerfully tearing off chunks of its victim's flesh. The belief became, and remains, a graphic metaphor for hypocrisy. We see it when Othello, maddened by the 'green-eyed monster' jealousy, cruelly rails against the hapless Desdemona in *Othello*:

O devil, devil! If that the earth could teem with woman's tears, each drop she falls would prove a crocodile. (4.1)

Meanwhile, in *Antony and Cleopatra*, Marc Antony teases the inquisitive Lepidus, who wants to know what manner of creature the Egyptian crocodile is, giving him meaningless answers and ending with:

And the tears of it are wet. (2.7)

References to the crocodile's tears date back at least as far as the first-century Roman essayist Plutarch. Bartholomaeus Anglicus, a thirteenth-century French monk, writes:

If the crocodile findeth a man by the brim of the water, or by the cliff, he slayeth him there if he may, and then weepeth upon him and swalloweth him at last.

The story spread in England after the fantastical accounts of the travels of the mysterious Sir John Mandeville were circulated in the fourteenth century. Calling crocodiles 'serpents', the author of *The Travels of Sir John Mandeville* writes:

These serpents slay men, and they eat them weeping; and when they eat they move the over jaw, and not the nether jaw, and they have no tongue.

Shakespeare's contemporary Edward Topsell had his own rather different theory about the crocodile's reputed tears, suggesting the cunning creature would pretend to be in distress in order to elicit the sympathy of its victim, then pounce when least expected. In his view:

> *There are not many brute beasts that can weep, but such is the nature of the crocodile that, to get a man within his danger, he will sob, sigh, and weep as though he were in extremity, but suddenly he destroyeth him.*

The naval commander and ruthless pioneer of the slave trade Admiral Sir John Hawkins reported how, in the Caribbean, he had observed the crocodile would 'cry and sobbe like a Christian body' to lure its prey within range. Shakespeare takes up that suggestion too when, in *Henry VI, Part 2*, the formidable Queen Margaret complains about Humphrey, Duke of Gloucester:

> **Gloucester's show beguiles him as** [in the same way] **the mournful crocodile with sorrow snares relenting passengers** [sympathising victims]. (3.2)

Although crocodiles do not weep as such, they possess lachrymal glands which produce tears, lubricating a transparent membrane that acts as a second eyelid. Scientific observations in recent years have confirmed that tears do indeed appear when the animals are eating, especially while they are out of the water. The reason remains unclear but one thing is for sure – it is not out of sympathy for the feelings of the unfortunate dish upon which they are banqueting.

❋ ❋ ❋

Apothecaries themselves – the equivalent of a blend of today's GPs and pharmacists – have been around for a long time too, at least in terms of human history. Their profession can be traced back to the Babylonians of four thousand years ago. In England, apothecaries became an organised group of traders with the formation of the Guild of Pepperers, formed in London in 1180. The guild, which originally attempted to regulate the purity of spices, evolved into the Worshipful Company of Grocers in 1345. By Shakespeare's time, tensions had developed between general grocers and apothecaries over who could sell what.

Grocers sold foodstuffs. Apothecaries specialised in mixing herbs, spices and altogether more unsavoury ingredients into compounds that were designed, with varying degrees of success, to relieve the sick. Knowledge of which combinations supposedly worked and which didn't resided entirely in their heads and personal notes – the first *London Pharmacopoeia*, which helped standardise treatments, did not appear until 1618. It was with great pride that they celebrated being granted their own City of London livery company, the Worshipful Company of Apothecaries, by James I just a year before the *London Pharmacopoeia*'s publication. Among the physicians contributing to the *London Pharmacopoeia* was William Harvey, remembered today as the first person to accurately describe the circulation of the blood.

Despite the apothecaries breaking away from the grocers' company, or perhaps because of it, trade disputes became even more frequent than they had been in the past. A key area of contention was the growing demand for perfumes among the burgeoning middle classes of London in those days long before piped water and sanitation arrived. The stenches of the great city were everywhere, emanating from piles of sewage, rotting offal and fish, the overpowering smells of bad breath and personal body odour, the stink of tanneries and, as Sir John Falstaff himself complains in *The Merry Wives of Windsor*:

Thou mightst as well say I love to walk by the Counter-

gate [the entrance of a notoriously foul-smelling prison in Southwark], **which is as hateful to me as the reek** [smoke] **of a lime-kiln.** (3.3)

Blackheath, south of the Thames, was noted for its lim-ekilns, which busily produced lime for use in building materials in the ever-expanding capital, churning out toxic fumes in the process. The kiln operators were under strict orders to halt production whenever the Queen was holding court at nearby Greenwich Palace, lest the acrid smoke they produced should drift under Her Majesty's delicate nostrils. Depending on wind direction, it was said that anyone travelling to London could smell the capital from twenty miles (32km) away. Little wonder the rising middle classes were happy to spend money on products that were claimed to mask offensive odours. In *The Merry Wives*, Falstaff croons to Mistress Ford:

What made me love thee? Let that persuade thee there's something extraordinary in thee. Come, I cannot cog [deceive] **and say thou art this and that, like a many of these lisping hawthorn-buds** [foppish young men], **that come like women in men's apparel, and smell like Bucklersbury in simple time; I cannot: but I love thee; none but thee; and thou deservest it.** (3.3)

Bucklersbury was a street off Cheapside which was well known for the grocers and apothecaries who sold perfumes or treatments there. By 'simple time' Falstaff means summer, when the business of gathering and purveying herbs (known as 'simples') was at its height. Bucklersbury would have been at the epicentre of a major trade dispute because, while grocers could sell perfumes but not medicinal treatments, apothecaries could sell both perfumes and treatments. Interestingly, in *King Lear* it is an imagined apothecary, not a grocer, to whom the maddened monarch appeals when he cries out:

There's hell, there's darkness, there's the sulphurous

pit; burning, scalding, stench, consumption. Fie, fie, fie! Pah, pah! Give me an ounce of civet, good apothecary, to sweeten my imagination. There's money for thee. (4.6)

Civet, also known as civet musk, was an exotic and highly valued perfume. It was made using oil excreted from the anal glands of the civet cat, a mammal native to Africa and Asia. Civet oil was still something of a novelty among the newly affluent in Elizabeth's time, having been given royal respectability when the animal was brought into England and introduced to the court of Henry VIII. The cynical jester Touchstone reveals nothing but contempt for the stuff when he tells the shepherd Corin in *As You Like It*:

Learn of the wise, and perpend: civet is of a baser birth than tar, the very uncleanly flux [discharge] **of a cat.** (3.2)

Touchstone's revelation might not have been entirely appreciated by either the grocers or apothecaries keen to sell their sought-after and highly profitable perfumes.

17. A WHALE OF A TIME

A stranded sea 'monster' sparks huge interest and provides Will with a useful analogy

Chide him for his faults, and do it reverently, when you perceive his blood inclin'd to mirth; But being moody, give him line and scope till that his passions, like a whale on ground, confound themselves with working.

(*Henry IV, Part 2*, 4.4, 1597-98)

THE ailing King Henry IV pleads with his son Thomas of Clarence to be 'a hoop of gold to bind thy brothers in' and so prevent civil strife breaking out after his death. Thomas is particularly urged to remain close to his eldest brother Prince Hal, the heir apparent, who is notorious for his reckless carousing with Sir John Falstaff. But the king cautions Thomas to be diplomatic, allowing Hal space to thrash out his wayward spirits in the expectation that he will in time calm down and get on with the heady task of governing the country. Henry strikes the analogy of a beached whale, thrashing about on land until at last its energy is spent.

A similar concept of a grounded whale appears in *The Merry Wives of Windsor*, a comedy written about the same time as *Henry IV, Part 2*, and which also features Falstaff. When the outraged Mistress Ford protests to her friend Mistress Page that Falstaff has written identical love-letters to them both, she says of the corpulent knight:

What tempest, I trow [I declare], **threw this whale, with so many tuns** [barrels] **of oil in his belly, ashore at Windsor?** (*The Merry Wives*, 2.1)

Shakespeare made frequent use of Holinshed's popular historical *Chronicles of England, Scotland and Ireland*, the second edition of which had been published in 1587. Here is what Holinshed records about an incident involving a whale, which occurred in Kent on 9 July 1574:

> *The ninth of Iullie [July] at six of the clocke at night, in the Ile [Isle] of Thanet besids Ramesgate, in the parish of Saint Peter under the cliffe, a monstrous fish or whale of the sea did shoot himselfe on shore, where for want of water, beating himselfe on the sands, he died about six of the clocke on the next morning, before which time he roared, and was heard more than a mile on the land. The length of this fish was twentie two yards, the nether iaw [jaw] twelve foot the opening: one of his eies [eyes], being taken out of his head, was more than six horsse in a cart could draw, a man stood upright in the place from whence the eie was taken. The thicknesse from the backe whereon he laie, to the top of his bellie (which was upward) was foureteene foot, his taile of the same breadth: between his eies twelve foot, three men stood upright in his mouth, some of the ribs were six foot long, his toong was fifteene foot long, his liver two cart lode, into his nosetrils anie man might have crept: the oile being boiled out of the head was parmasitie, the oile of his bodie was whitish and sweet of tast.*

Holinshed's publisher notes in the margin of the page:

> *A monstrous fish (though not so monstrous as some reported) for his eies, being great, were in his head and not in his backe.*

Wild rumours that the animal's eyes were in its back or even in its tail may have later inspired a line in *The Tempest*, when the drunken Stephano stumbles across his friend Trinculo and Caliban hiding top-to-tail under a gaberdine cloak, and confuses the pair of them for a single monster. Offering the strange creature his flask, Stephano urges:

Drink, servant-monster, when I bid thee: thy eyes are almost set in thy head. (3.2)

To which Trinculo replies:

Where should they be set else? He were a brave [impressive] **monster indeed, if they were set in his tail.**

In an age when few people had seen such a fabled monster of the deep as a whale, the beaching in Thanet must have proved a sensation. Hundreds, if not thousands, of people ventured down to the shore to take a look. The spectacle would also have been widely reported with some details, as Holinshed's publisher implies, deliberately exaggerated by the ballad mongers who spread news around the country. Shakespeare's audiences would be familiar with the story.

An account was still being included in *The History and Topographical Survey of the County of Kent (Volume 10)*, published by W Bristow of Canterbury in 1800, which says:

In 1574, a monstrous fish shot himself on shore on a little sand, now called Fishness, where, for want of water it died the next day; before which his roaring was heard above a mile.

The subject of a grounded whale surfaces again in Shakespeare's late play *Pericles,* thought to have been co-written with George Wilkins. Complaining about the habits of 'rich misers,' a fisherman paints this vivid image:

Why, as men do a-land; the great ones eat up the little ones. I can compare our rich misers to nothing so fitly as to a whale; 'a [he] plays and tumbles, driving the poor fry before him, and at last devours them all at a mouthful. Such whales have I heard on o' the land, who never leave gaping till they've swallowed the whole parish, church, steeple, bells, and all. (2.1)

Whales are also referred to in *All's Well That Ends Well,*

Hamlet, Love's Labour's Lost, Troilus and Cressida and again in *Pericles* (3.1).

In contrast, the shark, that other great predator of the deep, is mentioned only in *Macbeth*, when the Third Witch includes 'maw and gulf [throat and stomach] of the ravin'd [glutted] salt-sea shark' among the unwholesome ingredients to go into their cauldron. Fascinatingly though, on two occasions Shakespeare takes the noun 'shark' and turns it into a verb with powerful effect, as we shall see in a later chapter.

See also: 40. The Island of Devils
46. The Usurer's Wife
48. The Stranger's Case

18. THE DUKE WHO MISSED DINNER

A comedy gets Elizabeth I chortling as it lampoons a right royal nuisance from the Continent

Bardolph: **Sir, the Germans desire to have three of your horses. The duke himself will be tomorrow at court, and they are going to meet him.**

Host of the Garter: **What duke should that be comes so secretly? I hear not of him in the court. Let me speak with the gentlemen. They speak English?**

Bardolph: **Ay, sir. I'll call them to you.**

Host of the Garter: **They shall have my horses, but I'll make them pay. I'll sauce them** [make them pay exorbitantly]. **They have had my house** [rooms in the inn] **a week at command. I have turned away my other guests. They must come off. I'll sauce them. Come.**

(*The Merry Wives of Windsor*, 4.3, 1597)

THE above extract from *The Merry Wives of Windsor* is (with the exception of the opening stage direction *Enter Host and Bardolph* and the closing *Exeunt*) Act 4, Scene 3 in its entirety. That's it. A whole scene is devoted to this short exchange between Sir John Falstaff's minion Bardolph and the Host (landlord) of Windsor's Garter Inn about some Germans. It takes audiences completely by surprise. They have heard nothing of these mysterious Germans in the play until this moment and they will not hear much of them again. As a result, the scene is often dropped by directors looking both to trim lines from their productions of this comedy of Elizabethan manners and avoid adding unnecessary confusion. So what could have inspired Shakespeare to put it in?

The Merry Wives shows distinct signs of having been written in a hurry. Unlike most of Shakespeare's works, it contains very little of his celebrated iambic pentameter. Just twelve per cent of its lines are in verse, the smallest proportion in any of his plays. Only four other plays contain less than fifty per cent blank verse and most have far more than that, several (such as *Richard II*) being entirely, or almost entirely, in verse. The likelihood is that he simply didn't have time to dash off anything but prose. If we are to believe the playwright John Dennis, who in 1702 staged his own production of *The Merry Wives*, the original was penned to an extremely tight deadline on the personal orders of Elizabeth I. Dennis says:

> *This comedy was written at her command, and by her direction, and she was so eager to see it acted that she commanded it be finished in fourteen days.*

Nicholas Rowe, writing in 1709, said the Queen had been so delighted with the larger-than-life figure of Falstaff when she first saw him in *Henry IV, Part 1* that she told Shakespeare she wished to see a comedy about the fat knight falling in love. We do not know whether Shakespeare broke off from writing *Henry IV, Part 2* in order to pen *The Merry Wives*, or whether he had already completed that second historical saga of Henry Bolingbroke's reign. It is clear, however, that *The Merry Wives* pre-dates *Henry V* (1599), in which all we hear of Falstaff is his reported death.

The Merry Wives probably had to be written, lines learned, rehearsals finished, and props procured ready for its first performance on 23 April 1597 – St George's Day. The date happened to be Shakespeare's thirty-third birthday (we think) but, more importantly from the Queen's point of view, it marked an important event in her own calendar, the Feast of the Most Noble Order of the Garter. Although the Feast was held annually, 1597 was the first time in four years that new members of the order were to be elected. They would then be formally installed at a ceremony in St George's Chapel at Windsor Castle the following month. The Order of the Garter is the most prestigious order of knighthood in Britain's honours system, appointments being made at the sovereign's sole discretion and limited to no more than twenty-four living members.

The order was founded in 1348 by Edward III and the most popular explanation of its origin involves the story of a Countess of Salisbury, whose garter slipped from her leg while she was dancing at a court ball. When courtiers around sniggered at her fashion *faux pas*, the king himself picked up the garter and handed it back to her, declaring '*Honi soit qui mal y pense*,' which translates as 'Shame on him who thinks evil of it' in the Middle French spoken by English monarchs at the time. The phrase became the motto of the order and remains so to this day. From that time on, the Order of the Garter became a central pillar of the English establishment.

The Garter Feast planned for that spring day in 1597 at the Palace of Westminster in Whitehall was to be one of exceptional splendour with, we believe, *The Merry Wives* booked as the entertainment to round off the event. No fewer than five new knights would be elected, including George Carey, Lord Hunsdon, recently appointed to the high office of Lord Chamberlain and none other than the patron of Shakespeare's own theatrical company, the Lord Chamberlain's Men. Apparent confirmation that *The Merry Wives* was written for this occasion comes from Mistress Quickly in the final scene. She orders the fairies to go over to Windsor Castle to prepare the place, giving them instructions to arrange prettily coloured flower petals spelling out the Garter's motto. In one of the play's brief bursts of poetry, she chants:

And nightly, meadow-fairies, look you sing, / Like to the Garter's compass [members of the order may encircle their heraldic arms with the Garter], **in a ring: / The expressure** [expression] **that it bears, green let it be, / More fertile-fresh than all the field to see; / And 'Honi soit qui mal y pense' write / In emerald tufts, flowers purple, blue and white.** (5.5)

Also among the knights elected during the Feast, presided over by Elizabeth herself, was a German nobleman known as Frederick of Mömpelgard. Unlike the other proud candidates, Freidrich I, Duke of Württemberg, to give him his full title, was missing both on the day of the dinner and at the installation that followed on 24 May. His absence was no oversight but rather a calculated slight by Elizabeth, who did not want him anywhere near her. He had, frankly, been a right royal pain in her neck for quite long enough. Mömpelgard was an occultist, alchemist and excessive egotist. The Queen had been obliged to endure his company when he visited England in 1592 and she clearly preferred not to have to do so again.

At the time of his visit, Mömpelgard (*pictured*) was the thirty-five year old heir apparent to his duchy. Foreign noblemen usually restricted their travels to seeing the palaces of Whitehall and Greenwich in London, perhaps adding excursions to Windsor, Richmond and Hampton Court, while travelling on horseback. Mömpelgard and his party had been granted an  exceptional royal warrant permitting them to requisition post-horses without charge when travelling along the old Bristol road to Windsor. In Act 4, Scene 3 of *The Merry Wives*, the Host is quite happy with the situation, believing he is going to do very nicely out of it. The Germans have booked out all the rooms in his inn and, as he understands it, now wish to hire horses, even if the identity of the duke involved remains a mystery. But things turn ugly for the Host two scenes later, when Bardolph reports that his erstwhile foreign guests have made off with the horses.

> *Host of the Garter:* **Where be my horses? Speak well of them, varletto.**
>
> *Bardolph:* **Run away with the cozeners** [swindlers]. **For so soon as I came beyond Eton, they threw me off from behind one of them, in a slough of mire; and set spurs and away, like three German devils, three Doctor Faustuses.** (4.5)

While the Host at first insists that the Germans are honest men who have merely gone off to meet the duke, his hopes are quickly crushed when Parson Evans breathlessly rushes in to tell him:

> **Have a care of your entertainments** [hospitality]. **There is a friend of mine come to town tells me there is three cozen-germans that has cozened** [swindled] **all the hosts** [inn-keepers] **of Readins** [Reading], **of Maidenhead, of Colebrook** [Colnbrook], **of horses and money.** (4.5)

In case there was any doubt who was being referred to, in the performance at the 1597 Garter Feast itself the term 'cozen-germans' was rendered as 'cozen-garmombles', a deliberately comical mangling of the name Mömpelgard. At least, that is how the line appeared when the comedy was first published, in the *First Quarto* of 1602, based on the original script. The word 'cozen' here is in itself a play on the two meanings of the word, as in 'cousin' the relative – the Queen called Mömpelgard 'Cousin Mumpellgart' – and 'cozener' as in the term Elizabethans used for a swindler. By the time *The Merry Wives* was included in the *First Folio* of 1623 the 'cozen-garmombles' reference had been replaced by 'cozen-germans'. In his splendid *Asimov's Guide to Shakespeare*, the scholar and author Isaac Asimov speculates:

I wonder if it may be possible that the reason this portion of the play is as incomplete and unsatisfactory as it is, is that it was censored after the initial performance to avoid creating an international incident.

The Host of the Garter's humiliation is complete when the well-connected Doctor Caius next appears and, in what can only be a reference to Mömpelgard, says in the mock French accent Shakespeare gives him:

It is tell-a me dat you make grand preparation for a duke de Jarmany [Germany]. **By my trot** [troth] **dere is no duke dat the court is know to come.** (4.5)

Although Württemberg was only a minor German duchy, it was Protestant, and during those troubled times Elizabeth was keen to cultivate whatever continental friends England could get. The problem was that Mömpelgard, who had succeeded to the title of Duke in 1593, was insufferably pompous. His obsession with becoming a member of the Order of the Garter, a privilege reserved for the most honoured citizens of the sovereign's personal choice, dated back to that visit to England in 1592. Offered a tour of the castle and grounds at Windsor, he took part in a service in St George's Chapel and was dazzled by the banners and escutcheons of members of the order that he saw hanging there. Mömpelgard wasted no time in badgering Elizabeth to admit him as a member.

It is not clear what promises were made, but when he returned home he immediately commanded coins to be struck showing him wearing the Collar of the Order of the Garter. It was an outrageously presumptuous act, which must have offended the Queen. In February 1594 he wrote to Elizabeth reminding her of his wish to be elected to the order. In case the point had not been made strongly enough, in March the following year he dispatched a party of ambassadors to London to press his case. They met the Earl of Essex and Lord Burghley, themselves both Garter Knights, who politely arranged two audiences with the Queen.

The tiresome Mömpelgard wrote again to the Queen in July 1595 and sent yet another ambassador to London in October that year to keep up the hectoring. In April 1596, Elizabeth had finally had enough. Not wishing to offend a continental ally, she grudgingly gave in and the duke was nominated for election to the order. So it was that at the Garter Feast twelve months later he was designated a knight-elect – *in absentia*, because no one had bothered to tell him the sumptuous event was taking place.

We can now see that Shakespeare knew exactly what he was doing when he included those curious passages about the Germans in a play he apparently wrote especially for the after-dinner entertainment. His audience, including Elizabeth herself and Lord Hunsdon, delighted that his own players were presenting the well-received comedy, would have been shaking with laughter at the ridicule being heaped on the pesky duke who hadn't been invited to dinner.

Mömpelgard, no doubt feeling more than a little miffed at missing out on the beano, wrote to the Queen in 1598 and again in 1599 to enquire about his installation as a Knight of the Garter and the regalia he should have received. Apart from the antipathy she felt for her 'Cousin Mumpellgart', Elizabeth had shrewd political reasons for keeping him hanging on. Her delay in obliging helped secure the duke's continued allegiance at a time when English merchants faced restrictions in dealing with the cities of the continental Hanseatic League.

Mömpelgard must have at last got the message because he did not bother asking again until after Elizabeth died in April 1603. News of her death was something he had clearly been waiting for. Only three months later, having allowed a respectable interval for the nation's mourning, he wrote to her successor, James I. In August 1603, the Württemberg ambassador in London began pestering the new king for an answer to the duke's enquiries, by which time James evidently wanted the whole business to go away. In November, a lavish installation ceremony for the duke took place with much panoply in his capital Stuttgart, courtesy of an ambassador sent from London by James.

Mömpelgard, crashing bore as he was, had finally got his way. Little could he have known, however, that his insufferable vanity would be immortalised when Shakespeare's comedy was passed down through generations of theatre goers, even if the episode is so easily overlooked in modern productions of *The Merry Wives of Windsor*.

19. GILLIAN, THE FAT OLD WITCH

Falstaff's disguise when he flees a jealous husband is based on a notorious 'sorceress'

Mistress Ford: **What ho, Mistress Page! Come you and the old woman down. My husband will come into the chamber.**

Ford: **Old woman! What old woman's that?**

Mistress Ford: **Nay, it is my maid's aunt of Brentford.**

Ford: **A witch, a quean, an old cozening quean** [thieving strumpet]**! Have I not forbid her my house? She comes of errands, does she? We are simple men; we do not know what's brought to pass under the profession of fortune-telling. She works by charms, by spells, by the figure** [astrology]**, and such daubery** [pretence] **as this is, beyond our element** [our understanding] **we know nothing. Come down, you witch, you hag, you! Come down, I say!**

(*The Merry Wives of Windsor*, 4.2, 1597)

SIR John Falstaff has been caught out by Francis Ford, an upright citizen and jealous husband, who believes the fat knight is having an affair with his wife. In fact, Ford's wife and her friend Mistress Page have conspired to humiliate Falstaff for his unwanted amorous advances. During an earlier close call, the knight had been smuggled out, right under Ford's nose, in a basket of dirty laundry and dumped unceremoniously into the Thames. The trick will not work twice. This time the two merry wives disguise him as 'the fat old woman of Brentford'. It seems Ford has heard of the old woman's notoriety as a witch, for he has previously banned her from the house. As Falstaff makes his way down the stairs, Ford sets about beating him, believing him to be the old woman, shouting:

Out of my door, you witch, you hag, you baggage, you polecat, you runyon [mangy creature]! **Out, out! I'll con-jure you, I'll fortune-tell you.**

While upstairs, Mistress Page had wrapped a large muffler around Falstaff's face to hide his bushy beard. As the knight makes his hurried exit a witness, Parson Hugh Evans, catches a glimpse of the grey hairs. He exclaims in his Welsh brogue:

I think the 'oman is a witch indeed. I like not when a 'oman has a great peard. I spy a great peard under her muffler.

The parson is convinced. Any hint of a beard on a woman's face was a sure sign she must be a witch in those superstitious times. The extract from *The Merry Wives of Windsor* – the only play Shakespeare set in the England of his own day – which opens this chapter is taken from the *First Folio* of 1623. In it, Mistress Ford describes the old woman as 'my maid's aunt' of Brentford (then usually spelt 'Brainford' or a close variation). But when we look at the earliest printed copy of the script, which appeared in 1602, we find something remarkable. The *First Quarto*, thought to have been a pirated version reconstructed from someone's memory of Shake-speare's script (scholars have fingered the actor who played the Host of the Garter inn as the main suspect) also includes a name for the old woman. It is 'Gillian'. The name had dis-appeared when the play was reprinted in 1619, to be replaced simply with 'my maid's aunt' of Brentford. So if Shakespeare included the name Gillian in his original manuscript, where did he get it from?

We also have a surname for the 'aunt', which survives into the *First Folio*. Mistress Page, assisting Falstaff-in-drag to descend the stairs, says: 'Come, Mother Prat. Come, give me your hand.' Prat or Pratt was considered a common English surname (rather like Smith) and it gives Shakespeare the opportunity to insert another line for a laugh when Ford threatens 'I'll prat her' as he begins beating Falstaff. The writer John Heywood had used the surname for a character in his play *The Pardoner and the Friar, the Curate and Neighbour Pratte*, which dates from before 1533.

In *The Merry Wives*, Gillian is variously referred to as the 'old woman', the 'fat woman', the 'wise woman' and 'the witch' of Brentford. It may be no coincidence that in February 1599, two years after *The Merry Wives* debuted, the theatre impresario Philip Henslowe paid two writers, Thomas Dowton and Samuel Rowley, five pounds and ten shillings for the scriptbook for a new play to be performed by the Admiral's Men, who were rivals to Shakespeare's own Lord Chamberlain's Men. The title of that play was *Friar Fox and Gillian of Brentford*. Sadly, Dowton and Rowley's play has long since been lost and we know of its existence only because Henslowe meticulously kept a diary of his transactions, which is an invaluable resource for today's scholars.

Friar Fox and Gillian of Brentford featured among a flurry of plays apparently about witches that were in fashion during the closing years of the sixteenth century. Other titles staged by the Admiral's Men at that time included *The Witch of Islington* (circa 1597), *Mother Redcap* (1597), and *Black Joan* (circa 1598) all, sadly, also now lost. Gillian turns up again in a 1604 play titled *Westward Ho*, by Thomas Dekker and John Webster, when a character named Clare says: 'I doubt [have no doubt] that old hag [witch] Gillian of Braineford has bewitched me.'

The Merry Wives appeared less than twenty years after four poor and elderly women, known as Mother Stile, Mother Dutten, Mother Margaret and Mother Deuell, had been hanged for practising witchcraft in Windsor. Mother Deuell, a spelling uncomfortably close to 'Devil', probably stood little chance of a sympathetic hearing by virtue of her unfortunate name alone. Their trial at Abingdon Assizes on 26 February 1579, based largely on the evidence of one of them, sixty-five year old Elizabeth Stile, was widely publicised in a sensational pamphlet titled *A Rehearsal both strange and true of hainous and horrible activities committed by Elizabeth Stile, Alias Rockingham, Mother Dutten, Mother Deuell, Mother Margaret, fower* [four] *notorious witches.*

The British Library has a copy in its collection and a woodcut drawing on the cover shows two elderly women, one of whom is holding a small and decidedly ugly demon, which has horns, wings, vicious looking claws and a tail.

The pamphlet (*pictured*) regales its readers with graphic accounts and yet more lurid woodcuts depicting the women's supposed diabolic goings on in genteel, middle-class Windsor (of all places). In 1597, King James VI of Scotland, who would become James I of England, published his own major treatise, *Daemonologie*, describing the practices of witchcraft and associated dark arts. Shakespeare would draw heavily on James' book when writing *Macbeth* (1606).

* * *

A somewhat different light is shed on Gillian of Brentford in a play titled *Summer's Last Will and Testament* by Thomas Nashe, which appeared in 1600. The title character Will Summer – based on the Will Sommers who had been court jester to Henry VIII and died in 1560 – introduces himself to the audience. He asks: 'What can be made of Summer's last will and testament? Such another thing as Gillian of Brainford's will, where she bequeathed a score of farts amongst her friends.' And thereby hangs another tale.

Will Summer's speech harks back to a ribald and hugely popular ballad titled *Jyl of Braintford's Testament*, written around 1535 by Robert Copland. The poem appears to be a parody designed for the enjoyment of all those people poor enough to have nothing to leave in a legal will. It tells the story of Jyl (otherwise Gill or Gillian), a widow in Brentford, who clearly enjoys crude jests.

The will she makes consists entirely of leaving curses and farts to twenty-five types of people who have acted foolishly. A typical verse will give you the tenor of Copland's poem:

With that she groned as panged with pain / griping her bely with her hands twain / And lift up her buttok somwhat awry / and like a handgun, she let a fart fly.

Examples of Gillian's crude bequests are:

He that doth drink ever more / and will not shift to pay therefore / shall have a fart to set on his score. / He that lendeth a horse with all things meet / and on his own voyage goeth on his feet / shall have a fart. / He that doth his weapon lend / and have nothing himself to defend / shall have a fart, and there an end.

In addition, the unfortunate curate who helps her compose the will receives a fart-and-a-half in payment for his pains. Copland's ballad clearly struck an earthy chord, becoming so popular that his son William had printed at least two sell-out editions of it by the 1560s. Even Shakespeare's reference to 'Mother Prat' in *The Merry Wives* may hint at a connection with *Jyl of Braintford's Testament*. Besides being a reasonably common surname at the time, 'prat' was a slang word for a buttock cheek. When Master Ford threatens 'I'll prat her' he is probably kicking Falstaff's posterior, much to the groundlings' amusement. Gillian makes one more appearance, in an anonymous 1620 collection of stories titled *Westward for Smelts*. There she is a fishwife who tells how she fools a jealous husband by taking his wife's place in bed while the wife herself is committing adultery with another man. Interestingly, that story is set in Windsor, just like *The Merry Wives*.

❊ ❊ ❊

In Shakespeare's day Brentford was a resort in the countryside up-river from London, ideal for a day's ride on horseback or boat trip out of the noisy, seething cauldron that was life in the City. The town sat a dozen miles or so along the Thames from St Paul's. Brentford's largest hostelry by far was The Three Pigeons. After the theatres were closed by government edict in 1642, John Lowin, who had been a highly regarded actor in Shakespeare's company, is said to have retired to become landlord of the Three Pigeons. A large, well-built man, he is thought to have played the title role in *Henry VIII*, one of Shakespeare's last plays, written in collaboration with John Fletcher.

Accommodation at the Three Pigeons ran back to the River Brent, which flows into the Thames in the town, and stabling was provided for up to one hundred horses. The inn became such a celebrated landmark that it is mentioned in a surprisingly large number of plays by Elizabethan and Jacobean writers. Brentford itself, with its regular flow of well-heeled visitors, was a centre for seedy 'away day' goings-on, a place hidden from neighbours' prying eyes, where Londoners could dally with their mistresses or with prostitutes. Inventing its own identity as a sort of country resort, the town even put on alternative entertainments, such as horse races and puppet shows.

'We will turn our courage to Braynford, westward my bird of night ... we'll tickle it at The Pigeons,' says Subtle when he proposes to run away with Doll in Ben Jonson's *The Alchemist* (1610). 'Thou art admirably suited for the Three Pigeons at Braintford,' Laxton says to Moll Cutpurse in *The Roaring Girl* (1611) by Thomas Dekker and Thomas Middleton. In a later scene in that play, Mrs Openwork reports how her husband 'this very morning went in a boat with a tilt [canopy] over it to the Three Pigeons at Brainford, and his punk [prostitute] with him'. According to Dekker and Webster's *Westward Ho*, a landlord at the Three Pigeons is known as Dogbolt. A character named Linstock, suggesting a merry jaunt, says: 'Let's to mine host Dogbolt's at Brainford then. There you are out of eyes, out of ears [unseen and unheard]; private rooms, sweet linen, winking attendance, and what cheer you will.'

For many years a local legend persisted that the Three Pigeons was a regular haunt of both Shakespeare and his good friend and rival Ben Jonson. An etching (*pictured*), made by W N Wilkins in 1848, shows the stables and part of the inn. Sadly, the place closed in 1916. After sporadic use for other purposes, the building fell into disrepair and was badly damaged by fire twice, in 1920 and again in 1933, being finally demolished in 1950. It is beguiling to imagine Shakespeare and Jonson quaffing a mug or two of ale together beside a smoky fireside there, discussing their latest plays and arguing over much else besides. When the Three Pigeons disappeared so too, in all probability, did one of the last extant buildings outside of Stratford-upon-Avon with a close connection to Will Shakespeare.

See also: 32. The Curious Case of Falstaff
37. Something Wicked Comes

20. THE DOCTOR AND THE WELSHMAN

*An outrageous ban by the co-founder of a Cambridge college may
have given Will a bright idea*

You jack'nape [monkey], **give-a this letter to Sir Hugh. By gar**
[By God], **it is a shallenge: I will cut his troat in dee park; and
I will teach a scurvy jack-a-nape priest to meddle or make**
[interfere] **... By gar, I will cut all his two stones** [testicles]; **by
gar, he shall not have a stone to throw at his dog.**

(*The Merry Wives of Windsor*, 1.4, 1597)

DOCTOR Caius, a bad-tempered French physician, hands a
written challenge to a messenger named Simple, with instructions to deliver it to the Welsh parson Sir Hugh Evans. Caius
is infuriated because he has learned Evans is courting the fair
Mistress Anne Page on behalf of ineffectual young Abraham
Slender. Caius has his own designs on Anne, doomed though
they are sure to be. The character of Sir Hugh Evans is thought
to have been inspired by Thomas Jenkins, one of Shakespeare's
boyhood teachers at Stratford-upon-Avon.

The play even contains a scene full of *double entendres* in
which Evans tests a pupil, tellingly called William, on Latin
declensions. (Latin was firmly on the curriculum at Stratford
Grammar School, despite a scathing Ben Jonson later rebuk-
ing Shakespeare for having 'small Latin and less Greek'.) *The
Merry Wives* was entirely of Shakespeare's own invention, he
plumbed no source material as with so many of his other
plays. So where did he come up with the unusual name of
Caius for his Welshman-hating doctor?

A real Dr John Caius (*pictured*) had served as royal physician to Edward VI, Queen Mary and Elizabeth I, until his death

in 1573. Elected no fewer than nine times to the position of president of the illustrious College of Physicians, he is best remembered as the second founder of Gonville and Caius College at Cambridge University. (Edmund Gonville did his bit by originally founding the college in 1348.)

Caius refounded the college in 1557 with a handsome infusion of funds, intending it to become a centre of excellence in medicine. He had been born plain old John Kays in Norwich but, after spending time studying in Italy, Germany and France, he adopted the much grander sounding Latin moniker of Johannus Caius (and became known as John Caius). The character's name in *The Merry Wives* is traditionally pronounced 'Ky-us'. Today the college Caius co-founded is pronounced Gonville and 'Keys'.

Among other improvements at Cambridge, the good doctor built Caius Court, which for sanitary reasons he designed to have only three sides set at right-angles, rather than the traditional quadrangle. Or as he put it …

Lest the air from being confined within a narrow space should become foul.

Sometime after taking up his role as Master of the newly refounded college, Caius wrote a statute declaring that the institution must reject any candidate to be a fellow or scholar who …

Is deformed, dumb, blind, lame, maimed, mutilated, a Welshman, or suffering from any grave or contagious ill-

ness, or an invalid that is sick in a serious measure.

His inclusion of Welshmen among a list of unfortunate medical afflictions was clearly intended to be offensive. Caius had originally appointed a Welshman named Hugo Glyn, a proctor of the university, as president of his newly endowed college. That was in January 1559, but their happy relationship does not appear to have lasted long. By July of that year the first two names listed as residents of the college in the University Register are 'John Caius, *Custos*' and 'Hugo Glyn, MD (*absens, in componendis litibus*)'. The Latin phrase concerning Glyn translates as 'absent, in settling lawsuits'.

By the middle of October, the Welshman was absent in every way. He appears to have left the college in haste on 15 October 1559, abandoning a number of valuable books which he donated to the library. He then put some distance between himself and Cambridge, and is next heard of practising medicine in Chester, one hundred and seventy miles (274km) away. Whether, as seems likely after such a promising start, there was a falling out between the two men, and what the nature of that quarrel was, is entirely unknown. But given the evident dislike Caius, a doctor, took to Welshmen in his founding statute, what more appropriate name could Shakespeare have chosen for a physician who loathes Sir Hugh Evans, the caricature of an archetypal Welshman in *The Merry Wives*?

✳ ✳ ✳

During his lifetime Caius established a reputation as the foremost authority on a malady known to Elizabethans simply as 'the sweats' or 'the sweating sickness'. He published a paper on the disease, which had an alarmingly high mortality rate among those unfortunate enough to contract it. The precise nature of the infection remains a mystery to this day. Wherever it struck, it quickly became an epidemic and took a devastating toll on the local population. The sickness began with a headache, giddiness, shivering, and severe pains throughout the body. After one to three hours the victim developed high fever, a drenching sweat, often with an offensive smell, delirium and rapid heartbeat. Towards the end there was exhaustion and an irresistible urge to sleep, which Caius suggests should be deterred by a carer tugging on the patient's ears and nose to keep them awake. Death usually followed within eighteen hours of onset. In some alarming cases, it came with even more rapidity. According to the chronicler Edward Hall:

This malody was so cruel that it killed some within two houres, some merry at dinner and dedde at supper.

Other victims simply dropped dead in the street. In his *Chronicles*, Raphael Holinshed writes:

A newe kynde of sickness came through the whole region, which was so sore, so peynfull, and sharp [sudden] that the lyke was never hearde of to any manne's rememberance before that tyme.

Caius's *A Boke* [Book] *or Counseill against the Disease Commonly Called the Sweate or the Sweating Sickness* was published in 1552, and it is thanks to him that we know even what little we do about the affliction. He discovered that the mysterious disease appeared in England for the first time shortly after Henry VII arrived at Milford Haven, Wales, in 1485 with the army that defeated Richard III at Bosworth. 'The sweats' broke out on 19 September that year and by the end of October it had killed several thousand people.

The second outbreak occurred in 1506-7 and spread to Calais, where it became known as *Sudor Anglicus* or 'the English sweats'. The third appeared in 1517, at a time London was described as crowded with foreign artisans. 'The sweats' was back as an epidemic in London in 1528, severe enough to force Henry VIII to flee London until it subsided. That outbreak spread across the Channel to Hamburg, where it killed a thousand people within a month of arriving, thence to Danzig and along the Baltic coast to Scandinavia and Russia. The disease returned to England for the last time in 1551, during the reign of Henry's son Edward VI. He followed his late father's example and left town. A diarist named Henry Machyn records:

> *The vii [seventh] day of July [1551] begane a nuw swet in London ... The x [tenth] day of July the Kynges grace removyd from Westmynster unto Hamtun courte, for ther ded [died] serten [certain] besyd the court, and caused the Kynges grase to be gone so sune, for ther ded in London mony marchants and grett ryche men and women, and yonge men and old, of the new swett ... The xvi [sixteenth] day of July ded of the swet the ii [two] yonge dukes of Suffoke of the swet, both in one bed in Chambrydge-shyre ... and ther ded from the vii [seventh] day of July unto the xix [nineteenth] ded of the swett in London of all dyssesus [diseases] ... [eight hundred and seventy-two] and no more in alle.*

The young nobles to whom Machyn refers were Henry Brandon, aged sixteen, who died just hours before his brother Charles, thirteen. They were the sons and heirs of Charles Brandon, Duke of Suffolk. Youth and wealth provided no immunity, in fact 'the sweats' appears to have taken an unusually high toll among the rich. 'Many died in the Kinges courte,' wrote Edward Hall, including two lords 'and many knightes, gentlemen and officiers.' After the 1551 outbreak subsided, the disease is heard of no more.

Having described the symptoms and history of 'the sweats', Caius struggles to find a cause, chiefly blaming dirty conditions, 'impure spirits in bodies corrupt with repletion [overeating]', and 'evil mistes and exhalations drawn out of the grounde'. People should live quietly, he urges with a curious touch of nostalgia, 'as men were wont to do in the old world when this countrie was called merye England'. For prevention he recommends fresh air, sweet-smelling clothes – which presumably implies clean clothes – and plenty of outdoor exercise. Numerous herbs are suggested as a remedy for sufferers, including wild tansy, wormwood and feverfew. In a rather charming final disclaimer, Caius makes it clear if anything is the will of God, then it is beyond his powers to explain:

> If other causes ther be supernatural, theim I leve to the divines [ministers of religion] to serche, and the diseases thereof to cure, as a matter with out the compasse of my facultie.

Symptoms of 'the sweats' distinguished it from malaria (then known as 'ague'). Dengue fever, which like malaria is spread by mosquitos, has been suggested as the cause, but the case is far from proven. Another possibility is hantavirus, which is spread by rodents, although transmission from person to person is rare. In an article published in *New Scientist* in 2004, the American biologist Edward McSweegan suggested anthrax may have been the culprit, contracted from spores present in raw wool or infected animal carcasses. McSweegan arrived at his suggestion after studying the symptoms of ten victims of bioterrorism attacks, although anthrax spores must be inhaled to cause illness and, again, the malady cannot be spread from person to person. Whatever it was, 'the sweating sickness' remained active among people's fears during Shakespeare's lifetime. No one could be sure it would not return at any time, with further devastating effect. The brothel keeper Mistress Overdone mentions the disease among the litany of woes she rattles off in *Measure for Measure*:

Thus, what with the war, what with the sweat, what with the gallows and what with poverty, I am custom-shrunk [short of clients]. (1.2)

Perhaps of even greater interest is the Epilogue to *Henry IV, Part 2*, in which Shakespeare promises to bring back the hugely popular character Sir John Falstaff in his next play,

Henry V:

One word more, I beseech you. If you be not too much cloy'd with fat meat, our humble author will continue the story, with Sir John in it, and make you merry with fair Katherine of France; where, for anything I know, Falstaff shall die of a sweat, unless already 'a [he] be killed with your hard opinions. (5.5)

For once, Shakespeare doesn't keep his promise. All we hear of Falstaff in *Henry V* is a moving account from Mistress Quickly about how he died. Although there is no mention of a doctor attending Sir John, it would hardly be surprising if Caius's pioneering work on 'the sweats' came to mind when Shakespeare needed to kill the fat old knight off. The disease was, after all, prevalent during the period in which Falstaff supposedly lived. (Falstaff and Mistress Quickly also both appear in *The Merry Wives.*)

21. HERNE'S HAUNTED OAK TREE

Had Will seen a historic tree at Windsor ... or is an 'ancient' legend all a myth he cunningly invented?

There is an old tale goes that Herne the hunter, sometime [once] **a keeper here in Windsor forest, doth all the winter-time, at still midnight, walk round about an oak, with great ragg'd horns. And there he blasts** [blights] **the tree and takes** [bewitches] **the cattle, and makes milch-kine** [milking-cows] **yield blood, and shakes a chain in a most hideous and dreadful manner. You have heard of such a spirit, and well you know the superstitious idle-headed eld** [people in olden days] **received and did deliver to our age this tale of Herne the hunter for a truth.**

(*The Merry Wives of Windsor*, 4.4, 1597)

THE scene is a forest in Windsor at midnight. Sir John Falstaff has turned up disguised as the legendary hunter Herne, to the point where he has even donned a set of deer antlers ('great ragg'd horns'). While Falstaff is eagerly expecting a romantic tryst with the wives of the play's title, he is unaware that a plot has been laid to teach him a humiliating lesson. After he arrives at the great oak tree which is the appointed meeting place, a group of children emerge dressed as fairies and elves, led by the parson Sir Hugh Evans, Mistress Quickly and Falstaff's erstwhile companion Pistol. The children begin a ceremonial dance around Falstaff then, to his horror, take turns to pinch him and burn him with their candles.

It is unclear where Shakespeare found the legend of Herne. Some scholars believe the figure derives from a pagan Celtic or Anglo-Saxon god, and connections have been made with the mythical 'Green Man' of English folklore. The eighteenth-century Shakespearean actor Samuel Ireland thought Herne had been a local historical figure – hence 'sometime a keeper here in Windsor forest' – whose unquiet spirit haunted the park as a result of an untimely death.

The antiquarian James Halliwell-Phillipps, writing in the nineteenth century, maintained Herne was actually a hunter named Horne, who was put to death for poaching during the reign of Henry VIII. The earliest printed version of *The Merry Wives* does actually use the name 'Horne' not 'Herne' although, since it was a pirated quarto edition, it may not be entirely reliable. While Shakespeare gives the impression that he is harking back to some sort of elemental pagan deity whose origins are lost in the mists of time, no references to Herne exist in any writings that predate, or are contemporary with, his comedy. There has, therefore, to be a strong possibility that he simply made up the myth himself.

Shakespeare certainly displays an intimate knowledge of the Windsor area, with mentions of such localities as Frogmore, the Garter Inn, and Datchet Mead on the bank of the Thames. The centrepiece of all the nocturnal activity is Herne's Oak, a tree the play implies is ancient and revered, although it too is mentioned in no other surviving contemporary writings. Did Shakespeare and his audience know of such a celebrated grand old oak at Windsor? Uncertainty over whether the tree ever existed has not deterred enthusiasts from attempting to pinpoint where it might have stood. While Windsor Great Park has its supporters, others prefer a spot north of Frogmore House in the Home Park (formerly known as the Little Park), because of its proximity to the castle. They base their case on these lines spoken by Master George Page in *The Merry Wives*:

Come, come; we'll couch i' [lie hidden in] **the castle-ditch till we see the light of our fairies.** (5.2)

According to Halliwell-Phillipps, the 'general opinion'

was that Herne's Oak ...

> *Was accidentally destroyed in the year 1796, through an
> order of George III to the bailiff Robinson, that all the un-
> sightly trees in the vicinity of the castle should be removed;
> an opinion confirmed by a well-established fact, that a per-
> son named Grantham, who contracted with the bailiff for
> the removal of the trees, fell into disgrace with the king for
> having included the oak in his gatherings.*

However, an engraving now in the Royal Collection
(*pictured*), depicting a dead-looking leafless tree with sheep
grazing in the foreground, appeared in the *Gentleman's Magazine* in March 1840 and is titled *Herne's Oak, Windsor Little Park*.
Its publication sparked a letter in the magazine's April edition
from Edward Jesse, a writer on natural history who served as
deputy surveyor-general of the royal parks and palaces.

HERNE'S OAK, WINDSOR LITTLE PARK.

Jesse insisted:

*His late Majesty George IV constantly asserted that Herne's
Oak had not been cut down by George III, but that it was still
standing. I have been constantly assured by a member of
the Royal family, not only that Herne's Oak had not been cut
down by command of George III, but that the King was in
the constant habit of pointing out the present tree as the real
Herne's Oak.*

If it had not succumbed to the axe wielded by the 'person named Grantham,' according to another account the old tree was blown down in high winds on 31 August 1863. A saddened Queen Victoria is said to have planted a young oak barely two weeks later, on 12 September, to mark the spot. So exactly where Herne's Oak stood, if it ever stood anywhere at all, is still anyone's guess.

22. THE GREAT GLOBE ITSELF

London's most famous theatre began life with 'stolen' timbers spirited across the Thames

But pardon, gentles all, the flat unraised spirits that have dared on this unworthy scaffold to bring forth so great an object. Can this cockpit hold the vasty fields of France? Or may we cram within this wooden O the very casques [helmets] **that did affright the air at Agincourt?**
(*Henry V*, Prologue, 1599)

ON THE bone-chilling night of 28 December 1598, while most Londoners were safely tucked indoors celebrating the Christmas festivities, a dozen or so determined men descended on a run-down theatre in Shoreditch. With quiet efficiency, they set about dismantling the entire building, guided only by the light of flickering lanterns. The group worked feverishly all through the night, taking the structure apart, plank by plank and beam by beam. Passers-by and neighbours who enquired what was going on were assured that a refurbishment programme was under way and that the theatre was going to be rebuilt 'in another form'. Any stranger who became troublesome was warned off by intimidating guards armed with swords and daggers, posted around the perimeter of the site.

Taking the old theatre apart would prove an even harder task than the men had bargained for. It had been constructed using mortise and tenon joints, each length of timber slotting into the next by way of a wooden peg that locked perfectly into a rebate. The joints had become tighter with the passing years, as if the wood had almost fused together. Yet by the time the steely grey light of dawn broke the next morning, the men had loaded the half-ton oak beams and panelling on to carts hauled by sturdy horses, and set off south towards the river. Their destination was a waterfront warehouse belonging to a master carpenter named Peter Street, where the material they had salvaged would be stored. Street had personally supervised the night-time raid. He knew a thing or two about theatres, and that one in particular, because he had been involved in building it twenty-two years earlier for the actor and impresario James Burbage.

The Theatre, as it was prosaically called, had been an extraordinary innovation, the first of its kind to be built in England. Plays had traditionally been performed by touring troupes of actors in inn yards until the enterprising Burbage had the bright idea of getting the audience to come to them instead. The problem was that first purpose-built theatre stood on land belonging to one Giles Alleyn. Burbage had taken a twenty-one year ground lease on the site at the time. It was when the lease expired in April 1596 that things started to turn ugly.

Alleyn, living the life of a wealthy country gentleman in Essex, proved a difficult absentee landlord. Negotiations to renew James Burbage's lease staggered on for many months after its expiry date, all the time a recalcitrant Alleyn imposing increasingly onerous conditions. He almost doubled the ground rent and then even claimed to own the building itself. When Burbage pointed out a clause in their original contract by which he had cannily retained ownership of the structure, Alleyn insisted that a condition of any new lease must give him the right to tear down the building and, insultingly, put the timbers 'to some better use' after just five more years of tenancy.

The stress was all too much for James Burbage, who at the age of sixty-six was already an old man. He dropped dead on 2 February 1597, leaving the problem for his sons Cuthbert and Richard to sort out. The brothers – Richard was by now a celebrated actor in his own right – were resolved not to give up their father's struggle. Together with friends among the Lord Chamberlain's Men, who included Will Shakespeare, they hatched their breathtakingly audacious plot. They would spirit the Theatre away under the cloak of darkness during the Christmas holiday season, when Alleyn could be guaranteed to be out of London. Nothing remotely like it had been attempted before.

When the weather started to improve early the following spring, Peter Street began shipping the stored timbers by barge to Southwark. There on the other side of the Thames, the Burbage brothers had found a replacement site, on which they had agreed a thirty-one year ground lease. Despite being set in marshy ground, the new plot was, like Shoreditch, beyond the reach of the kill-joy City of London authorities who would forbid construction of any theatre within their boundaries. It was, in fact, just down the road from Philip Henslowe's thriving Rose theatre, where the rival Admiral's Men performed, meaning the South Bank was destined to become the epicentre of Elizabethan theatrical life.

Since the Burbages could not afford to build the new theatre by themselves, a consortium was formed. It would have the resources to construct something even bigger and better than the Theatre had been. The brothers would own one-half of all the shares, the other half going to Shakespeare and fellow actors John Heminges, Augustine Phillips, Will Kempe and Thomas Pope between them. They each put up the money for their stakes and signed a legal contract of shareholding on 21 February 1599 (although Kempe would drop out later that year and sell his stake to the others). The name they gave to the new theatre was the Globe.

The grasping landlord Alleyn was furious when he learned what had happened. He promptly launched legal action, with the case being heard by judges in the Star Chamber. In the lawsuit, Alleyn accused Cuthbert Burbage of 'unlawfully combininge and confederating himselfe with the sayd

Richard Burbage, and one Peter Streat, William Smyth, to the number of twelve,' alleging – all in one mind-boggling sentence – that they:

> *Did aboute the eight and twentieth daye of December ... ryotouslye assemble themselves together, and then and there armed themselves with divers and manye unlawfull and offensive weapons as, namely, swords, daggers, billes, axes, and such like, and so armed, did then repayre unto the sayd Theatre, and then and there, armed as aforesayd, in verye ryotous, outragious and forcyble manner, and contrarye to the lawes of your highnes realme, attempted to pull down the sayd Theatre, whereupon divers of your subjectes, servauntes, and farmers, there goinge aboute in peaceable manner to procure them to desist from that their unlawfull enterpryse, they the sayd ryotous persons aforesayd notwithstanding procured then therein with greate vyolence, not only then and there forcyblye and ryotouslye resisting your subjectes, servauntes, and farmers, but also then and there pulling, breaking, and throwing downe the sayd Theatre in verye outragious, violent, and riotous sort, to the great disturbance and terrefyeing not onlye of your subjectes sayd servauntes and farmers, but of divers others of your Majesties loving subjectes there neere inhabitinge; and having so done, did then alsoe in most forcible and ryotous manner take and carrye away from thence all the wood and timber thereof, unto the Banckysde in the parishe of St Marye Overyes, and there erected a newe playehouse with the sayd timber and wood.*

Alleyn demanded a total of eight hundred pounds in damages, and it is a measure of his vindictiveness that he included forty shillings for 'trampling the grass'. Litigation dragged on for two years, but eventually the Burbages were vindicated and the intractable landlord received nothing for his troubles. On Bankside, meanwhile, Peter Street and his workmen faced a daunting task on the boggy ground, first laying a foundation of brickwork upon which to build the new theatre. According to Ben Jonson, the area around was 'flanked with a ditch and forced out of a marsh'. Once the foundations were complete, construction took another ten weeks.

Although hampered by unexpected delays, the Globe rose on the South Bank horizon during the spring of 1599. Lath and plaster fill was applied to the framework and the walls were coated with whitewash. On the outside was a fine mural depicting Hercules bearing the Earth's globe on his shoulders. The cost of construction came to seven hundred pounds. When he saw the finished building, the initially sceptical Jonson rapturously declared it to be 'the Glory of the Bank'. Meanwhile, Shakespeare had been busily sharpening his quill to produce plays to put on the new stage.

The first production to open, probably in June 1599, was almost certainly his historical blockbuster *Henry V*, a tale of epic grandeur with Richard Burbage playing the hero king. At the very beginning of the drama Shakespeare inserted a Prologue in which a narrator named Chorus modestly urges the audience to augment with their imaginations such glorious scenes as are beyond the abilities of author and actors to portray in 'this wooden O'.

The 'wooden O' was, of course, a reference to the shape of the Globe itself, which was actually a polygon with either eighteen or twenty sides. The groundlings were admitted to stand in the central courtyard, with no shelter if it rained, for a penny each (it was cheap, about the cost of a loaf of bread). Wealthier patrons paid a few pennies more to enjoy seating and cushions in the tiered galleries. Peter Street had needed to bring in considerably more timber than the material that had been salvaged from Alleyn's site because the new theatre was much larger than the old one, able to accommodate as many as three thousand spectators. From forests in Berkshire, he used barges on the Thames to ship timber beams that had been cut into lengths and stored long enough to be seasoned and ready for use.

Shakespeare demonstrates a thorough understanding of the process of construction in *Henry IV, Part 2*, written the previous year, which reflects the planning he and his fellow actors faced when they conceived their plot to tear down the Theatre and replace it with the Globe. In the words of the play's Lord Bardolph (not to be confused with Falstaff's companion Bardolph):

> **When we mean to build we first survey the plot, then draw the model; and when we see the figure [design] of the house, then we must rate the cost of the erection; which if we find outweighs ability, what do we then but draw anew the model in fewer offices [with fewer rooms], or at least desist to build at all? Much more, in this great work – which is almost to pluck a kingdom down and set another up – should we survey the plot of situation and the model, consent upon a sure foundation, question surveyors, know our own estate how able such a work to undergo, to weigh against his opposite [the adverse factors]. (1.3)**

We also see a familiarity with the intricacies of carpentry and joinery in similes such as 'to be disjoint and out of frame' (*Hamlet*, 1.2) and 'but let the frame of things disjoint' (*Macbeth*, 3.2), and the need for timber to be seasoned before it can be put to such uses as decorative panelling, when Jacques advises the jester Touchstone in *As You Like It*:

> **Get you to church and have a good priest that can tell you what marriage is; this fellow will but join you together as they join wainscot [wood panelling]. Then one of you will prove a shrunk panel, and like green timber warp, warp.** (3.3)

Once open, the splendid theatre rapidly made a name for itself and curious crowds streamed across London Bridge or queued to be rowed across the river to Southwark to see the latest production. Shakespeare had proved up to the task of supplying the new material the Globe needed, and his dramatic tale of treachery in ancient Rome was on offer that autumn. A Swiss tourist named Thomas Platter, visiting England from his native Basel, obligingly records in his diary for 21 September 1599:

> *After dinner, about two o'clock, I went with my party across the water, and in the straw-thatched playhouse we saw the tragedy of the first Emperor Julius Caesar, very pleasingly performed with approximately fifteen characters. At the end of the play they danced together admirably and exceedingly gracefully, two in each group dressed in men's and women's apparel. The places are so built that they play on a raised platform, and every one can well see it all.*

Within Platter's helpful account lies an ominous clue to the fate that lay in store for the Globe.

See also: 23. Disaster and Rebirth

23. DISASTER AND REBIRTH

Will's own lines prove grimly prescient when his beloved theatre is destroyed in a disastrous fire

Our revels now are ended. These our actors, as I foretold you, were all spirits and are melted into air, into thin air: and, like the baseless fabric of this vision, the cloud-capp'd towers, the gorgeous palaces, the solemn temples, the great globe itself, yea all which it inherit, shall dissolve and, like this insubstantial pageant faded, leave not a rack [a trace] behind. We are such stuff as dreams are made on, and our little life is rounded with a sleep. (*The Tempest*, 4.1, 1610-11)

ON HIS magical island, with these words the magus Prospero resolves to break his staff, drown his books and abjure his potent powers. *The Tempest* is the last work Shakespeare completed alone (although he would collaborate with others on a handful of later plays) and the scene has come to be regarded as a poignant valedictory by the man from Stratford as he turned his back on the stage. Ironically, 'the great globe itself' could presciently have read 'the great Globe itself'. After fourteen years of thrilling the crowds, on the afternoon of Tuesday, 29 June 1613, 'the straw-thatched playhouse' once visited by Thomas Platter dissolved and left not a rack behind.

Thatch had been chosen for the roof of the three-tier gallery when the Globe was constructed because it was cheaper than tiles, the whole project having already taken longer and cost more than originally planned. In the those words of Lord Bardolph in *Henry IV, Part 2*: 'When we see the figure of the house, then we must rate the cost of the erection; which if we find outweighs ability, what do we then but draw anew.' Yet as the ageing Shakespeare's theatrical career drew to a close, that act of economising came back to bite the company.

Just as a play about one king named Henry (Henry V) had opened the Globe, so a play about another Henry (Henry VIII) would close it. With Elizabeth I having been dead for ten years, it was deemed safe at last to stage a production dealing with her father's controversial divorce from Katherine of Aragon. Shakespeare wrote the play, titled *All Is True* but known to us as *Henry VIII*, in collaboration with John Fletcher, the rising talent chosen to succeed him as house playwright. A history of the English theatre by John Downes titled *Roscius Anglicanus*, published in 1708, includes an anecdote that the sturdily built actor John Lowin was playing Henry VIII and 'had his instructions' from Shakespeare himself.

At the point in the drama when Henry enters Cardinal Thomas Wolsey's home, a cannon was fired for dramatic effect. No cannon ball was involved as standard practice was to use gunpowder and stuffed paper wadding. Tragically, a piece of the wadding flew across the courtyard and lodged in the thatched roof opposite, where it smouldered unnoticed as everyone below focused their attention on the play. In a letter dated 2 July 1613, the diplomat and politician Sir Henry Wotton gives an eye-witness account of what happened:

> *The King's players had a new play, called All is True, representing some principal pieces of the reign of Henry VIII, which was set forth with many extraordinary circumstances of pomp and majesty, even to the matting of the stage; the Knights of the Order with their Georges and garters, the Guards with their embroidered coats, and the like: sufficient in truth within a while to make greatness very familiar, if not ridiculous. Now, King Henry making a masque at the Cardinal Wolsey's house, and certain chambers being shot off at his entry, some of the paper, or other stuff, wherewith one of them was stopped, did light on the thatch, where being thought at first but an idle smoke, and*

their eyes more attentive to the show, it kindled inwardly,
and ran round like a train, consuming within less than an
hour the whole house to the very grounds. This was the fatal
period of that virtuous fabric, wherein yet nothing did per-
ish but wood and straw, and a few forsaken cloaks; only one
man had his breeches set on fire, that would perhaps have
broiled him, if he had not by the benefit of a provident wit
put it out with bottle ale.

In using the word 'train' two centuries before the steam locomotive was invented, of course, Wotton's analogy is expressing the concept in the same sense as the trail of material that is dragged behind a bridal gown. He continues by reporting that 'the house' was filled with people who had 'enough to do to save themselves, having but two narrow doors to get out'. Within two hours the Globe was completely destroyed and the conflagration also consumed a neighbouring ale house, probably the one from which the life-saving bottle of beer had been purchased. An anonymous ballad commemorating the fire later circulated, identifying Richard Burbage, Henry Condell and John Heminges among the actors who fled the stage in the commotion, although there is no mention of Shakespeare. It offers a further insight into the panic that ensued, and also tells how props and costumes, such as hairpieces ('perrywigges') and jackets ('jerkins'), were consumed by the flames:

Out runne the Knightes: out runne the Lordes / and
there was great adoe / some lost their hattes & some
their swords / then out runne Burbidge [Burbage] too. /
The reprobates thoughe druncke on Munday / pray'd for
the foole & Henry Condye [Condell] / Oh sorrow, pitti-
full sorrow, and yett all this is true. The perrywigges &
drumme-heads frye / like to a butter firkin / a wofull
burneing did betide / to many a good buffe ierkin. / Then
with swolne eyes like druncken fflemminges [Flemings

> *had a reputation of heavy drinking] / distressed stood*
> *old stuttering Heminges.*

Just in case anyone missed the moral of the tale, the ballad writer also warned 'you stage strutters all' to learn the Globe's lesson and save up enough money to build roofs with tiles instead of thatch. We have to wonder how many of Shakespeare's precious manuscripts and much-loved reference books may have gone up in smoke. It must have been with a broken his heart that he rode home to Stratford-upon-Avon and into retirement that summer.

The shareholders had become extremely wealthy men in the years since the Globe first opened, they still held the remainder of the ground lease, and between them they stumped up the one thousand four hundred pounds needed for the theatre to be 'new builded in a far fairer manner than before'. It opened the following year and this time they included a tiled roof. But it is difficult to escape the conclusion that it all happened without Shakespeare. Quite possibly he sold his shares to the others after the fire, because there is no mention of them in his will when he died in April 1616.

The Globe went on to amuse, entertain and educate its audiences until 1642, when Oliver Cromwell's dour Puritans seized control of Parliament and finally achieved their long-held ambition of closing all the theatres. Two years after that, the building was torn down and replaced with tenement housing. An illustration of the rebuilt Globe (*pictured*) is preserved in a panorama of London painstakingly drawn by the Dutch artist Claes van Visscher, which was published in Amsterdam in 1616.

* * *

That would have been the end of the story had not the American actor and film director Sam Wanamaker come along. The story goes that, arriving in London in 1949, he climbed into a taxi and asked to be taken to Shakespeare's Globe theatre. 'Where?' replied the cabbie. 'Never heard of it.' After wandering around several rubble strewn post-war bomb sites and disused warehouses in Southwark, Wanamaker was shocked to discover that the spot on which the Globe once stood was indicated only by a nondescript plaque on a nearby brewery. He later recalled:

> *Underneath the plaque was a large pile of garbage, which seemed to sum up the situation. I simply could not imagine why the British had done nothing else to mark the site.*

Twenty years on, steeled with the same resolve that had driven the Burbages, Shakespeare, Heminges, Condell and the others in 1598, Wanamaker began his campaign to rebuild the Globe. He would need every ounce of that resolve, because his battle turned out to be just as tortuous as the one the Lord Chamberlain's Men had waged. Wanamaker told the author Norrie Epstein, in an interview for her 1993 book *The Friendly Shakespeare*:

> *I was an American and an actor – and not a Shakespearean actor – so the Brits assumed that the only thing I could possibly have in mind was something like Disneyland.*

Trenchant opposition came from left-wing local councillors in the working-class district. When a site was earmarked for the reconstruction, the council decided it wanted the land for a social housing project instead. The news media portrayed the bitter debate as a conflict between everyday people and elitist artists, a theme underlined when, astonishingly, someone asked: 'What has Shakespeare ever done for Southwark?' Wanamaker told Epstein:

We had a lease on the site but the local council took the land away from us, so we sued them. We got back the land in the courts and it cost them nine million pounds, which they could have used to build public housing on a nearby site that was available.

Even then, Wanamaker was warned by sage heads that the differences between sixteenth- century building techniques and the demands of modern fire safety regulations would make reconstruction impossible. Others declared that no customers in their right minds would be willing to pay to stand for up to three hours or sit on hard wooden benches watching a Shakespeare play. Then there was the small matter of forming a trust to raise the millions of pounds the project would cost. Wanamaker also needed to appoint an architect capable of delivering on the plans. He found the right person in Theo Crosby.

Despite gloomy predictions that the whole thing would be a financial disaster, the Globe finally began to rise again on the South Bank. Traditional building techniques were employed and the design of the original theatre was researched in great detail to ensure the reconstruction was as authentic as possible. A thatched roof was installed, the first to be granted planning permission in London since the Great Fire of 1666, but this time incorporating a state-of-the art sprinkler system. Today's health and safety requirements mean the replica is allowed to accommodate only one thousand three hundred people, rather than the three thousand who crammed inside in Shakespeare's day.

The new theatre, known as Shakespeare's Globe, opened in 1996 but, sadly, Wanamaker did not live to see that day.

He died of prostate cancer in 1993. More than seven hundred actors attended his funeral in Southwark Cathedral. In 2003, the actress Zoe Wanamaker, Sam's daughter, unveiled a blue plaque outside the theatre in honour of her father. The opening production of the first official season in the spring of 1997 was, just as at the original Globe, *Henry V.*

The story of the Globe was already extraordinary enough before Sam Wanamaker added another remarkable chapter. If there is such a place as Heaven, I have a feeling he and Will Shakespeare spend their time there endlessly chewing over the building's design intricacies. Wanamaker's single-minded vision of restoring the 'wooden O' in which Shakespeare and his companions accomplished their greatest feats has created one of the most cherished cultural jewels London can boast today. The theatre is now a world-class attraction that receives no public subsidy thanks to the millions of pounds it takes in ticket sales (some financial disaster!), helps disseminate a love and understanding of the plays of William Shakespeare, and has delighted generations of theatre-goers by presenting some of the greatest works ever created in world literature. It's as if it never went away.

What effect 2020's calamitous coronavirus outbreak will have on the Globe's long history remains to be seen, but even a pandemic will surely prove just another challenge that enthusiasm, adaptability and dedication will overcome, just as plague and fire proved to be in Will's own lifetime.

See also: 24. Kempe's Nine Days' Wonder

24. KEMPE'S NINE DAYS' WONDER

The nation's most celebrated comic storms off in a huff and Will reveals why in his greatest tragedy

And let those that play your clowns speak no more than is set down for them. For there be of them that will themselves laugh, to set on some quantity of barren spectators to laugh too, though in the meantime some necessary question of the play be then to be considered. That's villainous and shows a most pitiful ambition in the fool that uses it.

(*Hamlet*, 3.2, 1599-1601)

WITH this heartfelt admonition Hamlet makes clear how much he detests those improvising comedians who play up to the delighted whoops of the groundlings, heedless of whatever storyline the writer of the play is attempting to convey. So does William Shakespeare. Hamlet is addressing his remarks to the troupe of players who are visiting Elsinore. Shakespeare's rebuke is aimed squarely at one man.

Will Kempe (also spelt Kemp) was the unrivalled comedy sensation of his day. Eager fans flocked to see him perform, a stocky figure whose outrageous and earthy antics on stage could be guaranteed to start the crowd laughing, no matter what play he was appearing in at the time. He would spontaneously crack cheeky jokes, dance an impromptu jig, make 'a scurvy face' or obscene gesture, play lewd tricks on unsuspecting actors sharing the stage, break into unscripted song or crude doggerel verses, and relish arguing with hecklers in the audience. There was a term for such slapstick ad-libbing: it was known as 'gagging'.

Some playwrights even lazily incorporated instructions to their clowns to extemporise, writing in stage directions such as 'Enter Forrester ... speake any thing and exit' (*The History of the Tryall of Cheualry* [Chivalry], anonymous, 1605) or 'Jockie is led to whipping over the stage, speaking some words but of no importance' (*The Second Part of King Edward IV* by Thomas Heywood, 1600). It meant less work for the scriptwriter. Any clown worth his salt would be sure to get the laughs and so attract more penny-paying groundlings into the theatre.

Kempe was heir to the figures of Vice and the Lord of Misrule in the Mystery Plays of old, and to the tradition of Commedia dell'Arte, that carnival-like theatrical style which had spread across Europe from Italy, with its rumbustious knockabout humour and exaggerated pantomime characters such as Harlequin. His admirers loved it. Shakespeare grew to despise it.

From time to time Kempe would delight an audience by throwing in one of his well-worn catchphrases. Hamlet singles out this particular practice for censure when hammering home his point:

And then you have some again that keeps one suit of jests [set of catchphrases], **as a man is known by one suit of apparel, and gentlemen quote his jests down in their tables** [notebooks] **before they come to the play, as thus: 'Cannot you stay until I eat my porridge?' and 'You owe me a quarter's wages', and 'My coat wants a cullison** [heraldic emblem],' **and 'Your beer is sour', and blabbering with his lips and thus keeping in his cinquepace** [a lively five-step capering dance] **of jests when, God knows, the warm clown cannot make a jest unless by chance, as the blind man catches a hare.** (3.2)

We know of that tirade against catchphrases only because it appeared in print when *Hamlet* was first published in what is now called the *First Quarto*, dated 1603. Also known to scholars as the 'Bad Quarto' because it comprises a mangled version of the text that is thought to have been cobbled together from memory by at least one of the actors who took part, this unauthorised edition was pirated by a printer seeking to cash in on the enormous popularity of the play. Nonetheless, it contains some revealing inclusions that are missing from later editions. The passage about catchphrases is one of them. It portrays a jarring image of Kempe bellowing out such lines as 'Cannot you stay until I eat my porridge?' and 'Your beer is sour,' screwing up his face in mock disgust to delighted guffaws from the audience, while other players on stage attempt to create an atmosphere of dramatic tension or act out a scene demanding gravitas.

Besides the distraction, such impromptu ad-libbing ran the very real risk of getting the author and theatre company into serious trouble. All plays for public performance were required to receive official approval and, despite the liberties some writers allowed their clowns, anything that went off-script was technically illegal, with authorities ever watchful for the slightest hint of sedition. An Act of the Common Council of London in 1574 regulating performances spelled out that no unauthorised material could be 'enterlaced, added, mynglydd [mingled], or uttered in anie suche play'.

Will Kempe no doubt resented any lecturing about how to practise his art from a scribbler busily trying to 'hold a mirror up to nature' and obsessed with evolving styles of writing and acting that were changing drastically from those of the good old days. He had been winning the adulation of audiences long before the wet-behind-the-ears young fellow from Stratford even arrived in London. The first record we have of Kempe as an actor is with a theatre company called the Earl of Leicester's Men in May 1585. He then travelled to the Continent and played at the court of King Frederick II of Denmark. It may have even been the tales with which Kempe regaled his fellow players about the time he spent in Frederick's castle at Elsinore that inspired Shakespeare to pen *Hamlet.*

Kempe was already a star turn in his own right by 1590, when the writer Thomas Nashe dedicated his book *An Almond for a Parrot* to him, with the glowing tribute:

To that most comical and conceited [ingeniously witty] cavalier, Monsieur du Kempe, jest-monger and vice-regent general to the ghost of Dick Tarleton.

No greater compliment could be paid to a comic than acclaiming him successor to the legendary funnyman and Elizabeth I's own jester Richard Tarlton, who had broken the nation's heart when he died in 1588. Kempe was offered a high-profile platform to show off his improvisational skills at Philip Henslowe's Rose theatre in 1592, in a new comedy titled *A Knack to Know a Knave.* Among the likely authors of *A Knack* was Robert Greene, the ex-university man who that same year sneeringly dismissed the grammar school-educated Shakespeare as 'an upstart crow'. The show was a huge success, returning a handsome profit for Henslowe and its stars Kempe and Edward Alleyn, while in the process bolstering Kempe's reputation as the leading comic actor of his day.

Two years later Kempe, along with the great tragedian Richard Burbage, Shakespeare and five other 'sharers', founded the Lord Chamberlain's Men, a theatrical company under the patronage of Henry Carey, the first Baron Hunsdon. As Elizabeth I's influential Lord Chamberlain, Carey was in charge of choosing courtly entertainments for Her Majesty. Shakespeare had already proved a competent playwright, making a name for himself with his Henry VI trilogy and *Richard III*, his gory melodrama *Titus Andronicus*, and a couple of comedies.

Relations between Shakespeare and Kempe appear to have rubbed along without incident for several years. There is evidence Shakespeare created certain comedic parts specifically for him, among them Peter in *Romeo and Juliet,* the clown Costard (probably) in *Love's Labour's Lost,* and Bottom in *A Midsummer Night's Dream.* In all likelihood, Kempe also played Launce with his unruly dog Crab in Shakespeare's early comedy *The Two Gentlemen of Verona*. In December 1598, the players were forced to up sticks from the Theatre at Shoreditch and shift across the river to Southwark, where they opened their newly built Globe in the summer or autumn of 1599. It was a new beginning for the Lord Chamberlain's Men. The simmering tensions with Kempe came to a head not long after.

* * *

Among the first plays presented at the Globe was Shakespeare's comedy *Much Ado About Nothing*. Early texts reveal that when the play opened Kempe was cast as Dogberry, the bumbling constable who, despite his own crushing ineptitude, unwittingly cracks open the conspiracy at the heart of the drama and brings the villains to book. In Dogberry, Shakespeare artfully crafted a pompous, long-winded but hopelessly inept officer of the law given to pretentious malapropisms (or rather, dogberryisms) – 'Oh villain, thou wilt be condemned into everlasting redemption for this' is a typical example – who delights in strutting about the stage as he exercises his petty authority.

The seventeenth-century antiquarian John Aubrey tells us Shakespeare and Ben Jonson assiduously gathered 'humours [temperaments] of men daily wherever they came'. Aubrey says Shakespeare encountered the real-life constable who inspired Dogberry at 'Grendon in Bucks', thought to be the village of Long Crendon, which straddled the playwright's oft-travelled route between London and his family home at Stratford-upon-Avon. That is entirely believable. It has been suggested that Shakespeare's officers of the Watch, typified in Dogberry, Elbow (*Measure for Measure*), and Dull (*Love's Labour's Lost*), are the most realistic characters he ever drew.

From a letter William Cecil, Lord Burghley, wrote to

Sir Francis Walsingham, Elizabeth I's powerful 'spymaster', we know such incompetence was no rare thing among those charged with preserving the Queen's Peace. Burghley paints a picture that could have come straight from the pen of Shakespeare himself as he created Dogberry. The letter – written around the time of the Babington Plot in 1586, when a hue and cry was going on to find all of the conspirators who had sought to depose Elizabeth and replace her on the English throne with the Catholic Mary, Queen of Scots – turns a vivid spotlight on a world Shakespeare knew and would portray with merciless humour.

Sir, as I came from London homeward in my coach, I saw at every town's end the number of ten or twelve standing with long staves, and until I came to Enfield I thought no other of them but that they had stayed for avoiding of the rain, or to drink at some alehouse, for so they did stand under pentices [penthouses, the overhanging upper storey on many Tudor buildings] at alehouses. But at Enfield, finding a dozen in a plump [group], when there was no rain, I bethought myself that they were appointed as watchmen, for the apprehending of such as are missing. And thereupon I called some of them to me apart, and asked them wherefore they stood there. And one of them answered, 'To take three young men.' And demanding how they should know the persons, one answered with these words, 'Marry, my Lord, by intelligence of their favour.' 'What mean you by that?' quoth I. 'Marry,' said they, 'one of the parties hath a hooked nose.' 'And have you,' quoth I, 'no other mark?' 'No,' saith they. And then I asked who appointed them. And they answered one Banks, a head constable, whom I willed to be sent to me. [I said] 'Surely, sir, whoever had the charge from you hath used the matter negligently. For these watchmen stand so openly in plumps as no suspected person will come near them; and if they be no better instructed but to find three persons by one of them having a hooked nose, they may miss thereof.'

In *Much Ado*, the villainous Don John's henchman Borachio actually says to his companion Conrad, as if in echo of Burghley's observations:

Stand thee close then under this pent-house, for it drizzles rain, and I will, like a true drunkard, utter all to thee. (3.3)

The delicious paradox of the comedy, as one critic has pointed out, is that Dogberry is the one person who discovers the 'Nothing' there is 'Much Ado' about. The exchanges between the constable and his assistants Verges, Hugh Otecake and George Seacole, and then the play's rambling trial scene in which the flustered constable takes offence at being called 'an ass' by Conrad, are hilarious enough. Such scenes needed no distracting slapstick buffoonery from Kempe to embellish them. What had worked on stage in the days of Tarlton no longer suited the more sophisticated scriptwriting Shakespeare was evolving for the new theatre. This collision of cultures was highlighted even four decades later by a writer named Richard Brome, whose 1638 play *The Antipodes* features a lord named Letoy, who is lecturing a clown called Biplay over the way he ignores his fellow actors and engages directly with the audience:

Letoy: *But you, Sir, are incorrigible, and take licence to your selfe to adde unto your parts your owne free fancy, and sometimes to alter or diminish what the writer with care and skill compos'd; and when you are to speake to your co-actors in the scene, you hold interloqutions with the Audients.*

Biplay: *That is a way my lord has bin allow'd* [was traditional] *on elder* [olden-day] *stages to move mirth and laughter.*

Letoy: *Yes, in the dayes of Tarlton and Kempe, before the stage was purg'd from barbarisme and brought to the perfection it now shines with.*

At some time during *Much Ado*'s opening run in 1599, Kempe declared he was quitting the role of Dogberry, resigning from the Lord Chamberlain's Men, and selling his shareholding in the Globe. The move to the new theatre on the South Bank had all started on such a high note that it is difficult to avoid concluding he must have been involved in an acrimonious showdown with Shakespeare and the others. After Kempe walked out of the door, an actor was hurriedly recruited to step into the breach as Dogberry. His name was Robert Armin. Physically smaller than Kempe and an altogether more cerebral comic, he brought his own considerable talents to the part.

It is clear that Armin (*pictured*) was much more attuned to what Shakespeare was looking for, because he remained with the company until his death in 1615. He had a fine singing voice and it was for him that Shakespeare went on to create such insightful, witty characters as Feste in *Twelfth Night*, Touchstone in *As You Like It*, and the Fool in *King Lear*. All were a very different kind of fool than anything Shakespeare had created before and Kempe, with his irrepressible urges to break into impromptu tomfoolery, could never have carried them off to the playwright's satisfaction.

Once Kempe had gone, with consummate skill Shakespeare transmuted the crude clowning convention he had inherited into something vastly more sophisticated, and the playwright was probably paying Armin a well-deserved compliment when, in *Twelfth Night*, Viola says of Feste:

This fellow is wise enough to play the fool, and to do that well craves a kind of wit. (3.1)

After outlining the qualities essential in a good fool, Viola concludes:

This is a practise as full of labour as a wise man's art. For folly that he wisely shows is fit, but wise men, folly-fall'n, quite taint their wit. (3.1)

Kempe's dramatic resignation must nevertheless have come as a shock to his fellow shareholders in the Globe. While Shakespeare and those actors accustomed to being upstaged by the clown's antics during a performance may have muttered a sigh of 'good riddance,' they must also have been apprehensive. For all his faults, Kempe had been box office gold. Among other parts he had, in all likelihood, played Shakespeare's greatest comic creation, Sir John Falstaff, in the Henry IV plays and *The Merry Wives of Windsor*. Indeed, it may have been Kempe's unexpected departure that obliged Shakespeare to renege on the promise he had made at the end of *Henry IV, Part 2* to bring Falstaff back in *Henry V*, where we instead hear only of the fat knight's death.

The Globe was still struggling to establish its reputation in the face of fierce competition from Philip Henslowe's Rose theatre just down the road, where Edward Alleyn and the Admiral's Men were always packing in the crowds. In that respect, Kempe's leaving must have proved a setback.

❋ ❋ ❋

If Kempe's critics thought he would go quietly, they had another think coming. After selling his stake in the Globe, he launched into one of history's most spectacular public relations exercises. On 11 February 1600, the first Monday in Lent, he set off dressed in costume from outside the Lord

Mayor of London's house, pledging to morris dance all the way to Norwich in fewer than ten days of travel. Although he would be permitted rest days in between the dancing days, Norwich, then England's second largest city, was a hundred and twenty miles (193 km) to the northeast.

This daunting self-challenge, laid down by a popular celebrity, captivated public imagination. A large crowd of cheering well-wishers saw him off amid a carnival atmosphere, offering him 'sixpences and groats and hearty prayers'. Much more money was at stake, because Kempe had opened a book on whether he could do it. Wagers were placed and he stood to scoop odds of three-to-one if he succeeded.

A man named George Spratt was appointed to accompany him all the way to ensure there was no cheating, together with one Thomas Slye, banging out time on a tabor – a small drum carried on a strap around the neck. Also in attendance was a servant called William Bee. A contemporary illustration (*pictured*) shows Kemp accompanied by Slye on their merry way.

Kempe thwarted the doubters by completing his dance to the mayor's house in Norwich on Saturday, 8 March. Although it was twenty-six days since he set off, he had actually travelled on only nine of those days. He was greeted by the mayor himself with great ceremony when he entered the city. Musicians played and a poem of welcome was read out. Crowds poured into the market place to see him, the throng becoming so dangerous that the mayor ordered officers to clear a way for him. At journey's end, Kempe had to leap over a churchyard wall to get away from the mobbing fans.

Having won his wager, and with an eye to coining another small fortune, he published a book in 1600 about the whole adventure, calling it *Kemp's Nine Daies Wonder*. It was as he expected, a best seller and copies still exist, giving a detailed account of how he endured 'exceeding paine' after straining his hip on the second dancing day, fell into a pot hole near Braintree, and was stranded by snowfall at Bury St Edmunds. In Sudbury, after a strong, tall butcher offered to join him all the way to Bury but quickly gave up, Kempe tells how a 'lusty country lass' danced with him for a mile and was rewarded with a crown piece to buy herself a drink.

He makes an oblique reference to the Globe when he writes: 'I have danced myself out of the World.' In an addendum, he also finds time to take an ill-tempered dig at his critics, including 'my notable Shakerags,' which sounds remarkably like an allusion to Shakespeare. (Robert Greene had famously coined the derogative name 'Shakescene' in his diatribe against the playwright.) Kempe must have considered his own reputation had been impugned by tittle-tattle because the cover of his book includes the pointed subtitle:

Wherein is set downe worth of note: to reprooue [reprove] the slaunders [slanders] spred of him: many things merry, nothing hurtfull.

Kempe would never again act in any play by Shakespeare. After *Nine Daies Wonder* he left England to tour Europe. He is thought to have spent time in Germany and may have travelled as far as Italy, where he reportedly met the English adventurer Sir Anthony Shirley. The money had clearly run out in 1601, when he turns up in the accounts book of Philip Henslowe at the Rose borrowing twenty shillings. In 1602, Kempe joined Worcester's Men, the third acting company in London after the Lord Chamberlain's Men of Richard Burbage and Will Shakespeare, and the Admiral's Men of Philip Henslowe and Edward Alleyn. After a lifetime in which his name became one of the most famous in the land, he faded into obscurity and in all probability died during a severe outbreak of the plague in 1603. An entry in the burial register of St Saviour's Church, Southwark, dated 2 November of that year, reads simply: 'William Kempe, a man.'

Kempe's achievement is remembered in Norwich to this day, with a commemorative plaque along a walkway known as Will Kemp Way, a monument in Chapelfield Gardens carved by the Suffolk sculptor Mark Goldsworthy, and a locally based troupe of morris dancers who call themselves Kemp's Men. A dance called *Will Kempe's Jig* survives, with music that was first published in 1651 and, in the year 2000, the four-hundredth anniversary of the Nine Days' Wonder was marked by morris dancers from all over the country who re-enacted his feat by themselves dancing from London to Norwich.

But that is not quite the end of the story. Between the years 1598 and 1602, to celebrate their Christmas festivities, scholars at St John's College, Cambridge University, staged three plays, now known as the Parnassus Trilogy. The anonymous academic author takes every opportunity to mock and satirise actors and scribblers, singling out Shakespeare for special attention with at least ninety-five references to his works.

Shakespeare and the Lord Chamberlain's Men almost certainly performed at both Oxford and Cambridge when they went on tour in 1601. A preface to the *First Quarto* publication of *Hamlet*, dated 1603, tells us the tragedy had been acted 'in the two universities'. The shocking presence of such low-born and base persons in their hallowed halls clearly horrified some in the privileged world of academia. *The Return to Parnassus; the Scourge of Simony*, the third play of the Christmas trilogy, thought to date from Christmas 1602, takes a shameless swipe at such *nouveau riche* reprobates having acquired wealth enough from their scurrilous activities to invest in property and even achieve a veneer of gentility. (Shakespeare had been granted a family coat of arms in 1596 and bought New Place, the finest house in Stratford-upon-Avon, the following year.) The play declaims:

England affords those glorious vagabonds / That carried earst [once carried] their fardels [heavy packs] on their backes, / Coursers [horses] to ride on through the gazing streetes, / Sooping it in their glaring Satten [satin] sutes, / And Pages to attend their Maisterships: / With mouthing words that better wits have framed, / They purchase lands, and now Esquiers are made.

Kempe and Burbage are even cheekily impersonated. In one exchange, intended to be biting satire, the actor playing Kempe says to the actor playing Burbage:

Few of the University [scholars] plaies well, they smell too much of that writer Ovid, and that writer Metamorphosis, and talk too much of Proserpina and Jupiter. Why here's our fellow Shakespeare puts them all downe, I [aye] and Ben Jonson too.

Kempe and Burbage are here being mercilessly portrayed as barely literate idiots, convinced in their ignorance that Metamorphosis is an author and that Shakespeare and Jonson, neither of whom had a university education, are far superior writers to any university men. The play's academic audience must have whooped with scornful pleasure on hearing such lines.

In truth, the theme of high-handed intellectual snobbery that runs right through the Parnassus plays merely continues what Greene had started in 1592 when, in an address to his fellow 'university wits', he launched his bilious attack on the 'upstart crow' Shakespeare. Worse still, it continues to this day among many of the conspiracy theorists who insist that the indescribably precious corpus we know as Shakespeare's texts cannot possibly be the work of a grammar school-educated boy from Stratford-upon-Avon.

See also: 7. Greene With Envy
15. Eastern Promise
22. The Great Globe Itself
45. Alas, Poor Tarlton

25. CUT-PURSES AND COZENERS

Sharp-witted thieves, conmen and vagabonds plague every town ...
and turn up on stage

**But, my lads, my lads, tomorrow morning, by four o'clock,
early at Gadshill! There are pilgrims going to Canterbury
with rich offerings, and traders riding to London with fat
purses. I have vizards** [visors or masks] **for you all; you have
horses for yourselves ... If you will go, I will stuff your
purses full of crowns.**
(Henry IV, Part 1, 1.2, 1596-7)

POINS excitedly informs his friend Prince Hal and the fat old
knight Sir John Falstaff that there are rich pickings to be had
early the following morning if they agree to ambush a party of
pilgrims and traders travelling along the highway at Gad's Hill.
Hal, the future Henry V, is enjoying his riotous youth, rebel-
ling against the wishes of his father Henry IV. But Poins' plan is
actually an elaborate plot to embarrass the cowardly Falstaff,
who will himself be robbed of the spoils once the hold-up has
been carried out.

A bit of highway robbery was something Shakespeare's
audience would consider totally unsurprising. England in
Elizabethan times was a wild and dangerous place, where robbers and bandits might be waiting around any bend in the road
to pounce on unwary travellers. While we think of highwaymen such as Dick Turpin as an eighteenth-century phenomenon, their forerunners were enjoying a flourishing business
two hundred years earlier.

Gad's Hill, on the London to Canterbury road, was a favourite spot for skulduggery. Falstaff's exploits are commem-
orated to this day in the name of a public house called the Sir

John Falstaff on the A226 at Gad's Hill, Rochester. The British Museum's Lansdowne Manuscripts collection includes an account of one particular highway robbery at Gad's Hill, carried out by two thieves named Custall and Manwaring. The robbers had good horses and one of the men wore a 'vizard grey beard' to disguise his face. The hold-up, which for some reason was significant enough to be recorded despite Gad's Hill being no stranger to such felonies, took place in 1590, six years before Shakespeare wrote *Henry IV, Part 1*.

Equally notorious was Shooter's Hill, closer to London at Blackheath. Further from the capital, the wilds of Newmarket Heath in Suffolk, and Salisbury Plain in Wiltshire, were among other places to be avoided. A favourite tactic of the robbers was to recruit a network of accomplices among workers at the inns where travellers were known to rest overnight. All it took was a tip-off about how many were in a party, what riches they were carrying, and what time the next morning they would be setting off, and the trap was set and ready to be sprung.

The country was a kind of Wild West, teeming with rogues, vagabonds and beggars. Among them were disbanded soldiers and seamen, some horrifically injured in battle and unable to earn a living. Equally desperate were families turfed out of their homes and a subsistence living by wealthy landowners who had appropriated arable land in order to enclose it for keeping sheep. Then there were 'masterless men,' those who had no employer and no reliable income; others who simply chose not to work but preferred the temptation of easy pickings from thievery and fraud; and the 'Bedlam beggars,' as the insane were known, both genuine and those who feigned madness in order to win the sympathy of strangers. There were myriad reasons for turning to a career of crime and, although it brought with it the spectre of branding, whipping, the stocks, or even the gallows if caught, the chances of getting away with villainy were acceptably high for most of its practitioners. For some, crime seemed the only option.

Matters had been made much worse by the dissolution of the monasteries during the reign of Henry VIII. Many abbots and other churchmen had tended to show a kindly face to the poor and wretched, either as sympathetic landlords or by charitable acts as simple as offering food and drink to the needy who knocked on their doors. By Elizabethan times the old spirit of giving was fast disappearing as an aspiring and increasingly prosperous middle class of merchants and tradesmen emerged, people determined to hang on to the wealth they had acquired by dint of their own hard work. A series of disastrous harvests in the 1590s, grain-hoarding and the soaring cost of food compounded the misery.

While the threat of war with European foes was ever present, fewer soldiers were needed than had been for the continental expeditions of previous generations, which meant the low-class thief had less of an opportunity to plunder possessions from a defeated enemy abroad. In *Henry V*, for example, which is set around the Battle of Agincourt in 1415, we learn that Falstaff's old acquaintance Bardolph is to be hanged for stealing a crucifix from a French church. Bardolph's offence was to ignore King Henry's edict that his newly acquired Gallic subjects were to be treated with respect. But the inveterate pilferer Bardolph had merely been doing what he and his kind always did. The prospect of loot was the incentive that had driven him and his companion Nym to France in the first place. As the Boy in the play complains:

> **They will steal anything, and call it purchase. Bardolph stole a lute-case, bore it twelve leagues, and sold it for three-half-pence. Nym and Bardolph are sworn brothers in filching, and in Calais they stole a fire-shovel ... They would have me as familiar with [picking] men's pockets as their gloves or their handkerchers. (3.2)**

At the end of *Henry V*, with the fighting over and facing

an end to his military exploits in France, a disgruntled Pistol shares a confidence with the audience, including the kind of punning on the word 'steal' that is a hallmark of Shakespeare:

> **Old I do wax; and from my weary limbs honour is cudgelled. Well, bawd** [pimp] **I'll turn, and something lean to** [become a] **cut-purse of quick hand. To England will I steal, and there I'll steal.** (5.1)

In *Henry IV, Part 1*, Falstaff even puts in a plea to Hal for thieves like himself to be allowed free rein when the prince becomes king:

> **But, I prithee, sweet wag, shall there be gallows standing in England when thou art king? And resolution** [a thief's courage] **thus fobbed** [thwarted] **as it is with the rusty curb of old father antic** [that old fool] **the law? Do not thou, when thou art king, hang a thief.** (1.2)

The incorrigible reprobate also takes pride in his chosen profession of stealing:

> **Why, Hal, 'tis my vocation, Hal; 'tis no sin for a man to labour in his vocation.** (1.2)

He goes so far as to urge the prince to promote thievery to the status of a respectable way of making a living:

> **Marry, then, sweet wag, when thou art king, let not us that are squires of the night's body be called thieves of the day's beauty: let us be Diana's** [the moon's] **foresters, gentlemen of the shade, minions of the moon; and let men say we be men of good government, being governed, as the sea is, by our noble and chaste mistress the moon, under whose countenance we steal.** (1.2)

Thankfully for England, his plea fell on deaf ears.

❋ ❋ ❋

While highwaymen lay in wait along the untamed heaths and woodlands through which travellers must pass on mud-filled roads, in the towns and cities robbers, thieves and conmen adeptly carried out their own style of villainy. The thousands of rustics who trudged into London every year to seek a living in what was by far the country's biggest city were especially vulnerable. Newcomers in the capital were likely to find themselves befriended by wily tricksters, who would seek to win their confidence and then dupe them out of money or possessions or, worse still, violently rob them.

A favourite ruse of the tricksters was to feign friendship, perhaps even mimicking a rural accent similar to the newcomer's, and pretending to be a distantly related 'coz' (the word was a shortened version of 'cousin', a term used much more loosely than today and implying any sort of relationship, however distant). Over time the verb 'to cozen' evolved, meaning to swindle someone. A confidence trickster or sneak thief was a 'cozener' and victims would complain that they had been 'cozened'. (A possible alternative source of the English word 'cozen' is the sixteenth-century Italian verb *cozzonare* meaning 'to cheat'.)

To gull an unsuspecting subject was also known as 'cony-catching'. A cony was a countryman's name for a rabbit, in this case the 'cony' being the very human victim of theft. The dramatist Robert Greene, who notoriously consorted with some of London's most unsavoury characters, penned a series of pamphlets spelling out the techniques of cony-catchers. He tells us villains included nips (cut-purses), foists (pickpockets), lifts (shoplifters), and courbers (thieves who used a hooked pole to haul goods out through a window). Each respected the others' art.

The nips and foists would hang around wherever crowds were likely to gather. The slang name for one's fingers, as Hamlet tells us, was 'pickers and stealers'. Many people kept their purses (or wallets) tied to their belts with string. All the thief had to do was watch carefully when a purse was taken out to be used and note whereabouts on the person it was stowed away for safety. As Greene puts it:

The nip spieth what every man hath in his purse & wher in what place, and in which sleeve or pocket he puts the boung [purse], and according to that so he worketh.

Sometimes an accomplice was used to distract the victim, and it was a moment's effort to pick a pocket or slice through the string of a purse with a knife and make off with the loot. The skilled thief was so good that the victim often did not even realise the purse was gone. In 1598, a German lawyer named Paul Hentzner, who was visiting London, went along to Bartholomew Fair, one of the city's best-known summer attractions. He recorded in his notebook:

While we were at this show, one of our company, Tobias Salander, Doctor of Physic, had his pocket picked of his purse, with nine crowns [a coin denomination], which, without doubt, was so cleverly taken from him by an Englishman, who always kept very close to him, that the Doctor did not perceive it.

If Doctor Tobias Salander felt foolish, he was far from alone.

One of Shakespeare's biggest rogues and, like Falstaff, his most colourful characters, is the pedlar-cum-pickpocket Autolycus in *The Winter's Tale*. He, like Falstaff, is proud of what he regards as the superior wit that enables him to prey on the gullible. Anything is fair game for a man named after the son of Mercury (in classical myth the god of thieves and pickpockets) and he tells us without shame:

My traffic is sheets; when the kite builds, look to lesser linen. My father named me Autolycus, who being, as I am, littered under Mercury, was likewise a snapper-up of unconsidered trifles. (4.3)

He is happy to steal the laundered sheets that house-holders left draped over hedges to dry and bleach in the sunshine – just as a kite might take pieces of linen to line its nest – then sell them in the next village he comes to. Autolycus lives by the maxim:

What a fool Honesty is! And Trust, his sworn brother, a very simple gentleman! (4.4)

Then he spells out the skills an accomplished thief needs:

I understand the business, I hear it: to have an open ear, a quick eye, and a nimble hand is
necessary for a cut-purse; a good nose is requisite also, to smell out work for the other senses. I see this is the time that the unjust man doth thrive. (4.4)

Vagrancy was a risky business. While the crime of highway robbery could lead the offender to the gallows, vagabonds – the able-bodied poor who refused to work – faced being 'grevouslye whipped and burnte through the gristle of the right eare with a hot yron of the compasse of an ynche about'. An attempt was made to deal with the problem when Parliament introduced the landmark Poor Relief Act of 1601, known to historians as 'the Elizabethan Poor Law'. It provided for the disabled poor in each parish to be cared for in almshouses, the unemployed but able-bodied poor to be set to work in an institution known as a House of Industry, and the idle poor and vagrants who refused to work to be committed to a House of Correction or prison until they mended their ways. The Act also levied a 'poor rate' on property owners and occupiers, the revenue to be used to support the destitute. The law had limited success, with little by way of structure in place to ensure it operated consistently throughout the country.

Still the thieving went on, human nature being what it is.

Easy targets were fairs and markets, the bustling area around the cathedral church at St Paul's, and even Tyburn when hundreds gathered to watch the grisly spectacle of a public hanging. Other favourite venues of the nips and foists were the theatres, where it was easy to slip unnoticed among the crowds who had their eyes on the actors. It all came as no surprise to disapproving Puritans, who had written off the playhouses as unspeakable dens of iniquity and debauchery where all manner of sinful goings on took place. A delightful passage in *The Compleat Gentleman* by Henry Peacham, a book first published in 1622, proves particularly   revealing:

A tradesman's wife of the Exchange, one day when her husband was following some business in the city, desired him he would give her leave to go see a play; which she had not done in seven years. He bade her take his apprentice along with her, and go; but especially to have a care of her purse; which she warranted him she would. Sitting in a box, among some gallants and gallant wenches, and returning when the play was done, returned to her husband and told him she had lost her purse. 'Wife,' quoth he, 'did I not give you warning of it? How much money was there in it?' Quoth she, 'Truly, four pieces, six shillings and a silver tooth-picker.' Quoth her husband, 'Where did you put it?' 'Under my petticoat, between that and my smock.' 'What,' quoth he, 'did you feel nobody's hand there?' 'Yes,' quoth she, 'I felt one's hand there, but I did not think he had come for that.'

See also: 26. Tom o' Bedlam
48. The Usurer's Wife
49. If You Want to Get Ahead

26. TOM O' BEDLAM

Madmen ... and those who feign madness ... menace the country-side while demanding alms

Whiles I may scape [escape]**, I will preserve myself; and am bethought** [have decided] **to take the basest and most poorest shape that ever penury, in contempt of man, brought near to beast. My face I'll grime with filth, blanket my loins, elf** [matt] **all my hair in knots, and with presented nakedness outface the winds and persecutions of the sky. The country gives me proof and precedent of Bedlam beggars, who, with roaring voices, strike in their numb'd and mortified** [insensible to pain] **bare arms pins, wooden pricks, nails, sprigs of rosemary; and with this horrible object** [spectacle]**, from low farms, poor pelting** [paltry] **villages, sheepcotes, and mills, sometime with lunatic bans** [curses]**, sometime with prayers, enforce** [demand] **their charity.** (*King Lear*, 2.3, 1605-6)

EDGAR is on the run. Wrongly accused of plotting to kill his father, the Earl of Gloucester, and attempting to kill his brother Edmund, he escapes his pursuers by disguising himself as a 'Bedlam beggar'. Thousands of such beggars roamed the land in Shakespeare's day, seeking alms with pleas or threats, and sometimes a combination of both. They were so common a sight that, by feigning madness, Edgar is satisfied he will not arouse suspicion wherever he goes. 'Bedlam' today means any scene of madness or chaos, but for centuries the word referred to Bethlem Hospital (a corruption of the name 'Bethlehem'), later renamed Bethlem Royal Hospital, and its inmates. 'Bethlem' evolved into being pronounced 'Bedlam' by Londoners. It was the first asylum founded in England that dedicated itself to catering for – or at least coping with – the mentally deranged in an age long before psychiatry. The hospital operates to this day, although on a different site and in a vastly different way, more than six hundred years after its doors first opened.

The place was well known enough to the groundlings for Shakespeare and contemporaries such as Ben Jonson, John Webster, Thomas Dekker and Thomas Middleton to refer to it in a large number of their plays. 'To Bedlam with him! Is the man grown mad?' declares Lord Clifford, when Richard Plantagenet (who will become Richard III) asserts his right to the throne as the Wars of the Roses rage in Shakespeare's *Henry VI, Part 2* (5.1). Henry himself responds with: 'Ay, Clifford, a bedlam and ambitious humour makes him oppose himself against his king.' King John turns the name into an insult while arguing with the lady Constance, insisting she must be mad as he shouts: 'Bedlam, have done' in *King John* (2.1). In *Henry V*, the belligerent Pistol snarls at Fluellen the Welshman: 'Ha! Art thou bedlam?' (5.1).

The reference to 'Bedlam' in *King Lear*, a play set in Britain before the Roman conquest, is one of Shakespeare's anachronisms. The hospital was founded as the Priory of Our Lady of Bethlehem in 1247, during the reign of Henry III. By 1402, it was taking in London's insane, who were known as 'lunatics' because their mood swings were believed to be influenced by the phases of the moon (Luna being the name of the Roman goddess of the moon). After Henry VIII dissolved the monasteries, Bethlem, as it was by then known, was granted an exemption from destruction because of the work it did. Instead of pulling the place down, Henry handed its governance over to the City of London.

The 'Bedlam beggars' were originally patients allowed out of restraint on a daily basis, wearing an identification badge on their arms, to beg for money to help pay for the hospital's upkeep. Male 'Bedlam beggars' were known as 'Tom o' Bedlam' or 'Poor Tom', Tom being one of the most common names for a man. Their female equivalents were dubbed

'Bess o' Bedlam' or sometimes 'Joan o' Bedlam'. Appearing on the streets and highways in far greater numbers than the genuine patients were vagrants who had absolutely nothing to do with the hospital, but who feigned madness in order to soften hearts or frighten householders into handing over food, clothing or money. It was notoriously difficult to tell who was truly mad and who was simply pretending to be so. In Shakespeare's plays, while King Lear, Ophelia and Lady Macbeth do actually lose their minds, Edgar and Hamlet put on convincing performances when affecting madness for their own purposes.

Those vagrant 'Bedlam beggars' who were simply pretending to be mad came to be known as 'Abraham men' because many of them claimed to be on release from the hospital's Abraham Ward. The epithet can be traced back to 1561, when it was coined by a printer named John Awdely, who published a detailed guide to the tactics of beggars titled *The Fraternitye of Vacabondes*. The warning was echoed five years later by the writer Thomas Harman, in a popular book titled *A Caveat or Warning for Common Cursitors, Vulgarly Called Vagabonds*. Harman writes:

> *These Abraham men be those that feign themselves to have been mad, and have been kept either in Bethlem or in some other prison a good time.*

If not given alms out of pity, Harman warned, they had no hesitation in becoming threatening, exploiting fears that the mentally ill were dangerous. In a publication titled *O Per Se O, Or a New Cryer of Lanthorne and Candle-light*, Shakespeare's contemporary Thomas Dekker warns that the Abraham 'cove' is a 'lustie strong roague' who often walks about wrapped in a sheet and sleeveless jerkin. He goes without trousers 'for both his legges and armes are bare'. He has 'a face staring like a Sarasin [Saracen or Turk, notorious for their ferocity], his hayre long and filthily knotted, for hee keepes no barber,' and he carries a staff of ash or hazel. Dekker goes on:

And to colour their villanie the better, every one of these Abrams hath a severall gesture in playing his part: some make an horrid noyse, hollowly sounding: some whoope, some hollow [holler], some shew onely a kinde of wilde distracted ugly looke. Some daunce, but keepe no measure, others leape up and downe.

He cautions that 'these, walking up and downe the countrey are more terrible to women and children' than the sight of sprites such as hobgoblins. 'These Abram ninnies' wander in such frightening shapes from village to village 'that when they come to any doore a begging, nothing is denyed them,' Dekker says. In 1673, the author Richard Head wrote in *The Canting Academy or Devils Cabinet Opened* that Abraham Men…

Used to array themselves with party-coloured ribbons, tape in their hats, a fox-tail hanging down, a long stick with streamers, and beg alms; but for all their seeming madness, they had wit enough to steal as they went along.

By 1675, the patience of Bedlam's governors with the Abraham Men finally ran out. They published a public notice in the *London Gazette* declaring:

Whereas several vagrant persons do wander about … pretending themselves to be lunatics under cure in the Hospital of Bethlem, commonly called Bedlam, with brass plates about their arms and inscriptions thereon. These are to give notice that there is no such liberty given to any patients kept in the said Hospital for their cure, neither is any such plate as a distinction or mark put upon any lunatic during their being there, or when discharged thence. And that the same is a false pretence, to colour their wandering and begging, and to deceive the people.

As late as 1737 the *Dictionary of Thieving Slang* was defining 'Abram-men' as 'shabby beggars ... pretending to be besides themselves, to palliate their thefts of poultry, linnen, &c.'

In *King Lear*, Edgar has chosen his desperate disguise because it provides such a plausible cover. Edgar goes on, however, to paint a grim picture of the life that awaited Tom o' Bedlam outside the hospital, tormented, as it was supposed, by devils.

> **Who gives anything to Poor Tom? Whom the foul fiend** [the Devil] **hath led through fire and through flame, through ford and whirlpool, o'er bog and quagmire ... Bless thy five wits, Tom's a-cold. O do, de, do, de, do, de: bless thee from whirlwinds** [storms], **star-blasting** [evil influence of a star or planet] **and taking** [infection or evil influences]. **Do Poor Tom some charity, whom the foul fiend vexes.** (3.4)

It gets worse:

> **Poor Tom, that eats the swimming frog, the toad, the todpole** [tadpole], **the wall-newt** [wall-lizard] **and the water** [water-newt]; **that in the fury of his heart, when the foul fiend rages, eats cow-dung for sallets** [salads], **swallows the old rat and the ditch-dog** [dead dog thrown into a ditch], **drinks the green mantle of the standing pool; who is whipp'd from tithing to tithing** [parish to parish], **and stock-punish'd** [placed in the stocks] **and imprison'd.** (3.4)

Whipping was the standard punishment for vagrancy, and wandering undesirables would be whipped from one parish to the next until, supposedly, they ended up back in their own parish. The stocks awaited thieves and other miscreants. It is difficult to conclude whether Tom and Bess o' Bedlams were better off outside Bethlem or in it, care having long since been replaced by brutality in the institution. While the regime might honour the hospital's traditions with an element of religious devotion, whips, chains, manacles and stocks were all considered helpful to restoring a person's sanity. We glimpse Bedlam's pitiless cruelty in a late Elizabethan play by John Marston titled *Jack Drum's Entertainment*, when a character called Flawne says of a usurer named Mamon:

I'll even lay him up in Bedlam, commit him to the mercy of the whip, the entertainment of bread and water.

Drum says in reply:

The price of whips is mightily risen since his brain was pitifully overtumbled, they are so fast spent upon his shoulders.

In the 1604 comedy *The Honest Whore, Part 1* by Thomas Dekker and Thomas Middleton, a cleaner at the asylum tells us:

I sweep the madmen's rooms, and fetch straw for 'em, and buy chains to tie 'em, and rods to whip 'em. I was a mad wag myself here once, but I thank Father   Anselm. He lash'd me into my right mind again.

For more hopeless cases, confinement in a pitch-black room was considered efficacious. In Dekker's play *Westward Ho* a character named Justiniano speaks of 'pent-houses' – the overhanging upper floor of Tudor houses that were often only a few feet from the overhanging floor of a house on the opposite side of the street – that make 'the shop of a mercer [dealer in fabrics] or linen draper as dark as a room in Bedlam'. Shops were usually on the overshadowed ground floor below.

In Shakespeare's *Twelfth Night*, Sir Toby Belch persuades his fellow conspirators to take matters a step too far when pretending they believe the haughty servant Malvolio to be mad, saying:

Come, we'll have him in a dark room and bound. My niece is already in the belief that he's mad: we may carry

it thus, for our pleasure and his penance, till our very pastime, tired out of breath, prompt us to have mercy on him. (3.4)

The final indignity heaped on Bedlam's unfortunate inmates came from the wealthy citizens who paid a fee to be entertained by watching their antics. Although this horrific phenomenon reached its peak in the centuries following, it had already begun in Shakespeare's lifetime. In Jonson's play *Epicoene*, first performed in 1609, the pretentious Madame Haughty tells Epicoene (who is a boy disguised as a young woman) that when she is married she shall 'go with us to Bedlam, to the China Houses, and to the Exchange'.

The China Houses were shops in East London where exotic Eastern silks and porcelains were sold. The Exchange was what today might be called an up-market shopping mall in Cornhill. Four storeys high and surrounded by piazzas with marble pillars, it boasted more than a hundred shops, many of them milliners seeking to attract fashionable ladies. In short, three of the most popular City of London resorts where the well-to-do might while away their time included Bedlam, to watch the 'lunatics'. A writer named Richard Braithwaite, in *Barnabee's Journal*, listed 'the Bedlam poor' as one of the seven must-see sights in London.

Whether Bedlam served as anything more than a place in which to simply confine the mentally ill was questioned even in the early seventeenth century. A commentator named Donald Lupton came to a conclusion that was remarkably enlightened for his time:

Here live many that are cal'd men, but seldome at home, for they are gone out of themselves. Nature hath bin a steppe-mother to some, and misery and crosses have caused this strange change in others ... this House would bee too little, if all that are beside themselves should be put in here. It seemes strange that any one should recover here, the cry-

*ings, screechings, roarings, brawlings, shaking of chaines,
swearings, frettings, chaffings, are so many, so hideous, so
great, that they are more able to drive a man that hath his
witts, rather out of them, than to helpe one that never had
them, or hath lost them, to finde them againe. Certainely,
hee that keepes the House may be sayd to live among wilde
creatures. It's thought many are kept here, not so much in
hope of recovery, as to keepe them from further and more
desperate inconveniences. Many live here that know not
where they are, or how they got in, never thinke of getting
out. There's many that are so well or ill in their witts, that
they can say they have bin out of them, & gaine much by
dissembling in this kind; desperate that dare make a mocke
of iudgment. Well, if the Divell [Devil] was not so strong
to delude, & men so easily to be drawne, this House would
stand empty, and for my part, I am sorry it hath any in it.*

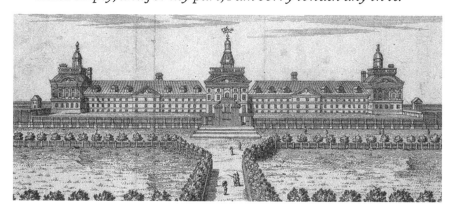

In 1676, coincidentally the year Donald Lupton died,
Bedlam moved from its site just outside Bishopsgate to much
larger premises at Moorfield. The new building (*pictured*) had
an impressive 540ft (165m) -long baroque façade inspired by
Louis XIV's Tuileries Palace in Paris. It was designed by Robert Hooke, a surveyor for the City of London and assistant to
Christopher Wren. Because of its truly monumental scale, the
hospital was dubbed by Londoners 'a palace for lunatics'.

Serious structural problems quickly became evident,

however. Construction had been carried out without proper foundations, and the ornate façade was so heavy that the building began cracking up. Water poured down the inside walls whenever it rained, prompting the satirist Thomas Brown in 1699 to ask 'whether the persons that ordered the building of it, or those that inhabit it, are the maddest'.

In 1815, the hospital moved again to Saint George's Fields in Southwark. The present Bethlem Royal Hospital, incorporated into the National Health Service, stands in Beckenham, Kent, a world away, in every sense, from its early days. The original Bedlam is now long gone, buried – along with the bones of many of its pitiful inmates – in the rubble beneath Liverpool Street Station.

See also: 25. Cut-purses and Cozeners

27. THE GEESE AND THE GOLDEN EGGS

Seedy brothels, syphilitic prostitutes and vicious pimps are an everyday feature of life in London

Brethren and sisters of the hold-door trade [prostitutes' pimps], **some two months hence my will shall here be made: It should be now, but that my fear is this, some galled goose of Winchester would hiss.**
(Troilus and Cressida, 5.10, 1600-2)

THE degenerate Pandarus – who has given the English language the word 'pander', meaning a pimp – laments his own demise in an epilogue to *Troilus and Cressida*, Shakespeare's retelling of a saga that dates back to Homer. Pandarus tells us he would have made his will earlier except that 'some galled goose of Winchester would hiss [complain]'. Despite the fact that the play was set amid the Trojan Wars two millennia ago, the groundlings would have immediately understood his reference to the world right outside the doors of the Globe.

'Winchester geese' was a contemptuous colloquialism for the hundreds of prostitutes who thronged the narrow streets and alleyways of Southwark, south of the River Thames and safely beyond the reach of the Lord Mayor's ordinances forbidding their activities in the City of London on the opposite bank. The epithet arose because most of Southwark's brothels – or 'stews' as the Elizabethans called them – were situated on land owned by the Bishop of Winchester. A 'galled goose' was a prostitute suffering from sexually transmitted disease, syphilis being so common among those unfortunate women that any man who caught it was said to have been 'bitten by a Winchester goose'. 'A Winchester goose' also came to mean a swelling of the groin that was a symptom of sexually transmitted disease, and that is the insult Duke Humphrey of Gloucester hurls at his bitter enemy the Bishop of Winchester in *Henry VI, Part 1*.

Winchester goose, I cry, a rope! A rope! Now beat them hence; why do you let them stay? Thee I'll chase hence, thou wolf in sheep's array. Out, tawny coats! Out, scarlet hypocrite! (1.3)

Bermondsey Abbey and the surrounding land in Southwark had originally been purchased in 1149 by Henry of Blois, Bishop of Winchester and brother of King Stephen, for his London residence. The abbey possessed a customary 'liberty', meaning the bishop was free to impose laws and taxes within his own boundaries. Two years later, he built what became a notorious prison called The Clink on his land ('clink' subsequently evolved into a slang name for any prison), and the area was known as the Liberty of the Clink. On the death of Henry of Blois the land remained the property of the bishopric and, because the 'liberty' was exempt from the regulations governing the City of London, it became fertile ground on which prostitution could flourish.

In 1161, King Henry II felt the need to introduce regulations to impose some order on the burgeoning stews of Southwark (so called because they began life as bath-houses). It was common knowledge that they offered what might be described as extra services and the king's new edicts regulated their activities, specifying that compliance was to be overseen by a bailiff and constables. Henry II's aim was not to stamp out prostitution but to keep it confined to the South Bank and out of the City itself.

By Shakespeare's day, successive Bishops of Winchester had been cheerfully pocketing the wages of sin through levying taxes and exacting rents on the brothel-keepers for four centuries. The stews jostled cheek-by-jowl with the theatres, bear-baiting rings and cock-fighting pits of Southwark, which by the close of the sixteenth century formed the epicentre of London's entertainment and 'red light' district. The thriving businesses were close neighbours in more ways than one.

The impresario Philip Henslowe, who founded the Rose theatre in 1587, was a shareholder in several brothels. So was his son-in-law Edward Alleyn, the celebrated lead actor of the Admiral's Men theatrical company. The pair jointly operated the Paris Garden, a large amphitheatre where bear-baiting events regularly packed in baying crowds of spectators. Prostitutes and pimps frequently mingled with the crowds watching performances of any description, considering them ideal targets for temptation. The playwright Thomas Dekker reckoned prostitutes frequented the theatres so much they knew the plays word for word and could even recite speeches from them 'by heart'.

So powerful was the lure of Southwark that the watermen were kept busy through all hours of the day and night, rowing eager clients across the river from the City. A favourite point of embarkation was the tellingly named Stew Lane, which led down to the river. It still exists today as a narrow alleyway. The journey may have cost customers the boatman's fare but it was less risky than walking over the bustling London Bridge, with its pick-pockets and cut-purses. Besides, the gates of the bridge were locked at dusk.

The presence of the stews crops up again and again in Shakespeare's plays, which simply reflects the prominent role they fulfilled in the licentious life of the capital. At the beginning of *Henry IV, Part 1*, for instance, Hal wakes a slumbering Sir John Falstaff, only to be gruffly asked what the time is. The Prince replies:

What a devil hast thou to do with the time of the day? Unless hours were cups of sack [white wine] **and minutes capons, and clocks the tongues of bawds** [brothel-keepers] **and dials the signs of leaping-houses** [brothels], and the blessed sun himself a fair hot wench in flame-coloured taffeta, I see no reason why thou shouldst be so superfluous to demand the time of the day. (1.2)

Falstaff himself later jokes that he 'went to a bawdy-house not above once in a quarter – of an hour' (3.3). In *Henry IV, Part 2*, the lecherous dotard Robert Shallow, now a respectable Justice of the Peace, wallows in questionable nostalgia when meeting up with Falstaff:

Shallow: **O, Sir John, do you remember since we lay all night in the Windmill in Saint George's Field?**

Falstaff: **No more of that, good Master Shallow, no more of that.**

Shallow: **Ha, 'twas a merry night! And is Jane Nightwork alive?** (3.2)

Their exchange prompts Falstaff's immortal line: 'We have heard the chimes at midnight, Master Shallow'. Jane Nightwork's name tells us all we need to know about her profession. Saint George's Field was a large open space that lay south of the Thames, between Southwark and Lambeth. A windmill appears there on a map of London made in 1600 by a surveyor named John Norden. There was also a brothel named the Windmill not far away in Paris Garden Lane, Southwark. Shallow persists with his tedious reminiscences, boasting:

By the mass, I was called anything; and I would have done anything indeed too, and roundly too. There was I, and little John Doit of Staffordshire, and black George Barnes, and Francis Pickbone, and Will Squele a Cotsole [Cotswold] **man – you had not four swinge-bucklers** [swash-bucklers] **in all the Inns of Court again. And I may say you we knew where the bona-robas** [high-class prostitutes, the words are from the Italian meaning 'good material'] **were, and had the best of them all at commandment.** (3.2)

Falstaff later complains about the 'lecherous as a monkey' magistrate, groaning:

I do see the bottom of Justice Shallow. Lord, Lord, how subject we old men are to this vice of lying! This same starved [scrawny] **justice hath done nothing but prate to me of the wildness of his youth and the feats he hath done about Turnbull Street, and every third word a lie.** (3.2)

While Southwark was the star attraction, prostitution had become established in other rapidly sprawling 'suburbs' north of the river that were also outside the old City of London boundaries. Turnbull Street (now Turnmill Street), a warren of dark alleys and courtyards which ran from Clerkenwell Green to Cowcross Street, was described as 'the most disreputable street in London, the haunt of thieves and loose women'.

Such was its reputation for depravity that to catch a sexually transmitted disease might also be known as being 'stung by a Turnbull Street bee'. In an outburst of violence in 1606, more than two hundred rioting 'unknown disturbers of the peace' attacked properties in Turnbull Street 'armed with stones and clubbes' before moving on to assail Cowcross Street.

Almost as notorious was a narrow street called Pickt-Hatch. According to Edward Sugden's classic *Topographical Dictionary* of 1925, it was 'an infamous resort of thieves and prostitutes' that lay at the back of Middle Row (formerly called Rotten Row) on the east side of Goswell Road, just south of Old Street, opposite the wall of the Charterhouse. Sugden says: 'The name was preserved for a long time in Pickax Yard, Middle Row.'

The term Pickt-Hatch, with several variations of the spelling, derives from the half-door (hatch) topped with sharp metal spikes (pickets) that became the hallmark of brothels.

Such a set-up meant the identity of anyone knocking could be established before the door was opened, and admittance after suitable bartering was at the discretion of the brothel-keeper. Ben Jonson's 1610 play *The Alchemist* features a character named Surly, who describes prostitutes as 'the decayed vestals of Pickt-hatch'. In *The Merry Wives of Windsor*, Falstaff snarls at his unwanted companion Pistol, ordering him to go away and return to his customary pastime of cutting purse strings among the crowds milling around the brothels:

> **At a word, hang no more about me, I am no gibbet for you.**
> **Go. A short knife and a throng! To your manor of Pickt-**
> **hatch! Go.** (2.2)

The capital's appetite for young women who could be lured into prostitution was insatiable. Particularly prized were new arrivals from the countryside, because they were presumed to be unblemished by 'the pox' that was so widespread. Shakespeare does not flinch from exposing the ugly industry in his late play *Pericles*. A distasteful conversation between an unnamed bawd (brothel-keeper), a pander and a servant named Boult, ostensibly in the city of Mytilene on the isle of Lesbos, turns a searing blowtorch on London's own repellent trade:

> *Pandar:* **Search the market narrowly. Mytilene is full**
> **of gallants** [men who are potential customers]. **We lost**
> **too much money this mart** [market time] **by being too**
> **wenchless** [not having enough prostitutes].
>
> *Bawd:* **We were never so much out of creatures. We have**
> **but poor three, and they can do no more than they can do;**
> **and they with continual action are even as good as rotten.**
>
> *Pandar:* **Therefore let's have fresh ones, whate'er we pay**
> **for them. If there be not a conscience** [here meaning
> professional strategy] **to be used in every trade, we shall**
> **never prosper.**

Bawd: **Thou sayest true: 'tis not our bringing up of poor bastards – as, I think, I have brought up some eleven** [to be prostitutes].

Boult: **Ay, to eleven** [years of age]; **and brought them down again. But shall I search the market?**

Bawd: **What else, man? The stuff we have, a strong wind will blow it to pieces, they are so pitifully sodden** [subjected to treatment in a sweating tub as a supposed cure for sexually transmitted disease].

Pandar: **Thou sayest true; they're too unwholesome** [diseased], **o' conscience. The poor Transylvanian** [a customer] **is dead, that lay with the little baggage** [prostitute].

Boult: **Ay, she quickly pooped** [overcame] **him; she made him roast-meat for worms** [he died]. **But I'll go search the market.** (4.2)

Shockingly, the text reveals that girls as young as eleven were considered old enough to become prostitutes. When the brothel-keepers light upon the innocent Marina, who is offered for sale by pirates who have abducted her, there is gleeful rejoicing. Treating the noble daughter of Pericles, Prince of Tyre, as no more than the prized commodity she has become, the Bawd orders:

Boult, take you the marks of her, the colour of her hair, complexion, height, age, with warrant of her virginity; and cry 'He that will give most shall have her first.' Such a maidenhead were no cheap thing, if men were as they have been. (4.2)

Shakespeare is thought to have co-written *Pericles* with George Wilkins. If he did, Wilkins was the very man to supply first-hand expertise on the whole seedy business. At one time Wilkins kept a tavern on the corner of Turnbull Street and Cowcross Street, close to the brothel quarter of Clerkenwell. His establishment was a haunt for prostitutes, for whom he acted as pimp. He was also a recidivist thug. He had impressively long form for court appearances, with some of the charges against him involving extreme violence against women – in all probability the prostitutes who worked for him. In one particularly repulsive episode, on 3 March 1611, three years after *Pericles* was first performed, Wilkins was accused of 'kicking a woman on the belly which was then great with child'.

Wilkins wrote a play titled *The Miseries of an Enforced Marriage* for the King's Men in 1605, although just how closely he and Shakespeare collaborated on *Pericles* in 1607-8 is an open question. Some scholars believe Wilkins wrote the first two acts and Shakespeare the last three. Perhaps Shakespeare was drafted in to complete the play. Court records no longer survive which might have told us whether Wilkins' contribution was interrupted by the overriding imperatives of the constabulary before he could finish what he had started.

Pericles proved a hugely popular production for the King's Men. Wilkins was certainly at liberty within a year of its first performance, because he rushed out a novel under his own name titled *The Painful Adventures of Pericles*, which derives its plot from the play. Wilkins' book was in all probability an unauthorised version of the story, including tracts filched from Shakespeare's contribution to the play, and aimed at making a fast buck for its author.

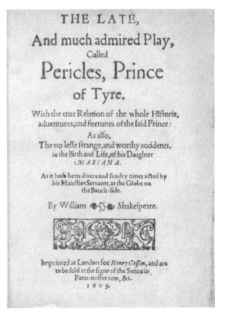

THE LATE,
And much admired Play,
Called
Pericles, Prince
of Tyre.

With the true Relation of the whole Hiftorie, aduentures, and fortunes of the faid Prince:

As alfo,
The no leffe ftrange, and worthy accidents, in the Birth and Life, of his Daughter
MARIANA.

As it hath been diuers and fundry times acted by his Maiefties Seruants, at the Globe on the Banck-fide.

By William Shakefpeare.

Imprinted at London for *Henry Goffon*, and are to be fold at the figne of the Sunne in Pater-nofter row, &c.
1609.

Wilkins died in 1618, two years after Shakespeare. Curiously, John Heminges and Henry Condell did not include *Pericles* among the plays in the *First Folio* of 1623, despite the fact that pirated quarto editions (*pictured*) had been published in the intervening years. The tragedy largely as we know it first appears as late as 1664, in the second impression of the *Third Folio* of Shakespeare's plays, under the title *The much admired play called Pericles, Prince of Tyre*.

✳ ✳ ✳

Syphilis was the ugly fate that awaited most prostitutes and their clients. The disease had rampaged through Europe for a century, possibly having been brought back from the Americas by the Spaniards and Portuguese. If that was the case, then the subjugated natives of the New World really did wreak their revenge on the colonisers from the Old. In an age long before antibiotics, the disease racked many of its victims with horrific torments that were relieved only by a premature death. Syphilis had reached epidemic levels by Elizabethan times and a barber-surgeon named William Clowes wrote in 1585 that London's handful of hospitals, such as they were, simply did not have enough room for the 'infinite multitude' of victims.

While using hot steam baths to make the patient sweat heavily was thought by some to help cure the disease (as in the excerpt from *Pericles* above), others preferred the administration of mercury, either orally or by rubbing into the skin. It was wryly said that an evening with Venus led to a lifetime of Mercury. The substance was so toxic that it created more health problems than it solved (in fact it solved none). Falstaff impudently turns the blame on to the wonderfully named Doll Tearsheet in *Henry IV, Part 2*, when he alludes to a belief that to grow fat and bloated was among the consequences of contracting sexually transmitted disease:

Falstaff: **You make fat rascals, Mistress Doll.**

Doll: I make them! Gluttony and diseases make them, I make them not.

Falstaff: If the cook help to make the gluttony, you help to make the diseases, Doll. We catch of you, Doll, we catch of you; grant that, my poor virtue, grant that.

Doll: Yea, joy, our chains and our jewels [you get back from us such 'valuables' as we have been given].

Falstaff: Your brooches, pearls, and ouches. (2.4)

In the wake of Henry II's strictures, efforts persisted on the part of the authorities to keep prostitution out of the City of London itself. In 1285, Edward I published a proclamation ordering forty days' imprisonment for any 'common whore' found dwelling within the old walls of the City. The measure must have met with only limited success, because in 1417 Henry V found it necessary to approve an ordinance abolishing the stews that had sprung up there.

In Southwark, the sex industry continued to flourish undisturbed until 1513 when Henry VIII – of all people – decided to impose a clampdown in an effort to put an end to the immorality, and consequent rampant syphilis, among his troops. As a moral crusade it marked the height of hypocrisy, since Henry himself was happy to receive a regular supply of hand-picked prostitutes for private gratification throughout his lifetime. His proclamation prescribed harsh treatment for all pimps and prostitutes, including an order for 'the branding of whores'. Such hypocrisy is alluded to in *King Lear*, during the mad king's ramblings:

Thou rascal beadle, hold thy bloody hand! Why dost thou lash that whore? Strip thine own back. Thou hotly lusts to use her in that kind for which thou whip'st her. (4.6)

Henry VIII went even further in 1546, not long before his death, sending shockwaves through the sex industry when he ordered the complete closure of all the brothels in Southwark.

Henry's clampdown had two unintended consequences: it immediately scattered prostitution to other areas outside the City walls north of the Thames, such as Clerkenwell, Smithfield and Shoreditch, and in Southwark itself it drove the trade underground. Now almost every alehouse in the 'liberty' became a covert front for illicit prostitution.

Throughout Elizabeth's reign the authorities battled unsuccessfully to restrict the growth of London, which was expanding at breakneck speed. With a population of around two hundred thousand it was ten times larger than the next biggest city, Norwich, as hopeful rustics seeking work poured in from the countryside every day. Particularly resented by residents were the lawless 'suburbs' outside the walls, where the City's legal writ did not run. They were rapidly filling up with hastily erected, ramshackle and crowded slums that housed tens of thousands more people than were living in the City itself, and they were considered ripe breeding grounds for the plague and other ills.

In 1603, Bills of Mortality began to be regularly published for the first time, listing the number of plague deaths – the disease claimed more than thirty-three thousand lives in London that year. On 16 September 1603, barely six months after James I had succeeded to the throne, the authorities acted. A proclamation was issued 'against multitudes of dwellers in strait [cramped] rooms &c in and about London, and for razing of certain newly erected buildings'. It called for the slums to be pulled down, thereby directly threatening many of the brothels. The panic that ensued was picked up by Shakespeare in *Measure for Measure*, which appeared the following year. Although set in Vienna, an exchange between the brothel-keeper Mistress Overdone and a tapster-cum-pimp known as Pompey Bum comes straight from the streets of London.

Pompey Bum: **You have not heard of the proclamation,**

have you?

Mistress Overdone: **What proclamation, man?**

Pompey Bum: **All houses [brothels] in the suburbs of Vienna must be plucked down.**

Mistress Overdone: **And what shall become of those in the city?**

Pompey Bum: **They shall stand for seed: they had gone down too but that a wise burgher put in for them.**

Mistress Overdone: **But shall all our houses of resort in the suburbs be pulled down?**

Pompey Bum: **To the ground, mistress.**

Mistress Overdone: **Why, here's a change indeed in the commonwealth! What shall become of me?** (1.2)

Pompey Bum assures the distressed Mistress Overdone, who is nine-times married and now a widow, that all will be well. In what sounds like an allusion to the deterioration of her eyesight as a result of syphilis – she was almost certainly a prostitute herself before she became a bawd – he says:

Courage! There will be pity taken on you: you that have worn your eyes almost out in the service, you will be considered. (1.2)

Her business will be able to continue undercover. He will provide a front as tavern-keeper and allow her to operate from his premises. It is precisely the way the brothels of Southwark had survived after Henry VIII's ordinance. The businesses were in any case symbiotic: the taverner was keen to ply brothel clients with drinks and over-priced food, and get them to 'treat' the girls at the same time. In his 1592 paper *A Disputation between a He Cony-catcher and a She Cony-catcher*, Robert Greene casts a light on the practice when a woman named Nan tells how she and her fellow prostitutes are required to encourage clients to buy expensive cakes and other sweet treats, saying:

First we feign ourselves hungry, for the benefit of the house,
although our bellies were never so full; and no doubt the
good pandar or bawd she comes forth like a sober matron,
and sets store of cates [cakes] on the table, and then I fall
aboard on them, and though I can eat little, yet I make havoc
of all. And let him be sure every dish is well-sauced [over-
priced], for he shall pay for a pippin [apple] pie that cost in
the market four pence, at one of the tugging-houses [broth-
els] eighteen pence.

A typical scene from a Tudor brothel (*pictured*) appears as a woodcut illustration in *A Book of Roxburghe Ballads*, published in 1847, which resides in the British Library. It shows patrons and bare-breasted prostitutes seated at a table, having been served food and alcohol.

Greene, who had his own close connections to London's seedy underworld, also portrays prostitutes as being adept at artful tricks with which to cheat or rob their lustful clients. After sounding an alarm about the diseases a man might catch he cautions that, if the prostitute herself fails to rob the customer while he is distracted, she will have a hidden male confederate lying in wait to complete the task. Not only purses were at risk, temporarily discarded clothing and other possessions were also considered fair game. Launching into a misogynistic rant, Greene warns:

> What flatteries they use to bewitch, what sweet words to inveigle, what simple holiness to entrap, what amorous glances, what smirking œillades [provocative looks], what cringing courtesies, what stretching adieus, following a man like a bloodhound, with their eyes white, laying out of hair: what frouncing of tresses, what paintings, what ruffs, cuffs and braveries, and all to betray the eyes of the innocent novice: whom when they have drawn on to the bent of their bow, they strip like the prodigal child and turn out of doors like an outcast of the world.

In 1593, the parson's son Thomas Nashe makes a similar point in his *Christ's Tears Over Jerusalem*, in which he also complains about the rampant corruption on the part of those in authority who allowed the brothels to flourish. Nashe writes:

> London, what are thy suburbs but licensed stews? Can it be so many brothel-houses of salary sensuality and sixpenny whoredom, the next door to magistrate's, should be set up and maintained, if bribes did not bestir them? Whole hospitals of ten-times-a-day dishonest strumpets have we cloistered together. Night and day the entrance to them is as free as to a tavern. Apprentices and poor servants they encourage to rob their masters. Gentlemen's purses and pockets they will dive into and pick, even whiles they are dallying with them.

There were many pejorative names for the prostitutes besides 'Winchester geese' and 'Turnbull bees'. One of those was 'nuns' and a brothel was a 'nunnery'. Hamlet tells Ophelia to 'get thee to a nunnery' and the question has long taxed scholars as to whether he is implying that she is a whore and should enter a brothel. In *Henry IV, Part 2*, the revolting Pistol snarls at Doll Tearsheet: 'Know we not Galloway nags?' A Galloway nag was a small horse that was easily ridden and therefore, by implication, a readily available prostitute. Autolycus, the wandering pedlar in *The Winter's Tale*, refers to prostitutes as his 'aunts' when he trills:

The lark, that tirra-lyra chants, with heigh! With heigh! The thrush and the jay, are summer songs for me and my aunts, while we lie tumbling in the hay. (4.3)

For the women themselves, a harsh and usually all-too-short life was followed by an ignominious death. The Church, which had profited so handsomely while they lived to line the coffers of the Bishop of Winchester, would at the end refuse them a Christian burial in sanctified ground. Most were interred in the Single Women's Graveyard – the name itself is a euphemism for prostitutes – at the junction of Redcross Way and Union Street in Southwark. Within a century, the corner patch had become a paupers' cemetery known as the Cross Bones Graveyard. By 1853, the graveyard was so full it could accept no more bodies and the London authorities closed it as a health hazard.

The place was pretty much forgotten about until the early 1990s, when Transport for London began digging there to construct an electricity substation while extending the Underground's Jubilee Line. Archaeologists investigating the site excavated a hundred and forty-eight skeletons, each of which told its own heart-breaking tale. Six in every ten were either women or perinatal babies – aged from twenty-two weeks into pregnancy to seven days after birth. One of the skeletons is thought to have been that of a child prostitute. It has been estimated that at least fifteen thousand bodies were piled on top of each other in the unsanctified cemetery over the years.

Today, locals have taken the Cross Bones Graveyard to

their hearts. Thousands of visitors have made a pilgrimage to the site, festooning railings with poems, flowers, colourful ribbons, letters, strings of beads and other impromptu mementoes in touching tributes. A small plaque has been erected, which shows a goose about to take flight and bears an inscription that reads, in part: 'Here local people have created a memorial shrine. The Outcast Dead. RIP.' It is a gesture of humanity far kinder than anything the poor souls buried there could have expected during their lifetimes.

See also: Cut-purses and Cozeners

28. THE WORLD'S MINE OYSTER

*Will lives in an exciting age of exploration when fearless exploits
open up a new era in map making*

**He does obey every point of the letter that I dropped to
betray him. He does smile his face into more lines than is in
the new map with the augmentation of the Indies. You have
not seen such a thing as 'tis.**

(Twelfth Night, 3.2, 1601)

THE housemaid Maria has placed a letter where it was sure to
be found by haughty manservant Malvolio, in which she has
artfully mimicked the handwriting of their mistress, the Lady
Olivia. Maria returns gleefully to her fellow conspirators,
Sir Toby Belch and Fabian, to report that Malvolio has been
gulled into believing Olivia secretly loves him and wishes to
see him dressed in cross-gartered yellow stockings and continually smiling. Maria tells how she has just witnessed Malvolio practising the unaccustomed smiling. If he really had
creased 'his face into more lines than is in the new map with
the augmentation of the Indies' then it would be lined indeed.

In 1569, the Flemish cartographer known to posterity
as Gerardus Mercator cracked the problem of how to project
the globe on to a two-dimensional map of the world. His
answer, so simple yet ingenious that it is still widely in use
today, was to represent the globe as if it were an unrolled cy-
linder. Although it increasingly distorted the size of territor-
ies the further away they were from the Equator – Greenland,
for instance, appears larger than Australia on modern maps
whereas in reality Australia is more than three times as big
– the so-called Mercator Projection marked a crucial break-
through in cartography. Its configuration allowed navigators

to plot journeys between any two ports using a straight line, called a rhumb line (from the Spanish and Portuguese words meaning 'direction'), following a constant bearing.

An English geographer named Richard Hakluyt (pronounced 'hackle-wit') celebrated England's prowess in maritime exploration by publishing in 1589 an epic volume titled *The Principall Navigations, Voyages, Traffiques and Discoveries of the English Nation*. The book was so popular that a revised and greatly enlarged second edition appeared ten years later, in the foreword of which Hakluyt strongly advocated the colonisation of Virginia. It also featured an entirely new map compiled by a talented cartographer named Edward Wright, who was one of the first to adopt the Mercator Projection as a basis for his own work.

Wright's map was the most accurate representation yet of the known world. It included much recently discovered detail of the islands of both the East and West Indies (hence 'the augmentation of the Indies'), and was criss-crossed by a lattice of helpful rhumb lines. Among the eager readers of Hakluyt's much talked about book was one Will Shakespeare, because it is Wright's map (*pictured*) with its rhumb lines that Maria has in mind when she describes the smiling face of Malvolio.

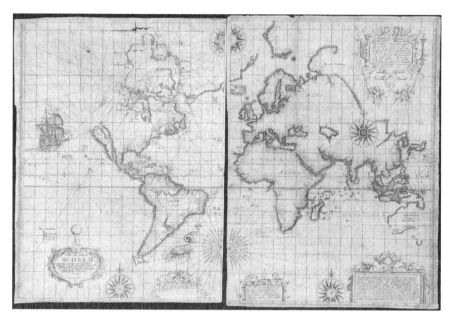

Although Shakespeare's geographical knowledge could at times be sketchy – Ben Jonson famously teased him for giving Bohemia a sea coast in *The Winter's Tale* – he never shied away from putting it to good use when it suited his purpose. He lived at a time when there was an explosion of interest in the world beyond Europe. To a large extent the oceans and what lay on their farthest shores remained a mystery. For a start, no one had the foggiest idea how deep the oceans were. Well might Rosalind say in Shakespeare's 1599 comedy *As You Like It*:

O coz, coz, coz, my pretty little coz, that thou didst know how many fathom deep I am in love! But it cannot be sounded. My affection hath an unknown bottom, like the Bay of Portugal. (4.1)

There is no Bay of Portugal, she means the Atlantic Ocean. Mariners traditionally sounded depths using a plumb line, a length of rope with a lead weight on the end (named from the Latin *plumbum* for lead). The unit of measurement was the fathom – one fathom was six feet (1.83m) – and when the lead weight touched the bottom the rope went slack. In the Atlantic, it seemed that however much the rope was lengthened it never reached the seabed. The ocean did indeed have 'an unknown bottom'.

Just as in space exploration today, an unquenched thirst for revelations about '*terra incognita*' and a sense that the human race stood on the verge of encountering hidden realms beyond the scope of current knowledge drove explorers onward. On 6 September 1522, fully four decades before Shakespeare was born, eighteen ragged survivors on one vessel, out of the two hundred and seventy men who had set off in five ships from Spain three years earlier, limped back into port having completed the first circumnavigation of the globe. Their Portuguese captain, Ferdinand Magellan, was not among them. He had been killed after being struck by a bamboo spear in a battle in the Philippines while attempting to convert the natives to Christianity.

On their journey, Magellan's ships had passed between the southern point of the mainland of South America and the archipelago known as Tierra del Fuego, through the strait that today bears his name. From there they sailed into what *As You Like It*'s Rosalind calls 'the South Sea of discovery,' which Magellan optimistically dubbed the 'peaceful' (or 'pacific') sea, now known as the Pacific Ocean. In 1580, Sir Francis Drake aboard the *Golden Hind* followed up with the first English circumnavigation. Eight years later, Sir Thomas Cavendish circled the globe again, and on his return jubilantly hosted Elizabeth I aboard his ship *Desire*, berthed in the Thames. Their beano celebrated both his success and England's defeat of the Spanish Armada that same year. It was a grand occasion.

* * *

Information about the Indies, both East and West, was of more than academic value. The centuries-old rivalry between the nations of Europe was nowhere being fought out more enthusiastically than on the high seas, in the competition to exploit newly discovered lands and native peoples. Pistol sums up the attitude of the times when he says in *The Merry Wives of Windsor*:

Why, then the world's mine oyster, which I with sword will open [to extract the pearl]. (2.2)

The Dutch were vying with the Portuguese and the English to control the valuable spice trade with the East Indies. Nutmeg and cloves from the so-called 'spice islands' were in particularly high demand in Europe, sought after both as condiments for food and for their medicinal properties (they were even thought to ward off the plague). The West Indies, meanwhile, largely controlled by the Spanish, yielded much-coveted tobacco and sugar cane. Elizabeth I herself was addicted to sugary treats, at the expense of her failing, blackened teeth. Both crops were grown on plantations that increasingly fuelled the burgeoning slave trade.

The shipping of captive natives across the Atlantic from West Africa into a life of misery was rapidly turning into a highly lucrative business. The Caribbean also offered rich pickings from Spanish and Portuguese ships returning laden with treasure from South America, which proved irresistible targets for English buccaneers like Sir Francis Drake. In 1585, Drake set off from Plymouth for the Caribbean with twenty-one ships, with the sole aim of spending several months plundering Spanish settlements and creating as much mayhem for Elizabeth's Spanish and Portuguese enemies as possible.

Ten years after Drake's West Indian escapade, Sir Walter Raleigh turned his sights towards finding the fabled gold of the lost South American city of El Dorado and the legendary women warriors known as Amazons. He led an expedition out of Plymouth, which captured a Spanish settlement on the island of Trinidad and turned it into a base for his operations.

Raleigh went on to navigate a series of inlets and rivers on the coast of Guiana (now the Venezuelan region of Guyana), despite being shadowed by the Spanish fleet.

Taking to small boats on the Orinoco and its tributaries, he succeeded in penetrating up to four hundred miles (640km) inland. According to one scathing contemporary, he 'conquered no lands, found no stores of wealth, and discovered little not observed by earlier adventurers'. Raleigh, however, was not a man to let such quibbles stand in the way of his declaring success, particularly as he was keen to get back into the Queen's favour after infuriating her some years earlier by secretly marrying one of her ladies-in-waiting without royal permission.

On his return to England he published an account of his feats, immodestly titled *The Discovery of the Large, Rich, and Beautiful Empire of Guiana, with a relation of the great and golden city of Manoa (which the Spaniards call El Dorado)*. The book was a shameless exercise in public relations in which Raleigh asserts:

> *The empire of Guiana is directly east from Peru towards the sea ... The country hath more quantity of gold, by manifold, than the best parts of the Indies or Peru ... and as many or more great cities than ever Peru had when it flourished most. I have been assured by such of the Spaniards as have seen Manoa, the imperial city of Guiana, which the Spanish call El Dorado, that for the greatness, for the riches, and for the excellent seat [position], it far exceedeth any of the world.*

As for the Amazons, he did not actually meet any of the formidable ladies but gave a lurid account of their reputed activities. Raleigh wasn't quite done with the hyperbole yet. Urging the colonisation of Guiana, he goes on to flatter the Queen with:

> *All the most of the kings of the borders are already become*

her Majesty's vassals, and seem to desire nothing more than her Majesty's protection and the return of the English nation.

Raleigh's sensational exaggerations find an echo in *The Merry Wives of Windsor*, written within two years of the adventurer's return, in which that inveterate reprobate Sir John Falstaff tries to cheat the wives of Master Ford and Master Page out of their life savings by affecting to love them. After pointedly describing Mistress Ford as 'a region in Guiana, all gold and bounty,' Falstaff says of the women he is targeting:

I will be cheater [a play on the words for 'escheator', an official involved in confiscating estates due to the Crown, and 'swindler'] **to them both, and they shall be exchequers to me. They shall be my East and West Indies, and I will trade to them both.** (1.3)

Around the same time as Hakluyt flourished, a precision craftsman named Emery Molyneux was producing England's first ever terrestrial and celestial globes. Two of his masterpieces were presented to Elizabeth I, after which he went on to construct others for sale to the gentry. Only six are believed to still exist, two of those being on view in the Middle Temple in London's Inns of Court. Another is in Petworth House, a National Trust property in West Sussex. Commonplace as globes may seem today, to the Elizabethans they were a revelation. Suddenly the earth and the night sky could be reproduced in perfect miniature.

Molyneux's globes began appearing in 1592, and in all likelihood they inspired one of the most gloriously funny interludes in Shakespeare's knockabout farce *The Comedy of Errors*, which has been variously dated between 1592 and 1594. In the exchange, the servant Dromio of Syracuse reports to his master Antipholus that a fat and 'greasy' kitchen wench he has never previously met shockingly claims he is her husband. We, the audience, know it is all a case of mistaken identity (she is actually married to Dromio's twin brother), but between them Dromio and Antipholus crank up the laughs with an unflattering exchange about the unfortunate woman.

Antipholus: **Then she bears some breadth?**

Dromio: **No longer from head to foot than from hip to hip** [her hips are as wide as she is tall]. **She is spherical, like a globe. I could find out countries in her.**

Antipholus: **In what part of her body stands Ireland?**

Dromio: **Marry, in her buttocks. I found it out by the bogs** [a swamp and also a crude term for the toilet].

Antipholus: **Where Scotland?**

Dromio: **I found it by the barrenness, hard in the palm of the hand** [which was covered in callouses].

Antipholus: **Where France?**

Dromio: **In her forehead; armed and reverted, making war against her heir.** [Shakespeare's wordplay on 'hair', as in she is going bald, and 'heir' contains an allusion to the Protestant Henry of Navarre, who had succeeded as Henry IV of France in 1589 only to find his claim rejected by his Catholic subjects, which led to a short civil war.]

Antipholus: **Where England?**

Dromio: **I looked for the chalky cliffs** [her teeth], **but I could find no whiteness in them; but I guess it stood in her chin, by the salt rheum that ran between France and it** [her chin was separated from her forehead by beads of sweat].

Antipholus: **Where Spain?**

Dromio: **Faith, I saw it not, but I felt it hot in her breath** [Spain was a country not seen though full of failed curses, as in the Great Armada of 1588].

Antipholus: **Where America, the Indies?**

Dromio: **Oh, sir, upon her nose all o'er embellished with**

> **rubies, carbuncles, sapphires** [covered in red welts and pimples], **declining their rich aspect to the hot breath of Spain, who sent whole armadoes of caracks** [fleets of treasure ships] **to be ballast at her nose.**
>
> *Antipholus:* **Where stood Belgia, the Netherlands?**
>
> *Dromio:* **Oh, sir, I did not look so low.** (3.2)

* * *

While riches clearly lay east, west and south, other adventurers were pressing north. Sir Martin Frobisher led three expeditions to Labrador and Baffin Island vainly seeking a North-West Passage that would link the Atlantic to the Pacific. The Dutch, meanwhile, were pushing back the polar frontiers around the large islands of Spitsbergen and Novaya Zemlya, the outline of which would also appear on Edward Wright's newly augmented world map.

Between 1594 and 1597, the Dutch navigator Willem Barents (*pictured*), hoping to find a North-East Passage to Asia around the northern coast of Russia, undertook the most determined attempts yet to explore the Arctic. On their third expedition to the frozen wastes, Barents and his crew became stranded by ice floes and were forced to endure a bitterly cold winter. They built a hut from lumber, which they carried from their ship, surviving on what rations they had with them and by hunting Arctic foxes and polar bears.

The seventeen men ended up being marooned for ten months and it was not until late the following summer that twelve survivors were rescued by another Dutch ship off Russia's Kola Peninsula. Barents himself died at sea on 20 June 1597, although in time the Barents Sea would be named in his honour. Ship's carpenter Gerrit de Veer, who sailed on Barents' second and third voyages, kept a diary of their experiences which became an instant success when it was published

in Amsterdam in 1598. The English too were captivated by reports of their polar adventures. Barents' crew had become the first known Europeans to spend a winter in the Arctic and Shakespeare could not resist an allusion as he was writing *Twelfth Night* in 1601. Cautioning the foppish Sir Andrew Aguecheek that his beloved lady Olivia is growing increasingly chilly towards him, the servant Fabian roundly warns:

> **You are now sailed into the north of my lady's opinion, where you will hang like an icicle on a Dutchman's beard, unless you do redeem it by some laudable attempt either of valour or policy.** (3.2)

The bearded Dutchman in question was, of course, Barents.

* * *

Five years after *Twelfth Night* made its debut, Shakespeare might have been found thumbing through his copy of Hakluyt again, as he composed lines for the First Witch in his Scottish thriller *Macbeth*:

> **A sailor's wife had chestnuts in her lap, and munch'd, and munch'd, and munch'd. 'Give me,' quoth I. 'Aroint thee** [begone], **witch!' the rump-fed** [big-bottomed] **ronyon** [scabby creature] **cries. Her husband's to Aleppo gone, master o' the Tiger. But in a sieve I'll thither sail and, like a rat without a tail, I'll do, I'll do, and I'll do. I will drain him dry as hay. Sleep shall neither night nor day hang**

upon his pent-house lid [eyelid], **he shall live a man forbid** [of sleep]. **Weary se'nnights** [seven nights or one week] **nine times nine shall he dwindle, peak and pine. Though his bark** [ship] **cannot be lost, yet it shall be tempest-tost.** (1.3)

Furious at being refused a feast of chestnuts by a sailor's wife, the witch vows revenge by planning to disguise herself as a rat in order to torment the woman's husband while he is at sea. (Witches were believed to have the ability to assume the shape of any animal they wished, but they would be tail-less since no part of a woman's anatomy corresponded to a tail.) The sailor is said to be the captain of the *Tiger*.

An account in Hakluyt's book of an epic adventure undertaken by a group of English merchants had turned a ship of that name into something of a legend. The story began when a 'gentleman merchant' of London named Ralph Fitch set sail aboard the *Tiger* on 15 February 1583 in the company of other traders, bound for the port of 'Tripolis' in Syria (now the Lebanese city of Tripoli) and thence overland to Aleppo. Among those travelling with him was a trader named John Newberry, who had been commissioned by Hakluyt to seek out a copy of a cosmography – a textbook of astronomical knowledge – written by a fourteenth-century Arab geographer known as Abulfeda Ismael.

A letter Newberry wrote to Hakluyt from Aleppo survives, in which he reports that he had not found anyone in either Tripoli or Aleppo who had heard of Abulfeda's *opus*, but that he would continue the search. He adds: 'Some say that it may possibly be had in Persia; but I shall not fail to make inquiry for it both in Babylon and Balsara [Baghdad and Basra], and if I can find it in either of these places, shall send it you from thence.' (Abulfeda, incidentally, has a crater on the Moon named after him.)

Aleppo, the western terminus of the Silk Road, was the

most important commercial centre in the Levant, a base for merchants from all over Europe who traded in the goods and spices that came from the most distant parts of Asia. Tripoli was the port that served Aleppo, along a route regularly traversed by long caravans of camels. A few weeks after their arrival in Aleppo, Fitch's party travelled on by camel to Bir on the Euphrates, where they purchased a large river boat and sailed it to Fallujah. From there they crossed a great plain – by night because of the heat – reaching Baghdad then Basra on the Tigris.

Onward they went to the Persian Gulf, until Fitch and three of his companions were arrested and thrown into jail by the governor of the Portuguese colony of Ormuz. They managed to regain their freedom and, after a chapter of further misadventures, Fitch ended up in Burma by way of India. He finally arrived home on 29 April 1591, eight years after leaving England, to discover that in his absence he had been pronounced dead and his will had been proved. Once back in London, he supplied a gripping account of his experiences to Hakluyt, who eagerly included it in his book. Newberry, having gone his own way, disappeared somewhere in the Punjab after leaving Lahore in September 1585, and is thought to have been robbed and murdered.

The *Tiger*, or another ship with the same name, turns up again in history on 27 June 1606 when she dropped anchor in Milford Haven, Wales, after another remarkable expedition. The vessel had set off from Cowes, on the Isle of Wight, in December 1604 under Sir Edward Michelborne, a 'gentleman adventurer,' her mission being 'to discover the countries of China and Japan and to trade with their people'. By August 1605, she was prowling the waters around Java and Sumatra, engaging in the shameless piracy of native craft.

Michelborne got more than he had bargained for, however, when he encountered a mysterious ship crewed by around ninety Japanese pirates, who had been happily pillaging their own way along the coasts of China and Cambodia. After the two vessels cautiously approached one other, the crews first parleyed then fraternised, and Michelborne agreed to a Japanese request to board the *Tiger* and inspect her. The strangers displayed an almost childlike curiosity in the English vessel until suddenly the mood changed.

They produced swords and knives and began ferociously attacking their hosts in an attempt to take control of the ship. What followed was a desperate struggle for life, in which the Englishmen were finally victorious, although not without considerable cost. Among the casualties was John Davis, a brilliant navigator and Michelborne's most valued lieutenant, who bled to death after being hacked to pieces by his assailants.

When the *Tiger* finally arrived in London she had been away for five hundred and sixty-seven days, or eighty-one weeks, which is 'nine times nine' seven-nights, exactly as 'predicted' by the witch in *Macbeth*. In Shakespeare's time a week was commonly known as 'a seven night,' just as two weeks were – and still are – referred to as a 'fortnight' (a shortened version of 'fourteen nights'). The ship's return became the talk of the taverns and Shakespeare appears to have conflated the story of the first sailing ('Her husband's to Aleppo gone, master o' the *Tiger*') with that of the second ('Weary se'nnights nine times nine shall he dwindle, peak and pine') for his own dramatic purposes.

As the century turned, and Elizabeth's reign gave way to that of James I in 1603, the lure of profits to be made from colonisation really began to take hold. Jamestown in Virginia (named after the new king) offered the most celebrated example, where conquest and long-term settlement could be exploited for England's prosperity. It was a model to be emulated. When Shakespeare and his collaborator John Fletcher penned *All Is True* in 1612, the play known to us as *Henry VIII*, they had none other than James in mind when Archbishop

Cranmer says:

> **Wherever the bright sun of heaven shall shine, his honour and the greatness of his name shall be, and make new nations. He shall flourish and, like a mountain cedar, reach his branches to all the plains about him. Our children's children shall see this, and bless heaven.** (5.5)

Those flattering though prescient lines presaged an empire which, for better or worse, reached its zenith three hundred years later by becoming so extensive that the sun was said to never set upon some part of it. Colonisation had come to stay.

See also: 29. The Bear Necessities
37. Something Wicked Comes
40. The Island of Devils

29. THE BEAR NECESSITIES

Theatre's most celebrated stage direction may originally have had a distinctly different significance

Exit, pursued by a bear.

(The Winter's Tale, 3.3, 1609-11)

IT IS the most jaw-dropping stage direction in the entire Shakespearean canon – and one of the most discussed. Shakespeare needed to kill off his character Antigonus, who has just abandoned the baby Perdita on the coast of Bohemia, and death by bear is undoubtedly an impressive way to do it. But where did he get the idea from and how was it staged? Was a real bear borrowed from a neighbouring bear-baiting pit in Southwark and hauled into the Globe? Did the actors just happen to have a bear costume hanging around that Shakespeare couldn't resist finding a use for? If it is any guide, Philip Henslowe, impresario at the rival Rose theatre, actually lists 'one bear's skin' in his inventory of 'all the properties for my Lord Admiral's Men', dated 10 March 1598.

To be sure, there were plenty of bears available in London in Shakespeare's day. Bear-baiting was not just a popular spectator sport among the hoi polloi, it had long been a favourite recreation of Elizabeth I herself. Together with bull-baiting, it was known as the 'Royal Game'. The Paris Garden, not far from the Globe itself, hosted the biggest bear-baiting spectacles, during which the poor creatures were tormented by mastiff dogs or beaten by men with whips, to whoops of delight from the excited crowd. The German lawyer Paul Henztner gives an account of the savage spectacle in his *Travels in England*, noting that the whipping of a blinded bear ...

Is performed by five or six men standing circularly with

whips, which they exercise upon him without any mercy,
and he cannot escape because of his chain. He defends him-
self with all his force and skill, throwing down all that come
within his reach, and are not active enough to get out of it,
and tearing the whips out of their hands and breaking them.

With his dreams crumbling around him, the besieged Macbeth likens his own plight to that of the stricken creature:

They have tied me to a stake. I cannot fly but, bear-like, I must fight the course. (*Macbeth*, 5.7)

Those bears which became veterans of many bouts were considered celebrities in their own right. The best known were given names, such as Tom of Lincoln, Ned of Canterbury, Don Juan, George Stone, Ned Whiting, and the old blind bear Harry Hunks. Most famous of all was the irascible Sackerson. When the ineffectual young man Slender seeks to impress Miss Anne Page with his prowess in *The Merry Wives of Windsor,* he boasts:

I have seen Sackerson loose twenty times, and have taken him by the chain. (1.1)

Only the Puritans raised any objections to the popular pastime not, sadly, out of concern for the animals' well-being, but simply because they held a profound distaste for anyone enjoying themselves in whatever way, particularly when some events took place on a Sunday.

Intriguingly, *The Winter's Tale* was not the only play performed around 1611 which featured a character being chased by a bear. An older romantic comedy titled *Mucedorus*, first staged in the 1590s, had been revived by the King's Men at the Globe in 1610. In *Mucedorus*, a clown named Mouse is frightened by a bear or, as Mouse puts it, 'some devil in a bear's doublet,' and in his comical attempt to escape, trips backwards over the creature's leg. In a later scene, a character named Segasto and his sweetheart Amadine, beautiful daughter of the

King of Aragon, run across the stage because they are – and here is the actual stage direction – 'being pursued with a bear'. Segasto flees but Amadine is rescued by the title character Mucedorus, Prince of Valencia, who later re-enters wielding a sword in one hand and the bear's head in the other (a prop, surely). The animal in *Mucedorus* was no ordinary bear, however. It was a never-before-seen white bear. We know that because one scene features this exchange:

> Mouse: *I saw her white head and her white belly.*
>
> Segasto: *Thou talkest of wonders to tell me of white bears; but, sirrah, didst thou ever see any such?*
>
> Mouse: *No, faith, I never saw any such; but I remember my father's words. He bad* [bade] *me take heed I was not caught with* [by] *a white bear.*

Mucedorus proved so popular that it appeared in print in no fewer than sixteen quarto editions over the years. Indeed, it is thought to have been the most performed and reprinted comedy in Early Modern English theatre. But did it have any direct connection with Shakespeare? Today, scholars as eminent as Jonathan Bate have become convinced Will had a hand either in writing or revising it. The play's revival in 1610 at the Globe included several new scenes. 'At least one of those scenes is, we think, linguistically full of his fingerprints,' Professor Bate told the *Guardian*.

But back to the bear. On New Year's Day 1611, Henry, Prince of Wales, son and heir of James I, bagged for himself the lead role in a festive extravaganza called *Oberon, the Faery Prince*, which was presented in the Banqueting Hall of Whitehall Palace before the king. Written by Ben Jonson and produced by the flamboyant Inigo Jones using all the most spectacular special effects he could devise, the show opened with the young prince riding on to the stage in a chariot drawn by two white bears.

Polar bears had a reputation for being particularly ferocious, which could only have added to the dramatic effect if they appeared in both *Mucedorus* and *Oberon, the Faery Prince*. The creatures had been discovered by Europeans as recently as 9 July, 1594, when the Dutchman Willem Barents encountered one for the first time while exploring the Arctic. The animal tried to clamber aboard one of his ships' rowing-boats, was shot with a musket and injured. An attempt to capture it and take it back to Holland failed when the bear escaped and rampaged, at which point it was killed. Only its pelt was brought home. An encounter with another polar bear the following year, on Barents' second Arctic voyage, ended even more disastrously when one of the animals pounced on a small landing party and savaged two sailors to death.

It is likely Shakespeare had read of this horror and seen a plate depicting the grisly scene in *The Three Voyages of William Barents to the Arctic Regions*, a book by Gerrit de Veer, a ship's officer who had sailed with Barents. The first English translation was published in 1609. De Veer's drawing (*pictured*) shows a polar bear sinking its teeth into a man's shoulder as he lies face down on the ground, exactly how a country yokel (whom Shakespeare casts as 'Clown') relates what he saw in *The Winter's Tale:*

And then ... to see how the bear tore out his shoulder-bone; how he cried to me for help and said his name was Antigonus, a nobleman ... and how the poor gentleman roared and the bear mocked him. (3.3)

A further encounter between Europeans and polar bears, which happened on 30 May 1609, may have had a direct bearing on the production of *Mucedorus* in 1610, as well as *Oberon, the Faery Prince* and *The Winter's Tale*, both in 1611. The English sealer Jonas Poole was exploring off Cherry Island, south of Greenland, when in his own words:

We slue 26 Seales, and espied three white Bears; wee went aboord for Shot and Powder, and coming to the Ice againe, we found a shee-Beare and two young ones. Master Thomas Welden shot and killed her; after shee was slayne, wee got the young ones, and brought them home into England, where they are alive in Paris Garden.

When Poole returned from his Arctic voyage in August 1609, he proudly presented the two captured polar bear cubs to James I. All the bears in London up to that point were brown European and Russian bears, so the appearance of the first white bears in captivity caused a sensation. The king in turn entrusted the animals to Philip Henslowe, who ran the Paris Garden as part of his bear-baiting empire, and granted him a royal warrant to look after them. They were kept caged, too precious to be used for bear-baiting. It would fit what we know of the entrepreneurial Henslowe's *modus operandi* if he then hit on the money-making idea of renting the animals out wherever they could be guaranteed to set gaping onlookers agog. Many people would happily pay good money to see such a sight. As Segasto in *Mucedorus* put it: 'Thou talkest of wonders to tell me of white bears; but, sirrah, didst thou ever see any such?'

Would two frightened bear cubs, sweltering in the unaccustomed heat so far from their Arctic home, be trusted to appear safely on stage and among crowds, even when restrained on a chain? The evidence certainly suggests they were present at the palace production of *Oberon, the Faery Prince* – they had been a gift to James I, after all – and quite likely in *Mucedorus* too. Raised by hand and still sexually immature, the young animals could have been docile enough to be considered effectively tame. Perhaps the Clown in *The Winter's Tale* gives us a clue in these lines:

I'll go see if the bear be gone from the gentleman and how much he hath eaten. They are never curst [bad tempered] **but when they are hungry.** (3.3)

Scholars suggest that such knowledge of bears' nature could have been possessed only by someone familiar with their behaviour in captivity. So perhaps that notorious stage direction, which still gives theatre directors a headache four hundred years later, should actually read: 'Exit pursued by a *polar* bear'.

See also: 28. The World's Mine Oyster

30. WEBS OF INTRIGUE

A reference to cobwebs shines a light on their vital role in the Eliza-bethans' treatment of wounds

I shall desire you of more acquaintance, good Master Cob-web. If I cut my finger, I shall make bold with you.
(A Midsummer Night's Dream, 3.1, 1595)

BOTTOM the weaver, encumbered with an ass's head foisted upon him by mischievous Puck, is astonished to be invited into the enchanted woodland bower of the beautiful fairy queen Titania. As he enters, he is greeted by her elfin attend-ants, Peasebottom, Moth, Mustardseed and Cobweb. 'If I cut my finger, I shall make bold with you,' he tells Master Cob-web. His comment is an allusion to the everyday Elizabethan practice of wrapping spider silk around an open wound, in the same way we might use a Band-aid or strip of gauze today. The useful medical properties of spider webs had been appreci-ated at least since the time of the ancient Greeks. Roman sol-diers injured in battle would wind spider web around limbs to protect cuts, or stuff a bundle of spider silk into wounds if they had sustained more serious injuries.

Spiders spin their silk through glands called spinnerets. Three spinnerets is the norm, although some spiders have four. The silk is initially excreted as a liquid but quickly hardens as it is drawn out of the gland. Spider silk possesses powerful adhesive qualities, so Bottom would have no diffi-culty getting one to stick around his finger. It is a remarkable material, having immense tensile strength – a strand of spider silk is stronger even than a strand of steel of the same gauge – as well as a high degree of elasticity. Significantly, the proteins from which the silk is made are rich in vitamin K, the so-called 'healing vitamin' essential for blood clotting. When applied to a wound, the silk may also act as a scaffold that stimulates the body's production of fibrin and platelet binding, speeding up the healing process. As long as they are clean, cobwebs are mildly antiseptic and biologically neutral, which means they will not irritate or be rejected by the body.

Today research is going on into the potential of utilising spider web material (dubbed 'webcillin') in medicine, including as a component of bandages and a basis for antibacterial ointment. Students at Gadjah Mada University in Indonesia have developed a compound they call Spidweb Gel for applying to damaged gums after dental extractions. Researchers at Tufts University in Massachusetts have used spider webs as scaffolds for regenerating damaged ligaments, particularly in knee injuries. Other scientists are experimenting with spider silk to make exceptionally fine sutures for stitches after surgery and for use in eye injuries. From all this we can conclude that Bottom was not the fool he appears to be.

It was not just cobwebs but the spiders themselves that were credited with healing properties in folklore. Gabrielle Hatfield, in her *Encyclopedia of Folk Medicine* (2004), records an old custom in West Sussex that a living spider rolled up in its own web should be gulped down as a pill to cure jaundice. In Ireland, there was a belief that swallowing a large living spider enveloped in treacle would cure ague (malaria). In Suffolk, the spider should be eaten alive inside a piece of apple to have the same effect. Henry Longfellow set his poem *Evangeline* in a village where tradition held that 'fever was cured by a spider shut up in a nutshell'. The spider web itself was said to possess narcotic properties, efficacious when eaten to treat certain fevers.

Folklore is riddled with many other superstitions about the creatures: if a spider lowers itself toward you at night, it is unlucky, if it does the same thing in the daytime, that means good luck is on the way; to brush a spider off someone playing a game of chance means they will lose; ominously, if a spider spins a thread and hangs on it in front of a door and is not killed, someone in the house will die before the year is out; spiders can show you where gold is hidden; spiders can be used to predict the weather; and on, and on. Spiders have long struggled to get over their image as creepy-crawlies, which can spark horror and even fear in some people. Despite Bottom's wish for more acquaintance with Master Cobweb, when Titania's fairy train sing her a lullaby, they are careful to warn the arachnids off:

> **Never harm, / Nor spell nor charm, / Come our lovely lady nigh; / So, good night, with lullaby. / Weaving spiders, come not here; / Hence, you long-legg'd spinners, hence! / Beetles black, approach not near; / Worm nor snail, do no offence.** (2.2)

Gossamer, those silvery threads seen stretching from bush to bush or floating through the summer air on a fine day, is mentioned in two of Shakespeare's plays. In *Romeo and Juliet* the priest Friar Laurence observes:

> **A lover may bestride the gossamer that idles in the wanton summer air, and yet not fall.** (2.6)

While in *King Lear*, when Edgar is trying to convince his blind father Gloucester that he has plunged from the top of a cliff at Dover, he says:

> **Hadst thou been aught but gossamer, feathers, air, so many fathom down precipitating** [falling], **thou'dst shiver'd** [you would have broken] **like an egg.** (4.6)

For all that, no one at the time seems to have connected gossamer with arachnids. We now know, of course, that the strands are spun by tiny spiders, but a different theory about their origin long prevailed. In *The Faerie Queene*, first published in 1590, Edmund Spenser calls gossamer 'the fine nets which oft we woven see of scorched dew'. As late as 1730, the Scottish poet James Thomson refers to gossamer as 'the filmy threads of dew' in his *Autumn*.

Spiders and their webs crop up throughout Shakespeare's works. In *Richard II*, the king refers to a long-standing belief that spiders and toads are highly venomous. As he sets foot again on the shores of his kingdom after crossing from Ireland to confront the rebellious Bolingbroke, Richard salutes the 'dear earth' on which he stands, urging:

Feed not thy sovereign's foe, my gentle earth, nor with thy sweets comfort his ravenous sense, but let thy spiders that suck up thy venom, and heavy-gaited toads, lie in their way, doing annoyance to the treacherous feet which with usurping steps do trample thee. (3.4)

Richard Plantagenet, Duke of Gloucester, on the other hand, compares his own feverish plotting to the spider's frantic spinning in *Henry VI, Part 2:*

My brain more busy than the labouring spider weaves tedious [elaborate] **snares to trap mine enemies.** (3.1)

In *King John*, Philip the Bastard interrogates Arthur's captor, Hubert de Burgh, over whether he has murdered the young prince, rival to John's throne. Hubert's hand in such a crime would be so heinous, Philip thunders, that:

If thou didst but consent to this most cruel act, do but despair. And if thou want'st a cord, the smallest thread that ever spider twisted from her womb will serve to strangle thee. (4.3)

In altogether lighter mood, when Bassanio, love-struck wooer of the fair Portia in *The Merchant of Venice*, opens a casket to discover a tiny portrait of his beloved, he rapturously declares:

Here in her hairs the painter plays the spider and hath

woven a golden mesh to entrap the hearts of men, faster than gnats in cobwebs. (3.2)

In *Richard III*, the deposed Queen Margaret rails against the current queen, Elizabeth Woodville, warning her not to trust Richard. It is the ugly shape of spiders and toads that she conjures up in a comparison to the misshapen villain:

Poor painted queen, vain flourish of my fortune! Why strew'st thou sugar [scatter sweet words] on that bottled spider [Richard], whose deadly web ensnareth thee about? Fool, fool! Thou whet'st [sharpen] a knife to kill thyself. The time will come when thou shalt wish for me to help thee curse that poisonous bunch-back'd toad. (1.3)

By 'bottled' she is probably referring to Richard's hunched shoulders resulting from the scoliosis that gave him a curved spine, although the eighteenth-century antiquarian Joseph Ritson thought the insult meant 'a large, bloated, glossy spider, supposed to contain venom proportionate to its size'.

In *The Winter's Tale*, the insanely jealous King Leontes, who mistakenly believes his wife Hermione and friend Polixenes have been cheating on him under his very nose, gives us Shakespeare's most nightmarish vision of an arachnid:

There may be in the cup a spider steep'd [soaking], and one may drink, depart, and yet partake no venom, for his knowledge is not infected. But if one present the abhorr'd ingredient to his eye, make known how he hath drunk, he cracks his gorge [vomits], his sides, with violent hefts. I have drunk, and seen the spider. (2.1)

Leontes is alluding to a belief prevalent in Shakespeare's time that a spider lurking in drink or food would poison whoever consumed it, but only if the person realised the creature was there. Other writers mention the superstition, including Thomas Middleton, whose play *No Wit Like a Woman's* includes the line: 'Even when my lip touch'd the contracting cup [of marriage], even there to see a spider?' Leontes is tormenting himself with the bitter thought that, if he did not know about Hermione's supposed adultery, he could continue living in happy ignorance. But since, as he believes, he has discovered that he is a cuckold, the detested knowledge is poisoning him. He has 'drunk, and seen the spider'. It is a striking example of Shakespeare's genius with metaphor.

31. KEEP THE HOME FIRES BURNING

A social revolution is under way as householders switch to burning coal instead of wood for heat

Thou didst swear to me upon a parcel-gilt [partly gilded] **goblet, sitting in my Dolphin chamber** [inn rooms often had names], **at the round table, by a sea-coal fire ... to marry me and make me**
my lady thy wife. Canst thou deny it?
(Henry IV, Part 2, 2.1, 1597-98)

THE much put-upon inn landlady Mistress Quickly has had Sir John Falstaff arrested for breaking his many promises to pay for her generous hospitality. She complains to the Chief Justice that the old rogue has eaten her 'out of house and home' and put 'all my substance into that fat belly of his'. Then she reminds Falstaff that he even swore to marry her and make her a 'lady'. Recalling the occasion on which he proposed, one detail in her account – the 'sea-coal fire' – shines a light on an environmental issue gripping Shakespeare's England as the sixteenth century drew to a close. If you thought energy crises were a product only of our own age, think again.

Sea coal, so called because it was transported to London by barges plying down the east coast from Scotland and New-castle-on-Tyne, was rapidly replacing wood in the hearths of the capital's homes. England's ancient forests had been plundered for hundreds of years. Besides winter firewood, their timber was in demand for house building and, particularly since the time of Henry VIII, the construction of large numbers of ships, both military and commercial. Trees had also been felled to clear land for increased agricultural use and, with the boom in wool prices, grazing sheep. Pressure on space and resources was intensifying, with the population of England and Wales doubling from around two million to four million in the century between 1500 and 1600. London, ever devouring the surrounding countryside, had gone from having around fifty thousand people to two hundred thousand in the same time.

In Scotland too, the most populous areas around the Firth of Forth had been largely stripped of their forests. By Shakespeare's day Birnam Wood, which famously comes to Dunsinane in *Macbeth*, would have been much diminished from the area it covered when the real Macbeth lived in the eleventh century. Today all that is left of the original forest is the five-hundred year old Birnam Oak, its ageing lower limbs supported by props, which stands amid a narrow strip of woodland on the south bank of the River Tay. The oak must have been a young tree at the time Shakespeare was born, almost four hundred miles (644km) to the south in Stratford-upon-Avon. Local legend has it that the playwright set eyes on Birnam Wood in 1589 as a member of a troupe of strolling players who were invited to Scotland by James VI (later James I of England). Deforestation was so intense during the reign of James that one wag observed tartly if Judas were to repent in Scotland he would be hard put to find a tree from which to hang himself.

In the two decades before 1600 the price of timber doubled. In contrast coal, mined cheaply near the surface, or gathered from the Durham and Northumberland coast where seams were exposed by the sea, was becoming increasingly available. Few had bothered digging and collecting coal while timber was so readily available for keeping the home fires burning, let alone shipping it all the way to the big population centres in the south of England. Now it provided a reliable source of heat for the citizens of London. Mistress Quickly was clearly fond of the stuff because she mentions it again, in *The Merry Wives of Windsor*:

Go, and we'll have a posset [spiced hot drink] **for't soon at night, in faith, at the latter end of a sea-coal fire.** (1.4)

The business of trading in coal boomed to the extent that in 1599 the government, realising it was missing out on a valuable source of revenue – surprise, surprise – slapped a tax on shipments. The switch to burning coal, however, inevitably brought problems in the form of increased air pollution. The coal had a high sulphur content and gave off copious volumes of sulphur dioxide fumes and soot particles when burned. Swirling acrid smoke stung the lungs and mingled with the stench of human dunghills, muck from horses and other animals, rotting off-cuts from butchers' shops, foul-smelling tanneries and coal-burning lime kilns, rendering the city air increasingly unpleasant to breathe. Struggling growers lamented coal smoke's deleterious effect on their vegetables. Drifting soot particles began to stain skin, clothes and buildings. In *Much Ado About Nothing* a member of the Watch is called George Seacole, a name Shakespeare surely chose to indicate a grubby and unwashed wanderer of the streets.

Many people realised the smoke was harming their health. Even by 1578, the Queen refused at certain times to travel into London from the palace of Nonsuch in the Surrey countryside, or green and pleasant Windsor, because she was 'grieved and annoyed with the taste and smell of sea coals' in the city. Brewers operating near her Palace of Westminster were required to burn wood and not coal on pain of being fined. As long ago as 1272, Edward I had forbidden the burning of coal in London because of the pollution it caused, but his proclamation had long since faded from public memory. For most Londoners, the necessity to keep warm in England's cold, damp winters as cheaply and efficiently as possible overrode environmental considerations.

Increasingly the brick-built fireplace was becoming a

focal point of the Tudor house, in bedrooms as well as living rooms, the word 'hearth' itself deriving from 'heart' in acknowledgement of its importance in the home. In *Cymbeline*, Iachimo hones in on the fireplace when describing Imogen's bed chamber, and in doing so reveals the elaboration that was going into design:

> **The chimney is south** [on the south side of] **the chamber, and the chimney-piece** [decorative carving or sculpture above the fireplace] **Chaste Dian bathing.** (2.4)

He goes on:

> **The roof o' the chamber with golden cherubins is fretted. Her andirons** [fire-dogs or iron supports in the fireplace] **– I had forgot them – were two winking Cupids of silver, each on one foot standing, nicely depending** [supported] **on their brands** [ornamental replicas of flaming torches].

Iron smoke hoods began to adorn hearths, the better to clear fumes from inside the room, while the need to disperse the sooty coal smoke into the winds that blew over the rooftops gave rise to another significant development in domestic architecture. Chimney stacks started appearing where there had never before been any. Wood smoke had traditionally emerged simply through a hole in the roof from the houses of all but the very wealthy.

The newly fashionable chimneys grew taller and ever more elaborate, evolving into what we now consider a quintessential feature of Tudor architecture. As bricks became cheaper, ornamental chimneys evolved into an aspiration of the rising middle classes in towns and villages, rather than the exclusive preserve of those who dwelled in palaces and manor houses. Shakespeare alludes to this fashion for building chimneys in *Henry IV, Part 1*. We learn from an early morning exchange between two carriers loading up their horses that an additional chimney has just been added to an inn in Rochester.

Telling the time by the movement of a constellation across the night sky, the First Carrier says:

Heigh-ho! An [if] **it be not four by the day, I'll be hanged. Charles' Wain** [Charles's Wagon, an old name for the Plough in Ursa Major] **is over the new chimney, and yet our horse not packed.** (1.2)

The existence of chimneys also gives us one of Shakespeare's rather charming anachronisms. In *Julius Caesar*, a tribune named Marullus orders a group of plebeians who are waiting to cheer on Caesar to disperse. He chides them for their disloyalty to Caesar's great rival Pompey, saying:

**Knew you not Pompey? Many a time and oft have you climb'd up to walls and battlements, to towers and windows, yea, to chimney-tops, your infants in your arms, and there have sat
the livelong day, with patient expectation, to see great Pompey pass the streets of Rome.** (1.1)

There were, of course, no chimney tops up which to climb in ancient Rome. William Harrison, Canon of Windsor, expressed his own appreciation of the innovation when he contributed a section titled *Descriptions of Britain and England* to the 1577 edition of *Holinshed's Chronicles*. Recording changes in his home village of Radwinter in Essex, Harrison noted:

There are old men yet dwelling in the village where I remain which have noted three things to be marvellously altered in England within their sound remembrance ... One is the multitude of chimneys lately erected, whereas in their young days there were not above two or three, if so many, in most uplandish towns of the realm (the religious houses and manor places of their lords always excepted, and peradventure some great personages), but each one made his fire against a reredos in the hall, where he dined and dressed his meat.

The recent prevalence of chimneys, Harrison added approvingly, meant houses were better aired. He listed it as one of the top improvements in the standard of living, alongside softer bedding material and an increase in imported luxury items such as tapestries, pewter and plate. Sadly, however, even the innovation of tall chimneys would not be enough to solve London's problems with air pollution. The situation deteriorated to the point where, within a generation of Shakespeare's death, the diarist John Evelyn in his *A Character of England* would write of the capital:

> *Such a cloud of sea-coal, as if there be a resemblance of hell upon earth, it is in this volcano in a foggy day; this pestilent smoak, which corrodes the very yron [iron] and spoils all the movables, leaving a soot on all things that it lights; and so fatally seizing on the lungs of the inhabitants, that cough and consumption spare no man.*

The smoggy winter days and nights for which London became notorious – smog being a combination of smoke and fog – and their devastating effects on its citizens' health would not be resolved for another three and a half centuries. The distressing events were dubbed 'pea soupers' after the artist John Sartain published an article in 1820 telling how he would 'slink home through a fog as thick and as yellow as the pea-soup of the eating house'. In 1871, a report in the *New York Times* described London as a city 'where the population are periodically submerged in a fog of the consistency of pea soup'.

Things came to a head with the 'Great Smog', which enveloped the capital from 5-9 December 1952. The pollution was so dense that transport, both public and private, ground to a halt and pedestrians collided with each other on pavements in visibility of less than a yard (0.9m). The smog even penetrated into homes and workplaces, and some cinemas were forced to cancel showings because the screen could not be seen from the seats. It has been estimated that up to six thousand people died as a result of that one event and more than a hundred thousand became ill due to the respiratory problems they suffered.

The outcome was the Clean Air Act of 1956, which banned the burning of coal in domestic fires in the capital and at last began to undo the harm of centuries. Across Britain, fine public buildings finally emerged from beneath the layers of sooty grime that had accumulated for generations as a national clean-up campaign got under way. With the worst of the smoke gone, the passing decades brought a new challenge. An exponential increase in the use of the internal combustion engine led London, along with other cities, to start the battle with air pollution all over again.

32. THE CURIOUS CASE OF FALSTAFF

*A run-in with the aristocracy forces Will to make a crucial change
to his most popular character*

**One word more, I beseech you. If you be not too much cloy'd
with fat meat, our humble author will continue the story,
with Sir John in it, and make you merry with fair Katherine
of France; where, for anything I know, Falstaff shall die of
a sweat, unless already 'a [he] be killed with your hard opinions; for Oldcastle died a martyr and this is not the man.**

(*Henry IV, Part 2*, 5.5, 1597-98)

THE fat old knight Sir John Falstaff is arguably the best loved
character Shakespeare ever created. He was as popular with
Elizabethan audiences as he is with those of today. He stole
the show when he appeared in both parts of *Henry IV*, which
were ostensibly historical dramas. Here, in an Epilogue directly addressed to the audience at the closing of *Henry IV, Part
2*, the author promises to bring back Falstaff in his next play,
Henry V. As things turned out, it was a promise that would be
broken. But what, you may wonder, is that last line all about:
'For Oldcastle died a martyr and this is not the man'?

Who in the world was Oldcastle, of whom we have heard
nothing before in this play? The line reads like a nervous legal
disclaimer, inserted to avoid potentially unpleasant consequences. Which is exactly what it is. Shakespeare had landed
himself in trouble with a powerful adversary, and it was the
very popularity of the larger-than-life comical character he
had created that was the cause. When *Henry IV, Part 1* first appeared on stage it proved hugely popular, not least because of
the antics of Falstaff, the profane and dissolute knight Shakespeare had originally called 'Sir John Oldcastle'.

Shakespeare came across the figure of Oldcastle in an earlier play of inferior quality, titled *The Famous Victories of Henry the Fifth*. In that drama, Oldcastle – based on a real-life soldier hanged then burned for heresy and treason in 1417 – had a minor role as a companion in Prince Hal's riotous youth. Shakespeare saw potential in the character and built him up into the personification of misrule, folly and impudent wit who dominates *Henry IV, Part 1*. Yet by the time *Henry IV, Part 2* appeared on stage, Oldcastle's name had mysteriously been changed to Falstaff. We know this both from contemporary testimony and from several tell-tale traces in the texts. In fact, an oblique reference remains (either carelessly or deliberately) in *Henry IV, Part 1*, where Prince Hal addresses Falstaff as 'my old lad of the castle,' an example of the sort of wordplay in which Shakespeare loved indulging.

In truth, Oldcastle had received pretty rough treatment in that earlier play, *The Famous Victories of Henry the Fifth*, partly because in real life he had been a Lollard, those followers of John Wycliffe regarded as heretics by the mainstream church. As far as Oldcastle's descendants were concerned, however, it was one thing for their ancestor's name to be casually impugned in a little-regarded history play, quite another for him to become a disreputable laughing stock in the eyes of the thousands of playgoers who now flocked to enjoy Shakespeare's blockbusters about Henry IV. Moreover, although Oldcastle had been burned as a heretic in the Catholic England of 1417, to the largely Protestant Elizabethans he might even be lauded as a proto-Protestant martyr.

In 1408, Sir John Oldcastle (*pictured*) had married a wealthy heiress named Joan Cobham, a member of one of the most prominent families in Kent. Their ancestral seat was Cooling Castle, near Rochester, and they owned several large manors spread across the south of England. In due course, Oldcastle became the fourth Baron Cobham. The problem for Shakespeare lay in the fact that in 1596-97, just as *Henry*

SIR JOHN OLDCASTLE, AFTERWARDS LORD COBHAM.

IV, Part 1 was taking to the stage, Oldcastle's descendant Sir William Brooke, the tenth Baron Cobham, happened to be a powerful figure at Elizabeth I's court.

Lord Cobham (Brooke), infuriated by Shakespeare's portrayal of his ancestor as a profane, riotous and cowardly clown, appears to have demanded that the character be removed from the play. Not wishing to meddle with a hugely successful production that was pulling in the crowds, Shakespeare proposed a compromise: he would change Oldcastle's name. He reached instead for another historical figure, Sir John Fastolf, described as 'a cowardly knight' who had played a small part in his own early drama *Henry VI, Part 1*. Handily, the real Fastolf had no powerful descendants to cause trouble. Changing a few letters, Shakespeare came up with the name Falstaff. Matters were clearly still not resolved to the satisfaction of Lord Cobham, however. Shakespeare and his company of actors must have feared that even the hurried name change might not be enough to stave off the threat of legal action or worse. Hence that distinctly odd disclaimer hurriedly inserted into the Epilogue of *Henry IV, Part 2*.

Lord Cobham's intervention backfired spectacularly when his protests became the literary scandal of the season and were regarded as a running joke. His son Henry Brooke (*pictured*), who succeeded to the title in 1597, becoming the eleventh Baron Cobham, found himself teasingly dubbed 'Sir John Falstaff' by rivals at court, the Earl of Essex among them.

Queen Elizabeth herself may have been amused by the

whole business. She is said to have admired Falstaff so much that she commanded Shakespeare to write a play about the knight falling in love. He obliged with *The Merry Wives of Windsor*, in which Falstaff is resoundingly humiliated by a pair of housewives. Indeed, Will appears to have been cheekily looking to get the last laugh, because in that comedy the jealous Master Ford, husband of one of the wives Falstaff attempts to woo, cooks up a scheme to secretly parley

with Falstaff using an alias, and thereby test his wife's fidelity. The alias Ford chooses is 'Master Brooke', none other than the family name of Lord Cobham.

The eleventh Baron Cobham took the latest jibe badly, and that name too was changed between early texts of the *Merry Wives* and the play's inclusion in the *First Folio* of 1623, where 'Master Brooke' has become 'Master Broome'. Unfortunately, the name change destroys at least one pun in the comedy. When Bardolph tells Falstaff, 'Sir John, there's one Master Brooke below would fain speak with you, and be acquainted with you, and hath sent your worship a morning's draught of sack [white wine],' Falstaff replies, 'Such Brookes are welcome to me, that o'erflow with such liquor.' The wordplay simply does not work when 'Brooke' is replaced with 'Broome'. As a result, in modern productions the name Brooke is usually restored (or rendered as 'Brook') to retain the comic effect of the line. The name game was clearly a battle Shakespeare would never win. Except, that is, among his appreciative public.

See also: 24. Kempe's Nine Days' Wonder

33. AN ACT OF SEDITION

A rebellion by the Earl of Essex almost gets Will and his fellow players arrested for treason

Richard II: To do what service am I sent for?

Edmund of Langley: To do that office of thine own goodwill which tired majesty did make thee offer: the resignation of thy state and crown to Henry Bolingbroke.
Richard II: Give me the crown. Here, cousin, seize the crown; here cousin. On this side my hand, and on that side yours. Now is this golden crown like a deep well that owes [owns] two buckets, filling one another, the emptier ever dancing in the air, the other down, unseen and full of water. That bucket down and full of tears am I, drinking my griefs, whilst you mount up on high.

Bolingbroke (Henry IV): I thought you had been willing to resign.

Richard II: My crown I am, but still my griefs are mine. You may my glories and my state depose, but not my griefs; still am I king of those. (*Richard II*, 4.1, 1595)

ENGLAND'S reigning monarch Richard II reluctantly accepts that the game is up and he must hand over his crown to the usurping Henry Bolingbroke, who will succeed him as Henry IV. Even so, Richard finds difficulty accepting his gloomy fate, and for a few moments there is an unseemly tug-of-war as he makes to offer Henry the golden crown, then pulls it back. Both men grasp the coveted prize, yanking it first one way, then the other, until Richard finally relinquishes his hold. It is a scene filled with high drama in which the tension veritably sizzles, and undoubtedly it held Shakespeare's audiences spellbound. It also almost got him arrested for high treason.

The history play about Richard II was written early in Shakespeare's career. It proved so popular that the Lord Chamberlain's Men put on at least forty performances. The script appeared in print for sale as a quarto edition in 1597, and demand was so great that it was reprinted twice the following year. Crucially, though, a scene was missing from those printed editions – the very one in which we see that tug-of-war over the crown and Richard being deposed. The Queen's spies were everywhere and, when word got back to the authorities of what was being depicted on stage, the censors quickly ordered the offending scene to be axed.

It was a nervous time. Spain's attacks on England had not ended with the scattering of the Great Armada in 1588. Another Spanish naval raid had taken place on Cornwall in 1595, the year the play first appeared. Catholic conspiracies were constantly suspected, and not without reason. In the government's view it was no time to have any portrayal of a rightful monarch being deposed, with all the implications that held for Elizabeth. Not until 1608, five years after the Queen's death, could that pivotal scene be reinserted when the next quarto edition of the play was printed.

So there can be little doubt that Shakespeare's company, the Lord Chamberlain's Men, felt distinctly uncomfortable on the morning of Friday, 6 February, 1601 when a high-powered delegation of followers of Robert Devereux, Earl of Essex (*pictured*), turned up at the Globe wanting a word. The men, Lord Monteagle, Sir Charles Percy, Sir Jocelyn Percy, Sir Gilly

Meyrick and two others, requested the actors stage a performance of *Richard II* the following day.

The company made clear they were not altogether happy about the proposal and, according to evidence their spokesman Augustine Phillips later gave his interrogators, they 'determyned to have played some other play, holdyng that play of Kyng Richard to be so old and so long out of use as that they should have small or no companye [audience] at yt'. That was a hastily concocted excuse, since it was not unusual for Shakespeare's early plays to be reprised years after their first performances.

Sir Gilly then sweetened the deal by offering to pay the company forty shillings over and above whatever they took at the box office, no small amount considering the groundlings paid just a penny per head for admittance. The only condition was that the contentious deposition scene had to be included. After some discussion, the actors agreed to accept the commission, dug the old scripts out of fusty trunks, and began frantically re-learning their lines. How, they would later ask, could they have suspected that an armed uprising was in the wind, and its leader would be Essex, the dashing, headstrong gallant who had risen to lofty heights in the Queen's favour only to fall again just as spectacularly?

To be sure, Shakespeare was sympathetic to Essex. The earl was, after all, a close friend and confidante of Henry Wriothesley, Earl of Southampton, who had long been a generous sponsor and admirer of Shakespeare's poetry and plays. The two earls had history together. In the summer of 1596, Essex and Southampton, craving feats of derring-do, had joined Sir Walter Raleigh on a daring naval expedition to Cadiz, in which they seized and pillaged the Spanish port, destroying fifty-three enemy merchant vessels.

As the English fleet approached the harbour, the Spanish had sought to fend them off using four of their strongest galleons, the *St Matthew*, *St Philip*, *St Thomas* and *St Andrew*. The

Spaniards were badly mauled and in the melee the *St Andrew* ran aground, where she was captured by the English and subsequently incorporated into the Royal Navy. On her arrival in England the vessel almost ran aground again, this time in the Thames Estuary. Shakespeare did not allow either incident to pass unremarked in the play he was writing at that time, *The Merchant of Venice*. Salerio, a friend of Antonio, the merchant of the title, says:

> **My wind cooling my broth would blow me to an ague** [fever] **when I thought what harm a wind too great at sea might do. I should not see the sandy hour-glass run but I should think of shallows and of flats, and see my wealthy Andrew dock'd in sand, vailing** [lowering] **her high-top lower than her ribs to kiss her burial.** (1.1)

In 1599, Elizabeth promoted Essex to the post of Governor-General of Ireland, with explicit instructions to put down an insurrection in Ulster that was being led by Hugh O'Neill, Earl of Tyrone. Commanding the largest English force that had ever been sent to Ireland, some sixteen thousand men, the handsome Essex rode out of London on 27 March to cheers from excited crowds, which stretched along the city's streets for four miles.

A popular figure, he was, like Hamlet, 'lov'd of the distracted multitude'. Church bells rang out and earnest prayers were offered up for his success. He had promised the Privy Council that he would crush O'Neill and return in triumph as the nation's hero. So high were everyone's expectations that Shakespeare could not resist inserting a reference to Essex in his new play about another English hero, *Henry V* (a fact that has helped scholars date the play to within a few months). In the Prologue to Act 5, Chorus declares:

> **But now behold, in the quick forge and working-house of thought, how London doth pour out her citizens! The**

mayor and all his brethren in best sort, like to the senators of the antique Rome, with the plebeians swarming at their heels, go forth and fetch their conquering Caesar in. As, by a lower but loving likelihood, were now the general [Essex] of our gracious empress [Elizabeth I], as in good time he may, from Ireland coming, bringing rebellion broached on his sword, how many would the peaceful city quit to welcome him!

In fact, when Essex did return from Ireland no one turned out to greet him. The expedition had been an unmitigated disaster. Rather than engage O'Neill in battle, he had negotiated a humiliating truce, causing Elizabeth to snarl that if she had wished to give away Ireland she need hardly have gone to the expense of sending Essex and an army there to do it. The earl sailed back to England in flagrant defiance of the Queen's orders to stay in Ireland and continue the military campaign, then rode pell-mell to London in reckless haste to explain himself. Around ten o'clock on the morning of 28 September 1599, he stormed into Nonsuch Palace in Surrey and burst unannounced into her private bedchamber even before she was dressed, seeing her without her layers of make-up and her wig. Thomas Birch, in his *Memoirs of the Reign of Queen Elizabeth*, published in 1754, writes:

> It was much wonder'd at in the court that he went so boldly to Her Majesty's presence, she not being ready, and he so full of dirt and mire that his very face was full of it.

It was an outrageous intrusion on the sanctity of the royal person and Elizabeth's revenge was swift. Essex was ordered to appear before the Privy Council the following day, where he was made to stand for five hours while being interrogated. He was accused of dereliction of duty for his conduct in Ireland and placed under house arrest. Secretary of State Sir Robert Cecil and Sir Walter Raleigh, both being his rivals at court, saw to it that he was stripped of all public office, lost his lucrative monopoly on the sale of sweet wines, and – the ultimate insult in Essex's eyes – banished from the Queen's presence. Shakespeare appears to allude to the ostracising of the earl, a former royal favourite, in his comedy *Much Ado About Nothing*, when Hero says of her cousin Beatrice:

Bid her steal into the pleached [intertwined] **bower where honeysuckles, ripen'd by the sun, forbid the sun to enter, like favourites, made proud by princes that advance their pride against that power that bred it.** (3.1)

The awful inevitability of Essex's downfall was probably also on Shakespeare's mind as he penned his Greek tragedy *Troilus and Cressida*, which he was working on at the time. When the hero Achilles is confronted by the decline of his own reputation, he muses:

What, am I poor of late? 'Tis certain greatness, once fall'n out with fortune, must fall out with men too. What the declined is he shall as soon read in the eyes of others as feel in his own fall. (3.3)

He could just as easily be talking about Robert Devereux. In *Troilus and Cressida,* Achilles continues by confessing that the honours anyone possesses are not intrinsic. They did not occur naturally but were given, and they will endure only as long as love and respect remain among those who bestowed them. He says:

And not a man, for being simply man, hath any honour, but honour for those honours that are without him [external to him] **– as place, riches, favour: prizes of accident as oft as merit – which when they fall, as being slippery standers** [having an unstable footing], **the love that lean'd on them as slippery too, do one pluck down another and together die in the fall.** (3.3)

Where Essex had once been eager to profess his undying

adoration for Elizabeth at any opportunity, he now became a bitter and resentful man. Lest he should blanch, he had a Machiavellian figure at his side always ready to egg him on in the shape of his malevolent secretary, Sir Henry Cuffe. Well practised in the art of deceit, Cuffe was described by the diplomat Sir Henry Wotton as 'a man of secret ambitious ends of his own' which he disguised under a 'semblance of integrity'.

So it was that on the afternoon of Saturday, 7 February 1601, the earl's friends and fellow conspirators took their seats on the Globe's benches to watch the performance of *Richard II* they had specially commissioned, complete with the scene depicting the monarch's deposition. Not only was the intention to boost their own morale for what was to come, but they hoped to arouse anti-Elizabeth sentiment among a wider audience. Essex, meanwhile, was shocked to receive a summons to appear again before the Privy Council, and concluded that Cecil and Raleigh were plotting to assassinate him when he turned up.

On the following morning, the tall, red-bearded earl left his home, Essex House, and rode into the City of London with around two hundred armed men, crying: 'For the Queen! For the Queen! A plot is laid for my life!' He confidently expected ecstatic citizens to rush out of their houses in their hundreds to join his crusade. True to character, however, even Essex's petulant rebellion turned out to be a slap-dash, ill-planned and utterly inept affair, and to his horror London's citizens merely looked on in puzzled bemusement as he passed. By nightfall, he and his fellow plotters had all been rounded up and arrested.

He was tried for high treason on 19 February. The indictment against Essex accused him of 'conspiring and imagining at London ... to depose and slay the Queen, and to subvert the Government', adding that he had 'endeavoured to raise himself to the Crown of England, and usurp the royal dignity'. He was found guilty and handed down the customary traitor's sentence of being hanged, disembowelled while still alive, and his body quartered.

Essex remained surprisingly dignified as sentence was pronounced and, when informed that his 'head and quarters' would 'be disposed of at Her Majesty's pleasure,' he calmly replied that it was fitting 'my poor quarters, that have done Her Majesty true service in divers parts of the world, should be sacrificed and disposed of' as his sovereign should direct ... 'whereunto with all willingness of heart I do submit myself'. His display of decorum led one observer to comment: 'A man might easily perceive that, as he had lived popularly, so his chief care was to leave a good opinion in the people's minds now at parting.'

At the last, the Queen's heart softened towards her old favourite and she ordered death by beheading, a less terrible fate than the one to which he had been sentenced. Essex was executed on 25 February on Tower Green, aged thirty-three. He appeared on the scaffold wearing a suit of black satin 'with a little ruff about his neck,' a black felt hat and velvet cloak. He forgave his executioner, was stripped of his cloak, and placed his head upon the block with outstretched arms. It took three blows of the axe to behead him. Shakespeare surely had the sentencing and execution of Essex in mind when, five years later, he gave Malcolm these lines about the Thane of Cawdor's execution in *Macbeth*:

> **I have spoke with one that saw him die: who did report that very frankly he confess'd his treasons, implored your highness' pardon and set forth a deep repentance. Nothing in his life became him like the leaving it. He died as one that had been studied in his death to throw away the dearest thing he owed** [owned] **as 'twere a careless trifle.** (1.4)

Sir Gilly Meyrick was sentenced to be hanged, drawn and quartered for his part in commissioning the illegal performance of *Richard II*. A similar sentence awaited Essex's aide Sir Henry Cuffe and several others. At his trial, Cuffe was alleged to be nothing less than 'the arrantest traitor that ever came to that bar', 'the very seducer of the earl' and 'the cunning coiner of all plots'. Just before Essex was executed he requested he might be allowed to confront Cuffe in the Tower, and reproached him with the words: 'You have been one of the chiefest instigators of me to all these my disloyal courses into which I have fallen.' Cuffe was quite likely the model for Shakespeare when he later came to create the malcontent Iago, author of the Moor's demise in *Othello*.

Shakespeare's good friend Southampton (*pictured*) was also arrested for his part in the plot and was fortunate to escape with life imprisonment, a sentence that would be overturned when he was set free by James I after Elizabeth's death in 1603.

The rebellion was over but, for Shakespeare and the Lord Chamberlain's Men, the reckoning was still to come. They were summoned by the Privy Council to explain their actions in staging *Richard II*, complete with the deposition scene, on the very eve of the abortive uprising. How much had they known? Amid official suspicions the actors may have been complicit in the conspiracy, Augustine Phillips, one of the original partners in the Globe, gave evidence as their spokesman.

Phillips related how they had been approached by Essex's supporters who, faced with the players' objections to staging the play, had offered the extra payment of forty shillings. He may also have pointed out that the visitors included high-ranking gentry, whereas the theatre company consisted merely of common players. 'Who were we to argue against such worthies?' he might have asked. It probably helped their cause that the company's patron was Lord Hunsdon, the Lord Chamberlain, who was a blood relative of the Queen. The Privy Councillors would hardly want any hint of suspicion cast over the most senior officer of the royal household. To their great relief, the theatre company were absolved of any complicity, and the Queen pointedly ordered them to perform a play in front of her on the eve of Essex's execution. There is no record of what the play was. Could it have been that Elizabeth, with an exquisite sense of irony, chose *Richard II*?

✽ ✽ ✽

Despite the leniency shown towards Shakespeare and his fellow actors, the Queen could be in no doubt about her own always tenuous position on the throne, even after four decades of rule. Since she was childless, there was no heir apparent. Age was creeping up on her and it was widely reported that in her later years she refused to have any mirrors positioned where she might catch a glimpse of her own deteriorating reflection. Elizabeth had come close to death when she contracted smallpox in October 1562, at the age of twenty-nine. The disease had left her face horribly pockmarked and half her hair had fallen out. She had never been a particularly attractive woman, and what little beauty she had was ruined.

She took to caking her face with white powder and wearing a red-haired wig. Unfortunately for her, the make-up mixture of egg, powdered eggshells, poppy seeds, borax and alum in the face coating also contained toxic white lead, which both ate into her skin and made even more of her hair drop out. As the years went by, she caked the powder on more and more thickly. According to one report, at Christmas 1600 her face was painted 'in some places near half an inch thick'. ('Now get you to my lady's chamber and tell her, let her paint an inch thick, to this favour she must come,' Hamlet says pointedly as he muses over the skull of Yorick). Elizabeth's teeth were stained and blackened, and several had broken off or been extracted, ravaged by her love of sugary treats. André Hurault de Maisse, an ambassador from the French king Henry IV, once observed:

> *Her teeth are very yellow and unequal ... many of them are missing, so that one cannot understand her easily when she speaks quickly.*

The more her looks deteriorated, the more obsequious courtiers flattered her. Portrait painters depicted her looking much younger and more beautiful than she really was. But the stark truth haunted her. Ben Jonson was one source of the story that she abhorred mirrors, saying: 'Queen Elizabeth never saw herself, after she became old, in a true glass.' Another was Elizabeth Southwell, who served as a maid of honour from 1599. Southwell wrote a manuscript after the Queen's death, in which she claims that the only mirror Elizabeth would look into had been specially designed to 'deceive her sight' until, one desperate night, she finally demanded 'a true looking glass' be brought to her. Southwell says:

> *She saw one night in her bed her bodie exceeding leane and fearfulle in a light of fire, for the which the next daie she desired to see a true looking glass, which in 20 yeares befor she had not sene but onlie such a one which of purpose was made to deceive her sight, which glas being brought her she fell presently exclaiming at all those which had so much commended her and toke yt so offensivelie that all those which had before flattered her durst not come in her sight.*

The deposition scene in Shakespeare's *Richard II* includes an episode in which the despairing Richard orders a mirror (a 'glass') to be brought to him and examines his own face in it.

Richard says to an attendant:

Give me the glass and therein will I read. No deeper wrinkles yet? Hath sorrow struck so many blows upon this face of mine and made no deeper wounds? O flattering glass, like to my followers in prosperity, thou dost beguile me! Was this face the face that every day under his household roof did keep ten thousand men? Was this the face that, like the sun, did make beholders wink? Was this the face that faced so many follies and was at last out-faced by Bolingbroke? A brittle glory shineth in this face. As brittle as the glory is the face. (4.1)

Then follows the dramatic stage direction 'Dashes the glass against the ground' and Richard declares:

For there it is, crack'd in a hundred shivers. (4.1)

Elizabeth can hardly have missed that striking parallel with herself and mirrors. As if the political atmosphere at the close of the sixteenth century were not febrile enough, in 1599 a historian named John Hayward published a treatise titled *The First Part of the Life and Raigne of King Henrie IV*, which also gave an account of Richard's deposition. Hayward unwisely dedicated the book to none other than the Earl of Essex and was subsequently ordered to explain himself before the Star Chamber. Suspecting Essex's own hand in the book, the Queen insisted that Hayward was only pretending to be the author in order to shield 'some more mischievous' person, and that he 'should be racked so that he might disclose the truth'.

Hayward was interrogated by Francis Bacon, who found no treason but did declare him guilty of 'felony'. The historian was sent to prison for his pains. The Queen summed it all up one day in 1601 while looking through documents with William Lambarde, Keeper of the Records at the Tower of London. Picking up some papers that related to the reign of Richard II, she turned to Lambarde and said wistfully: 'I am Richard II, know ye not that?'

The execution of Essex in February 1601 caused wide-spread public resentment. Although the citizens of London had not risen to support his rebellion, his popularity had not faded. Seditious broadside ballads were circulated after his death, pronouncing him a man of the people who had been cruelly conspired against by his enemies, Cecil and Raleigh.

For his part, Shakespeare appears never to have forgiven Elizabeth for executing Essex, who was such a close friend of his sponsor Southampton. When the Queen – England's great Gloriana – died after a momentous forty-four year reign, he wrote not one word of tribute to her. The omission did not go unnoticed by the dramatist Henry Chettle, the man who had once published Robert Greene's *Groats-worth of Wit* with its vicious diatribe against Shakespeare, the 'upstart crow'. Chettle complained:

> *Nor doth the silver tongued Melicert drop from his honied Muse one sable tear to mourn her death that graced* [rewarded] *his desert* [deserving], *and to his laies* [verses] *open'd her Royal ear.*

Melicert is a character in a novel titled *Menaphon*, which Chettle's late friend Greene had written in 1589. Scholars believe the allusion is to Shakespeare, not least because Chettle's lines go on to mention Will's poem *The Rape of Lucrece*.

Henry Chettle was dead by the time Shakespeare and John Fletcher penned their collaborative work *All Is True*, known to us as *Henry VIII*, in 1612. The play, a tribute to the Tudor dynasty, features a final scene that depicts Elizabeth's christening, in which Archbishop Cranmer heaps lavish praise upon Henry's baby daughter and predicts great glories ahead, both for her reign and that of her successor (that being James I, of course, in whose presence the play would be performed).

She shall be, to the happiness of England, an aged princess. Many days shall see her, and yet no day without a deed to crown it. Would I had known no more! But she must die, she must, the saints must have her; yet a virgin, a most unspotted lily shall she pass to the ground, and all the world shall mourn her. (5.5)

Those fawning lines in praise of Elizabeth do not sound much like Shakespeare to me. On 26 November 2019, *The Guardian* reported that Petr Plechac, of the Czech Academy of Sciences in Prague, had run an algorithm through *Henry VIII* which minutely scrutinised the rhythms of the text and the combination of words used. Plechac concluded, among other things, that Act 5, Scene 5 (paean and all) was solely the work of Fletcher.

See also: 36. Gunpowder, Treason and Plot

34. THE FACE IN THE PORTRAIT

Is Will teasing us with a cryptic hint to the identity of the elusive 'Dark Lady' of his desires?

Wherefore [why] **are these things hid? Wherefore have these gifts a curtain before 'em? Are they like to take dust, like Mistress Mall's picture?**
(Twelfth Night, 1.3, 1601)

WHEN Sir Andrew Aguecheek boasts he has hidden skills at dancing – including executing the 'back-trick,' a backward caper in a fashionable five-step dance known as the galliard – his fellow carouser Sir Toby Belch demands a demonstration. Sir Toby asks why Sir Andrew conceals such prodigious talent, as if it were 'Mistress Mall's picture,' stored away out of sight to gather dust. The reference clearly meant enough to Shakespeare's audience for the playwright to be confident it would raise a chuckle, which suggests there really was a 'Mistress Mall'.

In which case, who was she and why was her portrait so out of favour that no one would wish to look on it? It helps to know that to the Elizabethans 'Mall' was a diminutive form of the name 'Mary'. Which brings us to the most likely candidate, a woman who became involved in an unseemly scandal at Elizabeth I's court and who may, indeed, have an intriguing link to Shakespeare himself.

Mary Fitton (*pictured*), daughter of Sir Edward and Dame Alice Fitton of Gawsworth in Cheshire, was by all accounts a beauty. At the age of seventeen she was selected for a coveted role as one of Elizabeth's maids of honour. Maids of honour were junior to the ladies-in-waiting. Mary's duties were to attend to the needs of the Queen, both at court occasions and in her private chambers.

While it was an essential prerequsite for such young ladies to be deemed chaste maidens at the start of their service (they were all dressed in white to signify purity), their blushing honour might not, in fact, last long. Some knowing courtier or other was always hoping to tempt any pretty new arrival into his bed, as a result of which she might suddenly find herself the sub-

ject of both the latest scandal to rock the court and the wrath of the indignant Queen.

In 1595, around the time of Mary Fitton's seventeenth birthday, possibly even to mark her elevation to the royal household, a magnificent and almost full-length portrait was commissioned from a now unknown artist. It survives to this day. In it, she is fashionably and sumptuously dressed, wearing a white ornamented chest covering known as a stomacher, huge sleeves, and a skirt elaborately decorated with images of plants and garden creatures. On her head she wears a costly silver headpiece embedded with pearls. Little wonder, therefore, that her worried father commended her into the protection of his close friend Sir William Knollys, who was no less a figure than the Controller of the Queen's Household. Knollys, a fifty-year-old married man, responded effusively, pledging: 'I will be as careful of her well doing as if I were her own true father.' He promised to defend the 'innocent lamb' from the 'wolfish cruelty and fox-like subtlety of the tame beasts of this place'.

While Mary quickly became popular with the young men at court, who were entranced by her good looks and vivacious talents as a dancer, it was Knollys himself she had most cause to be concerned about. Beguiled by his young ward, he quickly became her wooer, expressing a desire to have children with her, and morbidly assuring her that he was expecting his actual wife, Lady Knollys, to die sometime in the near future. He even went so far as to dye his beard in order to impress her. For some reason the beard ended up in three colours – white at the roots, yellow in the middle, and black at the ends – causing him to be derided as 'Party Beard' by sniggering courtiers, among whom his infatuation was the cause of much mocking laughter.

Knollys was in all probability the inspiration for Shakespeare's po-faced killjoy Malvolio – the name itself may derive from a modulation of the Italian *Malavoglia*, meaning 'I want Mal' – who falls hopelessly in love with his young mistress in *Twelfth Night*. Some scholars have suggested that a court action taken in 1600 by a fiery Yorkshireman with the grand name of Sir Thomas Posthumus Hoby may have inspired the incident in *Twelfth Night* in which Malvolio protests about Sir Toby's drunken merrymaking. In the court case, Hoby complained that several of his neighbours had entered his house, freely imbibed, played at cards and ridiculed his Puritanism, before threatening to ravish his wife. Malvolio, who is accused in the play of being a Puritan, may well be a fusion of both Knollys and Hoby.

Possibly overcome by Knollys' attention, in 1599 Mary Fitton fled the court after suffering some kind of nervous breakdown, known to the Elizabethans as 'suffocation of the mother'. When she returned to royal service some months later, she decisively rejected his continued advances. But if Mary was to prove an unattainable dream for the old goat, she had a different reaction when courted by the young gallant William Herbert, aged twenty and heir to his father's title as Earl of Pembroke. Herbert appears to have been captivated by Mary in June 1600 when he saw her leading the dancing during a masque at a fashionable society wedding they both attended. A clandestine romance followed almost immediately. State papers later record how:

> *During the time that the Earl of Pembroke favoured her she would put off her head-tire [a kind of fascinator], and tuck up her clothes, and take a large white cloak and march as though she had been a man to meet the said earl out of the court.*

In other words, she sneaked out of the court disguised as a man in order to meet her lover, not unlike Viola in *Twelfth Night*. By July, Herbert had bedded her. She became pregnant and gave birth in March 1601 to a baby boy. Sadly the child died soon after, possibly as a result of the syphilis from which Herbert is suspected of having suffered. Despite admitting paternity, the cad 'utterly renounced all marriage' to her.

News of their affair outraged the Queen. Mary was dismissed from the court and Herbert was thrown into the Fleet prison. He succeeded in getting himself released a month or so later after petitioning Sir Robert Cecil, the Lord Privy Seal and Secretary of State, and Mary appears to have gone to live for a while with her married sister Anne at Arbury Hall, near Nuneaton. The scandal meant, however, that Mary, like William Herbert, was permanently banished from the Queen's presence. She was regarded as a thorough disgrace and her despairing father, Sir Edward, lamented that the whole affair had brought social ruin on the family.

Shakespeare probably wrote *Twelfth Night* just months after Mary was sent packing by the Queen. It is this fact that leads us to suspect Mary Fitton might well be the 'Mistress Mall' whose portrait Sir Toby Belch declares is now gathering dust, perhaps covered with a curtain, but in any case tucked safely out of everyone's sight in some forgotten room.

Undaunted by a scandal that would have marked the irredeemable downfall of anyone weaker spirited, Mary went on to enjoy a passionate affair with the married Vice-Admiral Sir Richard Leveson, a distinguished naval officer and politician, to whom she bore two illegitimate daughters. She later became the lover of one of Leveson's officers, Captain William Polwhele, and gave him a son. This was too much even for Mary's mother Alice, who effectively disowned her in a letter to her other daughter Anne, saying: 'Such shame as never had a Cheshire woman, worse now than ever. Write no more to me of her.'

Polwhele at length married Mary. Clearly her charm and beauty had not faded with the passing years because, after Polwhele's death in 1610, she was in turn courted by one Captain John Lougher of Pembrokeshire, described as 'a gentleman lawyer' and former Member of Parliament, who became her second husband. Mary herself died in 1647 at the grand old age, for those times, of sixty-nine. She is buried at the church in Gawsworth, the village of her birth, and – for those so minded – her ghost is reputed to haunt the splendidly timber-framed Gawsworth Old Hall, which was once the Fitton family home.

Yet that is not the end of the story as far as it concerns Shakespeare. In addition to being the father of Mary's first child, William Herbert, founder of Pembroke College at Oxford University, may have been the 'fair youth' to whom many of the sonnets are addressed. A patron of Shakespeare, his initials match the dedication of the verses, which reads: 'To Mr W H ... the only begetter of these ensuing sonnets'. What's more, when Shakespeare's friends and fellow actors John Heminges and Henry Condell published the *First Folio* in 1623, William Herbert and his brother Philip were the dedicatees, and may well have stumped up part of the considerable cost of producing the book.

As for Mary Fitton, she is one of a number of candidates to be the mysterious 'Dark Lady' for whom Shakespeare professes a deep and unrequited love in other sonnets. Leading the case for Mary as the subject of the poet's passion is *Sonnet 135*, in which the lover appeals to his mistress after having been rejected by her. Before indulging in bawdy wordplay on the double-meaning of the word 'will' (with a lower-case 'w') to mean 'penis', the sonnet opens:

Whoever hath her wish, thou hast thy 'Will', / And 'Will' to boot, and 'Will' in overplus ...

The lady has a Will, and another Will to boot, and a Will in 'overplus'. Could Shakespeare here be referring to Mary Fitton's three Wills ... William Knollys, William Herbert and himself? Intriguingly, Will Kempe – the comic who left Shakespeare's company and morris danced his way from London to Norwich in 1600 – dedicated *Nine Daies Wonder*, the book he wrote about his adventures, to 'Mistress Anne Fitton,' whom he described as 'Maid of Honour to Elizabeth'.

While Mary's sister was indeed called Anne, she was never one of the Queen's maids of honour. Moreover, she had been safely married from the age of twelve to one John Newdigate and living in the Warwickshire countryside. Did Kempe get Mary's name confused with her sister's? And why in the world was he (another Will) dedicating his best-selling work to either of them? If only the face in Mary Fitton's alluring portrait could speak, what fascinating secrets it might reveal.

35. THE WILD GOOSE CHASE

A bitter feud between three sisters over their father's estate may have led to 'King Lear'

Pray, do not mock me. I am a very foolish fond old man, fourscore and upward, not an hour more nor less; and to deal plainly, I fear I am not in my perfect mind. Methinks I should know you, and know this man; yet I am doubtful, for I am mainly ignorant what place this is; and all the skill I have remembers not these garments; nor I know not where I did lodge last night. Do not laugh at me; for, as I am a man, I think this lady to be my child Cordelia. (*King Lear*, 4.7, 1605-6)

WITH these words the broken, pathetic figure of King Lear greets his rescuers after waking from a long sleep of exhaustion. He has been through madness, driven to despair by the cruel machinations of his vixen-like daughters Regan and Goneril, to whom he gave his kingdom. The compassionate Cordelia, his third and youngest daughter, whom he had disinherited and driven out of his realm for her truth-telling honesty, has returned with an army from France to intervene on his behalf.

Shakespeare based his script for *King Lear* on several sources, including accounts by the twelfth-century chronicler Geoffrey of Monmouth and the historian Raphael Holinshed, as well as a play of inferior quality that had been doing the rounds from the pen of an unknown author, *The True Chronicle History of King Leir and His Three Daughters, Gonorill, Ragan and Cordella*. The story of the three feuding daughters and their ailing father was clearly an old one, which Shakespeare would turn into box office gold and the towering tragedy we know today. Yet it may have been an even more topical tale that first triggered his interest.

A lawsuit in which the three daughters of a certain Sir Brian Annesley argued over their father's lands and property became something of a *cause célèbre* just before Shakespeare began writing his play. The wealthy Annesley, described as a 'gentleman pensioner' of Kent, had been a loyal retainer of the late Elizabeth I and was living in retirement at his rural estate, which would now be within the London borough of Lewisham. Two of his daughters had married nobly, Grace to Sir John Wildgoose and Christinna to William, third Baron Sandys. The third daughter, intriguingly named Cordell, remained unmarried. In 1603 Lady Wildgoose, claiming their father had become senile, launched a legal action to have him certified insane and unable to manage his estate, thereby seeking power of attorney over his affairs. A bitter stand-off with Cordell ensued.

After an exchange of letters with Sir Robert Cecil, the Secretary of State, about the matter, Sir John Wildgoose, accompanied by two men named Tymothe Law and Samuel Lennard, descended on Annesley's home. On October 18, Wildgoose wrote again to Cecil:

> We repaired unto the house of Bryan Annesley of Lee, in the county of Kent, and finding him fallen into such imperfection and distemperature of mind and memory, as we thought him thereby become altogether unfit to govern himself or his estate, we endeavored to take a perfect inventory of such goods and chattels as he possessed in and about his house.

They were stopped in their tracks. Wildgoose went on to complain that Cordell Annesley ...

> Who during the time of all his infirmity hath taken upon her the government of him and all his affairs, refuseth to suffer any inventory to be taken, until such time as she hath

*conference with her friends, by reason whereof we could
proceed no farther.*

The defiant Cordell wasted no time in hitting back. In
her own letter to Cecil, dated 23 October, she complained that
if Wildgoose got his way he would have her

*Poor, aged and daily dying father ... begged for a Lunatic,
whose many years' service to our late Dread Sovereign
Mistress [Elizabeth I] and native country deserved a better
agnomination [recognition] than at his last gasp to be registered a Lunatic.*

Dutiful daughter as she was, Cordell pleaded that if, at
worst, her father 'must needs be accounted a Lunatic' that he
and his property should temporarily be placed in the care of
his old friend Sir John Croft ...

*Who out of the love he bare unto him in his more happier
days, and for the good he wisheth unto us his children, is
contented upon entreaty to undergo the burden and care of
him and his estate, without intendment to make one penny
benefit to himself by any goods of his, or ought that may
descend to us his children, as also to prevent any record of
Lunacy that may be procured hereafter.*

Cecil agreed that the respect owed to Brian Annesley
in his twilight days should overrule any case the two plaintiff
daughters might have. Things were left as they stood until
Annesley died in July 1604. Happily for Cordell, when her
father's will was read she enjoyed better fortune than does
Cordelia in the play Shakespeare was about to write. She inherited most of the estate. The furious Wildgooses contested
the will's validity but the Court of Chancery upheld it.

On 5 February 1607, Cordell married Sir William Hervey, a veteran of the campaign against the Spanish Armada in
1588. Their acquaintance must have been of some standing
because Hervey had been an executor of her father's will. And

therein lies a connection with Shakespeare. Hervey was the recent widower of Mary, the Dowager Countess of Southampton, and therefore the stepfather of Shakespeare's aristocratic friend and patron, Henry Wriothesley, Earl of Southampton.

Did the Annesley case inspire Shakespeare to turn to the Lear saga, possibly at Southampton's prompting? An essay in the *Philological Quarterly* of 1943 points out that in none of the versions of the King Lear story that were around before Shakespeare got his hands on it does Lear go mad. That was entirely his doing (Regan refers to Lear as 'the lunatic king'). Furthermore, when Lear's world crashes in on him, the Fool observes:

Winter's not gone yet, if the wild-geese fly that way. (2.4)

Given Shakespeare's irresistible urge never to pass up an opportunity of inserting a pun, is the Fool's line a tongue-in-cheek reference to the Wildgooses and their wild goose chase over Annesley's estate?

History offers another footnote to the Cordelia story. While Shakespeare was writing *King Lear* he was lodging with a family of Hugenots, those French Protestants who had fled their native country in the face of Catholic persecution, at a house in Silver Street in the parish of St Olave's.

Christopher Mountjoy and his wife Marie were doing nicely at creating decorative wigs and ornamental headpieces for well-to-do ladies about town, possibly also supplying the Globe with theatrical accoutrements. Living next door to the Mountjoys was an embroiderer named William Tailor (or Tailer). On 1 December 1605, a baby daughter born to the Tailors was baptised at St Olave's Church. They named her Cordelia.

Cordelia was the variation Shakespeare gave to the name spelt Cordella in the old play *King Leir* and Cordula in earlier history chronicles. Shakespeare's spelling was virtually unheard of at the time. Charles Nicholl, in his book *The Lodger Shakespeare*, charmingly suggests that perhaps the Tailors asked Shakespeare to suggest a name for their infant daughter as he worked on his latest play and that 'Cordelia' was his gift to them. Sadly, soon afterwards the plague took a devastating toll on St Olave's parish, including the houses in Silver Street. William Tailor and two of his sons died, though the parish registers suggest little Cordelia survived. So, thankfully, did Will Shakespeare.

36. GUNPOWDER, TREASON AND PLOT

Will feels the heat when Catholic conspirators attempt to blow up James I and his Parliament

To beguile the time, look like the time. Bear welcome in your eye, your hand, your tongue. Look like the innocent flower, but be the serpent under't.

(Macbeth, 5.1, 1606)

LADY Macbeth is urging her hesitant husband to appear every inch the genial host when the Scottish king, Duncan, arrives at their castle, yet secretly to be ready to strike a deadly assassin's blow. Shakespeare chooses his words carefully, aware they will resonate with another King of Scotland, one who happened to also be King of England, Wales and Ireland at the time he was writing. *Macbeth*, the only play he would set in Scotland, was especially created for James I, and its existence appears to be a direct result of the Gunpowder Plot against the king's life. Along with the famous witches, a subject of particular fascination to James, the theme of treason justly meeting its bloody end runs through the play like a thread. Shakespeare clearly felt he needed to declare his loyalty to the Crown to dispel any lingering doubts. The shadow of suspicion had passed him worryingly close by.

In 1605, James had been on the throne for two years since Elizabeth's death and in that time his Catholic subjects had grown increasingly restive. Although James was favoured to succeed the childless Queen because he was a Protestant, his mother Mary Queen of Scots had been Catholic. Accordingly, his Catholic subjects had hoped his rule would herald a new dawn when he travelled south from Scotland to take up his English throne. Yet no easing of the restrictions imposed under Elizabeth's regime on their freedom to follow the old faith had followed his accession.

The depth of their alienation was exposed on 4 November, when a tall, well-built Yorkshireman named Guido Fawkes was discovered skulking among thirty-six barrels of gunpowder that had been smuggled into the cellars beneath the House of Lords. There was more than enough explosive to blow the place to smithereens and, along with it, members of the government and James himself, who was due to preside over the State Opening of Parliament the following day.

Seized by armed guards, Fawkes was immediately subjected to excruciating tortures, during which he confessed his role in a plot to murder the king as the prelude to a Catholic revolution. As the thumbscrews tightened, he screamed out the names of his fellow conspirators. Soldiers were hastily despatched around the country to round them up. Among the plotters were notable figures from Warwickshire families, not least their leader Robert Catesby. He had grown up in Lapworth, a village twelve miles (19km) from Stratford-upon-Avon. Shakespeare's home county, it turned out, was a seething cauldron of Catholic discontent. The murderous plot may even have been hatched there.

Worse still, there were worrying connections with the Shakespeare family. Robert Catesby's father William, a zealous Catholic, was for many years a close friend of Will's father, John Shakespeare, himself staunchly Catholic until his death in September 1601. Indeed, William Catesby and John Shakespeare secretly shared highly illegal Catholic writings, some of which would be discovered hidden in the rafters of the Shakespeare family home in Henley Street by workmen carrying out renovations in 1750.

For his part, Robert Catesby had joined the Earl of Essex's rebellion against Elizabeth in 1601, for which he was fined the considerable sum of three thousand pounds but escaped with his life. Mary Arden, William Shakespeare's mother, came from a similarly devout Warwickshire Catholic family. Will's relative Edward Arden had been executed, along with Arden's son-in-law John Somerville, in 1583 for their involvement in an alleged plot against the life of Elizabeth I. (Their heads were perched atop poles over London Bridge lest he needed reminding of their 'treachery'.) Furthermore, Edward Arden had been the brother-in-law of Robert Catesby's mother Anne, meaning the playwright and the Gunpowder Plot ringleader were distantly related.

Family and hometown connections apart, it was widely known that Shakespeare's favourite London watering hole was the Mermaid Tavern in Cheapside. He and the landlord, William Johnson, were close friends. The Mermaid also happened to be where Robert Catesby and the other conspirators had met to discuss their plot to assassinate the king. Among the suspects hauled in for questioning by the authorities was Shakespeare's old friend and rival Ben Jonson, another regular at the Mermaid. Jonson had already had his own brushes with the law but he was released after protesting that, while he knew some of the conspirators, he had known nothing of the treason they were planning. Shakespeare himself, as a member of the King's Men – the company of actors created by James I out of the former Lord Chamberlain's Men – was surely grateful to know he had powerful friends.

The plotters are depicted in an engraving (*pictured*) by an unknown artist, which dates from around 1605. The implications if the plot had succeeded were unthinkable. England's experiment with Protestantism had begun under Henry VIII and, despite faltering briefly under the reign of Mary Tudor, it had been nurtured through Elizabeth's forty-four year reign. All that might have been overturned at a single, spectacular stroke. Spain, France and the Pope in Rome, the old enemies, would have been quick to exploit the turmoil that followed. A sense of paranoia now gripped London at the highest level. It was noted by the Venetian ambassador, who observed:

> *The King is in terror. He does not appear nor does he take his meals in public as usual ... the Lords of the Council also are alarmed and confused by the plot itself and [by] the King's suspicions. The city is in great uncertainty. Catholics fear heretics and vice-versa; both are armed; foreigners live in terror of their houses being sacked by the mob.*

James convinced himself that he had been spared for no less a reason than that he was God's chosen one. He told anyone who cared to listen that the discovery of the true nature of the diabolical plot had been his own, conceived through divine intervention. The vital clue that undid the plotters had come in an anonymous, cryptic letter received on 26 October by Lord Monteagle, a Catholic peer who, like Robert Catesby, had taken part in Essex's abortive rebellion in 1601. The letter from a well-wisher warned Monteagle to stay away from the opening of Parliament. Monteagle showed it to Sir Robert Cecil, the Secretary of State, who showed it to the King. James later claimed it was he himself who had picked up on a curious statement in the letter:

> *For though there be no appearance of any stir, yet I say they shall receive a terrible blow this Parliament; and yet they shall not see who hurts them.*

Puzzling over that phrase 'they shall not see who hurts them,' James said God had revealed to him what it meant. As a result, he ordered the cellars under Parliament to be searched.

To celebrate what was hailed as the king's miraculous escape, a silver medal (*pictured*) was struck. It economically served the dual purpose of also marking the expulsion from Protestant Holland of the Jesuits, a Catholic community long considered troublesome. On the front of the medal a snake is depicted, with its poisonous fangs extended and ready to strike. The creature slithers menacingly among a bed of lilies and roses, flowers that were symbolic royal emblems.

The design was meant to represent Catholic intrigue and deception, and was surrounded by a triumphant inscription in Latin that translates as: 'He who concealed himself is detected.' On the reverse is a design with another Latin inscription, addressed to the Almighty, which translates as: 'You [God], the keeper of James, have not slept.' It is to this medal that Shakespeare refers in Lady Macbeth's advice to her husband to 'look like the innocent flower, but be the serpent under't.'

The play's most telling reference to the conspiracy comes in a scene immediately after Macbeth has murdered Duncan. In a moment of high tension, a sudden loud knocking rattles the castle doors. A drunken porter shuffles to admit the night-time callers, complaining as he does so about the imagined guests he might have to let in. Although the scene is intended as light relief after the bloody deeds that have just taken place, the porter's grumbling contains mocking references to a man who, while not one of the Gunpowder Plot conspirators, had an intimate knowledge of the plotters and was even suspected by the authorities of being a ringleader.

The suspect in question was Father Henry Garnet (*pictured*), a Jesuit priest who had in fact tried to dissuade the plotters, fearful of the backlash against Catholics that would ensue. In the summer of 1605, Robert Catesby had met with Garnet and asked him about the morality of killing innocents if a cause was rightful.

On 24 July, a subordinate priest named Father Oswald Tesimond told Garnet about the existence of the plot, which Catesby had confided to him under the seal of confession. Garnet advised Tesimond that canon law forbade either priest from divulging what they had heard, but he wrote to the Pope urging his holiness to caution English Catholics against the use of force. Garnet did not directly mention the plot in his letter. He also appears to have personally attempted to persuade Catesby to abandon his plans.

As Jesuit Superior, the head of the Jesuit mission in England, Garnet had been a hated Papist thorn in the side of the establishment for some years, organising an underground network of priests, conducting forbidden Catholic ceremonies, and secretly publishing tracts the authorities considered both blasphemous and seditious. He had remained at liberty only by keeping on the move and sheltering in the homes of Catholic sympathisers. When the plotters were arrested, Garnet went into hiding. He was hunted down and arrested at Hindlip Hall, Worcestershire, on 27 January 1606, after being forced by attrition to emerge from an ingeniously concealed priest's hole. He was tried on 28 March that year, convicted of treason, and met the standard fate of being hanged, drawn and quartered, despite protesting his innocence.

During Garnet's trial, much was made by his prosecutors of his adherence to a controversial Jesuit doctrine known as equivocation. The doctrine permitted Catholics to lie under oath if necessary to protect their lives or those of other Catholics, without committing a sin in the eyes of God. Equivocation included techniques such as speaking part of a sentence out loud, then finishing it or adding a qualification silently in one's head, or saying one thing while thinking another. The listener might be misled, but the speaker could convince himself he had not lied before God if he had a 'secret meaning reserved in his mind'. In the eyes of the authorities, however, equivocation simply amounted to perjury, which in itself undermined the integrity of the courts and the English language, not to mention the sanctity of the *Holy Bible* on which the oath to tell the truth had been sworn.

All Garnet wished to do at his trial was clear himself of involvement in the plot. Instead, a treatise he had written on equivocation, found among the 'heretical, treasonable and damnable books' of one of the conspirators, Francis Tresham, was laid on the table before him and he was grilled at length about its contents. The subject of equivocation caught the attention of the chattering classes, no doubt some of them gathered around tables in the Mermaid Tavern, and Shakespeare cannot resist heaping ridicule on the argument in *Macbeth*. These are the porter's words as he answers the knocking on the castle doors:

> **Knock, knock, knock! Who's there, i' the name of Beelzebub? Here's a farmer that hanged himself on the expectation of plenty: come in time; have napkins** [handkerchiefs] **enow** [enough] **about you; here you'll sweat for't. [Knocking within] Knock, knock! Who's there, in the other devil's name? Faith, here's an equivocator, that could swear in both the scales** [of justice] **against either scale; who committed treason enough for God's sake, yet could not equivocate to heaven: O, come in, equivocator. [Knocking within] Knock, knock, knock! Who's there? Faith, here's an English tailor come hither, for stealing out of a French hose** [being stingy with his cloth]**: come in, tailor; here you may roast your goose.** (2.3)

The 'equivocator' is, of course, Father Henry Garnet. 'Here's a farmer that hanged himself' may be a reference to the name 'Farmer', one of Garnet's known pseudonyms while he was working undercover. The mention of napkins, or handkerchiefs, alludes to Catholic spectators at public executions who would use the cloths to mop up the blood of victims they considered to be martyrs. As for the 'English tailor,' a man who was interrogated in November 1606 for being in possession of 'Garnet's Straw' – a stalk of grain on to which Garnet's blood was said to have splashed and miraculously formed an image of his face – was a tailor.

Garnet was said to have consoled himself with wine during his relatively comfortable imprisonment before the trial. His prosecutors also taunted him with lurid suggestions that his relationship with a woman sympathiser named Anne Vaux, who had attempted to hide him at Hindlip Hall before his arrest, included sexual encounters in violation of his vow of chastity. These allegations may explain something else on the mind of the porter in *Macbeth*, when he goes on to declare that alcohol provokes three things:

Nose-painting [a flushed nose], **sleep, and urine. Lechery, sir, it provokes, and unprovokes; it provokes the desire, but it takes away the performance. Therefore, much drink may be said to be an equivocator with lechery: it makes him, and it mars him; it sets him on, and it takes him off; it persuades him, and disheartens him; makes him stand to, and not stand to; in conclusion, equivocates him in a sleep, and, giving him the lie, leaves him.** (2.3)

There is that word 'equivocator' again. Nevertheless, the most accomplished equivocators in *Macbeth* are surely the witches. Are they living beings or mere visions? Are they men or women? When the witches speak, their language is riddled with double meaning: When the hurlyburly's done, when the battle's lost and won ... Fair is foul, and foul is fair ... Lesser than Macbeth and greater ... Not so happy, yet much happier ... Thou shalt get kings, though thou be none.

Indeed, their equivocation in a world where 'nothing is but what is not' will prove the final undoing of Macbeth. The reassurance he finds when the witches conjure an apparition that tells him 'Laugh to scorn the power of man, for none of woman born shall harm Macbeth' comes to nothing when his opponent Macduff reveals that he was 'from his mother's womb untimely ripp'd', in other words born by caesarean section. Even the promise that 'Macbeth shall never vanquish'd be until great Birnam wood to high Dunsinane hill shall come against him' proves meaningless when his enemies break off branches of Birnam's trees and use them to camouflage their advance.

Shakespeare found the original story of Macbeth in

Raphael Holinshed's *Chronicles*, though he makes a significant change to the character of Banquo. While Holinshed writes that Banquo was Macbeth's accomplice in regicide, Shakespeare instead portrays him as a loyal follower of Duncan, the rightful king. He had good reason. James I considered himself to be descended from the historical figure of Banquo, Thane of Lochquhaber ('Thou shalt get kings, though thou be none' was the witches' prophesy for Banquo). True to form in writing *Macbeth*, Shakespeare chose not to pen some flattering song of praise giving thanks for the monarch's 'miraculous' survival. But having gone to great lengths to appease the fretful James with a tale about the downfall of traitors and the emptiness of equivocation, he also recognised there would be little point in putting it all at risk by gratuitously insulting Banquo, the king's royal ancestor.

See also: 33. An Act of Sedition
37. Something Wicked Comes

37. SOMETHING WICKED COMES

James I's obsession with witchcraft leads Will to write a disturbing supernatural thriller

[Thunder and lightning. Enter three Witches]

First Witch: When shall we three meet again / In thunder, lightning, or in rain?

Second Witch: When the hurlyburly's done / When the battle's lost and won.

Third Witch: That will be ere the set of sun.

First Witch: Where the place?

Second Witch: Upon the heath.

Third Witch: There to meet with Macbeth.

First Witch: I come, Graymalkin!

Second Witch: Paddock calls.

Third Witch: Anon.

All: Fair is foul, and foul is fair / Hover through the fog and filthy air.

[Exeunt] (*Macbeth*, 1.1, 1606)

CUE noises offstage to replicate thunder. In modern theatres, cue also stroboscopic lighting effects to mimic lightning. Add dramatic music and smoke machines hidden in the wings to belch out their miasma of mystery.

The extract above is short, sharp and wastes not one word in its pithy dialogue. It is also the opening scene – in its entirety – of Shakespeare's only play set in Scotland. *Macbeth* is thought to have received its first performance in 1606 in the presence of James I (*pictured*) and his visiting brother-in-law,

Christian IV, King of Denmark. The subject of witchcraft had become something of an obsession with James. Several years before he ascended the English throne on the death of Elizabeth I in 1603, he wrote a book titled *Daemonologie*, in which he explored the vexing subject. Among the matters the book covered were the sensational North Berwick witch trials of 1590-92, over which James, while simply James VI of Scotland, had personally presided.

When Shakespeare set out to write *Macbeth* he clearly reasoned that if the king was so fascinated with witchcraft he would give him a play saturated with the stuff, culminating in the ultimate triumph of good over evil. Better still, he would set it in the king's own northern homeland. Poring over the pages of *Daemonologie*, and adapting a reference to the 'weird sisters' in his old favourite, Raphael Holinshed's *Chronicles*, Will conjured up the spectre of the three grotesque witches to infuse his story of a Scottish king's assassination with an all-pervading air of satanic menace. He succeeded so spectacularly that generations of actors have since believed even mentioning the play's name is to risk invoking a fearful curse, a superstition which persists to this day. *Macbeth* is instead referred to in some theatrical circles as 'the Scottish play'.

James' morbid fascination with witchcraft was rooted in the dramatic events of May 1590. He was then twenty-three years old, having been King of Scotland since 1567, and was sailing home from Denmark with his new bride. She was Anne, a fifteen-year-old Danish princess who was the sister of Christian. As the happy couple sailed north-west across the North Sea, a ferocious storm blew up and pummelled the royal fleet. While the other vessels struggled on gamely towards Scotland, a 'contrary wind' struck the king's ship and blew it back in the direction from which it had come, separating it from the rest of the fleet. The waves were so huge they almost caused the ship to capsize.

Given that an attempt in the previous year by Anne herself to sail to James in Scotland had been thwarted by a storm which forced her fleet to take shelter in Norway, there could be only one conclusion. On both occasions the elements had been summoned into a frenzy at the command of the Devil, the king's sworn enemy. James considered himself not only to have been chosen by God to rule his subjects through Divine Right, but also to be Satan's chief foe on earth. The fact that their lives were spared, he insisted, was proof positive that he was being protected by the Almighty.

In Copenhagen, a witch-hunt immediately got under way to find the servants of the Devil who were responsible for conjuring up the tempest. Several unfortunate women were arrested and confessed under torture to being guilty of sorcery by raising both storms. When news of their confessions reached James, at last safely ensconced at Holyrood House with Anne, he instituted an exhaustive search for any Scottish witches who might also have had a hand in the evil plot.

He did not have far to look. A maidservant called Geillis Duncan, almost certainly just a teenager, had aroused the suspicions of her employer, a magistrate named David Seton, in the village of Tranent, nine miles (14km) east of Edinburgh. Seton heard rumours that Duncan was being credited with a curious ability to ease pain and suffering among the sick. What was more, she had a curious habit of sneaking out in the middle of the night for unknown purposes. In November 1590, Seton accosted Duncan and accused her of dabbling in witchcraft, taking it upon himself to interrogate her with increasing degrees of violence.

Her emphatic denials ended only when Seton, enthusiastically assisted by his son and others, subjected the poor girl to sadistic tortures which involved crushing her fingers with thumbscrews known as 'pilliwinks' and twisting a rope tightly around her head. Her tormentors then stripped her, shaved off every hair on her body, and examined her intimately in order to locate what was known as 'the Devil's mark,' a blemish said to signify a covenant between a witch and the Devil. At length they declared that they had found such a damning symbol on her neck. It was probably no more than a mole or birthmark, but it was enough. After that humiliation, the broken maid succumbed and confessed that she was indeed a witch. Under further torture designed to force her to identify her accomplices – for where one witch was discovered there were bound to be others – she reeled off a list of names in the hope that doing so would bring an end to her agony.

Among those Duncan fingered were Agnes Sampson, an elderly local woman who had a reputation as a midwife and healer; Euphame MacCalzean, who also appears to have practised midwifery as we hear of her being accused of using black magic to relieve 'the God-ordained pain' of women giving birth; Barbara Napier, who was alleged to have bewitched to death Archibald Douglas, the eighth Earl of Angus, after he succumbed to a mysterious disease for which his baffled physician could find no remedy; and Dr John Fian, a schoolmaster, who was a purported sorcerer, grave robber and head of the coven.

James himself presided over the interrogation of Agnes Sampson, 'which was the eldest witch'. She would not confess to anything, even under excruciating torture. Finally all her hair was shaven off and 'the Divels [Devil's] marke was found upon her privities [privates]'. From that time on, probably realising resistance was futile, she regaled her examiners with the most extraordinary stories of how she was among a coven of two hundred witches who had set out to sea in sieves – an ability with which only witches were credited – and sailed along the coast until they landed at North Berwick, where they indulged in drinking, ritual dances and general merry-making in the church until the Devil himself appeared. The gripping events at North Berwick were recorded in *Newes from Scotland*, a pamphlet printed in London in 1591, which was snapped up by an excited reading public. (Much of what the pamphlet contained would later find its way into James' book *Daemonologie*.) Amid the ungodly goings on, according to *Newes from Scotland*, the Devil 'did greatlye enveighe against the King of Scotland' and demanded pledges of unswerving loyalty from his servants:

> *At which time the witches demaunded of the Divel why he did beare such hatred to the King, who answered, by reason the King is the greatest enemy he hath in the worlde.*

There was worse to come. Sampson confessed that she had taken a black toad and hung it up by the heels for three days, collecting the venom that dripped from its body in an oyster shell in the hope that she could smear the fluid on an item of cloth belonging to the king and thereby cause him an agonising death. Then came the most crucial confession of all. She said it was because of a 'christened' cat, to which she had tied body parts taken from a dead man, that the great storm arose which almost sank the king's ship as it returned from Denmark. The plan would have succeeded, she claimed, 'if his faith had not prevailed above their ententions'.

James – once famously described as 'the wisest fool in Christendom' – initially expressed his doubts, replying that her stories were so far-fetched all of the accused could only be 'extreame lyars'. His view changed suddenly when Sampson, insisting she was telling the truth, reportedly took the shocked king to one side and revealed 'the verye woordes' that had passed between him and his bride Anne on the night of their wedding.

Newes from Scotland

A woodcut illustration from *Newes from Scotland* (*pictured*) shows a ship being sunk by witchcraft (top left); witches stirring a cauldron (top right); the Devil preaching from a pulpit to a coven of witches while Dr John Fian, a schoolmaster of Haddington, writes down his words (Fian was tried and executed for sorcery); and a pedlar (right and lower right) who was said to have discovered witches in the Scottish village of Tranent, only to find himself diabolically transported to a merchant's wine cellar in Bordeaux.

The upshot of this farrago of nonsense, which most of Sampson's interrogators had been only too eager to believe from the start, was a series of convictions at the so-called North Berwick witch trials and the grisly executions, mainly by burning at the stake, of Geillis Duncan and the people she had named. Torture to extract confessions from those accused of witchcraft was legal in Scotland but not in England at the time.

Those Duncan identified had been horrifically tortured to make them reveal further names, and as a result more than seventy people ended up being arraigned at the trials. In the last moments of her life, the terrified Duncan retracted her original confession. She declared it had been made only to stop the unbearable torments to which she had been subjected, a fact that might reasonably have called into question the veracity of all the names subsequently extracted from her under duress. Not that it did her, or them, any good.

Shakespeare had grown up in a society in which there was an implicit belief in the infernal powers of witches, a concept that had thrived since the Protestant Reformation and was pursued with particular zeal by the Puritans. Henry VIII's second wife Anne Boleyn – Elizabeth I's mother – had herself once been accused of witchcraft. Anne reportedly had six fingers on her right hand, which couldn't have helped. In 1542, six years after Anne's death, Henry passed England's first Witchcraft Act, which declared practising the dark arts to be a secular crime against the state rather than a spiritual matter to be dealt with by the clergy.

Lurid accounts of witches' activities flourished during Elizabeth's reign and in 1563 she made witchcraft a capital offence if it led to anyone's death. Her *Act Against Conjurations, Enchantments and Witchcrafts* declared that anyone would be subject to execution who used, practised or exercised 'any witchcraft, enchantment, charm, or sorcery, whereby any person shall happen to be killed or destroyed'. Lesser witchcraft offences were punishable by imprisonment.

Under Scotland's separate and more draconian laws, all offences of witchcraft, even consorting with witches, were punishable by death. In 1604, James I toughened up the law in England too, instituting an Act that made 'conjuration, witchcraft and dealing with evil and wicked spirits' of any sort a felony punishable by death, though hanging replaced burning at the stake. It was James' law that would empower the notorious excesses of England's Witchfinder General Matthew Hopkins a generation later.

One of the first women to be executed under the 1563 Act passed by Elizabeth was Agnes Waterhouse, better known as 'Mother Waterhouse'. She was tried in 1566 at Chelmsford along with two others, including her eighteen-year-old daughter Joan, who was acquitted. Waterhouse was convicted on the absurdly fanciful testimony of a neighbour's twelve-year-old daughter. Among the key pieces of evidence presented at the trial were claims Waterhouse, who lived in the Essex village of Hatfield Peverel, kept a 'familiar' – that is, a witch's pet – in the form of a cat named Satan, or Sathan, which she turned into a toad. Possession of a 'familiar', a malevolent spirit in the shape of an animal capable of carrying out the owner's commands, was an essential prerequisite for any self-respecting witch. 'Familiars' also figured prominently in the trial of the four accused Windsor witches, Mother Stile, Mother Dutten, Mother Margaret and Mother Deuell, at Abingdon Assizes in 1579.

In that case it was said Mother Dutten 'keepeth a spirite or fiende in the likenesse of a toade, and feedeth the same fiende, lying in a border of greene herbes within her garden, with blood whiche she causeth to issue from her owne flank'. Mother Deuell, described as 'a very poore' woman, 'hath a spirite in the shape of a blacke catte, and calleth it Gille, whereby she is aided in her witchcrafte, and she daily feedeth it with milke, mingled with her owne blood'.

Mother Margaret, a cripple 'dwelling in the almes house at Windsor, doeth feede a fiende named Ginnie, with crumbs of bread and her owne blood'. As for Mother Stile, said to be a morose woman given to falling out with her neighbours, she 'kepte a ratte, being in very deede a wicked spirite, naming it Philip, and that she fed the same ratte with bloode, issuing from her right hand, the markes whereof evidently remaine'. It is to such 'familiars' that *Macbeth's* weird sisters refer in that opening scene when the First Witch declares 'I come, Graymalkin!' and the second adds: 'Paddock calls.' Graymalkin was a common name for a cat. Paddock was a toad.

Further evidence against the four women of Windsor alleged that they practised a dark art known as 'image magic,' in which a picture or wax doll, known as a 'poppet', would be crafted. The poppet would then be stabbed through the heart and limbs with pins or sharpened sticks while curses were invoked against the person it was meant to represent. Coincidentally at the time of the trial in Abingdon, panic arose when three wax poppets, each about twelve inches (30cm) long and with pins stuck through them, were found buried in a dung heap in Lincoln's Inn Fields, London. One had the name 'Elizabeth' scrawled across the forehead and the others appeared to represent the Queen's closest advisors.

Elizabeth herself was on a 'progress' (or tour) of East Anglia at the time and she happened to be suffering severe pain from toothache, not surprisingly given her famed love of sugary treats. When news of the discovery of the waxen images reached her, she summoned her personal astrologer Dr John Dee to travel to Norwich from London in order to perform magic charms of his own. She was satisfied that would counter any spell put on her by the unknown makers of the poppets.

No fewer than twenty-six of Shakespeare's plays and three of his poems mention witches, witchcraft, or people being bewitched in one form or another. There were, after all, not yet any rational scientific explanations, let alone effective treatments, for pain, disease and infections. The years around the turn of the sixteenth century brought tempests that tore down buildings and sank ships. They heralded cold, wet summers, disastrous harvests and sickness among cattle that led to starvation and desperate people resorting to crime to stay alive. Mothers frequently died during childbirth, children often perished young – hence the demand for baptism within a few days of birth – and lifespans were often less than half those we expect today. While loose and immoral behaviour thrived as it had through the centuries, rampaging syphilis took a terrible toll and was regarded as God's punishment of the sinful. In towns and cities, the recurring terror of the plague was never far away. It was tempting to look for some-one to blame when things went wrong, misfortune struck, or accidents just happened. Sheer bad luck must have been caused by somebody's ill-will.

The people accused and convicted of witchcraft, of whom women made up the vast majority, were usually poor, powerless, elderly and widowed. To ease their loneliness they perhaps kept a pet such as a cat, which could all too readily be condemned as a 'familiar'. Sometimes such women had simply been good-hearted enough to help their neighbours in childbirth or by supplying traditional herbal mixtures they believed would help alleviate sickness and disease. Some-times they had fallen out with others, who then sought spite-ful revenge by inventing improbable stories about them.

Quarrelsome women neighbours were particularly vul-nerable to accusations of witchcraft. Sometimes they were ostracised for unsightly physical deformities or unseen men-tal impairment that made them oddballs in their small vil-lage communities. For an old woman to be seen as eccentric, to have piercing blue eyes or, horror of horrors, tufts of hair on her chin, could all be enough to mark her out for suspicion. In the words of Macbeth when he first encounters the weird sisters:

What are these so wither'd and so wild in their attire
that look not like the inhabitants o' the earth and yet are
on't? Live you? Or are you aught that man may question?
You seem to understand me, by each at once her chappy

[cracked skin] **finger laying upon her skinny lips. You should be women, and yet your beards forbid me to interpret that you are so.** (1.3)

Others might have sought notoriety by implying they had mysterious powers, believing it conferred upon them an enhanced social standing in their small communities while not realising where it would lead. A small number could even have been driven to dabble in the occult. Most were simply ordinary people who got caught up in waves of irrational mass hysteria that turned them into the victims of prejudice, misogyny and downright sadism. Well might the Second Witch in *Macbeth* incant:

By the pricking of my thumbs, / Something wicked this way comes. (4.1)

See also: 19. Gillian, the Fat Old Witch
28. The World's Mine Oyster
36. Gunpowder, Treason and Plot

38. THESE LATE ECLIPSES

*Strange phenomena are seen as heralding disasters but Will sounds
a note of scepticism*

**These late eclipses in the sun and moon portend no good to
us. Though the wisdom of nature** [scientific knowledge] **can
reason it** [offer explanations] **thus and thus, yet nature finds
itself scourged by the sequent effects. Love cools, friendship falls off, brothers divide, in cities mutinies, in countries
discord, in palaces treason, and the bond cracked 'twixt son
and father.**

(*King Lear*, 1.2, 1605-6)

THE Earl of Gloucester confides the superstitions that are
troubling him to his treacherous son Edmund, the very person who will betray him. Gloucester was not alone in holding
such beliefs. Eclipses had for centuries been regarded as heavenly harbingers of doom and misfortune. The message that
human life is governed by the chance alignment of heavenly
bodies had been peddled enthusiastically by, among others,
the occultist Dr John Dee, who wielded huge influence as
trusted court astrologer to Elizabeth I. Indeed, Elizabeth was
so in thrall to Dee's prowess that she allowed him to set the
date for her coronation on 15 January 1559.

Dee's standing declined rapidly after Elizabeth's death in
1603, however, when he and his dark arts were regarded with
distaste by her successor on the throne, James I. But in this
tense early scene in *King Lear*, Gloucester's warnings inject an
air of supernatural foreboding to which many in Shakespeare's
audience would have unquestioningly subscribed.

Some doubt surrounds exactly when Shakespeare wrote
the magnificent tragedy that is *King Lear* but we know for cer-

tain it was performed as court entertainment for James I on the Feast of St Stephen, 26 December 1606. Two eclipses that may have inspired Shakespeare's lines had occurred within weeks of each other the previous year: an eclipse of the moon on 27 September 1605, followed by an almost total eclipse of the sun, visible from all over the south of England, on 12 October. In fact, the previous seven years had seen an extraordinary convergence of eclipses. On 7 March 1598, a solar eclipse occurred in which the sun was totally obscured along a path stretching from Cornwall to Aberdeen, followed by a partial solar eclipse on 24 December 1601, a year that also saw two lunar eclipses.

Moonlight that continues to shine during lunar eclipses was purported to possess magical properties of its own. Among the potent concoction of ingredients that Macbeth's chanting witches seek for their cauldron's potent diabolical mix are:

Gall of goat, and slips of yew, silver'd in the moon's eclipse. (*Macbeth*, 4.1)

The sceptical Edmund in *King Lear*, however, will have none of it. Once his father is out of earshot, he delivers a mocking rejoinder, scoffing:

This is the excellent foppery [stupidity] **of the world that, when we are sick in fortune, often the surfeits** [excesses] **of our own behaviour, we make guilty of our disasters the sun, the moon, and the stars; as if we were villains on necessity, fools by heavenly compulsion, knaves, thieves, and treachers** [traitors] **by spherical predominance** [because a certain planet was most powerful at our birth], **drunkards, liars, and adulterers by an enforc'd obedience of planetary influence; and all that we are evil in, by a divine thrusting on** [supernatural force]. **An admirable evasion of whore-master man, to lay his goatish** [lascivious] **disposition to the charge of a star!**

(1.2)

Edmund's riposte may have been inserted simply to portray him as the self-serving cynic that he is, but – particularly coming during an age when the distinction between the science of astronomy and the mumbo-jumbo of astrology was non-existent – his dismissal of Gloucester's musings appeals to our modern sensitivities.

❈ ❈ ❈

The commonly held conviction that a person's character and fortunes were shaped by the star sign or planetary influences under which they were born, or which prevailed at any given moment, pervades Shakespeare's writings. Most people would have agreed with the Earl of Kent in *King Lear*, when he declares:

> **It is the stars, the stars above us, govern our conditions.**
> (4.3)

Romeo and Juliet are condemned to their tragic fate in the inevitable way 'star-cross'd lovers' must be. Romeo senses trouble even before he meets the love of his life:

> **My mind misgives** [I have a premonition] **some consequence yet hanging in the stars shall bitterly begin his fearful date** [its fateful course] **with this night's revels, and expire the term of a despised life closed in my breast by some vile forfeit of untimely death.** (*Romeo and Juliet*, 1.4)

At length, as the feared ending inexorably closes in, the resentful youth rages with a fist clenched to the sky:

> **Is it even so? Then I defy you, stars!** (5.1)

A desperate Pericles, Prince of Tyre, turns to pleading with stellar influences:

Yet cease your ire, you angry stars of heaven. (*Pericles*, 2.1)

While the loyalist Humphrey, Duke of Gloucester, makes his own impassioned entreaty to the heavenly powers for a change in fortune in *Henry VI, Part 1*:

Hung be the heavens with black, yield day to night! Comets, importing change of times and states, brandish your crystal tresses [tails] in the sky and with them scourge the bad revolting stars that have consented unto Henry's death! (1.1)

In an altogether lighter vein, that wayward drunkard Sir Toby Belch encourages his foolish friend Sir Andrew Aguecheek to show off his skills at dancing in *Twelfth Night* by appealing to their star sign.

Sir Andrew: **Shall we set about some revels?**

Sir Toby: **What shall we do else? Were we not born under Taurus?**

Sir Andrew: **Taurus! That's sides and heart.**

Sir Toby: **No, sir, it is legs and thighs. Let me see the caper. Ha, higher! Ha, ha, excellent!** (1.3)

Different parts of the body were thought to be endowed and controlled by various signs of the Zodiac. Taurus, the bull, was believed to govern the throat and neck (body parts revered by drinkers), though on this occasion the inebriated knights get their star signs and anatomical features hopelessly muddled. While the stars and planets shining at a person's birth could spell ill fortune, they might also be credited with bringing good luck and happiness. Also in *Twelfth Night*, the servant Malvolio rejoices at having received what he believes is a love-letter from Olivia, the mistress he serves, and his lucky stars get the credit:

I thank my stars, I am happy [in love]. **I will be strange**

[aloof], **stout** [proud], **in yellow stockings and cross-gartered even with the swiftness of putting on. Jove** [Jupiter, god of erotic conquest] **and my stars be praised!** (2.5)

Then there is this delightful exchange in *Much Ado About Nothing*:

Don Pedro: **Your silence most offends me, and to be merry best becomes you. For out of question, you were born in a merry hour.**

Beatrice: **No, sure, my lord, my mother cried** [in labour]. **But then there was a star danced, and under that was I born.** (2.1)

Among the dissenters to astrological superstition, however, is the down-to-earth Cassius, as he seeks to convince Brutus to join a plot to assassinate Julius Caesar in the Capitol.

Men at some time are masters of their fates. The fault, dear Brutus, is not in our stars but in ourselves that we are underlings. (*Julius Caesar*, 1.2)

Perhaps for the final word on the subject we should return to Edmund, that resentful illegitimate son of Gloucester's in *King Lear*, when in a tone dripping with sarcasm he snarls:

My father compounded with my mother under the Dragon's Tail [part of the constellation of Draco], **and my nativity was under Ursa Major** [the Great Bear], **so that it follows I am rough and lecherous. Fut! I should have been that I am had the maidenliest star in the firmament twinkled on my bastardising.** (1.2)

See also: 39. Comets and Prodigies

39. COMETS AND PRODIGIES

Events in the night sky spark an epoch in astronomy that is set to overturn the old order

When beggars die, there are no comets seen; the heavens themselves blaze forth the death of princes.

(Julius Caesar, 2.2, 1599)

CAESAR'S wife Calpurnia has spent a troubled night, tormented by wild dreams and ill omens she fears herald impending disaster. It is the morning of the Ides of March and she pleads with her steely husband not to go to the Capitol where, as we later see, his assassins plan to stage their bloody coup. What better harbinger of doom could there be than a comet, one of those cosmic balls of ice and rock that have been regarded throughout history with dread as they streaked across the sky? Shakespeare had good reason to write those lines for Calpurnia. A formidable comet had indeed appeared in the spring of 44BC around the time, or shortly after, Caesar was murdered. It duly became known as Caesar's Comet and was regarded by many Romans as a sign of the deification of the late warrior-turned-dictator.

The night sky was surprisingly busy during Shakespeare's lifetime and comets get a mention in several of his plays. In *Henry IV, Part 1*, for instance, the king chastises his wayward son Prince Hal for frequenting common taverns and spending time in the company of such wastrels as Sir John Falstaff, thereby dragging down the reputation of the Crown itself. Henry compares such behaviour with his own well practised policy of rarely venturing outside the royal palaces and grounds, so attracting throngs of cheering admirers whenever he did grace his subjects with an appearance. Henry says:

By being seldom seen, I could not stir but, like a comet, I was wonder'd at; that men would tell their children: 'This is he.' (3.2)

The boisterous Petruchio upbraids astonished on-lookers as he turns up mockingly dressed in outrageously inappropriate clothes for his wedding to Katherine in *The Taming of the Shrew*:

Gentles, methinks you frown. And wherefore [why] gaze this goodly company as if they saw some wondrous monument, some comet or unusual prodigy? (3.2)

Shakespeare himself witnessed the arrival of at least two spectacular comets in his lifetime. The Great Comet of 1577 appeared when he was thirteen years old and would have dominated the night sky in Stratford-upon-Avon, as it did across all of Europe. It shone so brightly that, like the full moon, its light could be seen through the clouds. A chronicler in Ireland wrote of it:

A wonderful star appeared in the south-east in the first month of winter. It had a curved bow-like tail, resembling bright lightning, the brilliancy of which illuminated the earth around, and the firmament above. This star was seen in every part of the west of Europe, and it was wondered at by all universally.

At her palace in Richmond, Elizabeth I snorted at the exhortations of her counsellors not to look on the comet for fear it should bring her ill health. In the words of the courtier Henry Howard, Earl of Northampton:

When divers, upon greater scrupulosity than cause, went about to dissuade her majesty from looking on the Comet which appeared last: with a courage answerable to the greatness of her state, she caused the window to be set open, and cast out this word 'Iacta est alia', the dice are thrown, affirm-

ing that her steadfast hope and confidence was too firmly planted in the providence of God to be blasted or affrighted with those beams, which either had a ground in nature whereupon to rise, or at least no warrant out of scripture to portend the mishaps of Princes.

The Queen's attitude in this instance was an enlightened one, considering the deeply superstitious age in which she lived and the high regard she held for the musings of Dr John Dee, her court astrologer. Among those observing the 1577 comet was the Danish nobleman Tycho Brahe from his observatory on the island of Hven. In a major step for astronomy, Tycho established that the comet was no 'exhalation' of earth's atmosphere, as most people believed comets to be, but was instead around three times further away than the moon.

Shakespeare was an established playwright aged forty-three when a second truly memorable comet swam into his ken. The year 1607 saw a visitation by the same comet that featured on the Bayeux Tapestry (*pictured*) and had appeared again many times since 1066. No one could know it then – and it would not be until 1705 that the astronomer Edmond Halley would calculate – that the comet which now bears Halley's name returned every seventy-six years.

It may, indeed, have been the appearance of Halley's Comet that Shakespeare had in mind when, in writing *Pericles* that same year, he gave to the chaste Marina these lines:

I am a maid, my lord, that ne'er before invited eyes, but have been gazed on like a comet. (5.1)

Comets were considered prodigies because they disturbed what was seen as the God-ordained order of things. More than twenty years before Shakespeare's birth, Nicolaus Copernicus in Poland had published a theory that the earth revolved around the sun, but his ideas were considered outrageous by most people and were slow to catch on. In Europe, the Catholic Church took a bleak view, condemning such talk as nothing less than heresy, as the pioneering cosmologists Giordano Bruno and Galileo discovered to their cost.

The Church held steadfastly to the vision of the universe expounded by the Greek thinker Claudius Ptolemy in the second century, which placed the earth firmly at the centre of all Creation, circled by the sun and everything else in the sky. That comfortable concept, with the sun and moon dutifully orbiting the terrestrial globe, is alluded to by Hermia in *A Midsummer Night's Dream*:

> I'll believe as soon this whole earth may be bored and that the moon may through the centre creep and so displease her brother's noontide with the Antipodes. (3.2)

All celestial objects were believed to be attached to invisible concentric spheres, which encompassed the earth as they revolved around it. It was as if we are looking up at the inside of a dome of many layers, all moving independently of one another. The usurping Claudius has this in mind when he speaks of Gertrude in these lines from *Hamlet*:

> My virtue or my plague, be it either which, she's so conjunctive to my life and soul that, as the star moves not but in his sphere, I could not but by her. (4.7)

Likewise in *King John*, the character Philip the Bastard asks:

> Now, now, you stars that move in your right spheres, where be your powers? (5.1)

In *Henry IV, Part 1*, when Hal, the Prince of Wales, comes

face to face with his arch-enemy Harry 'Hotspur' Percy – who is seeking to overthrow Hal and his father then stake his own claim to the throne – he issues this deadly challenge:

> **I am the Prince of Wales; and think not, Percy, to share with me in glory any more. Two stars keep not their motion in one sphere; nor can one England brook a double reign, of Harry Percy and the Prince of Wales.** (5.4)

Shakespeare never strays far from that traditional view of a geocentric universe, with 'the planets' – which included the sun and moon – all confined to their respective spheres. In *Troilus and Cressida,* Ulysses paints a picture of an orderly heavens in which all the celestial bodies 'observe degree, priority and place,' with 'the glorious planet Sol [the sun] in noble eminence enthroned and sphered amidst the other'. Ulysses then warns that any departure from such rigid conformity could only ever spell disaster:

> **When the planets in evil mixture to disorder wander, what plagues and what portents! What mutiny! What raging of the sea! Shaking of earth! Commotion in the winds! Frights, changes, horrors, divert and crack, rend and deracinate** [uproot] **the unity and married calm of states quite from their fixture!** (1.3)

In *Antony and Cleopatra*, a nihilistic Cleopatra even cries out:

> **O sun, burn the great sphere thou movs't in, darkling stand the varying shore o' the world.** (4.15)

She is calling on the sun to set fire to the sphere to which it is attached, drift away into the space beyond, and cast the world into endless night.

For all that, some modern commentators, notably the American academic Peter Usher, consider family connections Shakespeare had with the pioneering English astronomer

Thomas Digges to be of significance. In 1576, Digges published a diagram supporting the heliocentric theory of Copernicus, but going an important step further. He suggested there was no outer sphere for the fixed stars, making him the first to moot the truly revolutionary idea that the universe is infinite. Professor Usher points to such lines in *Hamlet* as:

O God, I could be bounded in a nutshell and count myself a king of infinite space, were it not that I have bad dreams. (2.2)

From this reference to 'infinite space' and other allusions, Usher suggests Shakespeare possessed a profound grasp of astronomical reality and imbued his greatest tragedy with elaborate allegories covertly expounding Copernicanism. Could it be so? Yet again, Shakespeare proves to be all things to all people.

❋ ❋ ❋

Like comets, the appearance of exploding stars shattered the neatly ordained pattern of how the heavens ought to behave, and Shakespeare also lived to see two spectacular examples of those. In 1576, when he was aged twelve, a new star burst forth where none had been before. It outshone the planet Venus, normally the brightest object in the sky apart from the sun and moon, and the sharp-eyed could see it even in the daytime. In Denmark, the ever-vigilant Tycho Brahe set about recording its activity. What we now know was a supernova – an old star dying with explosive force – became known as Tycho's Star. It was very likely the brightest stellar display since the supernova in 1054 that created today's Crab Nebula, and it shattered the illusion of a steady universe running like clockwork to a pre-ordained pattern. Tycho noted first seeing it on the night of 11 November 1576, writing in his diary:

I suddenly and unexpectedly beheld near the zenith an un-

accustomed star with a bright radiant light.

Tycho was looking high in the sky at the northern constellation Cassiopeia, which is not far from the Pole Star. Peter Usher and others have suggested that Barnardo, one of the guards shivering on the castle ramparts of Elsinore, is alluding to Tycho's Star when he is interrupted by the appearance of the Ghost in *Hamlet*:

Last night of all, when yond same star that's westward from the pole had made his course t' illume that part of heaven where now it burns, Marcellus and myself, the bell then beating one ... (1.1)

Astonishingly, a second supernova blasted its way into the night sky in 1604, which this time provided valuable data to the German astronomer and mathematician Johannes Kepler, and was accordingly dubbed Kepler's Star. First seen on the night of 9 October that year, it rivalled Tycho's Star for brightness and destroyed the last vestiges of the orderly and predictable universe that had held sway for well over a thousand years. All of which would have suited Kepler who, taking the Copernican model as his basis, went on to formulate his celebrated three laws of planetary motion, establishing that the planets not only orbit the sun but move in elliptical orbits and not perfect circles. After two supernovae within a generation, another one visible to the naked eye – and which put on an altogether much less spectacular display – did not appear until 1987.

Whenever Shakespeare mentions the planets – the word derives from the Greek word *planetes* meaning 'wanderers' because they move against the background of the fixed stars – it is generally in connection with the attributes ascribed to them by the ancients: Mars is warlike, Venus is the goddess of love, Saturn is aged or gloomy (saturnine), and so on. When the old knight Sir John Falstaff is pleading for a kiss from the prostitute Doll Tearsheet in *Henry IV, Part 2*, Prince Hal scoffs:

Saturn and Venus this year in conjunction! What says th' almanac to that? (2.4)

Shakespeare undoubtedly possessed a basic astronomical knowledge, as we see in a comical reference to planetary retrograde in *All's Well That Ends Well*. 'Retrograde' is the term astronomers use when a planet appears to go backwards across the night sky, which is entirely an effect of perspective caused by the planet's movements relative to earth's own path around the sun. This is the exchange when Helena engages in a skirmish of wit with the cowardly Parolles:

Helena: **The wars have so kept you under that you must needs be born under Mars.**

Parolles: **When he was predominant.**

Helena: **When he was retrograde, I think, rather.**

Parolles: **Why think you so?**

Helena: **You go so much backward when you fight.** (1.1)

The single other occasion on which Shakespeare uses the word 'retrograde' is in *Hamlet*, when Claudius tells Hamlet that his plan to return to university at Wittenberg is 'most retrograde to our desire'. Shakespeare also knew that at times the moon passed closer to the earth than at others, an effect of its own elliptical orbit. On those occasions it appeared larger and brighter than usual. What today is popularly known as a 'super moon' was often associated with increased incidents of 'lunacy', based on the notion that the moon could unsettle people's minds. In *Othello*'s final, murderous scene, the Moor laments:

It is the very error of the moon. She comes more nearer earth than she was wont, and makes men mad. (5.2)

The gravitational pull of the moon – 'the governess of floods' – and its effects on the earth's tides was also understood. Falstaff mentions it when he speaks of the plight of 'the moon's men', thieves like himself who profit most by night, in *Henry IV, Part 1*:

For the fortune of us that are the moon's men doth ebb and flow like the sea, being governed, as the sea is, by the moon. (1.2)

In *The Winter's Tale*, the servant Camillo cautions about a hopeless task:

You may as well forbid the sea for to obey the moon. (1.2)

The moon, incidentally, was traditionally believed to shed a vaporous foam, commonly known as 'moondrops' (or in Latin, *virus lunare*) on to certain herbs and other plants which could then be used in conjunction with incantations by witches. Hecate, a fearsome goddess of the underworld, tells the weird sisters in *Macbeth*:

Upon the corners of the moon, there hangs a vaporous drop profound; I'll catch it ere it come to ground. (3.5)

When Julius Caesar likens his own constancy of character to the immovability of the Pole Star, there is a hint that Elizabethan astronomers understood the stars were fiery suns in their own right:

I could be well moved, if I were as you. If I could pray to move, prayers would move me. But I am constant as the northern star, of whose true-fix'd and resting quality there is no fellow in the firmament. The skies are painted with unnumber'd sparks, they are all fire and every one doth shine. But there's but one in all doth hold his place. (*Julius Caesar*, 3.1)

While Polonius, reading aloud a love poem Hamlet wrote to Ophelia, recites:

Doubt thou the stars are fire; / Doubt that the sun doth move; / Doubt truth to be a liar; /

But never doubt I love. (*Hamlet*, 2.2)

Shakespeare's plays and poems contain more than one hundred and sixty references to the moon, moonlight, moonshine and moonbeams, many of them, as you might expect, romantic enough to make your heart ache. (Moonlight is mentioned in *A Midsummer Night's Dream* three times more often than in all the other plays combined.) References to the sun, sunshine, sunlight and such derivatives, top three hundred. The stars get dozens of mentions. While the playwright and poet may have spent much of his time watching his feet as he traversed the muddy, unpaved and filth-strewn streets of London, his thoughts were often not far away from the heavens above.

See also: 38. These Late Eclipses
42. The Man in the Moon

40. THE ISLAND OF DEVILS

Startling news from Bermuda leads Will to pen his last solo play ... and a touching valedictory

Safely in harbour is the king's ship; in the deep nook, where once thou call'dst me up at midnight to fetch dew from the still-vex'd Bermoothes, there she's hid.

(The Tempest, 1.2, 1610-11)

A TERRIBLE storm at sea, conjured by the magus Prospero from his island, has caused a great ship to be swept on to rocks, though by some miracle the entire crew have survived. Ariel, an ethereal spirit who serves Prospero, is reporting to his master how things have turned out. Midnight dew might be an essential ingredient listed in Prospero's learned book of spells but what of 'the still-vex'd Bermoothes'?

In this one line, Shakespeare gives us a vital clue to the events that inspired him to create *The Tempest,* the last play he was to pen alone. (He would collaborate on later works with other playwrights, notably John Fletcher, his successor as in-house playwright for the King's Men.) 'Still-vex'd' means continually racked by storms. 'Bermoothes' are the Mid-Atlantic islands of Bermuda.

On the summer's day of 2 June 1609, seven ships and two towed pinnaces (or tenders) belonging to the Virginia Company set off in high spirits from Plymouth, Devon. They were carrying six hundred or so would-be settlers together with supplies for England's new colony in the Americas. It was the largest fleet ever assembled for Virginia and they were proudly led out to sea by their flagship, the three hundred ton *Sea Venture*. She was the first vessel to be purposely designed as a ship for emigrants, providing accommodation below decks for large numbers of people who were not crewmen.

At the helm was Admiral Sir George Somers, and among the VIPs aboard was Sir Thomas Gates, newly appointed Governor of the fledgling colony that had been named after the 'Virgin Queen' Elizabeth. Seven weeks into the journey, on 25 July or St James' Day, the flotilla had the bad luck to get caught up in an Atlantic hurricane. The storm raged incessantly for two days and nights and, when it finally passed, just four of the ships managed to find each other. They limped on together to Jamestown, the settlement named after James I. There was relief in the ensuing days as more of the flotilla straggled into port. Of the flagship *Sea Venture* there was no sign and, after several weeks of anxious waiting, she was deemed lost with all hands.

When the tragic news reached England it caused deep shock and consternation. What no one other than the crew and passengers of the *Sea Venture* could know at the time was that she had not sunk, but had been flung by the storm on to a reef a little over half a mile (0.8km) off the main island of Bermuda. Holed and leaking badly, the ship was left stranded when the tide receded. All the souls aboard were thankful to be safe but fearful of what might lie in store. Bermuda had long been a place to be avoided at all costs. Ships traditionally gave it a wide berth, with generations of sailors ominously calling it the 'Ile of Divels'. Shrieks and eerie cries heard emanating from the island contributed to its fearsome reputation as a mysterious, godforsaken and bewitched outcrop in the middle of the ocean. One of those aboard the *Sea Venture* was the writer William Strachey, who was later to publish a lurid account of their experiences.

Strachey graphically relates the terrors of the storm, describing how the ship was tossed around helplessly as each towering wave was followed by a bigger one, the winds that howled, the sky that lowered pitch black 'like an hell of darkenesse', and torrential rain whose 'waters like whole rivers did flood in the ayre'. The wildness of the elements mingled with the screams of the settlers below who were being violently tossed around and seasick, many of them women and children who had never been to sea before. Strachey, himself a veteran of storms at sea, writes:

> *All that I had ever suffered gathered together might not hold comparison with this. There was not a moment in which the sudden splitting or instant oversetting of the ship was not expected.*

He goes on to tell of the joy when a cry went up that land had been sighted, and then the horror that followed when the crew realised what land it was.

> *I found it to be the dangerous and dreaded Ilands of the Bermuda. They were so terrible a place that they be called commonly The Devils Ilands, and are feared and avoided of all sea travellers alive, above any other place in the world.*

The survivors had little choice but to go ashore and Strachey later records their astonishment as it slowly dawned on them what a paradise the islands, to which it had 'pleased our mercifull God' to deliver them, actually were. He is determined to set the record straight:

> *I hope to deliver the world from a foule and general errour, it being counted of most that they can be no habitation for Men, but rather given over to Devils and wicked Spirits. Whereas wee indeed find them now by experience to bee as habitable and commodious as most Countries of the same climate and situation.*

Although Bermuda had no streams or rivers, the survivors discovered that by digging they could find fresh water enough for everyone to drink. A type of petrel unique to the islands, now known as the cahow (a name given to the birds in imitation of the cry they make) could easily be caught in their nests on the ground and, along with turtles and wild hogs, supplied plenty of toothsome food. Other than the wildlife, the islands were completely uninhabited. It soon became clear that the haunting call of the cahow was the very sound that passing sailors had for years taken to be terrifying shrieks from the devils that were believed to stalk the islands.

The *Sea Venture* survivors spent the next nine months cutting down native trees and, under the direction of Admiral Somers, they constructed two small ships. On 10 May 1610, they set sail and two weeks later cruised into the harbour at Jamestown, to the amazement of everyone in the colony. When news of their apparent return from the dead at last reached England, it caused a sensation. Finally back in London, Strachey circulated his manuscript in a letter to friends.

One of the financial backers of the Virginia project was Shakespeare's good friend and patron Henry Wriothesley, Earl of Southampton. Southampton may well have drawn Strachey's letter to the playwright's attention. A further record of the miraculous survival was written by one Sylvester Jourdain, who had also been aboard the *Sea Venture*. Several other accounts were also rushed into print to satisfy a public eager to read all they could about the extraordinary adventure.

By way of a historical footnote, it was that entirely accidental landing in Bermuda by the *Sea Venture* which led to the islands becoming a British colony. To this day Bermuda is Britain's oldest remaining Overseas Territory. The islands' coat of arms (*pictured*) features a creature with the head of a lion to symbolise Britain, a shipwreck, and the Latin motto 'Quo fata ferunt', which translates as 'Whither the Fates carry us'.

❊ ❊ ❊

As for *The Tempest* itself, we learn that Prospero and his daughter Miranda were living on their island for twelve years before the play opens. Prospero had been deposed from his position as Duke of Milan by his envious brother Antonio, in conspiracy with Alonso, the King of Naples, and he and the infant Miranda were cast adrift in a boat that washed up on the island. In the storm now conjured by Prospero – the tempest of the title – it is the turn of Antonio and Alonso, along with others of their ship's company, to be cast ashore on the island as their own vessel is wrecked. But wait. Milan? Naples? We are no longer in mid-Atlantic Ocean but in the Mediterranean Sea. Indeed, in reporting the shipwreck, Ariel goes on to tell Prospero what happened to other ships that were sailing with the vessel that was grounded:

> **And for the rest o' the fleet which I dispersed, they all have met again and are upon the Mediterranean flote** [sea], **bound sadly home for Naples, supposing that they saw the king's ship wreck'd and his great person perish.** (1.2)

Shortly after his arrival on the island, Prospero had discovered the airy spirit Ariel trapped in a tree. Ariel had been painfully imprisoned there through a spell cast by a dreadful witch named Sycorax, who formerly ruled the island. Sycorax had incarcerated the sprite in a 'cloven pine' as punishment for his refusing 'to act her earthy and abhorr'd commands'. Using his potent art, Prospero invoked his own magic to remove the spell and free Ariel.

We hear in the play that Sycorax originally arrived on the island because she was so wicked that, 'for mischiefs manifold' and sorceries too 'terrible to enter human hearing', she had been banished by the people of 'Argier,' from where she hailed. Argier was Algiers – yes, we are still in the Mediterranean. In Shakespeare's day the North African city was held by the Ottomans, so his audience might well suppose that if Sycorax had been too wicked even for such infidels as them to countenance, she must have been evil indeed. The nineteenth-century essayist Charles Lamb, who co-authored *Tales from Shakespeare* with his sister Mary, claimed that about fifty years before *The Tempest* was written just such a witch, whose name is not recorded by history, had been banished from North Africa.

✳ ✳ ✳

Sycorax might be gone but she left one unhappy legacy. She had been pregnant when she arrived on the island and 'the son that she did litter here, a freckled whelp hag-born,' as Prospero puts it, is named Caliban. Caliban is precisely the sort of man-monster the *Sea Venture*'s survivors expected to meet on Bermuda but, to their great relief, never did.

Shakespeare came up with the name as an anagram of 'canibal' (an optional version of the word 'cannibal' in that era of notoriously inconsistent spelling), having read John Florio's 1603 English translation from the French of Michel de Montaigne's essay *On Cannibals*. The very word conjured up an image of a wild, uncivilised savage, originating as it did from the Spanish '*canibales*', a variant recorded by Columbus of 'Caribes' – the name given to a people in the West Indies who were reputed to eat each other. The Caribbean Sea derives its name from the same source.

Shakespeare had first mentioned such a race in 1603, in *Othello, The Moor of Venice*, when Othello tells how, on his jaw-dropping adventures, he has seen 'the Cannibals that each other eat, the Anthropophagi'. Anthropophagi derives from two Greek words meaning 'man eaters', a race of wild men described in the fifth century BC by the Greek historian Herodotus. Centuries after Herodotus, the Roman historian Pliny the Elder took up the theme, writing in his *Naturalis Historia* of a cannibalistic race who lived north of the Asian province of Scythia:

The manners of the Androphagi are more savage than those of any other race. They neither observe justice, nor are governed, by any laws.

The fact that a translation of Pliny's work into English by Philemon Holland had been published in 1601, just two years before Shakespeare wrote *Othello*, is unlikely to be a coincidence.

Caliban has been enslaved by Prospero. In an acrimonious exchange, we learn how much they despise each other. Prospero rebukes the man-monster, revealing how at first he had 'used thee, filth as thou art, with human care, and lodged thee in mine own cell,' which lasted until 'thou didst seek to violate the honour of my child'. Caliban is unrepentant of his grotesque attempt to rape Miranda, snarling back: 'O ho, O ho! Would 't had been done! Thou didst prevent me. I had peopled else this isle with Calibans.' He complains in an aside that he has no choice but to obey Prospero, saying 'his art is of such pow'r it would control my dam's [Sycorax] god Setebos, and make a vassal of him'.

Shakespeare gleaned the name Setebos from a book published in London by the scholar Robert Eden. Eden wrote that Ferdinand Magellan, whose 1519-22 expedition was the first to circumnavigate the world, had seen Patagonian natives who worshipped a deity they called Setebos. Sir Francis Drake came across references to the same pagan god when making the second global circumnavigation in 1577-80. Never mind the scrambled geography, just throw in all the ingredients that make up a good story. Such is the magic of Shakespeare's style.

Yet, as also is his style, he creates in Caliban no simple, off-the-peg monster, but a character of contradictions, capable of surprisingly deep feelings. Modern audiences of *The Tempest* often identify in Caliban the plight of the world's dispossessed victims of colonialism as he plaintively protests to Prospero:

This island's mine, by Sycorax my mother, which thou takest from me. When thou camest first, thou strokedst me and madest much of me, wouldst give me water with berries in't, and teach me how to name the bigger light, and how the less, that burn by day and night [the sun and moon]: **and then I loved thee and show'd thee all the qualities o' the isle, the fresh springs, brine-pits, barren place and fertile. Cursed be I that did so! All the charms** [spells] **of Sycorax, toads, beetles, bats, light on you! For I am all the subjects that you have, which first was mine own king.** (1.2)

'Which first was mine own king' – who determined my own destiny until you arrived. This was revolutionary stuff. Such sentiments that ran counter to England's newly popular gung-ho spirit of global adventurism, colonial conquest, and taming heathen savages had never before been expressed on the stage. Caliban even adds for good measure:

You taught me language; and my profit on't is, I know how to curse. The red plague [plague sores could be red, yellow or black] **rid** [destroy] **you for learning me your language!**

As if all that were not enough, Shakespeare chooses the bestial and misshapen Caliban to deliver some of the most exquisitely beautiful lines in the entire play. So beautiful, in fact, that they inspired Danny Boyle's *Isles of Wonder* theme for the spectacular opening ceremony of the London Olympics in the summer of 2012.

Be not afeard; the isle is full of noises, sounds and sweet airs, that give delight and hurt not. Sometimes a thousand twangling instruments will hum about mine ears, and sometime voices that, if I then had waked after long sleep, will make me sleep again: and then, in dreaming, the clouds methought would open and show riches ready to

drop upon me that, when I waked, I cried to dream again.
(3.2)

See also: 28. The World's Mine Oyster
41. Fire in the Sky
42. The Man in the Moon
Epilogue: Our Revels are Ended

41. FIRE IN THE SKY

Alarming natural spectacles are ascribed to devils, mischievous spirits and even a protective saint

I boarded the King's ship; now on the beak [prow], **now in the waist** [amidships], **the deck** [poop], **in every cabin, I flam'd amazement** [struck terror by appearing as flames]. **Sometimes I'd divide, and burn in many places; on the topmast, the yards** [spars] **and boresprit** [bowsprit], **would I flame distinctly, then meet and join.** (*The Tempest*, 1.2, 1610-11)

THE airy spirit Ariel gives Prospero a gleeful account of how he 'flam'd amazement' by taking on the shape of a dazzling fireball and racing around every part of a ship carrying the King of Naples, as it battled through the tempest. Up and down the masts he flew, across the spars and sails, and around the deck, at times dividing into more than one blazing fork, then just as quickly reuniting, compounding the terror of all aboard.

Compare Ariel's words with those of William Strachey, one of the survivors of the *Sea Venture* when the vessel was shipwrecked off Bermuda in 1609. Strachey relates how during the storm the distressed sailors saw:

An apparition of a little round light, like a faint starre, trembling, and streaming along with a sparkeling blaze, halfe the height upon the maine mast, and shooting sometimes from shroud to shroud [rigging to rigging], tempting [attempting] to settle, as it were, upon any of the foure shrouds. And for three or foure hours together, or rather more, half the night, it kept with us, running sometimes along the maine-yard to the very end, and then returning ... but upon a sodaine, to-

wards the morning watch, they lost the sight of it, and knew not which way it made.

Both passages are perfect descriptions of the natural phenomenon known as St Elmo's fire. Shakespeare is thought to have read Strachey's account when it was circulated a year or so before *The Tempest* was written. He is also likely to have studied the epic work by Richard Hakluyt, *The Principall Navigations, Voiages, Traffiques and Discoveries of the English Nation*, the second edition of which appeared in 1599. Hakluyt includes this report of seeing the mysterious glow:

I do remember that in the great and boysterous storme of this foule weather, in the night there came upon the top of our maine yard and maine mast a certaine little light, much like unto the light of a little candle, which the Spaniards call the Cuerpo Santo [Holy Body]. This light continued aboord our ship about three houres, flying from maste to maste, and from top to top; and sometimes it would be in two or three places at once.

Shakespeare may already have come across mention of St Elmo's fire in a book published in London as early as 1555 by Richard Eden. The book included Eden's translation from Italian of an account of the historic first circumnavigation of the globe, led by Ferdinand Magellan in 1519. Magellan's fleet encountered the phenomenon on several occasions, especially during their stormy passage through the treacherous strait that now bears his name, as they left the Atlantic Ocean and entered the Pacific.

With modern scientific knowledge we know St Elmo's fire to be a form of plasma generated by discharges of atmospheric static electricity. It is seen mostly on tall, isolated structures such as ship's masts, and usually has a blue or violet glow. Although the fluorescence is relatively faint, set against the background of a pitch-black night at sea the effect is dramatic, and it can continue for several hours at a time.

The spectacle had been recorded since the time of the ancient Greeks and was believed by generations of fearful sailors to be caused by supernatural spirits – 'the superstitious seamen make constructions [imaginative explanations] of this sea fire,' Strachey writes.

In *The Tempest*, Ariel himself is transformed into just such a spirit. To the ancients sailing the Mediterranean, if only one glow of the fiery light was seen it was called 'Helena', after Helen of Troy. If the light branched into two before combining again, it was known as 'Castor and Pollux', after the legendary twin brothers of Helen. If only one branch was seen, it was regarded by sailors as a harbinger of doom. Two branches meant the tempest was nearing an end.

By Christian times, the phenomenon had evolved the name St Elmo's fire. There never was a St Elmo. The name is a corruption of St Erasmus of Formia who, sometime after his death circa 303 AD, was promoted to the role of patron saint of seafarers. According to legend, Erasmus continued preaching even after a thunderbolt struck the ground beside him, leading subsequent generations of sailors to pray to him for protection at sea. Seamen who witnessed St Elmo's fire during a storm began to believe the inexplicable light was a reassuring sign of the presence of their guardian saint, and that a miraculous deliverance was at hand.

They may have had a point. Today's science tells us that the atmosphere does not usually become so charged with electricity until a storm is almost over. Down the centuries the eerie glow has been recorded by characters as diverse as Julius Caesar, Christopher Columbus, Robert Burton (in *The Anatomy of Melancholy* of 1621), and Charles Darwin aboard *HMS Beagle* off South America, as well as being created artificially by Nikola Tesla in the laboratory.

❋ ❋ ❋

Just as seafarers encountered St Elmo's fire, so travellers by land had mysterious lights of their own to contend with. Wanderers at night could be amazed, enchanted, terrified, or a combination of all three when they suddenly witnessed the Will o' the Wisp, otherwise often known as Jack o' Lanthorn (Jack of the Lantern) or 'the fire-drake'. (The fire-drake was originally a dragon-like fire-breathing creature in Teutonic mythology.) While a traveller was out on a lonely highway, crossing marshes or fens, perhaps approaching a churchyard, a dancing flame might suddenly appear out of the deep darkness, first darting off in one direction, then doubling back upon itself, or dancing delicately over a single spot. It would look for all the world like someone in the distance was zigzagging around crazily while carrying a lantern.

Superstition inevitably arose that the Will o' the Wisp was a goblin, a wicked fairy or some other evil spirit seeking to mislead the unsuspecting traveller to follow its light into an impassable bog or over a perilous cliff edge. Sinisterly, if anyone approached the flame it would recede, as though beckoning them to follow. If they turned and walked away, it would seem to follow them. There could be no doubt that it intended harm. The phenomenon is also known as *ignis fatuus*, which translates from the Latin as 'fools' fire'. In *The Anatomy of Melancholy*, Burton speaks of …

> *Fiery spirits or devils are such as commonly work by fire-drakes, or ignes fatui, which lead men often in flumina et praecipitia [into floods and over precipices].*

Chemistry tells us the shimmering light is caused by emissions arising from decaying organic matter. Phosphine and disphosphane, gaseous derivatives of naturally occurring phosphorous, combust on becoming oxidised in the air and, in turn, ignite methane, which is present in much greater quantities, particularly over marshy ground. It was no coincidence, therefore, that the lights were most often seen on summer nights, when the gases were more likely to be rising from damp soil. Mysteriously, although the Will o' the Wisp shone like fire, it gave off no heat, which added to its unearthly qualities.

By Shakespeare's day, the phenomenon was well known and inextricably embedded in folklore. So well known, in fact, that a plethora of additional regional names had sprung up. It was known as Peg o' Lantern in Lancashire, Bob-a-longs in Wales, Spunkie (Scotland), Fire Faery (Hebrides), Jenny-burnt-tail (Northants and Oxfordshire), Kit-in-the-Candle-stick (Hampshire), Will o' the Wykes (Lincolnshire and Norfolk), Hobbledy's Lantern (Warwickshire), and Hinky-punk (Somerset and Devon), among more than sixty variations.

One belief had it that the lights were emitted by departed souls who, like the ghost of Hamlet's father, were locked in Purgatory. Anyone sighting the Will o' the Wisp was urged to find a church or other religious institution the following day and pray for their own soul, preferably leaving a generous donation before they left. Another tradition claimed the souls were those of children who had died before they could be baptised. In Buckinghamshire, the fiery flame was known as 'the Wat' and it was said to appear around prisons as an omen on the night before the trial assizes. Any prisoner unfortunate enough to see it should resign himself to being sentenced to the gallows the next day.

THE IGNIS-FATUUS, OR WILL-O'-THE-WISP.

An illustration of the Will o' the Wisp (*pictured*) by Josiah Wood Whymper appears in *Phenomena of Nature*, published in London in 1849 for the Society for Promoting Christian Knowledge.

Shakespeare makes the most of the terror struck by the Will o' the Wisp in *King Lear*, when the Earl of Gloucester approaches the king's little group of outcasts at night on the storm-blasted heath. Gloucester is carrying a lantern and, when the Fool hails his appearance with 'Look, here comes a walking fire,' Edgar takes his cue to crank up his masquerade as 'poor mad Tom', shrieking:

This is the foul fiend Flibbertigibbet. He begins at curfew and walks till the first cock [midnight]. He gives the web and the pin, squinies the eye, and makes the harelip, mildews the white wheat, and hurts the poor creature of earth. (3.4)

Shakespeare borrowed the name 'Flibbertigibbet' from *A Declaration of Egregious Popish Impostures* by the clergyman Samuel Harsnett, which had been published in 1603, two years before he wrote *King Lear*. Harsnett gives the name as an example of a demon and for Shakespeare it conjures up a suitably diabolical tone for the 'walking fire'. The catalogue of evils for which Edgar accuses the spirit of being responsible include 'the web and the pin' (cataracts in the eyes from the spider's web-like effect the victim sees), squinies (squints), a harelip (cleft lip), and mildew on 'white' (almost ripe) wheat.

Another allusion to the Will o' the Wisp turns up in *Henry IV, Part 1* when Sir John Falstaff cannot resist a dig at Bardolph's notoriously red nose, claiming it glowed so brightly it could be seen even in the dark. Falstaff says of their nocturnal escapades:

When thou rannest up Gadshill in the night to catch my horse, if I did not think thou hadst been an ignis fatuus or a ball of wildfire there's no purchase in money. (1.2)

Shakespeare again treats the Will o' the Wisp in a lighter vein in *A Midsummer Night's Dream*, when we learn that the beguiling light is none other than Puck, the mischievous helper of Oberon, king of the fairies. We know that to be the case because a fairy asks Puck if he is not 'that shrewd and knavish sprite' who does 'mislead night-wanderers, laughing at their harm'. Happy to torment the terrified 'rude mechanicals' when they flee the enchanted wood after seeing Bottom with his head transformed into that of an ass, Puck promises to take on a variety of frightening shapes and lead them on a madcap chase, just as the shape-shifting flames would:

I'll follow you, I'll lead you about a round, through bog, through bush, through brake, through brier: sometime a horse I'll be, sometime a hound, a hog, a headless bear, sometime a fire; and neigh, and bark, and grunt, and roar, and burn, like horse, hound, hog, bear, fire, at every turn.

(3.1)

Puck assumes the shape of a walking fire once more when he leads the love rivals Demetrius and Lysander a merry dance through the suddenly foggy wood. He chants:

Up and down, up and down, I will lead them up and down: I am fear'd in field and town: Goblin, lead them up and down. (3.2)

Prospero's airy spirit companion Ariel takes on a similar role in *The Tempest*, leading the drunken Stephano and his companions on a wild goose chase through 'tooth'd briers, sharp furzes, pricking goss and thorns' until they end up in 'the filthy mantled pool'. Afterwards, Stephano angrily reproaches Caliban, saying:

'Monster, your fairy, which you say is a harmless fairy, has done little better than played the Jack [o' Lanthorn] **with us.'** (4.1)

An attempt to identify some sort of scientific rationale for the fiery lights can be found at least as far back as 1596, when the Swiss theologian Ludwig Lavater published his pithily titled *Of Ghostes and Spirites, Walking by Night, And of Straunge Noyses, Crackes, and Sundrie forewarnings, which commonly happen before the death of men: Great Slaughters, and alterations of Kingdomes.* In a chapter headed 'That many naturall things are taken to be ghoasts', he writes:

Many times candles & small fires appeare in the night, and seeme to runne up and downe ... Sometime these fires goe alone in the night season and put such as see them, as they travel by night, in great feare. But these things, and many such lyke have their naturall causes ... Natural philosophers write that thicke exhilations aryse out of the earth, and are kindled. Mynes full of sulphur and brimstone, if the aire enter unto it, as it lyeth in the holes and veines of the earth, will kindle on fier, and strive to get out.

In 1616, the lexicographer John Bullokar published his *English Expositor*. The book was a kind of early dictionary, which sought to define difficult words to an increasingly literate population. Bullokar attempted to explain why some people claimed to see a dragon in the fiery shapes, writing:

Fire-drake; a fire sometimes seen flying in the night like a dragon. Common people think it a spirit that keepeth some treasure hid, but philosophers affirme it to be a great unequal exhalation inflamed betweene two clouds, the one hot, the other cold, which is the reason that it also smoketh, the middle part whereof, according to the proportion of the hot cloud being greater than the rest, maketh it seem like a bellie, and both ends like unto a head and tail.

John Milton took his own crack at an explanation in *Paradise Lost* (1667), describing the phenomenon in these terms:

A wandering fire, compact of unctuous vapour, which the night condenses, and the cold environs round, kindled through agitation to a flame, which oft, they say, some evil spirit attends, hovering and blazing with delusive light, misleads th' amaz'd night-wanderer from his way to bogs and mires, and oft through pond and pool.

In our modern age of urban sprawl, ubiquitous street lighting, drained marshland and vastly improved sanitation, sightings of the Will o' the Wisp are rare in the industrialised world. These days 'will o' the wisp' and 'flibbertigibbet' are expressions that mean only a passing fancy or a frivolous and flighty person, rather than magically dancing lights to beguile the traveller on a dark night. I can't help feeling we have lost something rather precious.

See also: 40. The Island of Devils

42. THE MAN IN THE MOON

'Heavenly' liquor and an ancient superstition combine to bestow supposedly god-like powers

Caliban: **Hast thou not dropp'd from heaven?**

Stephano: **Out o' the moon, I do assure thee. I was the man i' the moon when time was.**

Caliban: **I have seen thee in her and I do adore thee: My mistress show'd me thee and thy dog and thy bush.**

(The Tempest, 2.2, 1610-11)

LOST and wandering around Prospero's magical island after surviving a shipwreck, the royal butler Stephano stumbles upon resident man-monster Caliban. Stephano has been partaking liberally of the wine he carries in a flask, decanted from the barrel to which he had clung while making for shore. He offers Caliban a drink. Caliban tastes alcohol for the first time in his life and the effect is immediate. Overcome, he proclaims:

> **That's a brave god and bears celestial liquor. I will kneel to him**. (2.2)

Stephano is happy to play along with his new convert's adoration and indulges in a boast that was a favourite among unscrupulous adventurers happy to exploit the crude polytheism of the native 'Indians' in the New World. He claims he is the 'man in the moon', who has now come down to earth. Stephano is also following an established pattern in which early settlers would supply natives with alcoholic 'fire water' in return for being shown where to find fresh water, fish and other victuals. Caliban tells him how Prospero's daughter Miranda had pointed out 'the man in the moon' at a time when she was still trying to educate and civilise him. Stephano dubs Caliban his 'mooncalf'.

Legends of 'the man in the moon' are very ancient and common to many cultures around the world. While some beliefs were based on 'seeing' an imagined face, made up of the dark lava plains and brightly lit uplands and craters on the moon's surface, tradition in western Europe and the British Isles preferred the figure of a crooked old man with a bundle of sticks on his back. The 'man' often also carried a lantern and sometimes had a dog at his feet. Shakespeare has fun with that image in *A Midsummer Night's Dream* when Robin Starveling the tailor, one of the 'rude mechanicals' – the working men who put on a play for the wedding of Duke Theseus – takes on the role of Moonshine and spells things out to their uncomprehending audience:

All that I have to say is to tell you that the lanthorn [lantern] **is the moon; I, the man in the moon; this thorn-bush, my thorn-bush; and this dog, my dog.** (5.1)

The story of the imaginary stick-carrying figure is said to have originated with an Old Testament passage about a man who was punished by Moses for the offence of gathering firewood on the Sabbath. The *Book of Numbers* (Chapter XV, verse 32) tells us:

And while the children of Israel were in the wilderness, they found a man that gathered sticks upon the Sabbath day. And they that found him gathering sticks brought him unto Moses and Aaron, and unto all the congregation.

Although *Numbers* gives its own account of the classic Old Testament punishment meted out to the offender – God ordered him to be stoned to death – subsequent story tellers had it that he was banished to the moon and has remained stuck there, frozen in time, ever since. The stick-gatherer story began to be conflated with cautionary tales against thievery. In the early thirteenth-century, Alexander Nechum, Abbot of Cirencester, translated a verse from Latin that ran something like:

See the rustic in the moon / How his bundle weighs him down, / Thus his sticks the truth reveal / It never profits man to steal.

Another Bible-related story has it that the figure is Cain, the first murderer, who was exiled to the moon after killing his brother Abel. Either way, 'the man in the moon' loomed large in popular imagination. By Shakespeare's time he had become the subject of a nursery rhyme well known to children:

The man in the moon came tumbling down / And asked his way to Norwich; / He went by the south and burnt his mouth / With supping cold pease porridge.

But there was also another side to 'the man in the moon'. He symbolised drunkenness. This was because the redness often seen on the rising moon, an effect caused by diffraction of light waves in the earth's atmosphere, was redolent of the flushed faces of the inebriated. The moon, like the drunkard, was also a creature of the night, who often stayed up until morning. In Elizabethan London there were at least three taverns called The Man in the Moon. The figure was said to be particularly fond of claret wine. An old song, to be found in the British Museum's *Folio Collection of Bagford Ballads*, proclaims:

Our man in the moon drinks clarret, / With powder-beef, turnep, and carret. / If he doth so, why should not you / Drink until the sky looks blew? [daybreak]

✻ ✻ ✻

Stephano continues to relish his new-found status as a god, the authority for which resides almost entirely in his possession of the fiery liquor Caliban now craves. In what sounds suspiciously like a parody of religious custom, when Caliban declares 'I do adore thee', Stephano instructs his worshipper:

Come, swear to that; kiss the book. I will furnish it anon with new contents. Swear. (2.2)

Stephano's 'book' is no *Holy Bible*, but the mouth of the drinking flask. He promises he can refill it again and again from a 'whole butt' of 'sack', the barrel of wine he has hidden behind a rock. Caliban pledges in return:

I'll show thee every fertile inch o' th' island, and I will kiss thy foot. I prithee, be my god. (2.2)

In a fascinating essay titled *Why Caliban Worships the Man in the Moon*, published in the *Shakespeare Quarterly* in 1975, Raymond Urban, a graduate student at the University of North Carolina, suggests Caliban 'is being inducted into the religion of drunkards – a comic Bacchanalian sect that took the man in the moon as its god and the liquor bottle as its Bible'. It was a burlesque religion, Urban says, begun by vagabond clerics in medieval Europe for whom 'their favourite taverns became churches, the noisy drinkers a congregation of the faithful, and the Bacchic drinking-songs prayers and hymns'. Such sacrilegious notions had spread to England by the sixteenth century and would be well known to Shakespeare's groundlings. Urban adds that a Jacobean ballad called *London's Ordinarie* spelled out how specific inns had their regular clienteles (an 'ordinarie' or 'ordinary' was an alternative word for a tavern). The ditty includes the lines:

The Plummers will dine at the Fountaine, / The Cookes at the Holy Lambe, / The Drunkards by noon to The Man in the Moon, / And the Cuckolds to the Ram.

Bacchanalian rituals in taverns continued as late as the

nineteenth century, according to Frederick W Hackwood's classic *Inns, Ales and Drinking Customs of Old England*, published in 1906. He records how at coaching inns in Highgate, London – a popular spot for travellers to rest overnight – 'a quaint and curious custom prevailed'. The horns of stags, bulls or rams would be carried into a large room with great ceremony. When as many travellers as possible were 'collected in the parlour, the ceremony known as Swearing on the Horns was introduced,' Hackwood writes.

Into the parlour would march the host as swearer-in, solemnly clad in a black gown with white bands, and wearing a mask and wig; followed by his clerk, also gowned, and carrying the horns, and a large book from which the oath was read.

Newcomers being 'sworn' in were required to kiss the horns at various stages of the oath taking. Hackwood continues:

The origin of this ancient but absurd custom is veiled in obscurity. One account says it dates from the Reformation, and was originally intended as a parody on the admission of neophytes into the religious confraternities of the Catholic Church.

Among those partaking in the mock ceremony in the early nineteenth century was the 'mad, bad and dangerous to know' Lord Byron, who later wrote a short verse celebrating 'the worship of the solemn Horn, grasped in the holy hand of Mystery'. Byron goes on to add that, after the ceremony, men and maids would 'consecrate the oath with draught and dance till morn'.

❊ ❊ ❊

Caliban turns out to be not quite as naïve as Stephano believes. Wondrous as the wine is, the man-monster has another, altogether more sinister agenda. He seeks nothing less than the overthrow and murder of his hated master Prospero, and decides Stephano is just the god to do it. Caliban has it all worked out, urging his new master:

> **As I told thee before, I am subject to a tyrant, a sorcerer, that by his cunning hath cheated me of the island. Why, as I told thee, 'tis a custom with him i' th' afternoon to sleep. There thou mayst brain him, having first seized his books** [of magical spells]; **or with a log batter his skull, or paunch him** [stab him in the belly] **with a stake, or cut his wezand** [windpipe] **with thy knife.** (3.2)

Caliban adds what he hopes will clinch his case:

> **Most deeply to consider is the beauty of his daughter. He himself calls her a nonpareil: I never saw a woman, but only Sycorax my dam** [mother] **and she; but she as far surpasseth Sycorax as great'st does least.**

The absurd Stephano needs no more convincing. He promises to grant his subject's prayers. Revolution is in the air as he vows:

> **Monster, I will kill this man. His daughter and I will be king and queen – save our graces!**

If Shakespeare needed a real-life rebel on whom to model Stephano, he found one. *The Tempest* was almost certainly inspired by accounts of the settlers' ship *Sea Venture* being swept on to rocks off the coast of Bermuda. She was caught in a hurricane while on route to the new colony of Virginia in July 1609. Once on the island, most of the shipwrecked survivors readily accepted the authority of the Governor of Virginia, Sir Thomas Gates, stranded with them on the way to take up his appointment, and Admiral Sir George Somers, commander of the *Sea Venture*.

The castaways worked diligently on building new ships with which to continue their journey to Virginia. But six months after their arrival on Bermuda, mumblings of mutiny could be heard. At the centre of the plot was one Stephen Hopkins. He was a twenty-eight year old former tavern keeper from Hampshire, who argued that the authority of Gates and Somers had ended the moment the *Sea Venture* was wrecked and the pair no longer had any right to be giving orders to anyone.

Besides, Hopkins reasoned, the colony they were bound for was notoriously harsh and inhospitable, with land that needed much hard work to break in. Food and home comforts were in short supply there and it had a questionable climate, not to mention the ever-present threat of hostility from native 'Indians'. In contrast, the island to which fate had brought them had turned out to be little short of a semi-tropical paradise. He insisted that, if they were going to sail anywhere, it should be back to England.

Things didn't go Hopkins' way, however. Just as, in *The Tempest*, Caliban's plot is thwarted by Prospero after it is overheard by the ethereal spirit Ariel, so in real life Hopkins' uprising came to light before he could strike because Governor Gates got wind of it. Gates promptly had him arrested and charged with mutiny. Hopkins was found guilty and sentenced to death. Distraught, he began desperately begging for his life. One contemporary account records:

> *So penitent he was, and made so much moan, alleging the ruin of his wife and children in this his trespass, as it wrought in the hearts of all the better sorts of the company.*

After all the weeping and wailing on his part, Hopkins was granted a pardon by Gates. From Bermuda, Hopkins went on with the others to Jamestown, returned to England several years later, and then in 1620 sailed on the *Mayflower*. He was one of only a handful of people on that epic voyage who had previous experience of the New World.

Stephen Hopkins' parallels with Stephano are striking. There is his first name for a start: Stephen/Stephano. Could Shakespeare have given us a more blatant clue? When the *Sea Venture* ran on to the reef off Bermuda, Hopkins swam to the shore clinging on to a cask of wine. In his account of the shipwreck, the writer William Strachey relates how the sailors 'threw over-boord much luggage' and 'staved [pushed away with staves] many a Butt of Beere, Hogsheads of Oyle, Syder, Wine, and Vinegar' to lighten the vessel as she foundered (a hogshead being a large cask). In *The Tempest*, Stephano explains his survival by saying:

I escap'd upon a butt of sack [barrel of wine] **which the sailors heav'd o'erboard.** (2.2)

He later speaks of the hiding place 'where my hogshead of wine is'. Then Hopkins plotted an abortive uprising against the authority of Governor Gates, while Stephano leads Caliban's ridiculous attempt to overthrow Prospero. Hopkins had been part of early exploratory missions to make contact with the native 'Indians' in the New World. Stephano and his friend Trinculo, the king's jester, are the first survivors of their own shipwreck to encounter the native Caliban.

For all his roguish nature, before Hopkins signed up for his original voyage on the *Sea Venture* in 1609 he had, somewhat surprisingly, secured a job as clerk to a minister of religion. One of his regular duties was to read passages from the Bible and other religious works to a congregation that included members of the Virginia Company, which owned the vessel. Perhaps here too was Shakespeare's inspiration for Stephano's debauched 'kiss the book' parody of religious ceremony.

Like Stephano, Hopkins clearly had a fondness for alcohol. Having been an innkeeper in England, he took up a similar calling on his second sojourn in the New World. Shortly after his arrival in Plymouth Colony on the *Mayflower* he opened a tavern in Leyden Street. Such a business cannot have been popular with the colony's Puritan authorities, and testament to his proclivity for flirting with trouble is evident in their official records as the years passed. In 1637, he was fined forty shillings for allowing customers to drink and play the game of shuffleboard on his premises on a Sunday. The following year he was fined again for allowing people to drink excessively, and on two subsequent occasions he was fined 'for selling wine, beere, strong waters, and nutmeggs at excessive rates'.

Unlike Jamestown, which had been established solely with the objective of returning a profit to the Virginia Company's investors back in England, Plymouth Colony was the dream of the religiously extreme Puritans who called themselves Pilgrims and sought to chart out their desired lifestyle unhindered by naysayers. Hopkins was no Puritan and had been recruited on to the *Mayflower* as a 'Stranger' primarily because his previous contacts with the 'Indians' and knowledge of their language and hunting techniques would prove useful to the settlers. Hopkins is noted in history as a signatory to the Mayflower Compact, which established a rudimentary democratic process for running Plymouth Colony. He was married twice, fathered ten children, and died in 1644. The Hopkins are now regarded as one of the founding families of Plymouth, Massachusetts, and many of their descendants still live in the area. In all likelihood, Stephen Hopkins was also immortalised as Stephano, *The Tempest's* 'man in the moon'.

See also: 40. The Island of Devils

43. SUFFER THE LITTLE CHILDREN

The brazen daylight abduction of a schoolboy on a London street exposes a sinister secret

Hamlet: **What players are they?**

Rosencrantz: **Even those you were wont to take such delight in, the tragedians** [actors] **of the city.**

Hamlet: **How chances it they travel? Their residence** [permanent stay in the city], **both in reputation and profit, was better both ways** [in both respects].

Rosencrantz: **I think their inhibition** [restriction on the number of performances] **comes by the means of the late innovation** [new fashion for using boy actors].

Hamlet: **Do they hold** [retain] **the same estimation** [esteem] **they did when I was in the city? Are they so follow'd?**

Rosencrantz: **No indeed are they not.**

Hamlet: **How comes it? Do they grow rusty?**

Rosencrantz: **Nay, their endeavour keeps in the wonted pace** [their performances are as good as they always were]. **But there is, sir, an eyrie** [a nest of young birds] **of children, little eyases** [unfledged hawks, noted for their clamour], **that cry out on the top of question** [in shrill contention] **and are most tyrannically** [outrageously] **clapp'd for't. These are now the fashion...**

Hamlet: **What, are they children? Who maintains 'em? How are they escotted** [provided for]? **Will they pursue the quality** [profession of acting] **no longer than they can sing** [until their voices break]? (*Hamlet*, 2.2, 1600-01)

WHEN a troupe of players arrive to put on a play in the castle at Elsinore, Hamlet questions his university friend Rosen-crantz about why they are travelling at all. He is astonished to learn that audiences are abandoning the playhouses he once knew in 'the city' in favour of watching performances by young children, thus forcing traditional adult actors to take their shows on the road in order to make a living. Hamlet asks:

Do the boys carry it away? (2.2)

To which Rosencrantz replies:

Ay, that they do, my lord, Hercules and his load too.

A picture of Hercules carrying the globe on his shoulder – in Greek mythology he temporarily relieved Atlas of the bur-den – adorned an exterior wall of the Globe as a visual repre-sentation of the theatre's name. By his comment, Rosencrantz is implying that even the takings at Shakespeare's own theatre have been hit by the changing tastes of audiences.

To understand what was going on, we must consider the case of Thomas Clifton. On the morning of 13 December 1600, Thomas, the thirteen-year-old son and heir of a wealthy nobleman, left his home near St Bartholomew-the-Great church in London to walk the short distance to Christchurch grammar school. He had attended the prestigious school for several years, having 'been taught and instructed in the grounds of learning and the Latin tongue'. However, on that chilly winter day, less than two weeks before Christmas, Thomas never made it to his classroom. On the way to school he was set upon by a group of men, one of whom was named James Robinson. They knew his usual routine and had been lying in wait.

A court was later told that the men 'with great force and violence did seize and surprise him'. To his 'great terror and hurt' they 'did haul, pull, drag and carry away' the boy, from which we might surmise that he put up the best struggle he could. They took him to the former medieval Dominican

Priory of Blackfriars, part of which had been converted into an indoor theatre. Their intention was, in the words of the court case that followed, 'to use and exercise the said Thomas Clifton in acting of parts in base plays and interludes, to the mercenary gain and private commodity of ... the said confederates'. He had been press-ganged.

When Thomas's father, Henry Clifton, described as 'a gentleman' who also had a country seat at Toftrees, near Fakenham in Norfolk, discovered what had happened to his son, he stormed around to the old priory. There he confronted three men, identified in court as Nathaniel Giles, Henry Evans and Robinson, demanding his son's immediate return. If Henry Clifton was expecting contrition, he found none. Despite his repeated requests, the trio 'utterly and scornfully refused' to hand the boy back. When Clifton threatened that he would complain to the Privy Council about the abduction, Giles, Evans and Robinson replied 'in very scornful manner' that he could 'complain to whom he would, and they would answer it'. When Clifton protested that it was not 'fit' for a gentleman of his standing to have his son 'so basely used', the men 'most arrogantly then and there answered that they had authority sufficient so to take any nobleman's son in this land'. As for young Thomas, he was handed a scroll of paper containing his part in a forthcoming production, ordered to learn the lines by heart, and threatened with whipping if he failed to do so.

Giles, Evans and Robinson had a point. Sort of. A highly regarded organist and composer, Nathaniel Giles held the office of Master of the Children of the Chapel Royal. His duties included ensuring there were always enough boy choristers to fill the ranks of the choir. To that end, in 1597 he had received a warrant from Elizabeth I herself granting him sweeping powers 'to take such and so many children as he or his deputy shall think meet, in all cathedral, collegiate, parish churches, chapels or any other place or places ... within this our realm of England'. What was more, he could at all times commandeer 'necessary horses, boats, barges, carts, cars [carriages] and wagons for the conveyance of the said children from any place'. Little wonder that Henry Clifton's protests were met with disdainful defiance.

While the Queen's warrant was intended to guarantee a sufficient number of boy choristers, Giles had a lucrative private arrangement in place with Evans. It involved misusing his authority in order to supply suitable candidates to Evans' newly established Blackfriars theatre, which staged all its productions using boy actors. The young actors, like the choristers, were known as the Children of the Chapel. Noted playwrights such as Ben Jonson and Thomas Middleton were writing plays for them. Thankfully for Thomas Clifton, however, his father had a powerful friend at Court in Sir John Fortescue, Chancellor of the Exchequer and a member of the Privy Council.

Within twenty-four hours of the abduction, Henry Clifton had obtained a warrant for his son's release. He then took out a prosecution against the three 'confederates' before the Star Chamber, which sat at the Palace of Westminster and was composed of Privy Councillors and common-law judges. Clifton argued that the Queen's warrant 'for the better furnishing of the Royal Chapel with well-singing children' had been perverted by Giles and Evans 'to make unto themselves an unlawful gain ... to erect, set up, furnish and maintain a playhouse or place in the Blackfriars'. Robinson was a henchman.

Clifton had done his research. He further alleged that seven other boys had been 'unjustly taken' about the same time as Thomas, and named them as three grammar school boys, Nathan Field, John Chappell and John Motteram, and four apprentices, Alvery Trussell, Philip Pykman, Thomas Grymes, and Saloman Pavey. Sadly, Clifton could do nothing for them. As it turned out, Saloman Pavey died aged thirteen, three years after he was abducted, a fact we know because Ben

Jonson wrote a touching elegy in his memory.

Nathan Field, who adopted the stage as a profession after his voice broke, went on to become a noted actor in adulthood. He became so celebrated for his acting skills that a portrait survives of him (*pictured*), painted around 1615. We have no idea what became of the other boys.

While Henry Clifton got his son and heir back, the only defendant censured in the case was Henry Evans, who was forced to resign from managing both the theatre and the children, although he was allowed to retain his status as a sharer in the business. Nathaniel Giles did not receive so much as a reprimand. Records of the infamous case survive to give us a fascinating window on the scandalous mistreatment of boys to which Shakespeare was referring in *Hamlet*.

Further and more disturbing material on the subject came to light during research by Bart van Es, a Fellow of St Catherine's College, Oxford, who published his findings in a book titled *Shakespeare in Company* in 2013. Dr van Es uncovered a seedier side to the practice, citing performances in dimly lit theatres by troupes of children before predominately male clients which appear suspiciously close to paedophilia.

In contrast, although Shakespeare's own company at the Globe was obliged to use boy actors to play female parts since women were by law not allowed on a public stage, the youngsters were there of their own volition and were all properly apprenticed. 'Shakespeare actually comes out of this rather well,' says Dr van Es.

As for the Blackfriars theatre, when James I became king in 1603 the company of 'little eyases' obtained a royal patent from his Queen, Anne, and was renamed the Children of the Queen's Revels. Over the next few years, a series of controversial and satirical plays performed by the boys saw the company fall from royal favour. The loss of many of the youngsters to the recurring ravages of the plague decimated their numbers. In 1609, the King's Men, Shakespeare's company, took over the lease on Blackfriars and evicted the previous tenants, using the indoor theatre to complement the Globe for their own productions. That was not quite the end of the children's company, however. It moved to the newly opened White-friars theatre before finally collapsing around 1616.

The authorised press-ganging of children aged from six to their mid-teens to serve as choirboys had been going on since at least 1420. They were required both by the Chapel Royal and St Paul's Cathedral, where they were known as the Children of Paul's (who from the 1560s doubled as actors in performances at Elizabeth I's court). Possibly as a result of the Clifton case, in 1606 the warrant granted to Nathaniel Giles for 'taking up' boys for service of the Chapel Royal was amended to include a proviso that they were not to be used to act in stage plays, 'for that it is not fitt or decent that such as sing the praises of God Almighty should be trained or imployed on such lascivious and prophane exercises'.

Further change was slow in coming. Not until 9 May 1644, in the reign of Charles I, did Parliament see fit to pass *An Ordinance of the Lordes and Commons Assembled in Parliament, for the Apprehending and Bringing to Condigne Punishment, All Such Lewd Persons as Shall Steale, Sell, Buy, Inveigle, Purloune, Convey, or Receive Any Little Children.*

44. MURDER MOST FOUL

Will appears to have been influenced by a bizarre assassination when devising a murder plot

Sleeping within my orchard, my custom always of the afternoon, upon my secure hour thy uncle stole with juice of cursed hebenon in a vial, and in the porches of my ears did pour the leperous distilment; whose effect holds such an enmity with blood of man that, swift as quicksilver, it courses through the natural gates and alleys of the body, and with a sudden vigour it doth posset [thicken] and curd, like eager droppings into milk, the thin and wholesome blood.

(Hamlet, 1.5, 1599-1601)

THE ghost of Hamlet's father appears on the battlements of Elsinore Castle to tell his terrified son how he was so cruelly assassinated. The 'murder most foul' was committed by none other than his brother – Hamlet's uncle – Claudius, who is now ensconced on the throne of Denmark. Speculation has gone on for years among scholars about exactly what the poison might have been. It was named 'hebona' when an apparently pirated edition of *Hamlet*, now known as the *First Quarto*, was circulated in 1603. By the time the *First Folio* of Shakespeare's collected works appeared in 1623 it had become 'hebenon'. The mystery arises because there is no such known   poison.

A favourite suspect for 'hebenon' is henbane, extracted from the seeds and leaves of both *Hyoscyamus niger* (stinking nightshade) and *Scopolia carniolica* (European henbane). Both plants belong to the Solanacae family, which includes foods such as tomatoes, potatoes and eggplants. *Hyoscyamus* and *Scopolia*, however, contain the active ingredients hyoscyamine and scopolamine, used today in anticholinergic drugs that block the action of a neurotransmitter controlling involuntary muscle functions such as breathing. Scopolamine is particularly effective as a psychoactive agent because it crosses the blood-brain barrier with relative ease. Overdoses can result in delirium, coma, respiratory paralysis and death. The narcotic effects of henbane have been known for centuries and its use had long been associated with witchcraft.

Alternative suggestions for the poison that killed Hamlet's father are an extract of ebony – 'heben' being the Elizabethan word for ebony (from the Latin *hebenus*) – and yew, one of a number of trees early writers referred to as 'hebenus'. The leaves, bark and seeds of the yew are highly toxic. Ebony extract is not as potent and would come in the form of a resin, not the 'juice' to which the ghost refers. Henbane and yew are the most likely candidates in that they would work very quickly, just as described. However, it is doubtful that any of these poisons would produce other manifestations the ghost tells Hamlet afflicted his body immediately after the 'leperous distilment' was administered:

A most instant tetter [eruption of the skin in scabs and blotches] **bark'd about** [encrusted], **most lazar-like** [leprosy-like], **with vile and loathsome crust all my smooth body.** (1.5)

It is quite possible, of course, that Shakespeare threw in the ghost's description of such ugly symptoms simply for dramatic effect, and that he had no specific toxic substance in mind. Indeed, finding himself in need of a deadly poison for dramatic purposes, he may have cribbed the name from Marlowe's *Jew of Malta* (1590), which mentions 'juice of hebon'. Marlowe in turn possibly borrowed the name from Chaucer's contemporary John Gower, who apparently used 'hebon' to mean ebony.

The ghost's reference to the poison holding 'such an enmity with blood of man that, swift as quicksilver, it courses through the natural gates and alleys of the body, and with a sudden vigour it doth posset and curd, like eager droppings into milk, the thin and wholesome blood' contains the intriguing implication that Shakespeare was alluding to the circulation of the blood. Intriguing because *Hamlet* was written almost three decades before the physician William Harvey provided the first accurate description of blood circulation in his seminal work *De Motu Cordis* (the Latin title translates as 'Motion of the Heart'), published in Frankfurt in 1628. Harvey's book was written in Latin. An English translation did not appear until 1653.

Whatever the poison was, the fascination remains that Shakespeare chose to give the assassin such an unusual *modus operandi*. His *Hamlet* was based on a tenth-century Nordic saga telling of a Viking hero named Amleth. The saga was set down around 1200AD by a Danish historian known as Saxo Grammaticus ('Saxo the Literate'). It was taken up again during Shakespeare's lifetime as the basis for a play by a now unknown writer, possibly Thomas Kyd, whose version has, sadly, disappeared. By the time Shakespeare had finished with the story, the father character is murdered by poison poured into his ear, a grisly fate found nowhere in *Amleth*. So how did Will come up with such an unlikely plot device? There are a number of clues.

When a troupe of wandering players arrive at Elsinore, Hamlet requests a performance of an old play called *The Murder of Gonzago*. He then asks the lead actor to insert 'some dozen or sixteen lines' he will write. Hamlet intends to rename the play *The Mousetrap* (his wicked uncle Claudius being the mouse) and promises himself: 'The play's the thing wherein I'll catch the conscience of the king.' The players assure Hamlet they already know *The Murder of Gonzago*, and it is indeed possible that such a work did exist in Italy at the time but has since been lost. Hamlet says of that play:

The story is extant, and written in very choice Italian. (3.2)

The Anglo-Italian scholar John Florio, who was living in London, is believed to have been Shakespeare's source for much of his knowledge about Italy and Italian literature, and may have acquainted him with *The Murder of Gonzago*. There is a plausible link in that Florio was in the 'paie and patronage' of Henry Wriothesley, Earl of Southampton, who was Shakespeare's friend and patron. Indeed, it seems likely Southampton introduced Florio and Shakespeare to each other. If the original *The Murder of Gonzago* was extant 'in very choice Italian', it probably related the story of the murder of Francesco Maria I della Rovere, the Duke of Urbino, in October 1538.

The barber-surgeon who killed the Duke confessed under torture that he had dropped poison into his ear while he was asleep. Although the Duke's name was not Gonzago, the instigator of the murder was identified as one Luigi Gonzaga, a kinsman of Leonora Gonzaga, the Duke's widow. The Duke was a celebrated soldier and a portrait of him (*pictured*) by Titian hangs in the Uffizi Gallery in Florence. The painting depicts him proudly wearing his battle armour, in exactly the same way Hamlet's friend Horatio describes how the ghost appeared on the battlements at Elsinore, 'armed at point [correct in every detail], *cap-à-pie* [from head to foot]'.

In an added twist, on 7 May 1592, again in Italy, the Marchese Alfonso Gonzaga di Castelgoffredo was murdered at the instigation of his nephew, the Marchese Rudolfo di Castiglione, while he was resting at midday. Hamlet later says in his commentary that Gonzago is murdered by 'one Lucianus, nephew to the king'. Given the ability of Shakespeare's magpie-like mind to collect snippets of useful information from disparate sources, a combination of these two stories could well have given him the plot for his own version of *The Murder of Gonzago*, and thence *The Mousetrap*, as 'the play within a play'. The ingredients were all there: murder by poison in the ear while sleeping in the afternoon, culprit a close family member (Claudius), the horror compounded because of a faithless wife (Gertrude). Hamlet's mention of a murdering 'nephew' could even have been added to alarm Claudius by implying that he would be the next victim, Hamlet being the nephew of Claudius.

If all that were not enough, back in 1560 a royal surgeon called Ambroise Paré had been accused of assassinating Francis II, King of France, by blowing a poison in the form of a white powder into an abscess in his ear. Apparently the charge was without foundation and Paré survived his grilling. Then in 1601, about the time Shakespeare was writing *Hamlet*, Philemon Holland's English translation of *Natural History* by the ancient Roman writer Pliny the Elder appeared. In his classic masterpiece, Pliny recommended pouring oil of henbane into the ears for use in ear-ache, although he warned that it could cause mental disorder.

The next question that must be asked is this: would it actually be possible to kill someone by administering poison into the ear? The Italian anatomist Bartolomeo Eustachi, who died in 1574, had identified the tube that now bears his name, linking the middle ear with the nasopharynx and thus the respiratory and digestive systems. But the middle ear is separated from the outside world by the tympanic membrane we call the eardrum, which would form a barrier to any substance poured into the outer ear. In 1986, however, an article appeared in the *New England Journal of Medicine* claiming a large proportion of Europe's population had suffered from ruptured ear drums during the Renaissance, as a result of infections that ran their course several centuries before the discovery of penicillin. A Los Angeles neurologist named Lance Fogan subsequently pointed out in a paper of his own, titled *The Neurology of Shakespeare*: 'With a permanent hole in the ear drum, if someone poured warm poison into the ear it would go into the Eustachian tube, into the throat and into the stomach.'

Other researchers have demonstrated that even a ruptured eardrum may not have been necessary for the assassin's poison to work. In 1918, David Macht, a lecturer at Johns Hopkins University, published a paper titled *A Pharmacological Appreciation of Shakespeare's Hamlet: On Instillation of Poisons into the Ear*. Macht had conducted experiments introducing certain poisons into the ears of animals to see what the effect would be, if any. He summed up his research decisively: 'It may be stated here that the author has found that a number of poisons can be, and are, absorbed through the intact ear.'

Henbane was the favoured suspect in an article titled *Scopolamine and the Murder of King Hamlet* – Hamlet's father, the old king, was also named Hamlet – which appeared in the *Journal of the American Medical Association* in July 2002. Dr Basilio Kotsias of the University of Buenos Aires suggests it may have been well known around the royal court at Elsinore that Hamlet's father was suffering hearing loss as a result of a perforated eardrum. Just a few milligrams of scopolamine dropped into his ear could reach toxic levels in the blood. On the other hand, with what can only have been a wry smile after penning his meticulously researched scientific article, Kotsias concludes:

Finally, there exists the possibility that everything related to the apparition of the ghost on the platform before the castle of Elsinore was a product of Shakespeare's fantasy ... If this were true, our interpretation would result in pure fiction.

Quite so.

45. ALAS, POOR TARLTON

Hamlet's 'Alas, poor Yorick' speech sounds distinctly like a lament for a late, great comic actor

First Gravedigger: **A pestilence on him for a mad rogue! A** [He] **pour'd a flagon of Rhenish** [Rhine wine] **on my head once. This same skull, sir, was Yorick's skull, the King's jester.**

Hamlet: **Alas, poor Yorick! I knew him, Horatio. A fellow of infinite jest, of most excellent fancy. He hath borne me on his back a thousand times. And now, how abhorred in my imagination it is. My gorge rises at it. Here hung those lips that I have kiss'd I know not how oft. Where be your gibes now? Your gambols? Your songs? Your flashes of merriment, that were wont to set the table on a roar? Not one now to mock your own grinning? Quite chap-fallen** [a pun on feeling down in the mouth and a jawless skull]**? Now get you to my lady's chamber and tell her, let her paint** [her face in cosmetics] **an inch thick, to this favour she must come.**

(*Hamlet*, 5.1, 1599-1601)

IT IS one of the most memorable scenes Shakespeare wrote. The image of Hamlet holding the skull of Yorick at arm's length and reflecting on mortality in the churchyard has featured on so many theatrical posters that it has become iconic of the play itself. Indeed, Laurence Olivier's publicity shot for the black-and-white cinema film *Hamlet,* released in 1948 (*pictured*), must surely be one of the most enduring Shakespearean images ever to enter popular culture.

Clearly, Yorick had been a hugely popular jester who was able to make people laugh whenever he appeared. Who, then, might Shakespeare have had in mind when Hamlet launches into his address to the chap-fallen skull? There is an obvious

candidate.

Richard Tarlton (also spelt Tarleton) had been the comedy sensation of his day. His comic genius undoubtedly popularised the theatre with Elizabethan audiences. He is described as having had a flat nose and a squint in one eye, the perfect face for a bit of creative gurning.

A surviving drawing (*pictured*) shows him playing a pipe while banging on a tabor, or small drum, carried by means of a strap around his neck. He wears a floppy cap and is dressed as a country yokel. Even Tarlton's appearance could be enough to start an audience roaring. The writer Thomas Nashe noted that 'the people began exceedingly to laugh when he first peept out his head' from behind a curtain. Henry Peacham recorded a similar experience, writing:

> *Tarlton, when his head was only seene, / The Tire-house dore [dressing room door] and Tapestrie between, / Set all the multitude in such laughter / They could not hold [stop laughing] for scarse an houre after.*

Tarlton quickly became a favourite of Elizabeth I, who relished his company at her court. He was said to be the only person able to 'undumpish' her when she was depressed. Watching him perform on one occasion, she wept with laughter so much that she 'bade them take away the knave for making her laugh so excessively'.

True to the tradition of a court jester speaking truth to power, Tarlton told the Queen 'more of her faults than most of her chaplains, and cured her melancholy better than all her physicians,' according to Thomas Fuller's *History of the Worthies of England* (1662). In fact, his position gave him so much influence that, Fuller says:

> *Her highest favourites would in some cases go to Tarlton before going to the Queen, and he was their usher to prepare their advantageous access to her.*

Tarlton was also a talented writer, although sadly all his works, including at least one popular 1585 play titled *Seven Deadly Sins,* have since been lost. He wrote many songs and could instantly improvise doggerel, to such effect that his humorous verses became known as 'Tarltons'. He was a skilful acrobat and a qualified Master of Fencing. He was also the perfect man to deal with any hecklers in the crowd who might intend disrupting a show.

Following his death in September 1588, books titled *Tarlton's Newes out of Purgatorie* (1590) and *Tarlton's Jests* (circa 1592), along with several ballads, were published in an attempt to cash in on his popularity. Many people lamented that they would never see his like again, the poet Edmund Spenser saying of his death 'all joy and jolly merriment is also deaded'. So enduring was his fame that taverns were still being named after him, depicting the familiar figure with pipe and tabor on their inn signs, as late as 1798.

In 1587, Tarlton was among the touring players in the Queen's Men troupe who visited Stratford-upon-Avon to stage a production for the townsfolk. It may have been during that visit Shakespeare talked his way into joining the Queen's Men. If that was the case, Will would certainly have got to know the irrepressible Tarlton, that fellow of infinite jest who was wont to set the table on a roar, and who may well have jokingly carried the young fellow on his back as Yorick did Hamlet. The fact that Shakespeare began writing for the company from an early point is suggested by an eighteenth-century woodcut print of Tarlton, which describes him as 'one of the first actors in Shakespeare's plays'. He was succeeded as resident funnyman among Shakespeare's company of players by Will Kempe, who sought to emulate much of his stage routine. Little wonder, perhaps, that Tarlton should receive a touching tribute in the guise of Yorick in *Hamlet*, Shakespeare's greatest work.

The date of Tarlton's death leads us on to an argument that has raged for centuries: just how old did Shakespeare envisage Hamlet to be? Early in the play we get the clear impression that Hamlet is a young man, perhaps in his late teens or, at most, about twenty years old. He has, after all, forsaken his studies at university in Wittenberg in order to hurry home to Elsinore for the funeral of his father. He has been in love with Ophelia, an innocent, even naïve, young woman, who is probably only a little younger than him.

But when the gravedigger hands over the skull, he tells Hamlet that it has lain 'in the earth three-and-twenty years'. Hamlet, in his musings about the fun-loving Yorick, recalls: 'He hath borne me on his back a thousand times.' Which means that if Hamlet had been, say, seven years old when Yorick last playfully carried him on his back, the Prince must now be at least thirty, well into middle age given the average life expectancy in Elizabethan times. No young student he, but a mature man who might have been expected to be married and settled down with children of his own. So what's going on?

The first published copy of *Hamlet* that we know of was

a quarto printed in 1603. Scholars call that first edition the 'Bad Quarto' because it includes some text of inferior quality and, in an era of *laissez-faire* copyright laws, was probably put out by a pirate printer seeking to cash in on the tragedy's success at the Globe. The version published would most likely have been written down from memory, possibly by one of the actors who took a minor role. That seems plausible because it contains several stage directions that do not appear in subsequent editions. Intriguingly, however, in that first quarto edition the gravedigger tells Hamlet: 'Here's a scull [skull] hath bin here this dozen yeare.' Twelve years would coincide with the time that had elapsed between Tarlton dying in 1588 and Shakespeare writing the passage in 1600.

By 1604 Shakespeare's own theatre company, the King's Men, rushed out a quarto edition of their own, possibly with the aim of putting the first 'pirated' quarto out of business. The fact that only two copies of the 'Bad Quarto' survive suggests that the actors might even have bought up as many as they could get their hands on and destroyed them. Among the changes that appear in the second quarto, which contains a vastly improved script, the time that Yorick's skull has been in the earth has become the familiar 'three-and-twenty years'.

That is the way it stayed in subsequent quarto versions and the *First Folio*. If we give the author of the 'Bad Quarto' the benefit of the doubt and suggest that, despite his other memory lapses about the script, he remembered the gravedigger's 'dozen yeare' correctly, we then have to ask why that change might have been made.

I would suggest that Shakespeare may indeed have first written 'a dozen yeare' when he penned his tragedy, with the date of Tarlton's death in mind. Problems arose because the actor taking the part of Hamlet when the play hit the stage was the hugely popular Richard Burbage. He happened to be around thirty-two years old at the time, well into 'middle age' in that era of shortened lifespans. He is also said to have become somewhat portly by then. Imagine the hurried back-stage discussions going on when Burbage protested that he couldn't possibly deliver the line as written. He was hearing derisory chortles coming from the groundlings as he spoke about being carried on Yorick's back only twelve or so years ago. So the gravedigger's 'dozen yeare' was scratched out and changed to an altogether more credible 'three-and-twenty'.

See also: 5. Three-and-Twenty
12. The Dancing Horse
24. Kempe's Nine Days' Wonder

46. THE USURER'S WIFE

*Pedlars relate preposterous yarns in order to sell their ballads ...
some even contain a grain of truth*

Autolycus: **Here's one to a very doleful tune, how a usurer's
wife was brought to bed of** [gave birth to] **twenty money-
bags at a burthen** [at one time] **and how she longed to eat adders' heads and toads carbonadoed** [cut and scored across for
broiling].

Mopsa: **Is it true, think you?**

Autolycus: **Very true, and but a month old. Here's the mid-
wife's name to't, one Mistress
Tale-porter, and five or six honest wives that were present.
Why should I carry lies abroad?**

(*The Winter's Tale*, 4.4, 1609-11)

THE roguish pedlar Autolycus is typical of the legion of ballad-mongers who snapped up cheap copies of printed scuttlebutt and sold them for a tidy profit to eager and credulous
buyers in towns and villages outside London. In addition to
'an open ear, a quick eye, and a nimble hand' required for his
alternative occupation as a pickpocket and cut-purse, it helps
that he has an ear for a tune and a mellifluous voice. Autolycus sings 'as he had eaten ballads and all men's ears grew to his
tunes,' says an excited servant in *The Winter's Tale*. 'He hath
songs for man or woman, of all sizes; no milliner can so fit his
customers with gloves.'

Elizabethan and Jacobean England saw an explosion of
ballad writing. Ballads were penned about almost every significant event that happened and about a lot that didn't. They
were the way news – and what today might be called 'fake

news' – was spread around the kingdom. Some were merry, some were sad, some were hilariously funny, others tragic in their pathos. Almost all were sensational in one way or another. They were usually printed on 'broadsides', which were sheets of inexpensive paper, their texts augmented with wood-cut illustrations depicting an arresting scene from whatever melodrama the ballad related. The country's increasingly literate population had an insatiable appetite for them and, wherever there were buyers, sellers were to be found. So much so that the writer Henry Chettle complained in his *Kind-Harte's Dream*, published in 1592:

> *A company of idle youths, loathing honest labour and despising lawful trades, betake themselves of a vagrant and vicious life, in every corner of cities and market towns of the realm, singing and selling ballads.*

While tales of thwarted lovers, wronged maids, cuckoldry and quarrels between husbands and wives were ever-popular fare, preposterous yarns about mothers bearing deformed babies – *A Most Strange and Trew Ballad of a Monstrous Child Borne in Southampton* was one example – and hideous creatures that appeared out of the sea also kept their audiences riveted. If ballads were the newspapers and internet news sites of their day, there was no shortage of the sort of sensationalism that would have left even the editors of today's most titillating tabloids blushing. Ballads about true events such as the large earthquake that shook England on 6 April 1580, foiled conspiracies against Elizabeth I, and the defeat of the Spanish Armada proved a useful way of spreading news around the land. But these were swamped by the deluge of ditties that often lacked both accuracy and decency, and cared nothing for either.

The Court of Venus, a 1558 publication containing a collection of lusty ballads, was condemned by one critic who thundered: 'No filthy mind a songe can crave but therein he may find the same.' The attack probably did wonders for sales. A religious writer named Thomas Brice was moved to ask if the English people had turned into heathens. The Stationers' Company, the state institution that was legally empowered to prevent offensive publications, attempted to impose some discipline on the ballad industry. Ballads were supposed to be registered but many never were.

Flexing its muscles, on 3 December 1595, the Stationers' Company ordered seizure of the press and galleys of type belonging to one Abel Jeffes, for having printed 'divers ballads and things very offensive'. Fines were imposed on other offenders but many more writers and printers of broadsides flourished unhindered by the regulations. Becoming the subject of a scurrilous rhyme made up by vexatious enemies was a risk all well-known people ran. Shakespeare alludes to the problem in *Anthony and Cleopatra* when Cleopatra laments to her handmaiden Iris that after her death:

> **Saucy lictors** [petty officials] **will catch at us** [sing bawdy songs], **like strumpets; and scald rhymers** [scurvy poets] **ballad us** [compose ballads about us] **out o' tune.** (5.2)

In *Henry IV, Part 2*, Sir John Falstaff warns he will avenge the tricks Prince Hal and others have played on him by threatening:

> **Go, hang thyself in thine own heir-apparent garters! If I be ta'en** [arrested], **I'll peach** [turn informer] **for this. An** [If] **I have not ballads made on you all and sung to filthy tunes, let a cup of sack** [white wine] **be my poison.** (2.2)

Falstaff returns to the subject of ballads when Sir John Colville of the Dale surrenders to him after a battle, the cowardly knight being the first opponent of rank Colville happens to come across when his side is defeated. Vaingloriously boasting that he has vanquished Colville, Falstaff declares to Hal's brother Prince John:

Here he is, and here I yield him; and I beseech your Grace, let it be book'd [recorded] **with the rest of this day's deeds; or by the Lord, I will have it in a particular ballad else, with mine own picture on the top on't, Colville kissing** [my] **foot.** (4.3)

In *The Winter's Tale*, Autolycus knows his target audience. The rustics excitedly gather around when he appears in their village, peddling his bag full of tawdry knick-knacks and calling out:

Gloves as sweet [perfumed] **as damask roses; masks for faces and for noses; bugle bracelet** [threaded black glass beads], **necklace amber, perfume for a lady's chamber; golden quoifs** [tight-fitting caps] **and stomachers** [decorated chest coverings], **for my lads to give their dears: Pins and poking-sticks of steel** [rods that were heated and used to stiffen starched ruffs], **what maids lack from head to heel: Come buy of me, come; come buy, come buy; buy lads, or else your lasses cry: Come buy.** (4.4)

Purses are produced and waved in the air. Even as he plies feverish buyers with his over-priced tat, Autolycus watches whereabouts on the person each purse is stowed away, so he can later indulge in a little thievery to boost his takings. But it is his ballads – 'the prettiest love-songs for maid, so without bawdry' – that are in greatest demand. Touchingly, the fact that they are on printed sheets adds to their authenticity, according to the simple country girl Mopsa as she urges her sweetheart:

Pray now, buy some: I love a ballad in print o' life [on my life], **for then we are sure they are true.**

Autolycus does nothing to dispel her faith in the printed word, despite knowing full well the ballads are sheer hyperbole. 'Why should I carry lies abroad?' he asks with feigned innocence.

So what are we to make of the songs Autolycus sells? Clearly Shakespeare had his tongue planted firmly in his cheek as he invented outrageous fabrications that parodied the bombastic claptrap peddled by the ballad-mongers. Even so, the tales he cites may have been based on kernels of truth. The first ballad Autolycus speaks of, concerning the usurer's wife who gave birth to twenty bags of money and 'longed to eat adders' heads and toads carbonadoed,' may have alluded to Penelope Devereux, Countess of Devonshire. She is seen in a portrait (*pictured*) by the artist Nicholas Hilliard, dating from around 1590.

The ballad is not lent any veracity by Autolycus declaring 'Here's the midwife's name to't, one Mistress Tale-porter' because a 'tale-porter' simply meant one, especially a midwife, who spread tittle-tattle. Even so, the unfortunate Lady Penelope had been the subject of much gossip.

She was the daughter of Walter Devereux, first Earl of Essex, and his wife Lettice Knollys, and was the sister of Robert Devereux, second Earl of Essex, the man once so beloved of Elizabeth I. Penelope was considered by many to be the most beautiful woman to grace Elizabeth's court. She had a mane of golden hair and dark eyes, and would later be described by James I as 'a fair woman with a black soul'. The poet Sir Philip Sidney was an ardent admirer of her beauty and she is said to have inspired his sonnet sequence *Astrophel and Stella*, composed in the 1580s.

In March 1581, when Penelope was eighteen years old, her legal guardian Catherine, Countess of Huntingdon, secured the Queen's assent for her to be married to Robert Rich, third

Baron Rich. Penelope is said to have protested vigorously against the forced marriage but to no avail. Rich was deeply unpopular at court and, perhaps fittingly given his name, he appears to have come into a great deal of money by somewhat dubious means. He was widely rumoured to be a usurer, a man who lent money at exorbitantly high interest rates, which was illegal. In the fullness of time, Penelope bore him not money-bags but no fewer than seven children.

By 1595, she had begun a clandestine affair with the dashing Sir Charles Blount, Baron Mountjoy, by whom, astonishingly, she gave birth to another four children, all illegitimate. The scandalised Rich finally divorced her on grounds of adultery in 1605. Penelope and Blount promptly married in defiance of canon law, which did not permit remarriage where an ex-spouse was still alive, and as a result were banished in disgrace from the court of James I. She had held a coveted position as a lady-in-waiting to James' queen, Anne.

In the course of her turbulent lifetime, Penelope fended off a charge of treason because of implication in her brother's abortive rebellion against Elizabeth I, recklessly flirted with converting to Catholicism – a dangerous prospect in Protestant England – and became entangled in a bitter legal fight with Blount's family over his will after he died in April 1606. Because her marriage to Blount was not recognised in law, his family brought a charge of fraud against her in their battle to prevent her and her four illegitimate children inheriting under his will. She was condemned in their suit as a 'harlot, adulteress, concubine and whore'. The matter was resolved when Penelope herself died on 7 July 1607, at the age of forty-four. Was she the subject of Autolycus' preposterous ballad? History does not record her taste in adders' heads and toads carbonadoed.

Autolycus has further irresistible tales up his sleeve, as he tells his eager audience:

Here's another ballad of a fish that appeared upon the coast on Wednesday, the four-score of April, forty thousand fathom above water, and sung this ballad against the hard hearts of maids. It was thought she was a woman and was turned into a cold fish for she would not exchange flesh with one that loved her. The ballad is very pitiful and as true. (4.4)

'*Is* it true?' asks Mopsa's friend, the shepherdess Dorcas. 'Five justices' hands at it, and witnesses more than my pack will hold,' Autolycus blatantly lies. As for 'the four-score' (eightieth day) of April, that detail goes unnoticed by the peasants, which would have provoked laughter at their expense among Shakespeare's city-dwelling audience. The fishy tale may have occurred to Shakespeare after he learned of a ballad, which appears in the Stationer's Company Register, claiming to be 'the most true and strange report of a monstrous fish that appeared in forme of a woman from the wast [waist] upward, seene in the sea' on Friday, 17 February 1604. Mermaids had been part of folklore for hundreds of years but no-one knew anybody who had actually seen one.

Alternatively, in *The Annales of England,* the noted historian John Stow wrote that on 10 October 1583, at Caister in Norfolk, a fish 17 yards (15.5m) long was said to have flown through the air and landed 'forty thousand fathoms above water'. A fathom was 6ft (1.83m), which would have meant the fish either leapt 240,000ft (73,000m) into the air, or landed around forty-five miles (73km) inland. Stow has nothing to say on the subject of whether the fish had originally been a 'hard-hearted' woman.

See also: 25. Cut-purses and Cozeners

47. IF YOU WANT TO GET AHEAD

A surprising item becomes the ultimate fashion accessory for the well-travelled man-about-town

Clown: **This cannot be but a great courtier.**

Old Shepherd: **His garments are rich, but he wears them not handsomely.**

Clown: **He seems to be the more noble in being fantastical: a great man, I'll warrant. I know by the picking on's teeth.**
(*The Winter's Tale*, 4.4, 1609-11)

A COUNTRY bumpkin called simply 'Clown', as was customary in Shakespeare's day, tries to convince his father, the Old Shepherd, that the stranger they have just met is a nobleman who may be able to help them by using his influence at the royal court. The shepherd is not convinced, rightly as it will turn out. The man is none other than Autolycus, unashamed pedlar, conman and thief, who has recently swapped garments with Prince Florizel, the king's son. The clothes he wears are far more expensive than any peasant could afford but, as the shepherd points out, they do not sit comfortably on the roguish figure. Yet there is one small detail that clinches matters.

Extraordinary as it may seem to a modern audience, the fact that the man is ostentatiously picking his teeth with a toothpick marks him out as one who is accustomed to mixing in high circles. It suggests the user is wealthy and sophisticated, and has probably ventured to distant and exotic lands, a finely wrought toothpick being a must-have souvenir with which to brag of foreign travel.

In Shakespeare's early play *King John*, a character known

as Philip the Bastard has just been knighted by the king and dubbed Sir Richard Plantagenet, after it is revealed he is actually the illegitimate son of Richard the Lionheart. Left alone on stage to reflect on the various ways he can flaunt his sudden good fortune, the Bastard muses:

> **Well, now can I make any Joan a lady. 'Good den** [day], **Sir Richard!' – 'God-a-mercy, fellow!' – and if his name be George, I'll call him Peter, for new-made honour doth forget men's names; 'tis too respective** [attentive] **and too sociable for your conversion. Now your traveller, he and his toothpick at my worship's mess** [dinner table], **and when my knightly stomach is sufficed, why then I suck my teeth and catechise my picked man of countries** [question him about foreign lands]. (1.1)

The use of toothpicks of one sort or another has been traced as far back as the Neanderthals. Feather-quill toothpicks had been around for centuries, but by Elizabethan and Jacobean times the finest toothpicks of the gentry were elaborately fashioned in metal. The plain fact was that most people simply picked food detritus from their teeth with the point of a knife. Other than wiping the teeth with a wet cloth, rubbing them with crushed sage leaves or a 'tooth blanch' made from cuttlefish bone (available from any good apothecary), and swilling the mouth using water infused with rosemary flowers or a compound known as 'spirit of vitriol', there was not much more a person could do to observe oral hygiene.

Feather-quill toothpicks could carry their own risks for the unwary. The historian Diodorus of Sicily, who lived in the first century BC, tells how Agathocles, a despised King of Syracuse, was murdered in 289 BC. The assassin, a servant named Menon, had hatched what must be considered one of the more imaginative ways of bumping off a tyrant. According to Diodorus:

Now it was the king's habit after dinner always to clean his teeth with a quill. Having finished his wine, therefore, he asked Menon for the quill, and Menon gave him one that he smeared with a putrefactive drug. The king, unaware of this, applied it rather vigorously and so brought it into contact with the gums all about his teeth. The first effect was a continuous pain, which grew daily more excruciating, and this was followed by an incurable gangrene everywhere near the teeth.

Toothpicks came to be regarded as an essential item among the upper classes of the Roman Empire, although by Medieval times they had all but vanished. When the Renaissance blossomed across Europe in the fifteenth and sixteenth centuries, the toothpick made a stunning comeback, principally in those hotbeds of fashion, Italy, Spain and France. Cardinal Richelieu was said to have so detested the use of knives for picking teeth that he ordered all knifepoints ground down, giving rise to the curved profile on sterling flatware that persists today.

The toothpick then became a coveted status symbol. In the lively comedy *Much Ado About Nothing*, Benedick requests his master Don Pedro send him on a mission to the farthest corners of the earth in order to escape the sharp tongue of 'my dear Lady Disdain' Beatrice. With a melodramatic flourish, he asks:

Will your grace command me any service to the world's end? I will go on the slightest errand now to the Antipodes that you can devise to send me on. I will fetch you a tooth-picker now from the furthest inch of Asia, bring you the length of Prester John's foot, fetch you a hair off the great Cham's beard, do you any embassage to the Pigmies, rather than hold three words' conference with this harpy. (2.1)

Although we cannot take Benedick's hyperbole seriously, they are formidable offers, so let us look more closely at his list. By 'the Antipodes' – the word, meaning 'with the feet pointed opposite', was coined by the ancient Greeks who had realised that the earth was not flat – he was referring vaguely to the furthest side of the world, since the lands we now know as the Antipodes, Australia and New Zealand, had yet to be discovered by Europeans. Prester John (or 'John the Priest') was a legendary, and quite possibly mythical, ruler of a mysterious Christian kingdom in the Far East, beyond the borders of the Muslim Ottoman Empire. Stories about him had been circulating since the twelfth century. The Great Cham was none other than the ferocious Kublai Khan, grandson of Genghis Khan, who had extended the Mongol Empire across China. He famously sported a forked beard. The explorers Marco Polo and Sir John Mandeville had both written about him in hugely popular accounts of their travels. Although the central African rain forest Pygmies were not encountered by Europeans until the nineteenth century, the name is first used in Homer's *Iliad* to refer to a dwarfish race reputed to live in Ethiopia and southern Egypt. (A harpy, by the way, was a figment of Greek legend, being a vicious bird of prey with the face of a beautiful woman.) But there, among all the herculean tasks Benedick offers to undertake, is 'I will fetch you a tooth-picker now from the furthest inch of Asia.' A toothpick! What could be more exotic?

The toothpick could either be carried on a chain around one's noble neck, making it convenient for use at a moment's notice, or kept in an elaborate gold or silver case, which better enabled it to be shown off and one's wealth and status thereby flaunted. Sometimes it was worn attached to a hat or cap, although that fashion appears to have faded by the time Shakespeare wrote *All's Well That Ends Well*, around 1604. In that troubled comedy, the braggart Parolles unsuccessfully tries to persuade a gentlewoman named Helena to abandon her commitment to preserving her virginity, claiming such a notion is hopelessly out of date in contemporary society:

Virginity, like an old courtier, wears her cap out of fashion, richly suited but unsuitable, just like the brooch and the toothpick, which wear not now. (1.1)

Today the brooch and the toothpick retain their popularity, even if they lack the social status they once boasted. As for virginity, that is a matter for the mores of each generation.

48. THE STRANGER'S CASE

Will's moving contribution to a history play reflects the anti-immigrant protests of his own time

Grant them removed, and grant that this your noise hath chid down all the majesty of England. Imagine that you see the wretched strangers, their babies at their backs and their poor luggage, plodding to the ports and coasts for transportation, and that you sit as kings in your desires, authority quite silent by your brawl, and you in ruff of your opinions clothed. What had you got? I'll tell you. You had taught how insolence and strong hand should prevail, how order should be quelled; and by this pattern not one of you should live an aged man, for other ruffians, as their fancies wrought, with self same hand, self reason, and self right, would shark on you, and men like ravenous fishes would feed on one another.
(*Sir Thomas More*, 2.4, 1592-95; Shakespeare's involvement 1603-4)

RIOTERS have gathered in London, intent on setting fire to the houses of foreigners and driving them out of England, back to the countries from which they came. The crowd are in an ugly mood. They blame the 'strangers' – as migrants from Europe are known – for causing soaring food prices, stealing their jobs, distorting their culture, and any other ill that besets blighted lives. The only man deemed to stand a chance of calming them is the widely respected Sheriff, Thomas More. The mob agree to hear what he has to say, and More lets rip with one of the most extraordinary speeches Shakespeare ever wrote. Known these days as *The Stranger's Case* and popularised in performance by Sir Ian McKellen, the speech is timeless in its appeal to humanity and common decency in the face of suffering and abject misery. It also tells us a lot about Shakespeare himself.

The dark day in history depicted in the play is 1 May 1517, which became known as 'Evil May Day'. Henry VIII is on the throne and foreigners settling in England, most recently bankers from the Italian region of Lombardy and Flemish labourers from the Low Countries, have found themselves the target of increasing hostility from local people. The flames had been fanned a few weeks earlier by a clergyman named either Dr Beale or Bell, preaching at Paul's Cross. According to the chronicler Edward Hall, he declared:

> *This land was given to Englishmen, and as birds would defend their nest, so ought Englishmen to cherish and defend themselves, and to hurt and grieve aliens for the common weal.*

Sporadic assaults on foreigners began to occur and dire threats were circulated that on May Day 'the city would rebel and slay all aliens'. A ham-fisted effort by an alderman to disperse a group of young men on the eve of May Day only antagonised the disaffected. In the early hours of 1 May more than a thousand rioters, mainly apprentice boys, assembled armed with bricks and clubs. They marched to a district of the city where many foreigners lived. Mayhem broke out. When the residents, seeking to defend themselves, threw stones and poured scalding water from upstairs windows, the demonstrators invaded their houses, rampaging through the properties and looting whatever they could carry. A few hours later, troops quelled the riot and arrested more than three hundred people. While a handful of ringleaders were charged with treason, most of the demonstrators were pardoned by the king and released.

In contrast to the ugly events which actually took place that night, in the play Thomas More turns the protesters' arguments back on themselves by asking them to imagine what it would be like to be migrants. Here Shakespeare cranks up the power of More's oratory, and treats us to the breathtaking sublimity of his skills as a writer and the depth of his compassion as a human being:

> You'll put down strangers, kill them, cut their throats,
> possess their houses, and lead the majesty of law in line
> to slip him like a hound? Alas, alas. Say now the King, as
> he is clement if th' offender mourn, should so much come
> too short of your great trespass as but to banish you.
> Whither would you go? What country, by the nature of
> your error, should give you harbour? Go you to France or
> Flanders, to any German province, Spain or Portugal, nay,
> anywhere that not adheres to England, why, you must
> needs be strangers. Would you be pleas'd to find a nation
> of such barbarous temper that breaking out in hideous
> violence would not afford you an abode on earth? Whet
> their detested knives against your throats, spurn you
> like dogs, and like as if that God owed not nor made not
> you, nor that the elements were not all appropriate to
> your comforts, but charter'd unto them? What would
> you think to be us'd thus? This is the strangers' case and
> this your mountainish inhumanity. (2.4)

'Mountainish.' What a wonderful word. This speech is the only occasion on which Shakespeare uses it.

Although *Sir Thomas More* is thought to have originally been written between 1592 and 1595, it was considered by the authorities at the time to be too contentious to be performed in case it incited further riots. We have clear evidence of that because a curt note written by Edmund Tilney, the Master of the Revels, whose job it was to scrutinise and censor theatre scripts, appears in the margin of one of the pages. It reads:

Leave out the insurrection wholly and the cause thereof,

> *and begin with Sir Thomas More at the Mayor's ses-*
> *sions, with a report afterwards of his good service done*
> *being Sheriff of London upon a mutiny against the Lom-*
> *bards – only by a short report, and not otherwise, at your*
> *own perils.   E. Tilney.*

The official censorship effectively confirms that even in the 1590s, eight decades after Thomas More's confrontation with the May Day mob, anti-migrant sentiment was still running strongly in England. Following Tilney's intervention, and a few half-hearted attempts at rewriting the troublesome passages, the script was probably thrown into a theatre trunk and abandoned as a hopeless case. It would remain so as long as Elizabeth I remained on the throne. Shakespeare's contribution appears to have been made sometime in 1603-4, when an attempt was undertaken to revise the play after the Queen's death.

That, as it happened, was the same time he was living as a lodger in the Silver Street house of Christopher and Marie Mountjoy, which would have given him good reason to feel the pull of raw emotion as he wrote. The Mountjoys were Huguenot refugees, two among the thousands of French Calvinist Protestants who had been forced to flee their Catholic homeland in fear of their lives. Shakespeare's landlord and landlady were, in other words, among the very migrants being subjected to vicious barbs of resentment by many of his fellow citizens. The evidence suggests he was on friendly terms with the couple, and may even have become a confidante of Marie Mountjoy in what appears to have been an unhappy marriage.

✳ ✳ ✳

Tensions in the capital, forcefully subdued by the authorities after the riot of 1517 but never completely eradicated, had rumbled on through the passing decades. They were kindled again in the 1570s as a wave of persecuted Protestants fled to England from the Spanish-controlled Low Countries. In 1571, aggrieved locals petitioned the authorities in London, complaining of the strangers:

> *They are a commonwealth within themselves. They keep themselves severed from us in church, in government, in trade, in language and marriage.*

The petition, titled *A Complaynt of the Cytizens of London against the great number of strangers in and about this cytty*, contained seven demands, which included:

> *First, they ought not to take any lodgings or houses within the citty but to abide at the tables of freehostes, and to dwell in noe other place but with the said hostes to bee assigned. Contrary heerunto the marchant straungers take uppe the fairest houses in the Citty, devide & fitt them for their severall uses, take into them several lodgers & dwellers.*

Another demand was that the strangers 'ought not to sell any merchaundizes by Retayle,' nor should any of them use their skills as craftsmen in order to make a living. The petition was largely ignored by the authorities, although the summer of the following year brought new pressures. On the night of 23 August 1572 – the eve of the feast of Bartholomew the Apostle – in an astonishing demonstration of the evils Christians could cheerfully inflict upon fellow Christians, a state-sponsored mass slaughter of Huguenots began in Paris. The bloody mayhem went on well into the following day and, after fanning out to the French provinces, spluttered on for several weeks more. In what became known as the St Bartholomew's Day Massacre thousands of Protestants were butchered, and the flow of refugees seeking safety across the

English Channel turned into a flood.

Two decades later, memories of the outrage inspired Christopher Marlowe to write a savagely anti-Catholic play. His *The Massacre at Paris* was possibly based on accounts he had heard from Huguenot refugees arriving in his native city of Canterbury. Marlowe's play was first performed in 1593, which itself turned out to be a momentous year. With the plague now gripping London, continuing threats of invasion from Spain, and a series of disastrous harvests causing food prices to skyrocket, xenophobia took hold again. Foreigners were, after all, useful scapegoats in troubled times.

In the spring, anonymous posters – described by the Privy Council as a 'vyle ticket or placarde, set up upon some post in London' – appeared, exhorting violence against the strangers. The message was addressed to 'You beastly brutes the Belgians, faint-hearted Frenchmen and fraudulent Flemings,' accusing them of 'cowardly flight' from their homelands. To the government's alarm, the posters went so far as to complain that the Queen had permitted the migrants 'to live here in better case and more freedom than her own people'. The message then took a particularly sinister turn, threatening:

> Be it known to all Flemings and Frenchmen that it is best for them to depart out of the realm of England between this and the ninth of July next. If not then take that which follows, for that there shall be many a sore stripe. Apprentices will rise to the number of 2336. And all the apprentices and journeymen will down with the Flemings and strangers.

Worse was to follow. On the night of 5 May, further placards appeared, affixed to the wall of the Dutch Church in London, instructing the foreigners to 'Fly, fly and never return.' The message, written in crude doggerel, began:

Ye strangers yt [that] doe inhabite in this lande, note
this same writing doe it understand. Conceit it well for
savegard of your lyves ... Expect you therefore such a
fatall day shortly on you & youres for to ensewe as never
was seene. Since wordes nor threates nor any other
thinge canne make you to avoyd this certaine ill, weele
cutt your throates in your temples praying. Not Paris
massacre so much blood did spill.

The rabid poster was signed at the bottom 'Tamburlaine'. The name was an allusion to *Tamburlaine the Great*,
a hugely popular play Marlowe had written in 1587 about
a bloodthirsty Tartar despot who revelled in the mass murder of his enemies. Not surprisingly, the posters triggered
a wave of terror among the immigrant community, many of
whom did indeed flee London and the country itself. A letter
received from England on 16 May by Richard Verstegan, an
Anglo-Dutch publisher based in Antwerp, reported:

Great fear is thereby conceyved by the strangers. Great
companyes of them are already departed, and more daily
preparing to follow, so it is thought the most part will
away, our Councell not knowing how to protect them.

Verstegan himself estimated that at least ten thousand
strangers are 'determyned this somer to departe from England . . . for fear of some comotion to be made by the comon
people against them'. Fearing further riots, this time the government acted. Its first task was to find the authors of what
became known as the Dutch Church Libel, and investigators
were authorised to use torture to achieve their objective.
They swooped on the playwright Thomas Kyd, a former flat-
mate of Christopher Marlowe's.

While there was nothing to directly connect either man
to the posters, officials found a sheaf of highly blasphemous papers espousing atheism, in itself a treasonous matter.

Under torture, Kyd insisted the papers belonged to Marlowe. A warrant was issued for Marlowe's arrest and questioning. Less than two weeks later Marlowe himself was dead, killed in the brawl at Deptford.

It was against this tumultuous background, and the rampant xenophobia then gripping England, that Shakespeare wrote Thomas More's extraordinary, impassioned speech, railing against the 'mountainish inhumanity' of those who would persecute the strangers.

❋ ❋ ❋

Sir Thomas More is a particularly interesting play for reasons that are quite unrelated to its subject matter. The drama, which was never performed in Shakespeare's lifetime, contains the only example we have of a manuscript in his own handwriting. Six 'hands' have been identified in what was clearly a collaborative effort, which underwent several revisions.

The writers were Anthony Munday, who appears to have penned the original draft of the play; Henry Chettle, the man who had been forced to apologise to Shakespeare after publishing Robert Greene's 'upstart crow' diatribe against him in 1592; the playwrights Thomas Heywood and Thomas Dekker; an unknown person thought to be a professional scribe who copied out sections of the play; and Shakespeare himself, who is prosaically known by paleographers as 'Hand D'. It looks as though Shakespeare was drafted in to write that powerful speech of Sir Thomas More's.

Shakespeare's contribution is contained in three unspeakably precious pages of playscript, and 'Hand D' was identified by comparing the handwriting with his six surviving signatures on legal documents as well as the words 'By me' before the signature on his will. Those examples were enough to establish his authorship. Scholars have also noted distinct similarities in some of the phrases and themes he uses in *Sir Thomas More* compared with similar instances in other plays. Variations on *Sir Thomas More*'s concept of 'men like ravenous fishes would feed on one another,' for example, appear in *Coriolanus, Troilus and Cressida,* and *Pericles.*

Also among stylistic fascinations is the enjoyment Shakespeare clearly derived from turning nouns into verbs. He was engaging in such coinages from his earliest writing days. Consider, for example, a stanza in his 1592 poem *The Rape of Lucrece*:

The aged man that coffers-up his gold / Is plagued with cramps and gouts and painful fits; / And scarce hath eyes his treasure to behold, / But like still-pining Tantalus he sits, / And useless barns the harvest of his wits; / Having no other pleasure of his gain / But torment that it cannot cure his pain.

The commonplace noun 'coffer', meaning a trunk or chest, has become the rather more exotic transitive verb 'coffers-up', and 'barns' too has turned into a verb. In *Sir Thomas More* he puts the noun 'shark' to work as a verb in the lines 'other ruffians, as their fancies wrought, with self same hand, self reason, and self right, would shark on you'. Now compare *Hamlet,* when Horatio says:

Now, sir, young Fortinbras, of unimproved mettle hot and full, hath in the skirts of Norway, here and there, shark'd up a list of lawless resolutes, for food and diet, to some enterprise that hath a stomach in't. (1.1)

'Shark'd up'. What other words would work so splendidly to describe the macho young Fortinbras of Norway gathering together a band of cut-throat mercenaries with which to invade Denmark? Yet perhaps the most telling idiosyncracy is the way Shakespeare spells the word 'silence'. In an age of easy-going spelling before the discipline imposed by dictionaries, most people spelled the word as we do now. Occasionally it occurs as 'silens' and rarely as 'scilence'. Shakespeare spelt it 'scilens'. Since no original manuscripts other than *Sir Thomas More* survive in his handwriting, we might never have realised the significance of this quirk because compositors invariably corrected the spelling when the plays were published. Except in one case.

A cousin of Justice Shallow in *Henry IV, Part 2* is named Silence. When that play first appeared in print in 1600 as a quarto edition, thought to have been based on Shakespeare's own handwritten working playscripts (known to scholars as 'foul papers'), the character's name appeared as 'Scilens'. Because the word was the proper name of a person, and not a common noun occurring in the course of the text, a wary compositor appears to have left the spelling exactly as he found it. By the time *Henry IV, Part 2* appeared in the *First Folio* of 1623, the spelling of Silence's name had been corrected.

What has all this to do with *Sir Thomas More*? There, among those three handwritten pages, is the same curious spelling of 'scilens'. Perhaps that is how it was taught at Stratford Grammar School. For whatever reason he spelled the word that way, the anomaly reinforces the already strong evidence that those one hundred and forty-seven lines of *Sir Thomas More* were indeed written by Will Shakespeare. The writer's ability to empathise with the lot of the strangers, and the sheer humanity articulated in More's speech, surely clinches it.

See also: 9. A Great Reckoning

EPILOGUE: OUR REVELS ARE ENDED

WILLIAM Shakespeare died on 23 April 1616, which we believe was his fifty-second birthday. We can say only that we *believe* it was his birthday, because we don't know for sure. He was baptised in Holy Trinity Church, Stratford-upon-Avon, on 26 April 1564 and, since babies were traditionally christened within a few days of birth, 23 April is as good a guess as any. As it also happens to be the feast day of St George, the patron saint of England, that date conveniently fits the narrative when we celebrate the man who has come to be regarded as the quintessential personification of Englishness.

The only account we have of his death comes a generation later from John Ward, the vicar of Stratford-upon-Avon from 1662-81, who writes in his notes:

> *Shakespeare, Drayton [the Warwickshire writer Michael Drayton] and Ben Jonson had a merry meeting and it seems drank too hard, for Shakespeare died of a fever there contracted.*

We do not know how reliable Ward's report is, but Will's younger daughter Judith was married to a Stratford vintner named Thomas Quiney on 10 February 1616, so the occasion may still have been something to celebrate when the three old friends got together two months later. (Susanna had married Dr John Hall, a respected medical man, in 1607.)

Shakespeare is buried beneath an otherwise unremarkable stone slab in Holy Trinity, the parish church which sits in picturesque splendour beside the banks of the River Avon. The grave famously bears an epitaph of four lines which, according to legend, Will wrote himself. It reads:

> *Good friend for Jesus' sake forbear, / To dig the dust en-*

closed here. / Bless'd be the man that spares these stones, /
And curs'd be he that moves my bones.

If you sound the extra syllable 'ed' at the end of 'en-closed', as would have been done at the time, the second line acquires the scansion necessary for crude poetry. The epitaph is often described as 'the curse' of Shakespeare's grave. In another sense, it is a blessing. Since none of us are likely to move his bones, we are thereby all blessed. Shakespeare, however, had good cause to fear the indignity of his mortal remains being disturbed. By convention, when a suitable length of time had elapsed the dead were periodically dug up from their 'last' resting place and turfed out in order to make room for later occupants. Their bones would be cast unceremoniously into a large building known as a charnel house which, in Stratford's case, stood on the north side of Holy Trinity.

In 1795, the actor Samuel Ireland chillingly described Stratford's charnel house as having the 'largest assemblage of human bones' he had ever beheld. It is an image of death that appears to have haunted Shakespeare, possibly from the days of his childhood. The horror of it finds expression in his writing, from Hamlet's 'gorge' rising at the skull of Yorick to the nightmarish terrors of Juliet:

O, bid me leap, rather than marry Paris, from off the battlements of yonder tower; or walk in thievish ways; or bid me lurk where serpents are; chain me with roaring bears; or shut me nightly in a charnel-house, o'er-cover'd quite with dead men's rattling bones, with reeky shanks [stinking limbs] **and yellow chapless** [jawless] **skulls. Or bid me go into a new-made grave and hide me with a dead man in his shroud. Things that, to hear them told, have made me tremble.** (*Romeo and Juliet*, 4.1)

Destination charnel house was something Shakespeare desperately wanted to avoid, and his pithily worded epitaph seems to have done the trick. Which is just as well for the thousands of tourists who flock to Stratford every year, seeking a focal point at which to pay homage. Yet as Ben Jonson so eloquently put it, in his preface to the *First Folio,* Shakespeare's true memorial is the incomparable body of work in which we can relish his genius. In lines addressed 'To the Reader,' Jonson comments on the portrait of Shakespeare by the Flemish engraver Martin Droeshout, which appears on the page opposite his words:

> *This figure that thou here seest put, / It was for gentle Shakespeare cut, / Wherein the graver had a strife / With Nature, to out-do the life: / O could he but have drawn his wit / As well in brass, as he has hit / His face; the print would then surpass / All that was ever writ in brass: / But since he cannot, reader, look / Not on his picture, but his book.*

Shakespeare appears to have been well liked by his fellow actors and others who knew him. Even Jonson, never one to hold back when it came to a bit of robust sparring with his rival, was moved to say after his death 'I loved the man, and do honour his memory, on this side of idolatory, as much as any.' It is unlikely Shakespeare expected his playscripts to survive him, and in all probability many of them would not have, but for his friends John Heminges and Henry Condell and the *First Folio.* Will must have had his tongue in his cheek when he gave Cassius the line in *Julius Caesar* that runs:

How many ages hence shall this our lofty scene be acted over in states unborn and accents yet unknown! (3.1)

Yet even Shakespeare would surely have been astonished to know his comedies, histories and tragedies, written to lure Elizabethan and Jacobean crowds off the streets and into the theatre, were still being enjoyed more than four hundred years later, let alone in countries and languages he never dreamt of. It fell to Ben Jonson to sum up the timelessness of his friend's genius, in that particularly memorable tribute he added to the *First Folio*: 'He was not of an age, but for all time.'

Two examples, which have occurred within living memory, give proof of Jonson's prescient dictum. They come from utterly contrasting sources. The setting for the first was Hungary in the years immediately after the Second World War, when the brutal Communist regime that had replaced Nazi occupation was strengthening its iron grip on a benighted country. A production of *Richard III*, which opened at the National Theatre in Budapest on 13 December 1947 was looked on approvingly by the authorities. Not only was Shakespeare regarded as a safe bet when it came to theatrical productions, but the plot of *Richard III* could even be seen as allegorical of the overthrow of Nazi tyranny.

The Hungarian academic Veronika Schandl records how, among the play's characters, the monstrous Richard was compared with Hitler; Elizabeth, mother of the two young princes in the Tower, was seen as representing those mothers whose sons had been torn away by war; the Lady Anne, seduced by Richard, was symbolic of the traitors who fell for the 'broad-shouldered' SS soldiers marching through Hungarian villages. Schandl also notes how, with Europe slowly recovering from the horrors of fascism, the production was hailed by the critics, with one writing: 'We cannot believe that there has ever been a better time for receiving *Richard III* this clearly.'

But if the Hungarian authorities believed they could use Shakespeare entirely for their own propaganda purposes, they had a shock coming. When *Richard III* was revived in 1955, the play took on a wholly different significance. Although Richard was still played by Tamás Major, the same lead actor as in the 1947 production, something had changed in the mood of the audience. When the drama arrived at Act 3, Scene 6, the theatre erupted. The scene is so short that it can be overlooked by modern audiences. Indeed, it is often cut out altogether by directors who fail to consider it important enough to retain. It consists entirely of a scribe, known as

Scrivener, revealing how he was ordered to draw up an indictment against Richard's enemy Lord Hastings. Yet, he tells us, he had written up the guilty verdict fully twenty-two hours before Hastings was even accused. Then came the Scrivener's lines that caused uproar in the Budapest of 1955, a city already hungry for the political revolution that would manifest itself in the following year's ill-fated uprising against Soviet hegemony:

Why who's so gross [stupid] **that seeth not this palpable device** [obvious trickery]**? Yet who's so blind but says he sees it not? Bad is the world, and all will come to nought, when such bad dealing must be seen in thought** [thought about but not spoken of].

Shakespeare's words neatly summarised the way in which the Eastern-bloc governments routinely dealt with their opponents: staging show trials when convictions had already been decided on, then carrying out state executions to eliminate the trouble makers. Richard III himself had morphed from symbolising Hitler, as in 1947, to representing Stalin. Suddenly the National Theatre had a subversive production on their hands. The story was taken up by Tamás Major himself, who reflected in a retrospective book on how the commotion started as early as Act 1, Scene 1, when Lord Hastings comments on the rise of his enemies at court. Major writes:

After the first lines ... 'More pity that the eagle should be mew'd, while kites and buzzards prey at liberty,' the performance had to be stopped, and we couldn't go on for minutes as the crowd was cheering so loud. This was right at the beginning of the play, so we all sensed this was going to be a very risky production. And so it happened. Whenever the audience felt that the words could have a current double meaning, they literally 'pulled down the house,' particularly at the moment when Elemér Baló, the scribe

*[Scrivener], came in with the prefabricated verdicts. We
all feared that this would be the end; it was received with a
standing ovation. This just shows that Shakespeare does
not need to be made current, he makes himself current.*

A second instance of a sixteenth-century drama wreaking political havoc in our own times came in 2017, when the Shakespeare in the Park presentation, a popular annual summer attraction in New York's Central Park, was *Julius Caesar*. Production decisions, it has to be said, were provocative, but the storm that followed again turned a spotlight on just how relevant Shakespeare remains today. Caesar was played by Gregg Henry, who described his character as having become 'drunk with ego, drunk with power, drunk with ambition and the belief that he alone must rule the world'. Harmless enough, you might think, until you learn that Henry, who bears a striking resemblance to Donald Trump, wore a blond wig along with a sharp suit and red tie. Caesar's wife Calpurnia sported a Melania-style wardrobe and spoke with a Slovenian accent. The young Octavius Caesar was described as 'a Jared Kushner-like nerd wearing a bulletproof vest over his blue blazer'. The appearance of the cast caused much merriment among the audience, according to *The Guardian*'s correspondent Lois Beckett, 'but when Caesar's enemies took out their knives and killed the Trump-like leader on the senate floor, no one was laughing'. Beckett continues:

*All the rhetoric about Caesar's ambition, the danger he had
posed to the republic, suddenly seemed worthless. There was
only the horror of the violence, the shock of it, even to the
men and women who had plotted it and carried it out.*

The howls of outrage that followed were deafening. An outraged Fox News reported 'NYC Play Appears to Depict Assassination of Trump', adding for good measure that the Trump-like character had been 'brutally stabbed to death by women and minorities'. Trump's son, Donald Trump Jr, fired off an angry tweet, demanding: 'I wonder how much of this "art" is funded by taxpayers? Serious question, when does "art" become political speech & does that change things?' Horrified, two major sponsors pulled their support. Public Theater's creative director Oskar Eustis defended the show, insisting: 'Anyone seeing our production of *Julius Caesar* will realise it in no way advocates violence towards anyone.' Lost in the shouting was the voice of Stephen Greenblatt of Harvard University, one of the world's most eminent Shakespeare scholars, who added his support for the theatre. *The Guardian* reported him as saying the point of the play was that it can be dangerous to get what you think you want, and that the assassination of an unpopular leader 'could bring an end to the very republic you are trying to save'. Professor Greenblatt added: 'It's weird to have that, then, be the object of this kind of hysteria.'

Legion are the anecdotes told of great Shakespearean actors and memorable performances down the years. Just as Falstaff says in *Henry IV, Part 2* 'I am not only witty in myself, but the cause that wit is in other men,' so Will might equally make the same claim. Peter O'Toole, in his 1992 autobiography *Loitering With Intent*, tells with relish a tale of the legendary thespian Edmund Kean (1787-1833), during a production of *Richard III* at the Drury Lane theatre. Kean, who was appearing as Richard, and his good friend George Cooke, playing the Duke of Buckingham, had been out on the town before one particular performance. Neither man was noted for strict sobriety and, as Kean began slurring Richard's famous opening soliloquy 'Now is the winter of our discontent' his condition quickly became evident. At which point, someone in the audience stood up and yelled indignantly: 'You're drunk!' Kean turned for a moment to stare into the wings, where Cooke was struggling to remain upright by wrapping his arms around the prompter, turned back to gaze bleary-eyed at the audience, and called out: 'If you think I'm drunk, wait till you see the Duke of Buckingham.'

Shakespeare's influence has not been limited to the stage, of course. In the four-and-a-half centuries since he was born, the English language itself has been enriched beyond measure by the words and phrases he bequeathed us. Some he simply popularised and, because of the enduring quality of the plays he wrote, they are still quoted today. Many others were of his own devising or, at least, he remains the first known user. *The Times* columnist the late Bernard Levin once wonderfully summed up some of the everyday gems in an article titled *On Quoting Shakespeare*. A few of the examples Levin gives are 'It's Greek to me' (*Julius Caesar*), 'more sinned against than sinning' (*King Lear*), 'more in sorrow than in anger' (*Hamlet*), vanished into 'thin air' (*The Tempest*), the 'green-eyed monster' jealousy (*Othello*), 'a blinking idiot' (*The Merchant of Venice*), and so on, and on and on.

Levin's point was that you have almost certainly been quoting Shakespeare throughout your life, in most cases without even knowing it. Indeed, so commonplace have Shakespearean quotations become that the joke is told of a tourist visiting Stratford-upon-Avon who insisted on seeing a performance of one of his plays. After sitting through an evening of *Hamlet*, the tourist complained: 'I don't see what's so great about Shakespeare's writing. It's just a bunch of old clichés strung together one after the other.'

One man who never doubted Shakespeare's power with words was Sir Winston Churchill. When granting Britain's former Prime Minister honorary American citizenship in 1963, President Kennedy quoted the comment about Churchill made by Edward Murrow, the CBS correspondent who famously reported from wartime London: 'He mobilised the English language and sent it into battle.' Yet when it came to oratory, William Shakespeare also played his part in defeating Hitler.

It was no coincidence that Churchill's speech dubbing the heroic Battle of Britain pilots 'the Few' echoed Henry V's: 'We few, we happy few, we band of brothers' at Agincourt. In February 1943, Churchill closed a speech to the Eighth Army, who were celebrating their defeat of Rommel's Desert Rats at El Alamein, with the stirring words: 'After the war, when a man is asked what he did, it will be quite sufficient for him to say "I marched and fought with the Desert Army".' In *Henry V*, the king tells his followers:

And gentlemen in England now a-bed shall think themselves accursed they were not here, and hold their manhoods cheap whiles any speaks that fought with us upon Saint Crispin's day. (4.3)

It was Churchill, after all, who persuaded Laurence Olivier to make his film *Henry V* as a rousing morale-booster for a war-weary nation in 1944, the year of the D-Day invasion. In an article titled *How Much Did Churchill Owe to Shakespeare?* published in *The Spectator USA* of December 2018, James Gore-Langton even wonders whether the scene from *Henry IV, Part 2*, in which Falstaff recruits a rag-taggle troop of soldiers from among Gloucestershire bumpkins, may have provided Churchill's inspiration for creating the Home Guard.

Perhaps Shakespeare's ability to transcend time's barrier is most evident today when we watch the depressingly interminable news reports of wretched migrants and refugees struggling with 'their babes at their backs and their poor luggage' to escape war-torn and destitute lands. We see overcrowded, shoddy and leaking boats, crammed with suffering men, women, and children, tossed about on wild waves, desperately hoping to reach safety. We hear of vessels that have capsized, plunging with all the terrified souls aboard to the bottom of the sea. A photographer takes a heart-breaking picture of a dead toddler whose body is washed up on a seashore.

We read of ruthless 'people smugglers' and victims who suffocate to death, locked inside shipping containers, the very metal mobile prisons they were promised would carry them to survival, freedom and a better life. We witness angry protesters demonstrating against the 'strangers,' denying them the right to live and work in their towns and cities, the migrants accused of taking houses, stealing jobs, and being 'a commonwealth within themselves'. What could be more relevant today than those lines Shakespeare put on the lips of Thomas More as he rails against 'mountainish inhumanity'?

Will Shakespeare was not of an age, but for all time.

* * *

It is often remarked that we know tantalisingly little about the life of Will Shakespeare. In fact, given the selfless hours that researchers have spent poring over dusty documents down the centuries since he lived, we know a great deal more about him than we do about many of his contemporaries. That said, literary historians and biographers, like nature, abhor a vacuum, and many an anecdote has emerged over the years. Some may contain a grain of truth, while others must be relegated to the fanciful. Among the most appealing are allusions to his rural upbringing in Warwickshire. One such tale concerns Hamlet's philosophical reflection:

> **There's a divinity that shapes our ends, rough-hew them how we will.** (*Hamlet*, 5.2)

The story of how that may have originated came from the Ben Greet Players, a troupe of travelling actors who performed Shakespeare's plays on village greens, in parks and in the grounds of great country houses during the early decades of the twentieth century. (Greet himself ended up as manager of London's Old Vic and was knighted for his services to theatre.) In her 2009 book *Actors Talk About Shakespeare*, the

American theatrical producer Mary Z Maher relates an anecdote told by the late English film and television actor Nicholas Pennell:

I knew an actor who performed with Ben Greet's company in Stratford-upon-Avon. He went out for a drive one day and got hopelessly lost and came upon two men. The actor asked the men for directions back to Stratford, and then he asked them about their work. The thick-set hedges in England were made by cutting the hazel twigs in half on a slant-cut through the stem and then bending it and winding it in with other hazel twigs. The man said, 'Yessir, that's what we do, sir, he and I work together near thirty year now. He rough-hews them, and I shapes their ends.' Here was a stage image wedded directly to the earth and not available in most of the scholarly books.

Equally delightful, although distinctly more dubious, is a lively discussion about the beautiful funeral oration in Shakespeare's late play *Cymbeline*, which contains these lines:

Fear no more the heat o' the sun, / Nor the furious winter's rages; / Thou thy worldly task hast done, / Home art gone and ta'en thy wages: / Golden lads and girls all must, / As chimney-sweepers, come to dust. (4.2)

According to one account, 'golden lads and girls' was a Warwickshire dialect term for dandelions when in flower. 'Chimney-sweepers,' on the other hand, were dandelions on which the head has gone to seed, the so-called 'dandelion clocks' blown into the wind by passing children. The popularity of the suggestion can be traced back to 1971 and *The Pound Era*, a biography by Hugh Kenner of the poet Ezra Pound. Kenner wrote:

In the mid-twentieth century a visitor to Shakespeare's Warwickshire met a countryman blowing the grey head off a dandelion: 'We call these golden boys chimney-sweepers

when they go to seed.' And is all clear? They are shaped like
a chimney-sweeper's broom. They come to dust when the
wind disintegrates them. And as 'golden lads,' nodding their
golden heads in the meadows around Stratford, the homely
dandelions that wilt in the heat of the sun and would have
no chance against the furious winter's rages, but need never
confront winter because they turn to chimney-sweepers
and come to dust, would have offered Shakespeare exactly
what he needed to establish Fidele's death in Cymbeline as
an easy, assimilable instance of nature's custom.

The story came from Pound's friend Guy Davenport, who claimed to have heard it from the visitor to Warwickshire himself, one William Arrowsmith. Davenport may indeed have picked up a bit of local folklore, but it is something which cannot be traced back to Shakespeare's day. The chimney-sweep's brush as we know it was not invented until the early years of the nineteenth century. Throughout Shakespeare's lifetime chimney brushes were besoms, a traditionally shaped 'witch-style' broom consisting of a stout pole having stiff brushing ends made from holly stems. The explanation must be considered a myth. Rural rather than urban, but a myth nonetheless.

Most alluring of all, however, is the suggestion that in those final, reflective scenes of *The Tempest*, the last play Shakespeare would pen without the input of collaborative writers, we hear the playwright himself bidding farewell to the theatre and to us, his audience. Summing it all up are those those five simple words:

Our revels now are ended. (4.1)

Shakespeare plundered no literary or historical sources for the plot of *The Tempest*. Prospero and his island are creations born entirely of the playwright's fertile imagination. Just as the magus Prospero can weave spells of every kind with a wave of his staff, so Shakespeare can transport us to distant times and places with the stroke of his pen. Like Prospero, he could rightly claim:

> **I have bedimm'd the noontide sun, call'd forth the mutinous winds, and 'twixt the green sea and the azured vault set roaring war. To the dread rattling thunder have I given fire and rifted Jove's stout oak with his own bolt; the strong-based promontory have I made shake and by the spurs pluck'd up the pine and cedar. Graves at my command have waked their sleepers, oped, and let 'em forth by my so potent art.** (5.1)

Had he not 'bedimm'd the noontide sun' in the eclipses of *King Lear*? 'Call'd forth the mutinous winds, and 'twixt the green sea and the azured vault set roaring war' in *The Tempest*? Made 'the strong-based promontory' shake in the earthquake that supposedly heralded Owen Glendower's birth, according to *Henry IV, Part 1*? As for 'To the dread rattling thunder have I given fire and rifted Jove's stout oak with his own bolt,' did not a stage direction in *Cymbeline* instruct 'Jupiter descends in thunder and lightning, sitting upon an eagle: he throws a thunderbolt'? Hadn't he 'by the spurs pluck'd up the pine and cedar' when Birnam Wood came to Dunsinane in *Macbeth*? Graves, at Shakespeare's command, had 'waked their sleepers, oped, and let 'em forth' when Julius Caesar, Mark Antony, Cleopatra and a long array of England's long-dead kings and queens had stridden across the stage, to breathe and speak again. And there, in *The Tempest*, standing alone before the gaping crowd, he was giving it all up:

> **But this rough magic I here abjure, and, when I have required some heavenly music, which even now I do, to work mine end upon their senses that this airy charm is for, I'll break my staff, bury it certain fathoms in the earth, and deeper than did ever plummet sound I'll drown my book.**

Finally we see him in *The Tempest,* the poor, bare, forked thing that is unaccommodated man, pleading with us to at last let him go, and to think only well of him as he departs:

Now my charms are all o'erthrown, / And what strength I have's mine own, / Which is most faint ... / But release me from my bands / With the help of your good hands. / Gentle breath of yours my sails / Must fill, or else my project fails, / Which was to please. Now I want / Spirits to enforce, art to enchant, / And my ending is despair, / Unless I be relieved by prayer, / Which pierces so that it assaults / Mercy itself and frees all faults. / As you from crimes would pardon'd be, / Let your indulgence set me free. (Epilogue)

It is a valedictory Epilogue. The author has stepped outside of his narrative to address us directly, and he speaks from the heart. 'As you from crimes would pardon'd be, / Let your indulgence set me free.' We set you free, Will, just as you have set us free with your lessons in humanity, in compassion, in the pain of suffering, in the joy of laughter, in the forbearance of adversity, in the power of truth, in the conquest of evil, and in the eternal triumph of love. Thank you for everything.

PICTURE ACKNOWLEDGEMENTS

Prologue: **William Shakespeare**, engraving by Martin Droeshout: *First Folio*, 1623

1. **Robert Dudley, Earl of Leicester** by unknown artist, attr. Steven van der Muelen: Waddesdon Manor Rothschild Collection

Elizabeth I by George Gower, 1588: National Portrait Gallery

Lettice Knollys, attr. George Gower c. 1585: Collection of the Marquess of Bath, Longleat

3. **Ophelia** by John Everett Millais, 1852: Tate Gallery

4. **Clopton Bridge back-eddy**, sketched by Caroline Spurgeon for her book *Shakespeare's Imagery*, published by Cambridge University Press, 1935

7. **Robert Greene**, woodcut from *Greene in Conceipt*, a pamphlet by John Dickenson, 1598

9. **Christopher Marlowe** by unknown artist, 1585: Corpus Christi College, Cambridge

11. **Frost fair** from a pamphlet, 1608: STC 11403, Houghton Library, Harvard University

12. **Marocco** by John Dando appears in *Maroccus Extaticus*, a satirical pamphlet, 1595

13. **Roderigo Lopez**, engraving by Esaias van Hulsen: Wellcome Trust

15. **Sir Anthony Shirley**, engraving by Dominicus Custos,1600-04: Rijksmuseum

Abd al-Wahid bin Messaoud bin Mohammed al-Annuri, artist unknown, c. 1600: University of Birmingham

16. **Alligator's carapace** from *Historia Naturale di Ferrante Imperato*, published in Venice in 1672: Natural History Museum of Ferrante Imperato of Naples, Wellcome Collection

18. **Frederick of Mömpelgard**, reproduced in *The Elizabethan People* by Henry Thew Stephenson, published by Henry Holt and Company, New York, 1912

19. *A Rehearsal both strange and true of hainous and horrible activities committed by Elizabeth Stile, Alias Rockingham, Mother Dutten, Mother Deuell, Mother Margaret, fower notorious witches*: British Library

Stables of the Three Pigeons, Brentford, engraving by W N Wilkins, 1848

20. **John Caius**, 1563: Gonville and Caius College, Cambridge

21. **Herne's Oak:** Royal Collection

23. **The Globe** from a panorama of London by Claes van Visscher, Amsterdam, 1616: Library of Congress

24. **Robert Armin** from the cover of *The History of the Two Maids of More-Clacke*, 1609: British Library

Will Kempe from the cover of *Kemp's Nine Daies Wonder*, 1600

26. **Bethlehem Hospital**, 1676: Wellcome Trust

27. **Tudor brothel** from *A Book of Roxburghe Ballads*, 1847: British Library

28. **Edward Wright's Map**, 1599: Private collection/ Boston Public Library

Willem Barents, engraving, artist unknown

29. **Polar bear attack**, engraving from *The Three Voyages of William Barents to the Arctic Regions* by Gerrit de Veer, 1596

32. **Sir John Oldcastle**, engraving from *The History of Protestantism* by J A Wylie, 1889: Cassell

Henry Brooke, 11th Baron Cobham: Christie's

33. **Robert Devereux, Earl of Essex** by Marcus Gheeraerts the Younger, c. 1596: National Portrait Gallery

Henry Wriothesley, Earl of Southampton, attr. John de Critz, c. 1603: Private collection of the Duke of Buccleuch and Queensberry

34. **Mary Fitton**, artist unknown, c. 1595: Private Collection

36. **The Gunpowder Plot** conspirators, engraving by an unknown artist, c. 1605: National Portrait Gallery

Gunpowder Plot silver medal: Trustees of the British Museum

Father Henry Garnet: British Library

37. **James I**, attr. John de Critz, c. 1605: Museo del Prado

Witchcraft, woodcut from *Newes from Scotland*, 1591: University of Glasgow

39. **Halley's Comet**, Bayeux Tapestry

40. **Bermuda coat of arms**: Government of Bermuda

41. **Will o' the Whisp**, engraving by Josiah Wood Whymper for *Phenomena of Nature*, 1849: Society for Promoting Christian Knowledge

44. **Francesco Maria I della Rovere, Duke of Urbino** by Titian: Uffizi Gallery

45. **Richard Tarlton**, artist unknown: Harley Collection, British Museum

APPENDIX
Select Bibliography

A Life of William Shakespeare, Sidney Lee, Spottiswode, 1898, republished Oracle, 1996

A Shakespearean Botanical by Margaret Willes, Bodleian Library, 2015

Asimov's Guide to Shakespeare, Isaac Asimov, Wings Books, Random House, 1970

By Me, William Shakespeare, Robert Payne, Everest House, 1980

Encyclopedia of Shakespeare, Charles Boyce, Roundtable Press, 1990

Prefaces to Shakespeare's Plays, A L Rowse, Orbis, 1984

Robert Dudley, Earl of Leicester, Alan Kendall, Cassell, 1980

Shakespeare, Anthony Burgess, Jonathan Cape, 1970

Shakespeare, Bill Bryson, HarperPress 2007

Shakespeare, Peter Quennell, Weidenfield and Nicolson, 1963

Shakespeare, The Biography, Peter Ackroyd, Chatto and Windus, 2005

Shakespeare, The Invention of the Human, Harold Bloom, Riverhead Books, 1998

Shakespeare's England, R E Pritchard, Sutton Publishing, 1999

Shakespeare's Imagery, Caroline Spurgeon, Cambridge University Press, 1935, republished 1961

Shakespeare's Language, Eugene F Shewmaker, Checkmark Books, 1996

Shakespeare's Restless World, Neil MacGregor, Allen Lane, 2012

Shakespeare's Words, David and Ben Crystal, Penguin, 2002

The Friendly Shakespeare, Norrie Epstein, Penguin, 1993

The Lodger Shakespeare, by Charles Nicholl, Penguin, 2007

William Shakespeare, Anthony Holden, Little, Brown and Company, 1999

William Shakespeare, A Documentary Life, Samuel

Schoenbaum, Oxford University Press, 1975
Will in the World, Stephen Greenblatt, Jonathan Cape, 2004
1599: A Year in the Life of William Shakespeare, James Shapiro, Harper Collins, 2005

Some Useful Websites

http://www.opensourceshakespeare.org/
http://www.bardweb.net/content/index.html
http://www.shakespeare-online.com/
http://www.shakespearestudyguide.com/
https://www.shakespeareswords.com/Public/About.aspx
Agas map of London, 1561: https://www.british-history.ac.uk/no-series/london-map-agas/1561
Harrison's Description of Elizabethan England, 1577: https://sourcebooks.fordham.edu/mod/1577harrison-england.asp
Holinshed's Chronicles: http://www.gutenberg.org/files/44700/44700-h/44700-h.htm
Philip Henslowe's Diary: http://hensloweasablog.blogspot.com/
Stow's Survey of London, 1598: https://www.gutenberg.org/files/42959/42959-h/42959-h.htm
Sugden's Topographical Dictionary: https://archive.org/details/in.ernet.dli.2015.157431/page/n8

Printed in Great Britain
by Amazon